Neutrality in Austria

Contemporary Austrian Studies

Sponsored by the University of New Orleans and Universität Innsbruck

Publication of this volume has been made possible through grants from the Austrian Cultural Institute in New York, the Bank Gutmann AG in Vienna, as well as generous financial support from both Metropolitan College of the University of New Orleans and the University of Innsbruck.

Neutrality in Austria

Contemporary Austrian Studies

Volume 9

Günter Bischof, Anton Pelinka, & Ruth Wodak
editors

Transaction Publishers
New Brunswick (U.S.A.) and London (U.K.)

Library of Congress Catalog Number: 2001027043
ISBN: 0-7658-0774-2
Printed in the United States of America

Library of Congress Cataloging-in-Publication Data

Neutrality in Austria / Günter Bischof, Anton Pelinka, Ruth Wodak, editors.
    p. cm.—(Contemporary Austrian studies ; v. 9)
   Includes bibliographical references.
   ISBN 0-7658-0774-2 (pbk. : alk. paper)
    1. Neutrality—Austria. 2. Neutrality. 3. Austria—Foreign relations—
1955- 4. Austria—Politics and government—1945- I. Bischof, Günter,
1953- II. Pelinka, Anton, 1941- III. Wodak, Ruth, 1950- IV. Series.

JZ1582 .N48 2001
327.436—dc21   2001027043

Dedicated to

SYBIL MILTON

(October 6, 1941 to October 16, 2000)

CAS Founding Board Member

Table of Contents

TOPICAL ESSAYS

Austrian Neutrality

Introduction

This special issue is the result of many debates about neutrality and the relevance of neutrality in Austria as well as in other neutral states, now belonging to the European Union.

Neutrality in Austria has a long and complex history: First, it was seen as something which was accommodated to please the Allied Forces. Slowly, neutrality became integrated into Austria's official identity. And nowadays, it is very positively connotated for many, emotionally laden for all, although very few know what it actually means and entails. The recent debates in the media and the discussion about European Security Policies as well as the meaning neutrality acquired for the main political parties in Austria, were the reason for a research project, undertaken in the Wittgenstein Research Center "Discourse, Politics, and Identity," in the years 1997 – 1999. The project is interdisciplinary in nature, and the team consisted of political scientists, sociologists, historians, and linguists (see Liebhart and Benke/Wodak in this volume). The project on "Discourses on Neutrality" is the continuation of another study on the "Discursive Construction of National Identity" (Wodak et al. 1999), which showed that the issue of neutrality was functionalized for many political goals at different times during the past forty-five years, the Second Austrian Republic.

Our study used the discourse-historical approach: on the one hand, debates in the media and political speeches were studied (on Austria's National Day, 26 October), on the other hand, interviews and focusgroups were installed to investigate private and semi-private beliefs and opinions. The confrontation of these different and distinct public spaces made it possible to study the recontextuliazation of the meanings of "neutrality" and the ideologies involved. Specifically, it was also possible to interview two former Austrian presidents, who had both been involved with the creation and implementation of neutrality in 1955: Rudolf Kirchschläger and Kurt Waldheim. Their speeches were also analyzed, and thus self- and other assessment could be contrasted and analyzed: the reporting about the speeches, and the speeches themselves. The linguistic analysis makes hidden and coded meanings and connotations visible and demonstrates the different usage of neutrality throughout the years and in different phases of Austrian Foreign Policies.

Recently, neutrality has gained new prominence—and has produced a new paradoxon. In 1999, the war in Kosovo and former Yugoslavia has created a popular wave in favor of neutrality. More Austrians said "yes" to neutrality in public opinion polls than during the years before. The war in Austria's neighbourhood made clear what it would mean to belong to the North Atlantic Treaty Organization (NATO) and to have to send soldiers into battle. During the electoral campaign in summer 1999 the (old) coalition partners gained profile through different positions regarding Austria's neutrality: The SPÖ wanted to preserve it as a symbol of Austrian identity as well as an instrument of a foreign policy focusing on peace without membership in a military alliance. The ÖVP opted for a policy which should lead Austria into NATO. During the negotiations between SPÖ and ÖVP to reestablish their coalition in December 1999 and January 2000, the principal differences between the old partners regarding neutrality were visible, but not unbridgeable. A compromise which would have kept the future of neutrality open was already reached, when the negotiations broke down in spite of the agreement.

The coalition created on 4 February, 2000 is the alliance of two parties which aim openly at NATO-membership. This could have had an immediate impact on Austria's neutrality: The consensus between FPÖ and ÖVP to officially end Austrian neutrality by joining NATO is obvious. Paradoxically, an Austrian NATO-membership seems to be unintentionally prevented by this coalition, due to its composition. The 'sanctions', the EU-14 have started immediately as a response to the integration of the FPÖ into the government, are a rehearsal for the (un)willingness of the leading Western powers to accept an Austria run by the Freedom Party. It would not be plausible for NATO-countries like Germany, France, Britain, Italy, or Spain (not to speak of non-EU members of NATO, like Canada, which have joined the EU-14 in freezing diplomatic relations with Austria), to boycott this Austrian government diplomatically—but accepting it at the very same time as a member of NATO.

The future of Austrian neutrality is open—the government which wants to exchange the neutrality status for NATO-membership has significant problems to be accepted by NATO. And the opposition, defending what has been left of neutrality, is on much better footing with the governments within the EU and NATO, which would have to decide about an Austrian application to NATO-membership. The domestic divide, which is the result of the coalition between FPÖ and ÖVP, could have a rather paradoxical impact on neutrality.

But neutrality is not only a phenomenon to be seen from an exclusive Austrian perspective. It is interesting that none of the postcommunist countries has demonstrated any interest in declaring its international position as 'neutral'. The countries west of the former U.S.S.R. (plus the Baltic republics) are overanxious to join NATO. Unlike 1956, when the Hungarian government declared its neutrality according to the Austrian model—only to be crushed by Soviet tanks—none of the new democracies seems to perceive neutrality as a pattern worth following. The post-cold war era does not produce any incentives for becoming neutral.

In the years when the conflict between two blocs dominated international politics, neutrality was a credible solution for smaller states in specific geopolitical positions. To maximize national security, countries like Finland and Austria developed the combination of liberal democracy and non-alignment. The East-West-conflict is history, and neutrality has lost most of its attractivity—at least within Europe. A pattern so typical for smaller European democracies between the 1950s and the 1980s such as neutrality is not a value in itself anymore. The perception of Swiss neutrality is a good example for the purely instrumental character of neutrality. Immediately after 1945, Swiss (and Swedish and Irish) neutrality vis-à-vis Nazi-Germany was seen differently from Swiss neutrality during the cold war or from present Swiss neutrality. Before World War I, Belgium was considered a model for neutrality—like Switzerland. But the Belgian neutrality fell victim to German aggressions twice, and neutral Belgium became one of the founding nations of NATO.

Neutrality is not neutrality. Austria's neutrality of 1955 is not identical with Austria's neutrality today. As in instrument, neutrality changes its functions—as a consequence of general political change. Neutrality cannot be the same, when Austria is almost completely surrounded by NATO-members—compared with 1955, when Soviet forces stood sixty kilometers east of Vienna and U.S.-forces at the limits of the city of Salzburg.

This is neither an argument in favor nor against the future of Austrian neutrality. This perspective just underlines the political character of neutrality: It is not a political creed like "liberté, égalité, fraternité." It is not a value system like democracy. But it can be helpful, even decisive, to stabilize democracy; or to preserve freedom—under specific circumstances. Which values neutrality can help to maximize in the future—this debate will determine the survival or the end of Austrian neutrality.

Neutrality has different meanings. Austrian neutrality must or at least can be seen as a concept of International Politics; as s set of rules in International Law; as an instrument to strengthen Austrian identity; as a possibility to avoid victimization; as a doctrine permitting pacifists to be pacifists without declaring their pacifism; as a 'double standard' which allowed the country to be Western and non-Western at the same time; as an illusion to live on an island; as a possibility to mediate credibly international conflicts; as the politics of egotistical national cynicism. This and much more—this is, or this can be neutrality.

Therefore, it cannot be just one academic discipline which would be able to answer the complexity of questions. To deal with neutrality in all its aspects, a multidisciplinary viewpoint must be established. Neutrality is important for historians, as well as for political scientists; for economists, as well as for socio-linguists; for legal experts, as well as for philosophers. The complexity of neutrality makes it necessary to take a most complex approach.

Our study illustrates the manifold meanings neutrality has taken: the focus groups, using the methodology of semantic networks, manifest the complex meanings and narratives in which neutrality has become involved: the distinction from Germany after the war; a positive sense fighting unemployment; a guarantee of richness and social welfare; and many more domains which are touched upon in this volume. The generations differ, as well as gender and social class and political affiliation.

The question remains: what will substitute 'neutrality' if it is given up? What will retain its place? This is open for speculation.

The volume comprises papers from very different disciplines and also transcends disciplinary boundaries. This manifests our intention of the above mentioned project: we believe that complex issues, like neutrality, can not be studied from one perspective alone; issues of politics, sociology, history, cultural studies, and discourse analysis have to be combined, not in an additive way, but in an innovative and qualitatively different manner.

Two papers stem from the project "Discourses about Neutrality" of the Research Center "Discourse, Politics and Identity." The paper by *Karin Liebhart* analyzes two life histories which were recorded in narrative interviews, with two very significant figures of official life in Austria's Second republic: Rudolf Kirchschläger and Kurt Waldheim. Both were presidents of Austria, and both were present in 1955 when neutrality was implemented. Especially Kurt Waldheim got large international attention during the "Waldheim Affair", in 1986/87 when his former Wehrmacht past was disclosed (see Mitten 1992, Wodak et al. 1990). These data are unique because both men are already very old and probably the last witnesses of the beginning of Austria's new Second Republic. The second paper, by *Gertraud Benke* and *Ruth Wodak*, studies a TV debate in Austrian television (ORF) where the topic of "Nato and Neutrality" was discussed. This debate serves as a microcosm, as a possibility to view the differing positions and ideologies towards the significance of neutrality. Proponents of all positions are present, all political parties are invited to this discussion. The methodology was newly elaborated for the analysis.

Oliver Rathkolb, a historian, investigates international perceptions of Austrian neutrality in the course of fifty years. He very clearly states that the political changes throughout the past have influenced the significance of the concept of neutrality, specifically the cold war. He also states that Austrian neutrality cannot be perceived independently from major political power games.

David Irwin and *John Wilson* present a very different approach: a combination of Foucault's genealogy and an application of this theoretical framework to the history and debates on neutrality in Ireland. This paper is of particular importance to our volume because it serves as comparison to the Austrian history of neutrality.

Finally, we have included two papers by political scientists, *Heinz Gärtner* and *Paul Luif*, who both address specific of around the Austrian case. *Heinz Gärtner* presents a very interesting concept of change and proposes a "new neutrality," whereas *Paul Luif* narrates the history of Austrian neutrality from a constructionist point of view.

The essays by *Michael Gehler* and *Klaus Eisterer* provide two case studies by historians of Austria's *active* neutrality policy during the Hungarian crisis of 1956 and the Czech crisis of 1968.

In sum, all these papers together allow an understanding of the complex issue of neutrality: neutrality as part of the positive self-identification of Austrians, as something obsolete after the end of the cold war, and as an instrument of independence.

Anton Pelinka (University of Innsbruck)
Ruth Wodak (University of Vienna)

Transformation and Semantic Change of Austrian Neutrality
Its Origins, Development and Demise

Karin Liebhart

1. Preliminary Remarks on the Methodology

In his book *Das kulturelle Gedächtnis* the egyptologist Jan Assmann rephrases Maurice Halbwachs' theses about the social frame of collective memory (1985) and observes that the communicative memory within a social grouping is related to the recent past and tied to recalls of a "generational memory" (1992, p. 48).

With regard to establishing neutrality as a pillar of identity of the Second Republic in the collective memory of Austrians, Assmann's model assumes—far more than four decades after the mystified declaration of everlasting neutrality—special interest to current scholarship. A "sustainable memory referring to origins"—not merely though "in a modus of biographical memories" reminiscent of the frame of one's own experiences or the "recent past" (ibid., p. 52)—Austrian neutrality and its meaning have been transformed from the communicative into the cultural memory. This memory is directed towards "fixed points in the past" and "changes factual history into remembrances," into "a story being told in order to illuminate the presence by recalling the origins" (ibid.). The focus on Austrian neutrality as contributing to both cultural and communicative memory can be taken as an example of how the two forms of memory are often overlapping (ibid., p. 55): Everlasting neutrality—originally a (rather unpopular) idea of the political elite but a vehicle that eventually lead to full sovereignty—became, in the course of the Second Republic, the carrying idea in founding the identity of Austrians and is commemorated as *the* guarantee for success in foreign policy, the "Austrian way."

According to Assmann, retelling stories and memorial patterns stored within the cultural memory is the task of specific experts. The "cultural memory always has its specific supporters" because "contrary to the communicative memory the cultural memory is dependent on story tellers and needs careful introduction" (ibid., pp. 54). In the following, analyzed interviews quoted in excerpts present the opinions of "memory experts" as defined by Assmann. These experts facilitate insights in their specific explanation of the 'history of Austrian neutrality', serving as the fundament to the history of the Second Republic, and about their interpretation of the political functionality of everlasting neutrality. The selected interview partners, owing to their professional biographies (politicians and official representatives of the Second Republic, military personnel, political scientists with expert opinions on international security policy, journalists specialized in Austrian and foreign policy matters, and specialists in international and constitutional law), are proper authorities for handing down the meaning of Austrian neutrality, of interpreting and re-interpreting it. At the same time the experts interviewed are considered to be the mediators of their message, which is passed on publicly through media (electronic and written) or in the semi-public context of university, bureaucracy, or in a military setting. Finally, they are all 'time witnesses' who have either directly experienced the development of neutrality, or even partaken in drafting Austrian neutrality, who have commented and analyzed neutrality, or who have been concerned with Austrian neutrality politics as an identity founding factor defining Austrian domestic as well as foreign policy for many years of their lives. The experts interviewed in 1998 are:

- Major Reinhold Görg (public relations liaison officer of the Austrian armed forces in the federal state of Lower Austria);
- Dr. Georg Hofmann-Ostenhoff (journalist and head of the department of foreign policy of the news magazine *Profil*);
- Dr. Rudolf Kirchschläger (former president of the Republic of Austria over two periods of office, long-time and high-ranking civil servant at the Austrian ministry for foreign affairs, and former Austrian ambassador in Prague);
- Mag. Bernd Körner (civil servant at the Austrian ministry for the interior, member of several bilateral and multi-lateral commissions dealing with bureaucratic changes in conjunction with the Schengen agreement);
- Dr. Hugo Portisch (journalist and co-author of the popular TV-series *Austria I* and *II* and of numerous historical publications);
- Dr. Heinrich Schneider (political scientist, professor at the University of Vienna, and specialist on international security policy);

- Dr. Kurt Waldheim (former president of the Republic of Austria, long-time and high-ranking civil servant at the Austrian ministry for foreign affairs, former Secretary General of the United Nations).

The interviews were not held in standardized form but in the form of an open questionnaire following the concept of social interaction (cf. Maindok 1996, p. 109). Within the framework of these interviews data was generated interactively, in a way which is methodologically more refined than daily communication and depends on the continually changing interpretations of all parties involved (ibid., p. 9, 11, 20). The chosen approach follows those methods of collecting data which aim at the reconstruction of meaning, social sense, and semantic connections. Social realities are thus considered as parts of a logical and semantic unity which is constituted by the interpretations and actions of individual players. This implies that the situation of collecting data is itself kept sufficiently open to allow for the context of individual interpretations to be depicted by the interviewees and for particular utterances to be included into more comprehensive semantic systems. Maindok defines the expert interview as a "functional story telling" (1996, p. 15), whereby the questionnaire serves as an offer for an informed talk.

The experts were asked detailed questions about the "historical and actual meaning of Austrian neutrality." The talks lasted between ninety minutes and three hours. They were centered around key concepts or thematic clusters and, therefore, influenced by the methodology of problem-related interviews (Hölzl 1994, pp. 63). The following themes were discussed:

- the political context of the development of Austrian neutrality (the Austrian State Treaty, the re-gaining of full souvereignty, the guarantee of independence, the value of compliance in the face of the withdrawal of the allied occupying forces, the guarantee that Austria remains unassociated and superficially equidistant to the two cold war power blocs, the prevention of a renewed Anschluss to Germany);
- internal and external political functions of the neutrality issue in the history of the Second Republic, changes and transformations of the focal points, as well as interpretations in connection with a changing geopolitical surrounding;
- the meaning of neutrality to Austrians and its semantic change;

- The 'Austrian way' of interpreting neutrality in comparison to the politics of other neutral countries, with special focus on Switzerland as a model and counter-image at the same time;
- central data (of 1955, 1956, 1968, 1989, 1995, etc.), events and developments (the war in former Yugoslavia, the constitution of the Schengen agreement and the "fortress of Europe," European integration, the enlargement of the EU and of NATO), and their meaning to the Austrian politics of neutrality (continuities and/or breaks?);
- description of the status quo with regard to political trends and the discourses about them;
- estimation of future trends and options.

Most questions were kept general, though, to allow for utmost flexibility and to concentrate on those thematic fields of neutrality which resulted from the specific perspective of the participants. The interviewees were also incited to associate freely and to incorporate unconsidered aspects of the questionnaire. The interviewer gave conversational impulses (partly thematically related) but tried to shape the interview in such a way as to enable the interview partners to articulate their specific view as a 'reflected' opinion and to follow this view as the 'red thread' of their argumentation. This implies that the interviewer was open to clues from the interviewees in regard to their individual focus. The single talks are, thus, heterogenous and cannot be compared on a one-to-one basis. Such a comparison was not intended. The aim of the chosen approach was not a comparative analysis in its closer sense, and by no means was the intention to obtain representative results. The underlying intention was a 'multi-perspective approach' in order to obtain interpretations by 'central speakers' from within the neutrality discourse with special regard to the internal and external functions of Austrian neutrality and with particular attention to the reconstruction of the expert view on the transformation and semantic change of neutrality.

The interviews were interpreted according to qualitative methods in social sciences aiming at the reconstruction of the processes of semantic attribution and the construction of meaning (cf. Maindok 1996, p. 101). The results were accorded with the analysis of politico-scientific and historical literature about Austrian neutrality.[1]

2. The Expert Perspective

The perspective of participating experts on the historical development and semantic change of neutrality will be analyzed in regard to the following two aspects: The author tries, first, to reconstruct the experts' retrospective interpretation of Austrian neutrality and neutrality policy and, second, to analyze the description of the status quo of Austrian neutrality policy and discourse. Moreover, the options of future foreign policy and security policy discussed by the interviewees will be placed within a European context. The individual chapters are subdivided according to the dimensions pre-determined by the functionality of neutrality regarding internal and external policy. Citations illustrate and describe the expert opinions.

It should be mentioned in advance that some dimensions of Austrian neutrality are judged similarly by all experts interviewed, as for example the close link between Austrian neutrality and the identity of the Second Republic, its continuous high value on the subjective level, or the unanimous definition of neutrality as the 'price' of regaining independence. As to other aspects, the expert opinions differ greatly, especially in regard to future foreign-policy and security-policy options. The canon about the historical development seemingly includes some unalterable points of reference, which also emerge in the discourse of the elite. The interpretation of neutrality against the background of current political debates, however, refers to breaks and ambivalent moments within the historical and political design of the Second Republic.

2.1. Evaluation of the historical development

2.1.1. Neutrality as the price for freedom and national sovereignty

The interview partners mostly agree on the historical context of the declaration of Austrian neutrality. The declaration of Austria to assume everlasting neutrality is seen as a key demand to accede to national sovereignty and independence, especially from the part of the Soviet Union. Former President of Austria Rudolf Kirchschläger was as a high-ranking official at the department of international affairs and international law in the Austrian ministry for foreign affairs, part of the team that formulated the declaration of neutrality in the year 1955. As Austrian ambassador in Prague in 1968, and later as the minister for foreign affairs of the Republic of Austria, and finally as president of Austria over two periods of office (1974-1986), he considerably influenced and shaped the Austrian interpretation and politics of neutrality. He sees the primary political content of the declaration of neutrality in re-establishing a free, independent, and sovereign country. On several occasions Kirchschläger talks about this aspect of neutrality, which to him is significant: "From the beginning on I saw neutrality as a means of maintaining an independent status as it is explicitly stated in the neutrality law. This has always been the crucial point, independence." His successor as the head of state (1986-1992), and prior to that secretary general of the United Nations (1971-1981), Kurt Waldheim, also puts the regaining of national sovereignty into the center of attention and additionally points out the difficult circumstances under which the status of sovereignty was achieved: "I believe that for all of us, politicians as well as the population, the fundamental thing and the strongest desire in those days was to become a sovereign nation again. We were a country occupied by four different forces, the occupation was a hard period. ... It was a long process. Within the allied forces occupying Austria a multitude of different opinions existed ..., most of all it was the Soviet Union, which repeatedly had reservations, be it about the issue of settling the question of German property just as about the question of free movement across the borders ..." The foreign politics correspondent Georg Hofmann-Ostenhoff equally interprets the development of Austrian neutrality as the "price which we had to pay to the Russians in order to become independent." The political framework and its results later were presented to the Austrian population as positive assets, "as an integral part of the identity as an independent country." Hugo Portisch, journalist and co-author of the popular TV-series *Österreich I* and *Österreich II*, extensively describes the diplomatic efforts of individual Austrian politicians, interpreting them as the only possible political strategy in order to regain freedom, again with neutrality as the price to pay in exchange.

In the eyes of the interviewees neutrality also meant protection from a possible partition of the country into a western-dominated liberal democratic block and one under the interest sphere of a Soviet-oriented Communist block. According to the opinion of the experts, the Soviet Union saw in the establishment of Austria as a block-free country the guarantee that this young republic, a western country in its ideological and political orientation, would not become a western block member. Kurt Waldheim explicitly points out that the Soviet Union boycotted the talks about independence for a long time out of fear that Austria would join the western military alliance.

The experts today still debate whether the decision, from the Austrian side, to sign the neutrality declaration came about because of Soviet pressure, as the military officer Reinhold Görg thinks ("It surely is a historical lie to say that it came about because of free will"), or whether it originated from Austrian politicians themselves, who thought that neutrality was not a lesser evil but a good way out of the dilemma of occupation, as described by Kurt Waldheim. Görg interprets the political context as if it was solely within the decision-making of the Soviet Union. This view is quite popular among military personnel due to their clear-cut scenario of threat held up during the cold war. Such an opinion is not shared by other experts to the same extent, who, in turn, take a more ambivalent position. Kurt Waldheim remarks for example: "It was an Austrian idea, ... the then two great parties, Socialists and Christian Democrats, absolutely thought that this question should be seriously discussed." The belief in a successful political strategy and in the negotiating skills of the concerned politicians—both assumptions are firmly established in the collective memory of the Austrians, as, for example, Hugo Portisch illustrates by referring to the achievements of the minister for foreign affairs Karl Gruber—can also be said to influence the view of the experts interviewed. However, the interviewees are in concordance with each other that it was the party of the Christian Democrats, which at the beginning felt particular affinity to the idea of everlasting neutrality, whereas the Socialists hesitated and rather declined to follow such a course. Finally, though, according to all interviewees, both big parties agreed upon the option and accepted neutrality. According to Hugo Portisch, Julius Raab was one of the first politicians who accepted the thought of a neutral Austria. The Socialist Party for a long time held the position that Austria should at the most accede to demands of a block free existence and have no foreign military bases on its ground.

In order to regain national sovereignty, it was necessary for Austria to exhibit some characteristic forms of a bloc-free nation. This implied from the very beginning that Austria tried to woo western powers. This statement is ascertained by all interviewed persons: ideological equidistance was by no means Austrian governmental policy. Due to Austria's participation in the Marshall Plan it became evident that Austria, despite opposition from the Soviet Union, was always interested in maintaining its close Western orientation. Hugo Portisch considers the participation as a courageous act since it could have resulted in a partition of the country after the German model. The Soviets already considered Austria as a 'secret ally' of the West. Pertinent newspapers such as the *Volksstimme* and the *Blatt der Roten Armee (Red Army News)* publishing stories about the instalment of a new police force (the *B-Gendarmerie*), seemed to support these claims. The neutrality for the Soviets seemed a way of removing Austria out of the reach of western influence which saw "a pro-western Austria which also—mentally, seen from the perspective of the political public opinion, is willing to go along with the West—to judge by the whole political climate" (Hugo Portisch). In association with already neutral Switzerland, Austria could drive a wedge into NATO if it assumed neutral status. In addition to that, according to Portisch, Khrushchev was eager to follow a policy of détente in international relations and to initiate a departure in Soviet foreign policy from the Stalin era after Stalin's death in 1953. Within such a symbolic framework of détente, the Soviet attitude toward Austria could be seen as a signal for the possibility of implementing a free state at the border of the Soviet sphere of influence, like in the case of Finland.

Kurt Waldheim, Rudolf Kirchschläger, and Hugo Portisch vividly describe the joyous mood, which the political elite and the population exhibited during 1955, the year of signing the State Treaty and the declaration of neutrality. According to the interviewees, the exultant mood was mainly due to the joy of realizing that the occupation forces would leave Austria. "It led to this dramatic demonstration before the Belvedere, when Figl spoke the famous sentence 'Austria is free' showing the State Treaty to the people. I ... could feel the incredible emotion that was prevalent there. The people were exceedingly happy to be rid of the occupation forces, especially of the Soviets ..." (Kurt Waldheim). Hugo Portisch emphasizes the exultation of the people which arose when it became clear that "the allied forces will leave." Even though neutrality was considered a sacrifice, it "was accepted with much more approval."

The Socialist political leadership, however, continued to articulate the disadvantages of the agreement and their political anxiety: "We will turn away from our Western friends—they will turn away from us—we will loose our rank in their view ... The West no longer will be willing to support and protect us, we will be unable to enjoy co-operation with the West, and then great crises will reappear, and we will stay alone again, and without protection—unguarded ... and then they will come again—and nobody will be here to protect us" (Hugo Portisch). Portisch explicitly remarks that "after the experience of the terrible dictatorship of National Socialism" the Austrian people were afraid "of another dictatorship, of Soviet Communism" in the country. This was one reason why so many people, i. e. 95 percent of all voters, voted for the two major parties SPÖ (Sozialdemokratische Partei Österreichs, the Socialist Party) and ÖVP (Österreichische Volkspartei, the People's Party), not for the Communists, in the first free and democratic elections after the end of the war in November 1945. "The new dictatorship that was looming over us and was clearly identified was Communism, and it meant no finger licking adventure, this danger of a new whip hovering over us." The feeling of anxiety became stronger the more the Austrian people observed "the putsch in countries such as Romania, Hungary, Czechoslovakia, the blockade of Berlin, and the Korean War. All this was experienced as threatening by all Austrians, not just by the politicians," states Portisch.

The experts agree on the consideration that neutrality revealed all in all more advantages than disadvantages—at least right after the declaration was signed and during the first decades following. The outside effect of regaining an internationally renowned status as a small sovereign nation—a fact ascertained by the United Nations when Austria assumed membership in 1955—and the inside effect of creating feelings of national consciousness as a factor of identity are regarded as the most essential successes. Kurt Waldheim remarks on that point: "From now on we didn't have to ask permission from the four allied powers for every [laughs] small decision, but Austria was finally independent and could decide for itself what our politics ought to be—no matter if interior or exterior policy."

Rudolf Kirchschläger addressed the aspect of Austrian neutrality as a guarantee for preventing a renewed Anschluß to Germany, which is repeatedly mentioned in scientific literature in association with the guarantee of a pact-free existence. According to Kirchschläger, neutrality was thought of as a token, as "a form of added insurance" for the prevention of a renewed annexation by Germany, which was the concern of the U.S.S.R and of France.[2] Heinrich Schneider also brings up this aspect, but he stresses that this point has no standing today.

2.1.2. Switzerland as model and/or counter-image

The association of Austrian neutrality with the Swiss model, which is anchored in the wording of the neutrality law, is taken up by the experts in their interviews. On the one hand, the interviewees, for example Rudolf Kirchschläger, emphasize that Swiss neutrality stood model for the complete independence of Austria. In the negotiation talks about the State Treaty Austria succeeded best with the Swiss model because it symbolized classic neutrality, finds Waldheim. Switzerland is, in contrast to Sweden, Ireland, or Finland, constitutionally neutral. Kirchschläger remembers that the Swiss model insistence on total independence was the motivating force behind the official Austrian representatives for closely following the Swiss conception of neutrality. But he also mentions a second reason for the acceptance of the Swiss model. Very little had been known about neutrality in Austria at the time of the neutrality declaration and, thus, Switzerland was a welcome model and master to Austrian intentions: "For it was so if . . . at the beginning …—of the Moscow Memorandum—neutrality was mentioned, we had known very little about neutrality … and at first we totally kept to the comparison with Switzerland. … We studied Swiss history and we sought the contact with Swiss experts on neutrality—in order to define neutrality according to the Swiss example and not to any other model. … At the beginning we were very closely tied to Swiss neutrality because we had to learn." Hugo Portisch explains the proximity to the Swiss model with the experiences of World War I and World War II, "both of them triggered by Austria," which, as a consequence, "has paid dearly for it." This is the reason why Austrians "had strongly desired not to get involved in conflicts any more, to finally assume the status of the Swiss," "not to have enemies …, not to get involved in wars," and "to stay outside of it all like Switzerland had stayed outside." In this context Portisch also remarks that neutrality "definitely could not" fall back on Austrian traditions, quite the reverse. "We always had been very quick to take sides. We had always been strongly opinionated, always for one group and against another, we always had had enemies, too, that were clearly identifiable such as the Turks, the Prussians …, intermittently … the Russians." Therefore, the declaration of everlasting neutrality also complied with the desire of renouncing to take sides.

On the other hand, the interview partners state that from the beginning on Austria interpreted and handled neutrality differently from Switzerland. Furthermore, in contrast to Switzerland, Austria never showed any abstinence in international politics. Owing to the restrictive interpretation of the everlastingly neutral status, Switzerland did not join the United Nations and until recently it has also not been integrated into the European Council. Switzerland practiced "total abstinence … from world and also European politics" (Hugo Portisch). According to Portisch, this is the reason why Austrians, due to their interpretation of neutrality, always "felt a little more comfortable ... than the Swiss." Austrian neutrality politics showed more flexibility, thinks Waldheim, but the Swiss history of neutrality is hardly comparable with the Austrian history because of the different historical context. This is also confirmed by Reinhold Görg, who refers to the "centuries-old traditions of freedom" in Switzerland, "which cannot really be compared to Austrian traditions." However, Austria has still taken its neutrality quite seriously, says Waldheim. In the course of the raising of U.N. security forces and the active service of U.N. peace-keeping forces, Austria, in contrast to Switzerland, has granted help on the basis of the U.N. charter and has actively participated with its own military units.

From the experts' perspective, Switzerland has thus a twofold importance for the conception of Austrian neutrality and Austrian neutrality politics. On the one hand, due to its exemplary effect Switzerland is considered to be the 'master' from which Austria received the general orientation at the beginning. On the other hand, there exists also a difference in interpreting and politically implementing neutrality. Even if Switzerland is somewhat stricter in its interpretation of neutrality, this also narrows down the scope of foreign policy, which has never been regarded as an option to be imitated by Austria. The Second Republic did not consider neutrality as "sitting still," but, on the contrary, as the commitment to active humanity, as Rudolf Kirchschläger believes.

2.1.3. "Touchstones" of Austrian neutrality:
Hungary in 1956 and Czechoslovakia in 1968

In this context, two events are particularly referred to by the interview partners: the failed Hungarian Revolution in 1956 and the suppression of the Prague Spring in 1968 by troops of the Warsaw Pact, as well as the resulting consequences for Austria bordering on the 'Soviet Imperium'. The two examples are considered evidence of the independent Austrian way of interpreting neutrality, the emancipation from the model of Swiss neutrality, and the regaining of an internationally renowned status for the young Republic of Austria. Due to its humanitarian engagement in 1956, a year after the constitutional profession of everlasting neutrality, Austria has been able to gain international prestige, to step out of the shadow of Switzerland, and to

show a distinctive image, says Rudolf Kirchschläger. Other experts
remark on that point as well. A liberal asylum policy towards Hungarian
refugees, a social and humanitarian engagement, as well as the stance
Austria took within the U.N. signing resolutions against Soviet politics
in Hungary, brought Austria international respect.

The myth of 1956 very likely played a role in the construction of
Austrian identity, and may still continue to do so: "Due to the Hungarian
Revolution—because of our strong humanitarian ... engagement—due
to our very liberal asylum policy—and the fact that we had been co-
sponsoring U.N. resolutions against the Soviet Union—and taking the
risk ... of an uncertain response by the Soviet Union—This had actually
only been the beginning for us— to gain a distinctive image in the eyes
of the West and the rest of the world. ... Without the Hungarian
Revolution—I think we would have stood in the shadow of Switzerland
for much longer," says Rudolf Kirchschläger. Kirchschläger considers
the year 1956 to be the 'masterpiece' of Austrian neutrality, as the
political practice distanced Austria from the Swiss model[3]: "Once I said
that I had approached Switzerland as an apprentice ... but—relatively
early— and indeed caused by the Hungarian Revolution ... we graduated from apprenticeship—to become a journeyman—and one who
already worked very independently—because our neutrality in 1956
when the Hungarian Revolution had taken place had already
grown—away a bit from the Swiss model ... we have seen neutrality to
be a commitment, a means of implementing humanity ... we use
neutrality as politics of independence—to the common use—of the
single individuals ... that´s where our liberal asylum policy comes
from." Kirchschläger recalls the historical role specific to Austria as a
country neighboring member states of the Eastern bloc: "We do have a
relatively strong personal component—to citizens—in the Communist—let´s briefly say ... Eastern states ... and—we were— much more
able ... to do something for these people—to organize family reunions,
to grant marriage certificates etc.—than pact states— ... inevitably.
Towards us they rather made gestures—and this has been conveyed to
others—then one easily says—well, because we are Austrians, aren't
we?"

Kirchschläger also thinks that the border kept open to the West in
1956 was an encouragement to the Hungarian revolutionaries. This
statement is corroborated by Hungarian literature which underlines the
modeling impact of neutral Austria on the modeling conception of the
future foreign policy of Hungary during the government of Imre Nagy

in 1956 (cf. Litván/Bak 1994, pp. 97-104). Hugo Portisch claims that not only did this contribute to starting the Hungarian Revolution, the Prague Spring is also hardly conceivable without neutral Austria as Czechoslovakia's neighbor: "Well, I believe we had great modeling character." Most of all, the Austrian population was totally sympathetic towards the revolutionaries: "The Hungarian Revolution was like this, the people were wildly sympathetic, the Russian embassy had almost been stormed along with Communist Party headquarters and so on, there was an incredible solidarity, 180,000 refugees were taken in immediately without visas or questions asked whatsoever."

For Rudolf Kirchschläger the Austrian commitment to individual humanism in granting asylum to refugees in 1968 was also a main factor for political decision-making. The political risk Austria was facing then, as seen in the past and in retrospective, was small, says Kirchschläger. At the request of the interviewer Kirchschläger refers to the humanitarian tradition of Austria, so highly esteemed by him, and explains why, as Austrian ambassador to Prague in 1968 during the suppression of the Prague Spring, he disregarded the directive from the ministry for foreign affairs not to issue any more visas to Czechoslovakian refugees fleeing from Soviet troops: he believed this directive breached the commitment to humanitarian engagement imposed by Austrian neutrality. Kirchschläger interprets this order—which thereafter was soon retrieved—as the response of overanxious members of the Austrian government, who thought that the members of the Warsaw Pact could possibly march to Yugoslavia via a shortcut through the mountainous country of Austria, instead of taking the route across the Hungarian lowland plain. "I only know—that I— received a Telex—where the order came—not to issue any more visas to ... Czech citizens. [I thought] our neutrality always—had had a very strong humanitarian component ... and that we shouldn't break with the tradition now ... this (the refusal of issuing visas) would have been a break (with the humanitarian traditions) that's why I have not ... followed—the directive." Kirchschläger thinks that the careful politics pursed by the Soviet Union at that time were underestimated. However, other interview partners, like Kurt Waldheim, who in 1968 was Austrian minister for foreign affairs, emphasize the precarious political situation of Austria, potentially being marched through by Warsaw Pact troops in the aftermath of crushing the Prague revolutionaries: it was a risk to provoke the Soviet Union.

Georg Hofmann-Ostenhoff is the only interviewee to state explicitly how important the events of 1956 and 1968 were for the Austrian self-consciousness. He estimates the danger to national sovereignty and to the freedom of Austria, that may have existed at that time to be rather small if at all present. No longer was there imminent danger from 1956 onwards, nor were there any plans to attack Austria. The borders of Yalta were generally accepted, and the United States did not intervene in Hungary in 1956 or in Czechoslovakia in 1968. The Soviet Union did not take efforts to intervene anywhere else in Europe for that matter, either. But Hofmann-Ostenhoff emphasizes the importance of 1956 and 1968 for the Austrian national self-consciousness as a free, Western-oriented nation. In 1968, he thinks, "people were generally happy not to be in the East."

2.1.4. The era Kreisky and the 'Austrian way'

Politico-scientific and historical literature about the development of the political system and the political culture of the Second Republic, as well as the building of Austrian identity, repeatedly refers to the 1970s and the 'Kreisky era' as the 'Austrian way'. They see active neutrality politics connected with this trade mark.

The special role and function of the Socialist Chancellor Bruno Kreisky in regard to the high rank, the image, and interpretation of Austrian neutrality politics is emphasized by all interview partners. Hugo Portisch and Rudolf Kirchschläger both stress that in the 1970s the Republic of Austria was internationally accepted because of the merits of Bruno Kreisky and his foreign policy. Kreisky interpreted neutrality politics as security politics and, thus, created a stable position of international renown for Austria. Kreisky brought about a "great turning point in the way of thinking," Portisch claims, not because he was less pro-Western than others, "but because he was a real cosmopolitan and worldly man" and a "thoroughly clever politician," who recognized that "through neutrality Austria was able to gain a special role, especially when the cold war got colder ... or warmer." Kreisky knew exactly "where the lines of power were located within Europe" and "what was necessary to be done for the protection of the nation," Portisch says. For him, this is one reason why Kreisky followed the strategy "of defining neutrality policy as security policy." Austria should become acceptable and be of value to all sides—this strategy would also protect the state. Kreisky "had brought out the maximum of the neutral status for

Austria," and this was one reason why he became the world wide respected politician he was. Georg Hofmann-Ostenhoff also holds the opinion that the Kreisky era was highly significant to Austrian neutrality, lauding Kreisky´s—often ambivalent—ability to balance: "In my view this was the only era in which Austrians felt at ease in their own country, ... were satisfied with being a small country, ... since Kreisky in some way managed to reconcile Austria with the rest of the world. Because he played a role that was accepted— in the Near East and the U.N. and ... the Third World ... and a clever Ostpolitik and so forth."

Heinrich Schneider considers Kreisky's politics of neutrality to be the foreign policy dimension of the 'Austrian way', and part of the reason of state of the Second Republic to still have an impact. Although Kreisky´s foreign policy was not neutrality politics in its closer sense, Austria, as a NATO member, would not have had the same impact, Portisch observes. Hofmann-Ostenhoff doubts whether Kreisky´s active foreign policy was insolubly tied to Austria´s neutral status, or whether it was only possible because of its neutral position. He believes that the same type of politics would also have been conceivable within the confines of the Western defense alliance. Heinrich Schneider also remarks that under Willy Brandt Germany followed a similar political pattern.

The end of Kreisky´s political career, especially his death, also brought about the end of this particular politics of active neutrality, says Hofmann-Ostenhoff. Immediately—following the concept of Middle Europe—a path was taken that was leading towards Western Europe. Kreisky always maintained that his politics were based on the neutral state of Austria. Hofmann-Ostenhoff finds, however, that the political opportunities of the Kreisky era were not so much determined by neutrality, but by the specific historical situation and Kreisky´s personality: "It was a fortunate—historical—constellation—in which the particular personality of Bruno Kreisky could play a particular role. His Near Eastern politics had nothing to do with neutrality ... It was due to his biography and his sensitivity to it, and coincidences like his meeting with Arafat one time."

The characteristic connection of outside political functionality of neutrality, due to the equation of Austrian foreign policy with active neutrality politics, and inner political functionality through the trademark of the 'Austrian way' is repeatedly dealt with in scholarly literature and is also referred to by the political scientist Heinrich Schneider: "Bruno Kreisky managed to subsume the entire foreign policy under the heading of active neutrality politics and—what is much more important—Kreisky managed to anchor the official party line (the upward swung "S" under the heading of 'the Austrian way')—within the minds of so many citizens of this country, thus identifying and merging it with the reason of state of the Second Republic. To this day this has been the strength of Social Democracy. And Kreisky's politics of neutrality is nothing else than the foreign policy dimension in the Austrian way."

2.1.5. Neutrality as a safety shield

The question whether Austrian neutrality (at least historically) provided safety and protection for Austria and Austrian citizens, is answered differently by each expert. Heinrich Schneider, for example, says that "of course there was also ... the conception that neutrality indeed protected us." However, he emphasizes that since the turn in 1989, "after our comrades, friends, and colleagues from Hungary and Czechoslovakia for example showed us the plans about Warsaw Pact troops movements," it had been known "that it would have been just like the NATO faction in the Austrian military predicted and how the Austrian army always practiced in maneuvers. Red attacks blue, green intervenes. And it was also clear from the standpoint of international law, if a state is unable or unwilling to effectively defend its neutrality with military power in the case of a violation of neutrality, then the other party, the one affected by the violation, is allowed to take substitutive action. This was the thought, but it had not been taken into account, because everybody thought that, well, neutrality is a guarantee, nobody will ever do us any harm."

Hugo Portisch also disagrees with the supposed safety shield function of neutrality. In a concrete case, Austrian neutrality would have been ignored by the Warsaw Pact as well as by NATO, and Austria would have been marched through by troops of both pacts. Additionally, there was even some danger that tactical atomic weapons were used: "Neutrality surely would not have protected us from that." This view corresponds with the opinion of army officer Reinhold Görg, who ascertains: "To believe that neutrality so far has saved us from being drawn into a war is just being silly," since "today it is clearly evidenced that Austria ... of course would have been chosen as marching route in the war plans of the Warsaw Pact if it had come to a conflict between NATO and the Warsaw Pact." Austria cloaked itself "with the coat named neutrality," and, "thank God," nothing "of world political significance" happened in Europe, such as a European war in which Austria could have been involved. For Austrians, though, neutrality bore the connotation of feeling secure. Görg explicitly points to the ambivalence between the prevailing opinion that neutrality was an excellent safety factor and the observation that Austria had in fact no chance to defend itself.

Kurt Waldheim points out that the safety capacity of Austrian neutrality was never tried out: he doubts whether the great powers would have respected Austrian neutrality in the serious case of a war. The former president judges the historical meaning of neutrality, "especially for a small country, in a situation of historical tension as was the East-West conflict," to be higher "than in the situation given today." After the turn in the 1960s, when the United States had lost in reputation during the Vietnam War, the fear of conflicts rose in Austria, because of world political events like the construction of the Berlin Wall or the Cuba crisis. "One again was absolutely glad to be neutral and not necessarily to get involved." There was, according to Waldheim, "still a little bit of hope that under certain circumstances neutrality could protect from war."

Only Rudolf Kirchschläger holds the opinion that Austria's freedom and national sovereignty can actually be supported by a neutral status because, due to its functional role as a mediator, as an international meeting place, and a refuge to asylum seekers, it assumed special significance on an international level.

2.1.6. The special role in founding identity

All interview partners emphasized the historical meaning of neutrality for the construction of a specific Austrian role in the world arena. They refer to the world political constellation in the context of the cold war, which allowed for positioning neutral Austria between the two blocks. Heinrich Schneider for example indicates the "third way" Austria took, beyond U.S. capitalism and Soviet Communism, and which other countries also attributed to Austria. Following this "third way," neutrality was predominantly interpreted "as peace negotiation, as a paraphrase to the missions of understanding of this country," constituting an outside perception which was also readily engaged as a self-image by the Austrian population. "Of course, this was something the Austrians liked." "In the climactic period of the cold war, the position of being neutral and non-aligned had been ... a beneficial thing, indeed, not only an Austrian ideology." However, today the "role of an honest and balancing intermediary" has become obsolete. Due to changing geopolitical constellations it no longer presents a viable option: "Nobody today calls on Austria for a role as mediator. But now we assume ... an increasingly active role within the framework of the United Nations, and we are generally faced with a different constellation in Europe, where the trend is following interdependence."

As an asylum granting country Austria was particularly important "also to the West," according to Hugo Portisch: "Overall, it was always like this, that the West always said, this is a true democracy we can rely on." Portisch illustrates the statement by referring to the Austrian way of treating Hungarian asylum seekers in 1956 and of enabling the immigration of Russian Jews during the Kreisky era. The 'East' perceived the special role of Austria predominantly from an economic point of view. "The East said that they are important for business," a tradition which is continued until today by economic co-operations with the states formerly belonging to the Eastern block, says Portisch.

During the cold war, on a national and international level neutrality constituted "an element of appeasement, of stability." According to Waldheim, Austria was acknowledged as a stable and neutral country without domestic political turmoil, posing no threat to anyone and providing an excellent service as an intermediary: "And so with neutrality we had created something very worthwhile, which lastly became our national identity." Within this geopolitical constellation, neutral nations "have often been consulted and asked for their precious contribution to peace-finding endeavours or to negotiations." Waldheim recalls his experiences as U.N. secretary general, where he was able to view such developments from the outside. According to Rudolf Kirchschläger, Austria enjoyed a very good reputation in the international world of politics as well as with the United Nations because they could always call on Austria to send troops for international peace-keeping missions. In addition, Austria was internationally acknowledged and respected as a neutral country for its good mediation services to the world. Not only did this reputation make it possible to elect an Austrian secretary general to the United Nations, it also established the international reputation of Austria reaching far beyond the scope of a small nation. This connection of a neutral country assuming a special role as an internationally renowned refuge for asylum seekers, following humanitarian traditions, as well as its role as mediator in international conflicts, is in principle regarded as the great success of Austrian politics of neutrality. This was basically the idea that gave Austrians the feeling of being special.

All interview partners emphasize the important function of neutrality for the construction of Austrian identity and the development of national consciousness, which is also reflected in demographic surveys as well as the scholarly literature. This 'inner function' of Austrian neutrality is not even contested by opponents of neutrality and is still regarded as efficient by some experts. Georg Hofmann-Ostenhoff recalls that "in the Sunday speeches made by politicians" neutrality and Austrian identity were always tightly linked with each other. To many Austrians neutrality meant independence and had strong emotional connotations. Hofmann-Ostenhoff is the only interviewee speaking about another function of neutrality: "it created a historical twilight area—in which— Austria did not immediately jump from one camp into the next and did not immediately leave the Nazi dictatorship and take the part of the Allied war winners, but had some sort of moratorium phase where the people recognized, okay we are neutral. That was not bad for the psyche of the people." Hugo Portisch states in retrospect that "the people had the feeling to be special, special as a neutral nation in the middle of the cold war." Austria stood in some sense "in between the fronts," "did not adhere to one or the other side" and—despite ideological partaking in Western democratic principles—could by all means "be good with them all." Neutrality had "very considerably contributed to … establishing a proper Austrian identity." This explains why the issue of neutrality is still so vividly discussed: "for many Austrians, especially for the generation around 50, … it has become a part of their Austrian identity. This element is reflected in opinion polls." For this reason neutrality is still today—especially on the individual level of the citizen—a decisive factor: "psychologically, neutrality is still there, in the psyche of the people."

2.1.7. Political developments in Europe and Austria's neutral status

According to the experts, Austrian politicians after 1945 or 1955 agreed that "we belong to the West, we are pro-Western, we are for democracy, we are against dictatorships, we are against … the dictatorship in the East and we know where our friends are"—summed up by Kurt Waldheim. In economic terms, too, Austria was defined as a nation oriented towards the Western model. Despite this conviction, a widely distributed consensual understanding existed among the political elite about the impossibility of taking part in a Western economic alliance due to the commitment of staying independent on the basis of international law: "There was always a consensus. Never did ... one party take a decision on its own," says Rudolf Kirchschläger. Even within the party of the Christian Democrats many politicians thought: "Careful, ... let's stay with our neutrality, we fared well with it so far."

Although the party of the Christian Democrats steered towards the European Economic Community (EEC), as Georg Hofmann-Ostenhoff remarks, the predominant opinion at the time was "that this was not compatible with neutrality." The Socialists always particularly opposed the efforts to become a member of this community and did so well into the 1980s when they "first had to be coerced by the Christian Democrats." The efforts to obtain a closer connection with European Economic Community caused, at first, objections among the political elite of the two major parties, says Rudolf Kirchschläger. Supporters of neutrality were suspected to be particularly pro-Soviet and were shifted to "the left corner." But also the party of the Christian Democrats had some strong supporters of neutrality, who found close allies among the Socialists. Even after the election results of the 1960s, in which the Christian Democratic party succeeded to obtain the majority, a relatively broad consensus about the neutral status was still maintained. From the perspective of Kirchschläger, the problem of the Austrian membership within European dimensions at that time was solved by joining the European Free Trade Association (EFTA). Thus, the question of the compatibility of Austrian neutrality with the option of becoming a member of the European Economic Community lost for some time its relevance.[4]

2.2. Evaluation of the status quo and of the contemporary discussion

2.2.1. The political significance of the debate about neutrality

Some of the interviewees estimate the actual political importance of the discussion about abandoning or maintaining a neutral status as high. Hugo Portisch thinks that the meaning neutrality carries for many citizens can be deduced from its identity-founding role. The generation of 55-year-olds and younger grew up with neutrality and gained their personal identity "partly because of the neutral status of Austria." Georg Hofmann-Ostenhoff also admits that the discussion about neutrality touches the nerve of Austrian identity, regarding taboos and national consciousness, but he surmises that the problem will solve itself once the Social Democratic party also joins the NATO course. A real discussion about the meaning, the advantages and disadvantages of neutrality, though, cannot happen because Austria lacks a climate of open discussion. Due to "an all too under-developed culture of political discussion," the question of neutrality remains hidden behind other currently relevant questions such as the Euro and the NATO question. Also the question of how to deal with Neo-nazis and the issue of anti-faschism take precedence over a discussion about mentality, as the former are often addressed against the background of a latent Austrian feeling for German nationalism. This also causes fear among the people. Hofmann-Ostenhoff, however, understands "that ... politicians say ... now lets leave NATO for a while—it is enough for now ... we have enough ... to do with ... the opening of the East and ... the Euro and so on, ... so we don´t need another discussion." Heinrich Schneider agrees that no real neutrality debate is actually taking place and that Austrians show more interest in discussing other problems, such as unemploy-ment. The neutrality discussion is not a primary concern expected to be solved by the government. "One expects the government to tackle the unemployment question first and certainly only in a fourth, fifth or sixth case to deal with NATO or with other definitive decisions on security problems."

2.2.2. Political developments in the 1990s and the present meaning of neutrality

Threat scenarios only play a minor role in the current discussion about neutrality according to the opinion of the experts. As Austria is presently not threatened from any side, a potential situation of danger is not to be the decisive factor for maintaining or abandoning neutrality, nor for joining a collective European and/or North Atlantic security system. Hugo Portisch states ironically: "No one is threatening us at the moment, one could lie down and take a nap, and say—yes, if everyone else joins NATO, then we are fine, let the Czechs or Hungarians defend us [laughs] when it gets bad." Even the major of the Austrian army, Reinhold Görg, says that he is personally very confident about the future, for "we have actually never been as safe as we are now." Even in 1991, when aggressions escalated in former Yugoslavia, nobody seriously believed "that the conflict would spill over." Rudolf

Kirchschläger does not think either that Austria faces any danger, but his standpoint is that the integration into NATO would also not provide considerably more safety compared to the protection due to the neutral status: "But I ask myself … how much safer will we be then than we are now? … I think—it will not quite make any difference … I … don´t see the absolute necessity in this case."

From the perspective of security policy, it does not make any difference whether to maintain or abandon neutrality, thinks Hofmann-Ostenhoff: "It doesn't matter if we join NATO now, in two years, or in five years, overall one cannot see any threat in the future for us." The decision was purely a political one, a clear stand with the West: "It is clearly political and about the decision in favor of the Western powers … and not having the feeling, which somehow is a—typical Austrian whim, … that Austria could find its own … way to reach happiness."

Heinrich Schneider observes "strong tendencies of assimilation regarding Austria approaching the majority position within the EU," especially since Austria internationally signalled readiness for being integrated in a European-wide defense and security system. But the current discussion was influenced by a strategic mistake of the Christian Democrats, who, "since the end of 1996 and the beginning of 1997, have tried to make pressure following the motto of the ministry for foreign affairs that we still have to finish the matter in 1997 and not just in the first quarter of 1998 as it had been arranged." The haste of the Christian Democrats made the Social Democrats feel uncomfortable and this consequently pushed the general opinion towards the position of 'no' to NATO. After the NATO declaration of December 1994 that no longer the *if* but only the *how* of Eastern enlargement was to be discussed, and after the attempt to shape the CSCE (Conference on Security and Co-operation in Europe) into the form of an OSCE (Organization for Security and Co-operation in Europe) had failed, it became clear "that nothing works without NATO," for "all WEU member states, which are also NATO members, have declared that European safety and defense is only possible within the framework of NATO." Such a position undermined "the position which the chancellor massively held up during the last months before the 31st of March of this year [1998, K.L.]."

Georg Hofmann-Ostenhoff discovers a certain unreflected, if inviting, pacifism among some Social Democrats, "who lack any military way of thinking, nor do they want to discuss the subject that one is of course entering a military block." Neutrality was so likeable, he remarks, that Austria had "an army of operetta soldiers no good for anything." Social Democracy got used to "this idea of neutralistic pacifism": "Momentarily it is like that: pro-NATO is right and anti-NATO is left. ... to be for neutrality means to be left and ... there are only very few ... who are not along these party lines. And one side seems to be more militaristic and the other more pacifistic -, which does not quite correspond to reality." The political discussion followed a simple pattern of left versus right, or pro-NATO versus anti-NATO positions, even though the end of the cold war weakened the front lines, "which already at that time were no longer valid. But today it is even more complex and less clear to say what is left or what is right in ... many questions." Moreover, party loyalties diminished, and the Austrian political culture became more dynamic, "just as the voters." At the same time, however, they also became "much more confused, ... as old arrangements and securities are no longer working." But as Austrians were confronted with quite some changes "during the last years, like becoming a member of the EU, opening the borders to the East, abandoning the Austrian Schilling," there is good reason to say: "well, at least neutrality is still a stable value."

All interview partners except Rudolf Kirchschläger agree on the observation that, apart from its function as founding a postwar identity for the Austrian population, neutrality at present has only little value if any at all. But also its role of supporting the Austrian identity is decreasing in tendency or is at least ambivalent, says Heinrich Schneider. "Those values of course are slowly losing significance, ... two years ago or so there was this paradox situation that no more than 80 percent but still around 64-65 percent were for maintaining neutrality, but at least 79 percent were for joint defense." According to Georg Hofmann-Ostenhoff the political class is wrongly maintaining the illusion that Austrians were excessively attached to neutrality. He believes that Austrians would just as gladly abandon neutrality and accept NATO membership, as they got used to the Euro, if the two governing parties could just reach an agreement. The young generation on the other hand is quite indifferent about neutrality.

For Kirchschläger the disintegration of the blocks is no argument for declaring neutrality obsolete. First of all, one block, the USA, still exists, and second, one could also "have found another variation ... of neutrality." The fact that interpreting neutrality has become more flexible resulted, according to Kirchschläger, from the "developments in the East," "the ... breakdown of the Communist system ... at the end of the 1980s," but above all from a generational change in the Austrian political elite: "It ... was ... the personal component ... due to a change of personnel ... inevitably there was some inner alienation from neutrality ... because one—might not comprehend its deeper sense and meaning anymore." Such a development was also partly the result of the international isolation of the Austrian president Kurt Waldheim: "Austria had lost its significance as a country in between blocks and as a meeting place because of the campaign against President Waldheim, ... which was started in America. ... Meetings of the heads of state no longer took place in Vienna but in Helsinki.— ... Thus, Austria lost its reputation as a country in between blocks, as a meeting place, or at least this idea slightly vanished." At the end of the 1980s, those political voices gained the majority which, "on this occasion, together with neutrality wanted to abandon the State Treaty." Waldheim himself "never had this opinion ... because I ... have known about the value of the State Treaty ... and I have known about the value of neutrality."

Kirchschläger explicitly regrets the loss in significance of Austrian neutrality and states that neutrality lost its aura and its magnetism. At the same time he has no doubts about the absence of symbolic and practical political value of Austrian neutrality. Meanwhile, no nation assumes that Austria would stay neutral should the occasion arise because present Austrian politicians gave no indications of convincing the international community of the opposite. "From the standpoint of practical politics ..., we have given it up ... at present nobody, not even the most subtle mind, finds any purpose in our everlasting neutrality, ... and the reason for this is that it doesn't exist—for neutrality-needs—recognition ... from other nations ... the recognition of the Austrian capabilities ... to comply with the commitment of staying neutral needs to be recognized ... I don't know which nation to choose which still believes ... that we are still willing and able—to keep our neutrality in a serious crisis, also in a political crisis, and therefore neutrality no longer has any meaningful aura and people can feel this— saying 'Why, in such a case what do we need it for?—What is the sense of it?'"

2.3. Future options for a European security system and the future of neutrality

The way topics like neutrality and European security policy are handled by the Austrian government appears, from the outside, "decidedly ludicrous" and somehow like political muddling, says

Heinrich Schneider. Although it is definitely acknowledged "that there are some problems with domestic politics and with the cultivation of public opinion," Austria committed itself already in the early 1990s to cooperate with GASP and declared in 1992 to "draw adequate conclusions from the fact that the Western European Union is the defensive arm of the EU." The wavering position of the Austrians concerning the participation in an European and/or North Atlantic defense system shows a "lack of historical consciousness," according to Hugo Portisch. He explains that "historically we belong to this society of Western values and to the democratic community of nations, and the history of neutrality is one that points exactly in this direction." Heinrich Schneider deduces the Austrian hesitation from an "anti-American position." The desire to distance oneself from the USA is mainly linked to the imperial tendencies of the USA, to the turbo-capitalism with American coinage, and "to a certain ... barefootedness in dealing with military matters." Austria does not want "to be abused for any sort of interest of the superpowers once we are members of NATO." Georg Hofmann-Ostenhoff thinks that the "anti-American tendency," which he finds to be commonly held among Austrian Social Democrats, can be traced back to a specific "Russian connection." This friendship with Russia dates back to the period of the cold war, when big deals were made with the East (especially within the reach of state-owned enterprises). Therefore, one tended to comply with the Russian wishes for a neutral Austria, rather than approach the USA. This latent "anti-American" feeling is mostly a recent development: "Well, it wasn't always like that, when I 'as a radical left' was anti-American, at that time Social Democracy was pro-American." But as soon as America started playing a positive role, NATO, according to Hofmann-Ostenhoff, assumed mostly a "civilizing" function. From the "outside perspective" the Austrian debate about joining NATO seemed "curious." From this Hofmann-Ostenhoff deduces among other things, a general hostility towards progress on the part of the Austrians, which also became manifest in the debate about genetic technology. But nobody from abroad really paid any attention to Austrian interior politics because "Austria has actually little significance ... in international discussions." International newspapers only rarely report about Austria since "Austria is a boring nation that has no problems."

When confronted with the question of Austria's NATO membership or WEU integration, the interview partners hold different opinions. On the whole, though, most of them welcome such an option of security politics, although with differing intensity, and regard it to be a desirable option or an inevitable, but not primary, consequence of Austria's European politics.

"I think, first, neutrality ... is outmoded, second, it was not even necessary and is less so in the future and that ... it will be possible ... also to convince the population so that they finally say ... that we should leave the neutral boat and ... agree on a ... safety contract.... I believe Austria will be a NATO member in five years. Well, it is too late for that now, ... and we will take part in the next, the next round." This is how Reinhold Görg judges the situation. He reflects the military aim of Austria to match its military structure with NATO and to make the weapon systems compatible. Military representatives, in any case, want to be part of NATO or WEU—Görg has no doubt about this: "There will only be few soldiers who do not have the same opinion, that we were best protected joining an alliance of European security politics, be it WEU or NATO, one or the other doesn't really matter to me personally because I am no particular NATO fan who only co-operates with NATO or the Americans, but in a greater association we can achieve more than a single state could."

Georg Hofmann-Ostenhoff comments more enthusiastically: "I'm a NATO freak. Not because I'm militaristically inclined – but because I believe that presently neutrality is doing horrible things to people's minds. That they are still sticking to it. Austria has made a decision and it was that we belong to the West ... and with a vast majority. Yes? And from a historical point of view this is a very fundamental step because since the 18th century Austria had never clearly ... taken part in an alliance with the enlightened West, enlightened in the sense of the French Revolution, democratic relations, civil society and so on. ... And we do not have a special standing ... and part of such change would also be to join the Western alliance ... and most of all, and this seems significant to me, to have a clear relationship with America. NATO is the only organization existing at the moment which constitutes the connection between ... Western Europe and America, in the form of an organization. And America is still important for Europe." As long as Europe is unable to act in case of conflicts, says Hofmann-Ostenhoff pointing to the Iraq and Bosnia crises, it is good for the USA to play an essential role within Europe, and NATO is a good vehicle for that purpose: "In this century the Americans had to intervene in Europe twice." The idea of a separate European defense system independent of the USA "is not relevant at the moment, and only from a long-term perspective will it be possible to develop a European identity as a defense system having friendly relations to the USA. ... That means that the increasing European integration and an increasing national constitution, that is European national constitution, will result in a greater European weight. But this is a slow process. ... This means that as Europe becomes more integrated, that is politically integrated and capable of acting, relations between Europe and America can be shifted in favor of Europe. ... And as long as Europe is still in dire straits, meaning ... unable to act on essential matters, then the Americans are still here." Although there are no realistic ideas in Austria about what NATO is all about, this seems to be characteristic of Austrians since nobody had clear ideas about what the EU really meant either. Such processes also need time to develop and grow. The European consciousness is growing very slowly in other European countries as well. At some point in time it will be obvious to be a NATO member, "this won't be a problem," and, probably at the beginning of the next century, "neutrality will fall into oblivion." "Subcutaneously" some things are already happening today, remarks Hofmann-Ostenhoff: "Austria took part in missions of the United Nations—I believe 30,000 people have already taken part in U.N. missions abroad, and these are 30,000 people experienced in international organizations, ... this has some importance." However, neither Europe nor a European military or security alliance could ever gain such high emotional quality like "national pride or national or regional consciousness or patriotism, namely local versions of patriotism."

Kurt Waldheim also regards NATO as presently being the only viable alternative. WEU momentarily only exists on paper and "the only thing of practical relevance is NATO, the only alternative available to the western world from the point of view of military defense is NATO." For NATO "works," says Waldheim by indicating the Dayton talks: "Personally, as long-time (laughing) secretary general of the United Nations ([I always commit myself to) a solution by negotiations, that is not to a military solution, but to a solution through negotiations. But one must be realistic and recognize that unfortunately there are always situations arising where the opposing parties are unreasonable enough not to accept any such solutions by the way of negotiation at all." Therefore, Waldheim pleads for Austrian integration into NATO.

For Hugo Portisch a medium-term European security system is also hardly conceivable without NATO: "To believe ... that there will be a European security system without NATO—is an illusion for the next twenty years. As Europeans will never ... want to raise the money necessary for covering the expenses, the Americans bear the costs for the infrastructure, for the transport, for information, for commando structures and for military bases— ... NATO to a large part has also been ... an enterprise saddling the Americans with two-thirds of the expenses for European defense."

Only former president Rudolf Kirchschläger feels sorry about this development and discusses the feasibility of other options: "We could have stayed a bit more in the ... middle ... according to my opinion. That one does not necessarily have to belong to an alliance ... is demonstrated by the example of Ireland. ... Yes, I believe it had ... at that time ... possibly been a good point for coming to an agreement with the other neutral states—especially with—Switzerland and ... also with Sweden, for if one says ... as the Communist system has fallen apart ... so Austrian neutrality also has become—a non-valve—then I can only ask, well, yes, what was then the original message of the Swiss neutrality in comparison? Right from the beginning the German-French conflict has been the cause for Swiss neutrality in the course of the last century ... and—the German-French conflict—has actually been—at least let's hope so—overcome ... and nobody—says—well, Swiss neutrality has become invalid."

Some interview partners bring forth the argument of solidarity, which, as a demand from Austria being an EU member state, determines to a high degree the political and media discussion about Austrian neutrality. Hugo Portisch claims a neutral status to be a clear declaration for the West. Heinrich Schneider refers to the Social Democratic concept of solidarity and to the requirement that a comprehensive understanding of solidarity should also include the military aspect. The keenest opponent of neutrality, Georg Hofmann-Ostenhoff, regards neutrality as an ultimately immoral concept, referring to the example of Switzerland during World War II. Reinhold Görg assumes in his argumentation the key word of "bandwagon rider" for Austria and pleads for an active contribution to a European security and defense system. Kurt Waldheim also argues that within the framework of an integrated Europe Austria has to profess solidarity from the military point of view. Rudolf Kirchschläger holds the contrary opinion that solidarity was rather to be practiced on the individual, personal, humanitarian level or on the political and diplomatic level within the framework of the U.N. He further articulates his anger in view of the accusation that Austria had not shown solidarity and refers to the service

Austria did for humanitarian and international freedom as a reliable partner of the Western community of solidarity. Austria really must not be accused "of lacking solidarity. During the whole period of the Communist regime we have generously practiced solidarity—setting an example for other nations—against Communism—and also for the freedom of the individual ... we have shown more solidarity.—One can only think of the vote at the United Nations ... more solidarity with the West—than—certain other allied partners."

If Austria joined NATO, neutrality would in any case become obsolete. This statement is inarguable among the experts interviewed. Rudolf Kirchschläger sums up the evidence of this conjunction as follows: "One cannot [laughs] belong to a military alliance ... and at the same time stay an everlastingly neutral nation ... this is not possible, not with the best will in the world."

Gradually, and with more or less explicit regret, the experts interviewed, therefore, come to the conclusion that neutrality is a old-fashioned security option of the past (*Auslaufmodell*). "Thus, the only possibility left at this stage is to somehow join this mainstream or to go off into a corner to sulk, but [there is] no reliable and convincing alternative perspective," states Heinrich Schneider.

Arguments referring to security policy only scarcely influence the considerations of the experts interviewed. The central idea is rather the design of a new deliberate and clear Austrian self-image. Georg Hofmann-Ostenhoff points to this desire for a new construction of Austrian identity: "I am essentially concerned about the political aspect. Right? About the cognition ... that we are European."

Bibliography

Jan Assman, *Das kulturelle Gedächtnis. Schrift, Erinnerung und politische Identität in frühen Hochkulturen.* Munich: C.H. Beck Verlag, 1992.

Maurice Halbwachs, *Das kollektive Gedächtnis.* Frankfurt/M.: Suhrkamp-Verlag, 1985.

Erich Hölzl, "Qualitatives Interview," in *Verführung zum qualitativen Forschen. Eine Methodenauswahl*, ed. Arbeitskreis qualitative Sozialforschung. Vienna: WUV-Verlag, 1994, 61-68.

Herlinde Maindok, *Professionelle Interviewführung in der Sozialforschung.* Pfaffenweiler: Centaurus Verlagsgesellschaft, 1996.

György Litván and István Bák, *Die ungarische Revolution 1956. Reform – Aufstand – Vergeltung*. Vienna: Passagen Verlag, 1994.

Notes

1. In order to avoid overlaps with other contributions to the present volume (for example Gärtner, Luif, Rathkolb), the analysis of the specific literature is not considered in the following discussion. For such an analysis see the corresponding chapters in the "Topical Essays" section of this volume.

2. The prohibition of the annexation with Germany is documented in the Austrian State Treaty.

3. Kirchschläger holds the opinion that the Swiss model of neutrality was predominantly suitable for large-scale humanitarian actions like the International Red Cross.

4. Only an overview of the political discussions in the 1960s and, thus, the beginning of the approach of Austria towards the later EU is intended here. Further developments are dealt with in the chapter on the current situation of neutrality politics.

Neutrality versus NATO: The Analysis of a TV-Discussion on the Contemporary Function of Austria's Neutrality[1]

Gertraud Benke and Ruth Wodak

1. Introduction

On 1 Janurary 1995 Austria joined the European Union. This marked the end of the longstanding debate whether Austria's neutrality would allow the country to enter a supranational union. In the 1960s this was claimed incompatible on the grounds that economic dependencies would entail a breach of neutrality in times of crises, but in 1987 leading experts in international law declared it feasible.[2] With the end of the Cold War and the collapse of the Eastern block, neutrality was no longer considered an international necessity, as it had been when born out of the aftermath of the Second World War. Yet, in the meantime, neutrality had gained additional facets. Within Austria it had become a symbol of national identity,[3] most notably through the "active neutrality" policy of the former Socialist Chancellor Bruno Kreisky (1966 – 1983). His foreign politics were oriented towards 'the world,' the North-South conflict, the 'Near East.' When in the succeeding years a coalition between the two major Austrian parties was formed, and the People's Party (*Österreichische Volkspartei*, ÖVP) started to dominate foreign politics, the focus of foreign politics shifted to (Western) European states, and (especially after the breakdown of the Iron Curtain) neutrality lost its vital role in defining Austria's foreign politics. The People's Party became a driving force in the debate of Austria joining the European Union. The party saw no problem with Austria's neutrality and no need for a special provision to ask for membership. Moreover, with the end of the Cold War, it no longer saw the 'pressing need' to remain neutral.

In contrast, the Socialist Party (*Sozialistische Partei Österreichs*, SPÖ), looking back at almost two decades of successful politics of 'active neutrality,' wanted to ensure that Austria's neutrality would not be given up. This difference of opinion led to a major crisis of the coalition in 1988, which was only settled when the parties agreed, in a joint meeting on12 December 1988, on the further timetable for the decision.[4]

Thus, the conflict was pacified for the time being, and Austria eventually joined the European Union. In recent years, the member states of the European Union have started to discuss a joint (military) defense politics. Since most of the member states are also members of the North Atlantic Treaty Organization (NATO), the relation of such a military pact to NATO would most likely be very close. In any case, military pacts are undoubtedly precluded by Austrian neutrality. Therefore, if Austria is to join either one of the two pacts it has to give up its neutrality. However, in 1997 an unspoken agreement seemed to convey that, if Austria was to give up neutrality, it would join NATO—a decision based on the country's longstanding orientation towards the West, especially towards NATO member states.[5]

Yet, in 1997 the party positions briefly presented above are still firmly in place. There is still a coalition between the two major parties, with the People's Party predicting the imminent end of neutrality, and the Socialist Party preferring Austria to remain neutral. At the same time, however, both parties are not willing to risk a major conflict in public. The differences exist, but in a direct confrontation they are mitigated and negotiated, and a collegial atmosphere is retained.

In this essay we will analyze a TV discussion, in which politicians of each of Austria's major parties, as well as several other participants, met to discuss the topic of "Austria between Neutrality and NATO." As will be explained in more detail, this TV discussion provides a good example of the public discourse about neutrality at the time. In analyzing this show, we will seek to answer the following questions about the ongoing discourse:

- How do the involved politicians discuss neutrality? What are the positions of the parties (in particular the coalition parties) in this debate? Which arguments are put forward? How do the politicians try to address their audience and gain support for their perspective?
- How does the coalition negotiate different opinions in (possible) direct public confrontations?
- Who is successful in this discussion and why?

The following section will introduce the data and each of the participants. Next, we will present our methodology, and, in the succeeding section, provide an overview of the whole TV discussion, with a characterization of the roles the different participants played in the discussion. We will then turn to the analysis of the contributions of the coalition representatives, and analyze a short excerpt of their contributions. Their positions and discourse style will be contrasted with those of a participating 'expert.' In the final section, we will summarize our analysis, return to our research questions, and discuss some of the results in the framework of the meaning and changes of public space.[6]

2. The Data

On 23 February 1998 six people were invited by the Austrian National Broadcasting Service (ORF) to discuss "Austria between Neutrality and NATO" in a well known weekly TV discussion, a live broadcast called *Zur Sache* (roughly translated: "contending the issue"). This TV discussion airs every Sunday night at 10 p.m. on Channel Two of the National Broadcast Service, the channel generally oriented towards an educated and politically interested audience. The show addresses topics of public interest and usually features well known politicians and other public figures among its participants. It thus informs a wide public audience about current positions of the invited party members or government representatives. However, in most instances a 'discussion' in the sense of people presenting their opinions and possibly changing their points of view does not take place. Instead, one conferee usually states an opinion and is then contested until someone else takes over and changes the topic.[7]

On 23 February 1998 the aforementioned TV conference, which lasted about seventy-five minutes, was hosted by Peter Rabl (PR) of the ORF and his guests were (in alphabetical order):

- Georg Hoffmann-Ostenhoff (GO): a 'leftist' journalist and weekly editor of a foreign politics column in one of the most established Austrian weekly news magazines, "*Profil.*"
- Andreas Khol (AK): party leader of the People's Party and Member of Parliament.
- Erich Reiter (ER): head of a division within the defense ministry and consultant for the Austrian right wing Freedom Party (*Freiheitliche Partei Österreichs*, FPÖ) whose program is close to Le Pen's Party in France.

- Peter Schieder (PS): 'speaker' for the Socialist Party on foreign politics and Member of Parliament.
- Heinz Schmutzer (HS): unaffiliated, relatively unknown person, who initiated a political petition concerning neutrality. Passing of this petition would obligate the national assembly to hold a referendum, if it wanted to give up neutrality.
- Andreas Wabl (AW): 'speaker' of the Green Party on peace and Member of Parliament.

The Freedom Party, not yet mentioned in the introduction, has always had a right wing orientation. Since 1986 it has notably considered the Austrian nation an 'ideological' aberration because it regards Austria as part of the German nation. The FPÖ would like to see Austria join NATO. One can suspect that this position derives from still existing Anschluß dreams within supporters of this party. On the other end of the spectrum stands the Green Party, which promotes neutrality as the most peaceful international stance possible. For the Green Party joining a military treaty is equivalent to giving up a clear orientation towards peace and to accepting the logic of the arms race.

Most participants of the TV discussion reflect the position implied by their political affiliation, with the exception of GO, who is strongly in favor of Austria joining NATO, despite his leftist orientation.

3. Overview of the Discussion

At the beginning of the broadcast, a short section shows the participants advancing towards the building or walking up the stairs. A voice-over introduces them and presents a short position statement, summarizing the position taken by each of the participants. Next, PR introduces the topic and starts to address the participants one after the other, giving them a chance to lay out their general positions in a first statement. Then HS introduces the first question, asking what peace people are trying to defend by joining NATO. This leads to statements that question the peacekeeping role of a military organization (AW) and doubt that wars in the old sense will ever happen again in Europe (AK). PS finishes this discussion by asking ER whether the obligation to defend an ally (*Beistandspflicht*) would possibly be dropped by NATO. This shifts the overall discussion to the topic of NATO and the issue of security. ER and GO believe that NATO increases Europe's (and Austria's) security, but AW protests against NATO. In doing so, he also accuses PS, i.e. the Socialist Party, of supporting the People's Party in a policy of undermining the meaning of neutrality. This leads to a brief digression of AK and PS, in which they each state the overall political position of their party concerning the place of Austria in a future European security system. ER reintroduces the issue of NATO in a European perspective, addressing, in particular, the relation of NATO to Russia, which is seen as a possible destabilizing factor. Again, GO supports him.

PR changes the topic by asking AK whether his party would be willing to give up Austria's neutrality. AK's answer is rather cautious, declaring that his party will wait until the results of currently negotiated issues (within the EU) are available.

ER follows with a lengthy statement in which he declares neutrality obsolete. PS in turn questions the ideological purity of NATO. As can be expected, ER rejects such a notion (he claims to be speaking only of security issues). His position is then challenged by AW, who wants security to be understood in social and economic terms as well, and who addresses the issue of locating resources. AK counters that security cannot prevail without military security, to which PS replies that the real question lies with the legitimate agents of military measures (e.g. the United Nations).

Next, PR turns the discussion to the topic of costs, which AW has tried to introduce several times before. GO predicts that joining NATO will enable Austria to decrease spending for defense. PR presents some figures on defense expenses of European states in general. ER states that no serious calculations exist at the time, but he assumes that the defense budget can remain as it is. AW rejects all these estimations and cites a U.S. Congress budget report on the estimated costs of an expansion of NATO to include Eastern Europe. Based on this, he posits that joining NATO will obligate Austria to increase the defense budget considerably. This proposition is rejected by AK, GO, and, less emphatically, by ER, and possibly also by PR (see analysis below).

Then PS repeats the question of (military) obligations, which would ensue from Austria joining NATO, and ER refers again to the *Beistandspflicht*. AW shifts the topic briefly back to the issue of costs, and ER states that no one could force Austria to pay any particular sum, even if 'moral pressure' would be exerted. PR closes the discussion and introduces the final sequence, in which he asks the politicians about their stance on the poll promoted by HS.

Thus, we see that on the whole NATO is being discussed more than neutrality. NATO is introduced, questioned, and defended in various forms and under various perspectives, while neutrality never becomes the predominant focus of the interaction. Although arguments for or against neutrality are raised at several occasions during the discussion (see below), neutrality never becomes a topic in its own right (for any longer segment of the discussion).

4. Arguments

In the following part, we analyze the arguments put forward by different speakers. In this section, arguments which make a point in the topic under discussion are defined as statements with 'new' propositional content (this excludes statements, which simply support or refute a previous statement without adding new information).

If one categorizes the contributions of the individual speakers, one finds about five different classes of arguments: arguments concerning the function of neutrality (whether it still had a function, what that was etc.), arguments concerning NATO as the organization it is (as something positive and modern, ensuring security in Europe, etc.), arguments concerning the costs of joining NATO, arguments concerning (other) aspects of Austria joining NATO, and arguments concerning an expansion of NATO to include the Eastern European states.[8] Speakers differed remarkably in terms of their number/ratio of contributions to the different areas, and the evaluative stance taken towards the topics under discussion. Table 1 presents an overview of the breakdown of arguments put forward by the different speakers and their evaluative stance. It shows that speakers favoring neutrality contribute no positive evaluations of NATO (AW, HS, PR), and speakers clearly favoring NATO contribute no positive evaluations of neutrality (ER, GO). The assessment of the cost situation and of the statements about joining NATO also conforms to this picture. The only participant who does not clearly fall in these categories is AK. Although he clearly favors NATO, his stance towards neutrality features positive and negative evaluations.

Regarding the number of statements, ER contributes most arguments, followed by PS. HS has the least number of contributions among the participants, and becomes completely marginal in the discussion. With respect to neutrality, AK and PS contribute most statements, but ER and AW also contribute noticeably to this discussion. The discussion of NATO is clearly dominated by ER. He proposes almost twice as many

Table 1

Person	Functions of neutrality				NATO				costs				Aspects of joining NATO	Eastern expansion of NATO	Total
AK	10	2	5	3	4	3	1		1			1	0	2	17
AW	5	4	1		1			1	10	10			0	1	17
ER	7	7			11	4	7		4	3	1			7	29
GO	3	3			6	5	1		2	2	1		3 +	2	16
HS	2	2			0				1	1			2 -	0	5
PR	1	1							2	2					3
PS	9	5	4		4	4			2	2			4 -	2	21

Legend: In this table the first entry of each main column presents the total number of arguments proposed by the speaker about the respective subject. The first gray area shows the positive evaluative statements; the second gray field lists arguments which were neither positive nor negative (but providing e.g. information about general political developments); and the third gray column of each section presents negative evaluations. For costs, the first gray column indicates statements assuming raising costs; the second one refers to statements indifferent about costs; and the third reflects arguments about decreasing costs. In the column "Aspects of joining NATO" the plus stands for positive aspects proposed by the speaker, the minus for negative aspects. In this category people only had evaluative comments.

arguments about this topic as GO, who is another NATO proponent. Yet, a close look at ER's statements on NATO reveals that, although he contributes most arguments, the majority of them is not clearly evaluative (which might add to his image of being an expert, see Table 1). Finally, the topic of costs is strongly promoted by AW.

5. The Interactional Profile of the Discussion

A further important aspect of an analysis of this TV discussion is the interactional profile. This provides not only an important contextual characteristic, but constitutes also an explanatory level in its own right. Looking at the interactional dynamics, we uncover who has most to say, who is most attended to etc. Since people are very tightly linked to positions in a discussion such as the one we are looking at, tracking the interactional dynamics also constitutes an indirect means of tracing the success of the positions and ideologies pronounced.

To analyze the interactional profile, we divide the discussion into units. In each unit one speaker holds the floor, i.e. is the main speaker on a particular topic.[9]

For each of these units (henceforth referred to as 'floors') we also note how the main speaker gets the floor: through self-selection or an assignment by the moderator or another participant. We further observe who precedes and follows the present floor, who comments on the floor, whether the floor's initial statement is an 'answer' to a previous contribution, who tries to interrupt the present floor, and, finally, whether the current main speaker got into a 'conversation' with another participant. We code turn-sequences as conversations only if someone makes a comment to something the main speaker has said, and the main speaker addresses this comment in his following turn. Thus, a conversation consists minimally in only one turn of another speaker, and an 'answer' to this turn by the main speaker; in other cases a longer interaction would ensue.

While this analysis allows us to gain some insight into the interactional dynamics of this discussion, its methodological shortcomings have to be kept well in mind: naturally, the length of the 'floors' varies considerably from a few lines of transcript to up to two pages. This difference in length influences the number of possible interruptions, conversations, and comments. It is more likely that a longer floor will contain more such exchanges, even if a per minute count would result in the same or even reversed figures! For this reason, we do not count the frequency of any of these measures, but take only categorical notes: Who comments, interrupts, converses during the floor under consideration? We believe that the results of the analysis allow us to see at least who prompts a reaction from whom. They further provide us with a crude measure of strength. What is not considered in this analysis are unsuccessful tries to take over the floor (at the end or beginning of a floor) and unsuccessful assignments of the floor by the moderator.

5.1 Main speakers and their floors

Table 2

Speaker	Number of floors assigned by PR	%	Number of self-selected floors	Total
AK	7	100%		7
AW	6	100%		6
ER	5	56%	2	9
GO	2	29%	5	7
HS	5	83%	1	6
PS	2	18%	9	11
Mean:	4.5		Mean:	7.7

Table 2 provides an overview of the total number of floors for each participant, and whether their respective floor is self-selected or whether they are invited to speak by the moderator or somebody else.

The participants differ remarkably in the number of floors they hold during the entire discussion. AW and HS have little to say, AK and GO neither say a lot nor very little, and ER and PS have the largest number of contributions. PS and GO are both seldom invited to make a contribution, yet they frequently take the initiative themselves. In contrast, AK only speaks when invited by the moderator, as does AW (who also tries to speak at other occasions, but does not manage to get the floor). HS's contributions are also mostly invited by the moderator. ER speaks when invited by the moderator or someone else (PS)—he is the only participant who is invited to speak by another participant. Thus, despite his relatively low percentage of floors, which are assigned to him by the moderator, he does not have many self-selected floors either.

5.2 Sequence of speakers

Table 3

	Subsequent speaker					
Speaker	AK	AW	ER	GO	HS	PS
AK	1	1			2	3
AW	3			1		1
ER		2	1	2	1	2
GO		1	1		2	1
HS	1	1	1	1		1
PS	1		5	3	1	1

Table 3 shows who is speaking after whom, and who prefers to respond to whom. In other words, the columns signify the 'reaction' of a speaker to the previous speaker, e.g. AK seems to respond most to statements of AW, and he never follows up statements of ER or GO, the other two NATO proponents of this discussion.

AW himself never follows statements of PS, but he gets the floor after each of the NATO proponents. ER seems to be in a complementary position to AK, i. e. he never succeeds him and responds in particular to one proponent of neutrality, PS. For GO no clear preference for proponents of neutrality or NATO can be discerned, and HS predominately follows up NATO proponents. The only participant to follow up all other participants is PS (he also has the highest overall number of floors), but he responds more to NATO proponents than to proponents of neutrality.

The rows allow you to see who typically follows a particular speaker. Thus, one can see that PS follows AK more often than any other participant (three times). Further analysis of the data reveals that in those cases where PS did not immediately follow AK, he would often be the second subsequent speaker.

AK is the predominant speaker after AW; for ER no clear preferred following speaker is discernable, we can only see that AK never follows him. For GO and HS we do not find any clearly preferred subsequent speaker either. PS is mostly followed by ER or GO, that is by NATO proponents.

The relations we have just described can be depicted in the following diagram (Figure 1). This diagram shows who is speaking after whom using directed arrows. The line-strength indicates how frequently speaker A was following speaker B, a count of 1 was not included.

Figure 1

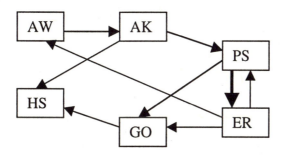

5.3 Responding

The sequence of speakers does not clearly indicate 'reactions' to a particular speaker or content. Speaker A might follow speaker B for a number of reasons. To look closer at particular reactions, we also note whether a contribution makes direct or indirect reference to a previous contribution, e.g. by addressing a particular previous speaker by name. The resulting table (Table 4) confirms the overall tendencies of the previously discussed sequence of speakers, with slight modifications in the details. Overall, the resulting picture shows stronger distinctions than the speaker-diagram.

Table 4

Speaker	.	PR	AK	AW	ER	GO	HS	PS
AK .		3		3				
AW		2			3	1		
ER	2	2		.5				4.5
GO	2	1					1	3
HS	3	1	1			1		
PS	5	1			3	1	1	

Again, AK responds predominately to AW; at the same time we find an equal number of responses to questions of the moderator. AW himself is more oriented towards ER, who responds mostly to PS.

Similar to ER, GO mostly replies to PS. HS does not show any clear preference for a particular participant, yet he only responds to NATO proponents. PS displays the highest number of contributions that are not responding to any particular previous contribution. At this point, we just want to note that he frequently introduces topics in form of questions instead of responding to already existing issues. If he actually answers somebody, it is foremost ER.

A diagrammatic representation results in the following picture:

Figure 2

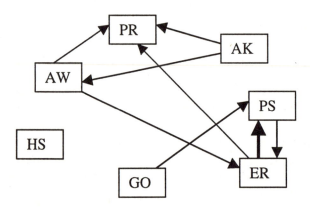

In comparison to the speaker-diagram we can note one particular difference: in Figure 2 the participants can clearly be grouped into two separate groups: on one side we have AK, AW, and PR, on the other PS, ER, and GO. We think this impression is foremost due to the fact that AK and PS never 'answer' each other. Thus, we find that PS frequently follows contributions of AK, but never directly responds to what AK has to offer. PS' statements are elaborating, enhancing, and reflect the opinion or perspective of his party (who is in a coalition with AK's party) without pointing out differences between their positions. He simply states their point of view. Thus, on a thematic level (in the macrostructure), it becomes obvious that both, PS and AK, discuss the same topic, however without direct references to the preceding talk or speaker ("We are of the opinion *as well* that …"), without being explicitly in disagreement or agreement. PS' contributions are foremost 'statements' addressed to all participants, statements which present the party's position and do not move against or towards AK.

5.4 Conversing

Another important category which picks up aspects of the responsiveness of participants to each other is 'conversing'.

Table 5: Having Conversations

Speaker	With	AK	AW	ER	GO	HS	PS
AK		\					
AW		3	\	2	1		1
ER		1	2	\			5
GO					\		3
HS					1	\	
PS		3		3			\

The analysis of conversing clearly shows the monologic character of AK's contributions. He is never involved in 'conversations' with other participants; instead he makes statements without addressing anybody in particular. At the same time he frequently converses with other participants—in particular proponents of neutrality—while they are holding the floor. In contrast to AK, AW gets into conversations with almost all participants while presenting his positions, but converses with ER only when somebody else is stating his point of view. ER is mostly involved with PS but also responds to AW when the latter has the word. Similarly, GO discusses with PS, when he (GO) holds the floor; but he himself gets rarely in discussions with other participants when they are speaking. HS is completely marginalized, and, finally, PS converses mostly with AK and ER.

In sum, we find the following picture: the interactional dynamics mirrors the 'battle-lines' between proponents of neutrality and proponents of NATO. Usually, there are only few reactions to contributions of speakers of one's own position—one reacts mostly to speakers of 'the other camp.' And most everyone has his preferred 'enemy.' We see a symmetric relationship between ER and PS, who follow each other, respond to each other, and converse with each other. In contrast, the interactions between the other participants are predominantly asymmetric. AK is oriented towards AW, but AW reacts mostly to ER. PS frequently 'follows' AK in the flow of the discussion (which indicates that he monitors AK), yet he does not take any open stance towards AK's contributions. HS is completely marginalized: his contributions are usually quite short and his arguments are frequently ignored. In one instance the moderator himself changes the topic completely after one of his statements. GO is another marginalized participant, who mostly reacts to ER (thus being the only one who responds to somebody with the same position in this discussion),[10] but prompts responses only from HS.

Thus, we judge this discussion as a typically political one, in which the participating politicians and administrators avoid discussing a particular topic, i.e. proposing arguments, challenging them, and working on an agreement. Rather they state their conflicting points of views and demarcate their topical 'territory.' The lay person and the journalist in the discussion, who follow a different discursive strategy, remain observers of this process. In this discussion, the main axis is constituted by PS and ER, who hold the highest number of contributions.

5.5 Comments

One further aspect of 'reactivity' to a particular speaker is the number of comments evoked by his contributions. (Naturally, the total number of contributions depends, to some extent, on the time someone is holding the floor.) Therefore, we have again opted for a categorical coding scheme: for each participant we noted the number of 'commenting acts' while holding the floor.

In general, we can observe that almost all participants to some degree comment on each other—with the sole exception of HS, who evokes almost no comments. His contributions are silently received, and often given way to a topical change.

The speaker who seems to elicit most responses is GO. More than anybody else, PS comments on GO's statements, which is not surprising considering that GO often follows and responds to PS's comments. Thus, PS reacts in turn to GO's response to him. Also AW evokes much response—most frequently from ER. Again, we see the same interactional pattern as before: AW follows and responds to what ER is saying, and ER in turn comments on AW's contributions. In a way, AW already foreshadows his later contributions with his frequent comments

Table 6: Comments (per floor)

Speaker	Commenter						Floor w/o Com	%	Total Floor	Total Com	Com/Floor
	AK	AW	ER	GO	HS	PS					
AK		2	1	1	2	2	2	29	7	8	1.14
AW	3		4	1	3	1	1	17	6	12	2.00
ER	3	6		1	3	4	2	22	9	17	1.89
GO	3	4	2		3	6		0	7	18	2.57
HS				1		1	4	67	6	2	0.33
PS	2	5	3	3	3		4	36	11	16	1.45

to ER's statements. He seemingly tries to preselect himself as the addressee and next respondent. This strategy appears successful considering that he never self-selects his contributions but gets his floors by assignment from the moderator.

Besides AW, also PS is very engaged in commenting on ER. In fact, his overall involvement with ER is even higher than appears in the table, as his 'comments' frequently lead to conversations, which do not figure in this table. PS's own contributions, though, are not commented on to the same degree (36% of his floors go by without any comment). Nevertheless, as he holds the highest number of floors in the overall discussion, the attention paid to him during the whole discussion is not lower than for the other participants. Moreover, he is often engaged in conversations, which naturally lowers the frequency of comments. In general, he is most frequently commented on by AW. ER's 'comments' often lead to conversations. PS himself repeatedly responds to contributions of other participants, in particular GO's.

The arguments put forward in the case of PS cannot be applied to AK. He does not engage in any conversation. 29% of his floors do not elicit any comments. This and his low number of responses to the other speakers make AK a rather peripheral participant in this discussion. His contributions are long, coherent, and do not evoke any reaction. He himself frequently comments on contributions of other participants without any discernable preference for any particular speaker.

5.6 Attempts to take over the floor
Last but not least, we have—again in a categorical fashion—taken a closer look at 'attempted interruptions'. An 'attempted interruption' is a speaker's response that appears, like a comment, but, if taken up, causes a change of topic or shifts the interaction to another participant (than the one presently holding the floor), e.g. by putting a question to a third participant.

53

Table 7: Interruptions

Speaker	Interrupter PR	AK	AW	ER	GO	HS	PS	Floor w/o Com	%	Total Floor Interruptions	Attempted Interruptions	%	Interruptions Every xth Floor
AK			3					4	57	7	3	43	2.3
AW	1						1	5	83	6	2	33	3
ER	2	1	2		2			4	44	9	7	78	1.3
GO			3			1	2	4	57	7	6	86	1.2
HS	1							5	83	6	1	17	6
PS	3	1		3		1		7	64	11	8	73	1.4
Total	7	2	8	3	2	2	3						

Again we find HS as the participant whose contributions are listened to without any reaction. Also, a very low frequency of attempted interruptions can be found in contributions of AW. It seems that in his case the high number of comments and responses indicate strong reactions to his statements, thus little attempt was made to change the topic or the main addressee.

As for AK, we interpret the low number of attempted interruptions again as indicator for his self-contained statements, which were not closely tied into the overall discussion. GO, PS, and ER all face a number of attempted interruptions. In detail, ER is interrupted by GO, who agrees with him and tries to take over the floor to elaborate on his statement; GO, in return, is interrupted by AW, who strongly disagrees with ER. PS is interrupted predominantly by ER (who disagrees) and by the moderator, who tries to control PS's relatively successful self-selections to be the next speaker. The main 'interruptors' are the moderator and AW. In that respect it is telling that AW attempts to take over the floor more often than he himself actually holds the floor. AW is unsuccessful in his attempts to gain the floor by himself; the floor was always assigned to him by the moderator.

5.7 Summary

In terms of the interactional dynamics, there are no clear groupings by any characteristics—the politicians differ remarkably from each other: AW repeatedly tries to get the word and fails in most instances; AK mostly waits to take over the floor from the moderator and is usually not interrupted; and PS speaks a lot, self-selects his turns, and is very much the focus of the discussion. The 'political lay person,' HS, is slighted in the discussion, and the political observer, GO, stays at the fringe. Most of the discussion turns to ER, an expert with a clear opinion and political preference. His main conversational partner is PS. Not surprisingly, participants who share an opinion (see arguments) generally do not converse with each other.

If the discussants are grouped according to opinions (PS, AW, and HS for neutrality; ER, GO for NATO; AK at odds), we see that each of the groups has a prominent speaker: PS for neutrality and ER for NATO. Choosing AW as his main conversational opponent, AK affiliates himself implicitly with the pro-NATO group. However, he does not attack PS.

6. Negotiating the Coalition

Not very long before this discussion, the political situation in Austria changed. The former Austrian chancellor, Franz Vranitzky, stepped down from his office, and Viktor Klima became the head of the Socialist Party and the new chancellor. Only about a month before the discussion analyzed here, the new chancellor presented his government's statement (*Regierungserklärung*).[11] The People's Party declared its support of the new government and its readiness to continue the coalition under the new leadership of the Socialist Party. In a newspaper article of the time, the head of the People's Party was said to be astonishingly supportive and welcoming of the new chancellor.[12] This constitutes an important context for the discussion. At the very time of the discussion, the parties of the coalition had been able to do away with a conflict, which had hurt the image of both parties. Now, they wanted to show unity, and the will and power to govern the country together. Yet, their positions regarding the measures to be taken to preserve Austria's security, as well as their attitude towards neutrality were quite different.

In the following section, we will present the programmatic positions AK (People's Party) and PS (Socialist Party) put forward in the discussion (which may differ from those presented in other media). This will be followed by the analysis of a short transcript of each of them, which will allow us to characterize the speakers in terms of their linguistic or rhetorical strategies. These strategies constitute another means for explaining why a particular position ends up being interactionally more successful.

6.1 AK's programmatic position:
Austria in a time of change

The main tenor of AK's arguments dealing with neutrality is "change": "Neutrality has a different function today, we are facing a new order in Europe." "Neutrality was valuable, it has a different meaning today, but it still does have a meaning." This change is presented as an overall loss of the importance or meaning of neutrality. At the same time, this change is accompanied by general change in European politics. The new developments in Europe, in particular the outcome of negotiations within NATO, are uncertain, and AK presents his party as cautiously waiting for the results of these debates before it will come to a decision about neutrality.

Yet, AK's position within the discussion suggests a preference for joining NATO: "One may not see European politics as being simply European; we are also facing peace-promoting actions within the U.N. In Europe, it is not neutrality which is called for today, but solidarity." "One should replace neutrality with active politics for peace." Moreover, AK believes in and stresses the necessity for military power as a means to enforce peace and provide security. His orientation towards NATO is in general positive: he contributes only favourable evaluative statements regarding NATO (e.g. "NATO has never unleashed a war."). These comments, together with AK's position statement at the beginning of the discussion—"Peace and security for Austria are of utmost importance"—lead to the implicit conclusion that, according to AK, Austria should indeed join NATO, which is in line with his party's later official statement.[13]

6.2 PS's programmatic position: an alternative future

In contrast to AK, PS tries to uphold the meaning of neutrality for the present. However, frequently succeeding AK in the discussion (see below), he seems to respond to AK's skepticism of the present-day importance of neutrality: "Neutrality has still a considerable meaning for our country." But for one statement—"Neutrality is our part to bring peace to the world"—his arguments for neutrality are either oriented towards the past, highlighting former accomplishments, or question the alternatives. His stance towards NATO seems skeptical, even though, he rarely expresses this skepticism directly. Instead he raises doubtful and sometimes rhetorical questions, such as "Is it indeed the case, that European security can only be won with NATO?" In particular, he wants to strengthen the role of the U.N. and is worried by a strong NATO, which can act internationally without being necessarily bound by international law and political guidelines (in the same sense as the U.N.).

PS's future vision for Europe strongly contrasts with that of AK but is not directly linked to the issue of neutrality. For instance, PS can imagine a European security system "in which the different organizations are closely linked with each other and cooperate without being part of each of the involved organizations." In other words, while PS does not take a strong stance for neutrality (and can even imagine abandoning neutrality in the long run, depending on the European political situation), his idea of the future is quite different from AK's. PS is much more oriented towards traditional international peace-keeping organizations which are not military pacts. He favors the U.N., OSCE etc., and tries to bring alternatives to NATO into the discussion. In this, however, we judged him not very successful.

Each of the two politicians, AK and PS, uses particular linguistic strategies to make his point and convince his audience.

AK

> "And I think the political petition is a really important matter, which is to be taken seriously. The aim is—I think we all agree on that—that Austria should not participate in any war in the future as well—we don't want a war at our borders, and we don't want a war in Europe. And we don't want Austrian soldiers abroad, and we don't want any foreign soldiers in Austria, and in the end we all strive for the goal—I hope you do as well—that the biblical prophecy—that swords will be made into ploughs and spears into ...—that this sometime , uh will come true. And THIS is the important question. And I think that neutrality—which has for us for many years been very beneficial—it has a different meaning today, we are facing a new order in Europe. ... And we simply have to check, if—everything is evolving this year, what—is the best to reach the aims which I have mentioned. ..."

Of all the politicians present, AK proves to be the one most prolific in using "all" and "we." In the quoted example, which is taken from his first contribution (right at the beginning), he starts with the quite sensible wish for peace of "all Austrians," and thus sets the stage for a discourse in which he can project the point of view of his party onto the whole of "us," onto something "all" (sensible) Austrians would wish for. Thus it is no longer transparent who is referred to in the last sentence, who has to check what is best: "we," the Austrians (as in the preceding discourse) or "we," the People's Party?

In this respect, AK's language displays the typical features of political discourse in which the audience is drawn into the perspective of the speaker.[14] Frequently speaking about "we," the Austrians, he occasionally slips in a "we," the People's Party, obliterating the different points of view. Moreover, AK's longer statements tend to be quite general and vague, or otherwise hedged. For instance, "we don't want war at our borders" is a common sense truth, used here to build up a line of argument, which ends with the vague statement that neutrality has a "different" meaning today. In other places, where AK takes a clear stance, he personalizes his position: "because I am personally of the opinion that our national defense costs us a lot of money right now, we don't spend enough to safeguard neutrality, but if we are members of a European peacekeeping system, we can probably save considerable costs."

AK frequently projects long statements, delays conclusions with insertions and digressions, which might—in conjunction with his vagueness, the "we" - discourse, and the use of common sense truths—explain the small number of interruptions and comments occurring during his statements.

PS

" ... but in the meeting on Wednesday, and we have all been there, all three of us—the issue was not neutrality itself, not whether the existing law should be changed, but the debate was, whether your proposal, whether the text of the *Volksbegehren* [referendum] is to be recommended or not. And all of the scientists who were there, and it has been a hearing of scientists, you were there yourself, with these university professors, they all were of the opinion that this text [of the referendum] would not contribute anything to neutrality. ..."

"Most were of the opinion, and in particular my party as well, even if neutrality has changed, even if the politics of neutrality is changing, neutrality has still a significant meaning for our country; one should uphold neutrality, and everybody who wants to do away with neutrality should say, what they would like to put in its place. Whether what they would put in its place would do the same for us, would get us the same, which neutrality does. And not only in legal terms. Not only legally, and not only politically. But also in terms of the thinking and feeling of the people. And we may not—only one more sentence [to PR]—and we may not forget, that neutrality also led to the Austrians becoming active, that they care about the world in a time, where one is used to think much more locally."

Although a politician himself, PS does not display "we"-discourse to the same extent as AK. In the first example, his "we" is much more oriented towards (some of) the participants, of the undergoing discussion. In this sense, the TV-audience only watches a debate among the participants, in which they have no projected role; in Goffmanian terms they are overhearers, not a targeted audience.[15]

This tendency continues in the second excerpt, which is dealing with a more programmatic presentation of the party line. In this statement, PS introduces his party's position with phrases, such as "most were of the opinion" and "my party," but he does not use "all" and "everyone" and "we". He speaks for "us," "the Austrians," to whom neutrality is still of importance. This addressed audience, "the Austrians," appears in a "patient position," i. e. it is not active but remains in a recipient position. This stands in contrast to the active "they" who try to do away with neutrality. "They" is also presented as threatening "us" by taking away the benefits of neutrality.

Here, PS uses the only general "we" of this whole section, but this "we" remains rather vague. Is it the people of the discussion group he is asking not to forget? Is it the general TV audience? Since he continues with "led Austrians ...," he makes a co-referential relation of "we" with "Austrians" rather unlikely, which is why "we" should not be interpreted to mean "we Austrians."

In short, throughout the whole section presented here PS does not use a single all-inclusive active "we." In his discourse "we" is the passive recipient of other people's doing, if it appears at all. At the same time PS presents his party and its position rather directly. In contrast to AK he sets up his party as an entity which clearly exists independently, and thus exists independent from "the Austrians" and "we." Whereas AK tries to melt both concepts into one, PS preserves the distinction and tries to present his party as the one which "serves" the people.

In studies of political discourse,[16] these different styles are frequently (and critically) interpreted as follows: The obliteration of the difference between the speaker and his audience by using the all-inclusive "we" leads to a loss of distance between the reader and the text. The reader or, in this case, listener might under the pressure of on-line processing simply accept what is being said. However, in doing so, the listener does not only accept the position of the speaking individual, but also a point of view, in which he or she is already situated. This discourse does not readily offer a position outside the discourse, which could be used to evaluate one's own position toward the subject. Thus, it takes extra mental, cognitive effort to distance oneself and critically reflect on whether one is truly part of this "we" and believes in everything "we" are said to do or believe. If the listener does not make this extra effort (which he/she will often not), he/she will end up with a model which already incorporates—unintentionally—his/her positioning, i. e. "opinion." Without further reflection and later critical examination of this model, the listener will in his/her beliefs and actions be informed by this model. Thus, the use of the all-inclusive "we" proves (under these theoretical assumptions) a very potent political means termed, in a critical perspective, 'populist discourse' (because it tries to politically "convince" the viewers with implicit, non-critical measures).

In contrast, PS's style of upholding the distinction between "the party" and "the people" allows a critical distance which invites one to think about whether the party's actions are indeed in one's interest. In critical studies this is often deemed the more 'enlightened' democratic discourse style, even though, in affording the critical distance, it is also considered less persuasive, less politically effective. In this discourse, it is the affiliation with the party ideology which takes active participation and reflection.

Thus, in terms of discursive studies of political discourse, AK would be regarded as populist and more successful, while PS's style would be conceived of as being 'morally superior' yet politically less effective.

As we have already discussed, there are very few instances of AK and PS interacting with each other. Both mostly direct their talk to someone else. However, to answer the question of how they negotiate the coalition in this discussion, we have also looked at instances in which PS and AK do interact. How do they manage disagreement, how do they negotiate the coalition?

In total we have found 26 segments in the texts, in which PS and AK talk at the same time or immediately follow each other. In four of these, they talk after each other but not relating to each other (they are both commenting on somebody else). In one further case, AK comments on somebody else's remark to PS (who is holding the floor).

The remaining 21 segments can be grouped into four classes:

- Either PS or AK talks about neutrality and the other disagrees or tries to weaken the expressed position (of the other).
- Or one of them talks about NATO, and again, the other one disagrees or tries to weaken the statement put forward by the first speaker.
- Or one of them speaks about any other topic and the other one agrees.

- Or both act in mutual agreement and momentary support of each other while taking a stance against a third participant.

Speaker	Neutrality	Nato	Agreement	Collaboration against third party
PS	1	2	3 agreeing, 3 elaborating	8
AK	1	-	5 agreeing	

Thus we can see, that in general the two politicians of the coalition cooperate with each other more than they debate with each other, as long as the subject matter does not concern their different points of view on 'neutrality' or 'NATO'. But even with these issues the difference of opinion is only moderately or indirectly expressed, as in the following example, which contains the most elaborate interaction of all these instances.

PS   We should not forget that neutrality also led to the fact that the Austrians became engaged, that they are caring about the world, that they – in a time when one is thinking much closer to home - kept

----
AK   but it is just this
PS   their perspective for the larger issues

AK   (issue xxxx)   that   the Swiss expert
PS   and that is a good thing for a country. That is good for

----
AK   has said that neutrality has lost its function.
PS   country<
?   yes

PR   what should in
AK   in this matter.
PS   the – Swiss expert (has) in this respect

PR   I:) (what should)   (xxx)   na=na m=m
PS   be critical   >(one) should talk about whether <

PR   (we)
PS   that is indeed the case and what should be put in in the place of neutrality
----

In this example, AK contests PS's claim by quoting the opinion of an "expert." He can thus defer the responsibility for his refutation to this expert: Although AK himself contests PS, it is the opinion of somebody else which stands in possible conflict with PS's statement. This move allows him to retain the image of joined action within the coalition, and, at the same time, to question PS. In response, PS does not start a debate about neutrality itself (as he could), or reject the content of the statement, but he redefines what was actually said in the reported statement. This, however, is a different matter altogether, and the two politicians may happily disagree or agree on this issue, without touching any of their respective party politics.

It is possible that both politicians were invited with the expectation that they would argue on some of the points. This could also explain why the discussion leader changes the topic at one point without any apparent reason to ask AK about his party's position on neutrality. But, as already reported, AK's answer is quite cautious, and can be readily accepted by PS, who is only led to affirm that "the meaning of neutrality has changed" (AK)—"but it still has one" (PS). In the same vein, we don not see PS making negative evaluative statements on NATO; his possibly critical statements are on several occasions put forward as questions to ER ("Will we have to fight, if we join NATO?" "What does it REALLY cost?").

In general we thus see that AK and PS do not confront each other. Their orientation toward each other and their difference of opinion show in other aspects: (a) as was already presented above, PS frequently tries to make a statement after AK, and (b) both of them choose another participant as opponent, to whom they react critically, and in interaction with whom they can express their position. In the case of AK this is AW; for PS this is ER.

6.3 ER: an expert in conversation with PS

In the following, we will analyze the interaction of PS and ER, as it is ER who holds the floor for extended periods of time. ER's talk differs linguistically from the talk of PS and AK. He displays many features of expert talk, which—at least in this interaction—prove to be a very effective register:[17]

ER: Uh, something, which the NATO, uh, which neutrality most definitely is not—Congressman Wabl—an up to date instrument of peace-maintenance. It is an ancient instrument of international law from a time, when war was still an acceptable means. Since we've got the U.N., there is no permissible war any more—which means, neutrality does not provide an additional security to the status of a normal country. Because everyone has the right not to be attacked.

However, neutrality does add something in contrast to one being not neutral, and these are obligations. The obligation not to join a military treaty and so on. And also the obligation to entertain a neutrality politics. It constrains without yielding in turn any specific advantages.

And now to you, Congressman Schieder. Naturally, you are completely right in that one has to respect people's feelings. And I know that a security advisor has an easier time to give good advice—and you have to put in action then. That there is a difference, I am well aware of. But, nevertheless it is the function of a security advisor, to be frank about the situation,

----

ER: and to state his reasons. In here we want to talk about the
PS: There must be place for debates

ER: dimension 'neutrality', which concerns the national security, in this there are a lot of people who talk/understand something different. For some this is an important element of Austrian national identity, for someone else ... and so on. Our neutrality conceived of as a security instrument is based on the federal law about neutrality and that states without doubt....

ER's talk in this and other instances features a lot of characteristics of 'scientific' language.[18] He uses many indirect, passive constructions (almost no "we," "they," but often "one" if there are agents mentioned at all), many nominalizations (in German) etc. Everything sounds factual; he does not utter opinions or points of view, but tells everyone the one and indisputable 'truth,' the 'plain facts.' When he mentions a range of opinions (about the possible meanings of 'neutrality'), he restricts his point of view explicitly to the one which a security advisor would give. In other words, he makes explicit reference to his expertise (as a security advisor) and implicitly asserts that every security advisor would be of this position, as it is the only rational one in terms of a national security policy.

In the course of the discussion, ER is very successful in establishing his position as an expert. Although he is originally introduced in affiliation with the Austrian Freedom Party, throughout the discussion he is more and more explicitly addressed with reference to his function within the defense ministry (at the beginning he is often addressed as "Mr. Reiter," towards the end frequently with the specific administrative title of his position within the ministry). As an expert with a seemingly unpartial position, he can dismantle neutrality (as in the transcript shown above) without being contested by the other participants.

In regard to PS, we see a change of the interactional style throughout the discussion. At the beginning, PS has a more antagonistic discourse behavior, which displays unmitigated disagreement, or refutations (example repeated from above):

ER: But, nevertheless it is the function of a security advisor, to be frank about the
    situation,

ER: and to state his reasons. In here we want to talk about the
PS: There must be place for debates

ER: dimension 'neutrality', which concerns the national security,
----

In this example, ER tries to assert himself as the unpartial security expert. PS rejects this self-presentation, indirectly stating that there is more than just one point of view.

In the following discussion, PS raises several critical questions, which call presuppositions of NATO supporters into question. His tone changes when he addresses a long question directly to ER. In the process of doing so, he actively seeks to establish a common ground (e.g. that NATO does have positive aspects), and addresses the question explicitly to ER in his function within the ministry. Already in the elaboration of that question, ER himself now starts to participate collaboratively in this discourse:

PS: article five of the NATO-treaty

PR: what does this exactly mean?
ER: *"Beistandsverpflichtung"*
PS: which is the obligation to offer support

PS: all states, if they are attacked...

In his subsequent answer, ER explicitly exempts PS when attacking some NATO opponents. For most of the remaining discussion, ER and PS collaborate in their interactions, while they are still clearly of different opinions.

ER: all military measures of NATO are to be stopped as soon as the *"Sicherheitsrat"* has
    takes measures to ensure the reconstitution of order and security.

ER: this is very much

PS: So, the issue are measures preceding measures taken by the U.N.

ER: aligned with the operations of the U.N. (xxxxxxxx) uh

PS: But that means we would have to fight for them

ER: This could happen. If it came so far. Uh. Of course, this

----

ER: is possible theoretically. In practice, however, things look different.
PS: This is the question, yes.

ER: Who would attack the NATO? And even more so: who would attack a bigger NATO?

In addition, PS and ER would occasionally give each other interactional support, using "of course," "sure," "yes," etc. Throughout the following discussion, PS directs a number of additional questions to ER, and is thus the only participant explicitly directing his questions to another conversation partner. The questions usually also contain the administrative title of ER, solidifying him as the expert. Since PS addresses his questions to ER as an expert on national defense, they usually concern NATO (and costs etc.) and do not deal with neutrality. Thus, as the principal speaker of the participants in favor of neutrality (for the moment), PS helps establish NATO as the dominant topic in this discussion, at the expense of the topic of neutrality.[19] In addressing ER solely in his administrative expert function, he participates in constructing ER as the impartial expert, although his affiliation to the Freedom Party is known to everyone present. AW's protests remain unheeded:

PS: ... Partnership for Peace in service for the U.N. – that is terrific. But you [ER] use that as a legitimization for article five. And is THAT right?

ER: Member of Parliament Schieder, it is not ideology when I say that in the end you need to be able to defend yourself, to defend a collective; this is not philosophy but security policy.

In brief, the two main speakers of this conversation (i.e. speakers with most floors) both end up talking most of the time about NATO, and the supporter of neutrality ends up deferring to the NATO-sympathizing expert. Nobody gives up his respective position, but in the overall picture NATO is very present, and the expert and NATO-proponent 'ranks' higher than the supporters of neutrality.

Only a study of the reception of this discussion could discern the exact nature of the impression that was left in the audience. However, it seems reasonable to suspect that NATO ended up being conceived as the more important and effective concept.

7. Conclusion

Although both representatives of the main coalition parties present their position programmatically, they do not insist on the program or on the ideologies behind these programs. In this paper we understand and define ideologies as clusters of beliefs and opinions.[20] Although the viewers know these ideologies and they are thus presuppositions, they are never made explicit. This leads us to conclude that the politicians of the governing parties avoid confrontation and prefer to transfer the conflict to other participants in the debate. This transfer leads in one case to an interaction between participants with different backgrounds and different interactional styles: namely a (military) expert and a politician. In the context of the topic under discussion, it is the expert whose style of speech proves to be more successful. Being drawn into the discussion in his role as an expert, the topic becomes constrained by the particular expertise he displays. In this discussion, this led one topical side of the proposed discussion (neutrality and NATO) to be much more prevalent. As is known for instance from theory on advertising, discourse presence can often be much more important than the expression of a particular stance or opinion towards a topic in raising awareness and attributing significance. Thus, the dominance of the expert topic might have well been received as "important" and looked upon favorably by the audience.

Notes

1. This paper is part of a project on the role of neutrality in the contemporary discourse of Austrian national identity, which is presently conducted at the Wittgenstein Research Center for Discourse, Politics, and Identity. Further information can be found at: http://www.wittgenstein.univie.ac.at/.

2. Waldemar Hummer and Michael Schweizer, *Österreich und die EWG. Neutralitäts-rechtliche Beurteilung der Möglichkeiten der Dynamisierung des Verhältnisses zur EWG* (Wien: Signum Verlag, 1987).

3. Neutrality changed its meaning and functions during the Second Republic: Starting out in 1955 as the Soviet precondition for a 'free Austria', it slowly became an integral part of Austrian national identity. See Ruth Wodak et al., *Zur diskursiven Konstruktion nationaler Identität* (Frankfurt am Main: Suhrkamp, 1998); Ernst Bruckmüller, *Symbole*

österreichischer Identität zwischen »Kakanien« und »Europa«. Wiener Vorlesungen (Wien: Picus Verlag, 1997); Gertraud Benke, "Neutralität im Wandel der Zeit," *Kursiv* 5 (February 1998), 14-21; Gertraud Benke and Ruth Wodak, "'We are no longer the sick child of Europe': An Investigation of the Usage (and Change) of the Term 'Neutrality' in the Presidential Speeches on the National Holiday (26 October) from 1974 to 1993," in *Challenges in a Changing World - Issues in Critical Discourse Analysis*, ed. Ruth Wodak and Christoph Ludwig (Wien: Passagen Verlag, 1999), 101-126.

4. Christian Schaller, "Die innenpolitische EG-Diskussion seit den 80er Jahren," in *Ausweg EG? Innenpolitische Motive einer außenpolitischen Umorientierung*, ed. Anton Pelinka, Christian Schaller, and Paul Luif (Wien: Böhlau, 1994), 27 - 256.

5. In 1998 the Socialist Party changed its position and is now willing to give up neutrality in favor of joint foreign and defense politics of the European Union if these take the shape of a peace-promoting European security system.

6. Norman Fairclough, "Democracy and the Public Sphere in Critical Research on Discourse," in *Challenges in a Changing World*, 63-85.

7. Ruth Wodak and Eva Vetter, "The Small Distinctions between Diplomats, Politicians and Journalists: the Discursive Construction of Professional Identity," in *Challenges in a Changing World*, 209-237; Fairclough, "Democracy"; Helmut Gruber, *Konfliktgespräche* (Oplanden: Westdeutscher Verlag, 1997).

8. Thus, a 'story' or account with more or less extensive evidence is counted as one argument not as two (or more). In problematic cases, the choice was to break a sequence of propositions down to the smallest units which make conversational sense as arguments for or against something in their own right.

9. We do not wish to claim that this division into units would be successful in all situations, but in this TV-discussion one person is usually the invited or self-selected speaker, who would address a particular topic at length. Though he would be interrupted by comments from the other participants, he would usually remain the center of the conversation. Nevertheless, the boundaries between such units are fuzzy, and there may be a number of turns, in which nobody can be considered the main speaker.

10. One might explain this by the particular party affiliations of the two participants, which would usually put them in a strong opposition. As noted before, GO's opinion was rather unusual considering his party preference; and given the strong emotions of many intellectual Socialists against the Freedom Party, it is not surprising that they should override the momentary thematic agreement.

11. "VP-Sanftmut, ein 'böser Geist' und 'intellekturelle Hochseilakte,'" *Die Presse*, 30 January 1997.

12. "Schüssel nach dem 'Down': Die letzte Chance der 'Firma'," *Die Presse*, 30 January 1997.

13. *Die Position der ÖVP zur Zukunft der österreichischen Sicherheitspolitik. Beschluß des Bundesparteivorstandes der Österreichischen Volkspartei.* (Wien: Bundesparteivorstand, 14 July 1997).

14. John Wilson, *Politically Speaking* (Oxford: Basil Blackwell, 1990).

15. Erving Goffman, *Forms of Talk* (Oxford: Blackwell, 1981).

16. Paul Chilton and Christina Schäffer, "Discourse and Politics," in *Discourse as Social Interaction. Discourse Studies,* vol. 2, ed. Teun A. van Dijk (London: Sage, 1997), 206 - 30.

17. Helga Kotthoff, "The Interactional Achievement of Expert Status. Creating Asymmetries by 'Teaching Conversational Lectures in TV Discussions," in *Communicating Gender in Context*, ed. Helga Kotthoff and Ruth Wodak (Amsterdam: Benjamins, 1997), 139 - 78; Wodak and Vetter, "The Small Distinctions."

18. Wolfgang U. Dressler, "Funktion und Textzusammenhang in der Wissenschaftssprache," in *Fachsprache und Kommunikation*, ed. Wolfgang U. Dressler and Ruth Wodak (Wien: Österreichischer Bundesverlag, 1989), 79 - 91; Wodak and Vetter, "The Small Distinctions."

19. The role of the moderator was important insofar, as he allowed this topic to take hold of the floor, whereas he curtailed other people and their topics – e.g. AW. In restricting the access or the topic-definition of others, he did not give them the space to show their expertise and establish themselves with their favorite topic.

20. Norman Fairclough and Ruth Wodak, "Critical Discourse Analysis," in *Discourse as Social Interaction. Discourse Studies*. vol. 2, ed. Teun A. van Dijk (London: Sage, 1997), 258 – 84.

International Perceptions
of Austrian Neutrality

Oliver Rathkolb

This article concentrates on outside perceptions of Austrian neutrality since 1955 in order to analyze the attitudes of the major players in the cold war and their interpretations of an allegedly clear cut concept of neutrality in international law. A deeper understanding of the much broader perception of neutrality as seen from the outside might be useful in the ongoing domestic debate about the future of Austrian neutrality in light of the end of the cold war and the membership in the European Union. Despite the fact that Austrian neutrality of 1955 is certainly a result of the first détente of the cold war and is a direct product of the Allied occupation between 1945-1955,[1] the ongoing discussions produce the myth that the Austrian government alone (sometimes with the Soviet Union) established neutrality and neutrality policy after 1955. In my point of view this is a typically isolationist and highly narrow-minded view.[2] In real-life politics neutrality policy is always influenced by the great power framework of neighboring countries, which decides the options and the decision making capabilities of the neutral state.

1955: Austrian (Split) Neutrality Is no Model at all
Immediately after his election, President Dwight D. Eisenhower reversed the total anti-neutrality policy of the Truman administration concerning Austria. From his point of view 'neutralization' of Austria alone—i.e. no neutralization of other 'split' countries such as Germany and non-alignment in the 'Third World' would close the gap between the conventional forces of the north-south line within NATO. Already as supreme commander of NATO he realized that, due to massive troop reductions in the three western allied zones of Austria and due to the

presence of estimated 30,000 Soviet soldiers in Eastern Austria, pro-Western Austrian conventional forces, comprising 65 000 soldiers under arms, could delay a possible attack of the Red Army and thereby assist NATO forces in mobilizing the north-south line between Western Germany and Italy through Austrian territory.[3]

It took Secretary of State John Foster Dulles, who preferred clear cut solutions in the cold war, until the end of the Berlin Conference of 1954 to accept the neutral status as an option for Austria. He agreed with President Eisenhower that Austria should accept a status like Switzerland and be prepared to defend neutrality with military forces. Dulles, however, tried to keep the Austrian delegation away from a 'neutrality declaration' in Berlin since he feared a 'negative' copying effect on Germany. Whereas Eisenhower knew that a military neutrality status of Austria would mean a strengthening of prowestern conventional forces in the region, Dulles even reversed the argument of the U.S. president and "noted that Austria could become an inviting invasion route to the South comparable to Belgium in 1914."[4] During the Berlin conference he realized that the post-Stalin nomenclatura had reversed the 'neutralization' propaganda, which Stalin had imposed in 1952. In 1954, the Austrian Communists were explicitly told not to continue their neutrality propaganda.[5] The hard-liners around Foreign Minister Molotov seemed not at all interested in a change of the status quo—not even with regard to Austria, which was certainly beyond the Soviet sphere of influence despite the presence of Soviet troops in Eastern Austria and Vienna. After Khrushchev had taken absolute power in the Kremlin, he continued to realize the options discussed by Malenkov and Beria after Stalin's death, especially to obtain détente.[6]

In May 1953 Malenkow already referred to Austria as part of a new strategy. He again focused on the Austrian bargaining chip, which Eisenhower, too, referred to in 1953 as an option for relaxation and for a follow-up summit meeting. In Malenkow's view the retreat of Soviet soldiers from Eastern Austria, to which Molotov was opposed, would not really weaken Soviet military strategic abilities although the Soviet Union would also have to give up the lines of communication and the allocation of troops in Hungary and Rumania.[7] He very well understood that Austria was completely integrated into the Western European economy and Western culture. At the same time the central postwar aim of the Soviet Union, separating Austria from Germany,[8] could be guaranteed by neutralization—even at the risk that, in case of conflict with NATO, Austria would side with NATO as a result of U.S. military assistance (at that time already well known due to the training and equipping of a nucleus Austrian Army, the *B-Gendarmerie*).

From the perspective of Moscow—until the late 1980s—Austrian neutrality was primarily a guarantee against a revival of West German 'imperialism' and a move against the Soviet border. At the same time Austria constituted a test case: If Austrian neutrality failed in peacetime, the probability of an attack against the Eastern block—as in 1938—would rise considerably. Before Gorbachev the World War II trauma of the Soviet Communist elites was so strong that they believed in a repetition of history.

Due to the conventional weakness of the Western military block the 'other' U.S., perception aimed more towards an all-out-conflict, not, as in the Soviet case, towards an early warning case. In 1955 Secretary of State Dulles urged the Austrian government to continue to build up an Austrian army under the guidance of U.S. experts and nearly exclusively based on U.S. armament and technology. He made it quite clear that this was a precondition for approval of the State Treaty by Congress. U.S. military assistance remained the nucleus of the Austrian army until the 1960s. From all we know, this pro-NATO concept in case of all-out-war was part of NATO strategy.[9] The military attaché in Vienna, Colonel Oden, reported in March 1956 that "Austrian military authorities consider active participation on the side of the West as their country's only possible course of action in the event of a general war. Their plans provide for the disposition of their forces and reserve so that ... they could fall back and defend the Klagenfurt basin and the Tyrol."[10] In case of a military showdown this would have resulted in a separation of Austria. This NATO concept of dividing the ideas of military neutrality and self-defense of Austria, however, was implanted by the Austrian general staff until the late 1950s and is referred to as 'split neutrality.' Efforts of the same military elite to establish a direct liaison office in Rome as early as November 1955 were blocked by U.S. diplomats as they could create—if known to the public or to Soviet intelligence—an excuse for the Soviet Union to question the neutrality status as such.[11]

At this point the military component of Austrian neutrality should be addressed. From the perspective of the U.S. an Austrian army should be able to suppress a domestic Communist coup d'état and to delay an attack from the Eastern bloc. This military neutrality was nevertheless contained since the military equipment was limited to the above-mentioned aims. At the same time the Austrian budget—reflecting the interests of the Austrian public—did not encompass the new needs for military spending until 1956 (and public opinion did not approve of this added expense). Only with outside pressure and foreign, U.S., assistance could these ten years of nearly no military spending be reversed to reach the level of comparable budgets of GNP. Still, Austria never reached the Swiss military budget nor comparable figures of smaller NATO countries or Sweden due to ten years of demilitarization. In addition, there was no need to completely change the postwar budget policy after 1955 due to the U.S. assistance.

Along the lines of international politics, the U.S. government, was also not interested in Austria, or Vienna in particular, as a meeting place for East-West détente and disarmament talks. The concept of neutrality should not find any more imitators. From the very beginning, John Foster Dulles opposed the Soviets' 'insistent pressures' to hold the summit meeting of 1955 in Vienna.[12] Even in 1958, when Chancellor Julius Raab tried to obtain the American approval for a more active role of Austria in the détente negotiations, Dulles objected.[13] The Austrian example of 1955 should not be enlarged by any sort of 'internationalization' of Austria. The establishment of the International Atomic Energy Agency (IAEA) in Vienna was therefore not considered a first sign of the 'internationalization' of Austria, but a special case. It was the result of a Soviet-American compromise (the U.S. aimed at the position of director general in this organization and therefore had to offer something to the Soviets, who had always wanted Vienna to become part of the international détente game) and reflected the fact that the Austrian government accepted U.S. leadership, offering very generous support for this institution in Vienna.[14]

While the superpowers were both convinced that Austrian neutrality would and should not change immediately, they disagreed on Austria's function as a communication place between East and West, which the Soviets wanted to reinforce and the Eisenhower administration tried to contain. The most skeptical European power, however, was Great Britain. Especially British diplomats saw the Austrian neutrality of 1955 as just another form of appeasement and forecasted it as a first step into pro-Soviet non-alignment. Sir Geoffrey Wallinger, the British Ambassador, noted that the Austrian Chancellor Julius Raab resorted to 'neutralism' and was convinced that this foreign policy, if continued, would only be the " ... first step to satellization."[15] This rather negative view, which prevailed in the Foreign Office in London, suddenly changed in 1956 as a result of Austria's distinct pro-Western political behavior during the Soviet intervention in Hungary. Austria thus proved that she was not on her way to non-alignment, but was clearly grounded in the Western camp regarding ideological battles. More than 170,000 refugees poured into Austria and the 'young' and small sovereign state was prepared to provide asylum—with large international financial and political assistance. Furthermore, Chancellor Raab directly attacked the Soviet Union, asking the Kremlin to "work cooperatively toward the ending of military hostilities and bloodshed," and requesting the "normalization of conditions in Hungary for the re-establishment of freedom in the sense of human rights."[16] Some Socialist members of the government, such as the Minister of the Interior Oskar Helmer, even went further, applauding the "Hungarian heroes" who "dare to rise against dictatorship and force ..." Raab tried to soften the very aggressive anti-Soviet media coverage in Austria. In general, though, the Austrian government stuck to the concept of military neutrality (one Soviet soldier was even killed when taken prisoner on Austrian territory) yet behaved "more Western than the West" and underlined the deep commitment to the West.[17]

Neutral Asylum Country—A Cold War Myth?

Another very important perception of Austria began to develop after 1956: Austria as a neutral asylum country. Especially after 1968, the year of the invasion in Czechoslovakia, this perception increased, but already in 1981—when many Polish refugees came to Austria—first signs of opposition appeared in Austrian society. Between 1956 and 1968 such prejudices were overruled by the cold war 'side show' and the international guarantees that the refugees will stay only for a short time and then emigrate to other countries like the U.S. or Canada. One could argue that in 1956 the economic situation was still tense, but, on the other hand, the Austrian economy started to import labor from Yugoslavia and Turkey already in the early 1960s. The Austrian population never felt prepared to support a considerable non-Austrian immigration segment, and thus Austria never developed extensive immigration laws or an immigration policy.

International media coverage, especially in 1956 and 1968, established a strong image of Austria as a neutral asylum country. Thus, in 1984, the perception of Austria as "an asylum country" is much stronger than that of "a political neutral country." Especially in Eastern Europe and the U.S.S.R. Austria was considered an asylum country, whereas 'political neutral' was a label more associated with Switzerland.

In Western Europe, France, Italy, and Switzerland still regard Switzerland as *the* 'neutral' and 'asylum' country; only Western Germany voted
for Austria in the category 'asylum'. In the U.S. the neutrality perception of Austria, when compared with Switzerland, is extremely low
(only 19% despite the possibility of double voting).[18]

"Keep the Peripherals out":
Neutrality Accepted, but Not 'Integrable'
into European Integration

That the new president, John F. Kennedy, chose Vienna among the
Soviet summit-suggestions (Stockholm and Vienna)[19] was a clear sign
that the Kennedy administration began to reverse the Dulles strategy of
containing neutrality (although they continued to contain non-alignment). But at the beginning this new strategy also included a "bitter
pill": The European strategy of Kennedy's Assistant Secretary of State
George F. Ball strictly opposed any form of association of the three
neutrals Sweden, Switzerland, and Austria with the European Economic
Union since this would endanger Ball's vision of a strong political and
military EEC.[20] George C. McGhee, member of the Policy Planning
Staff of the State Department, understood quickly that the neutrals might
turn to the Soviet bloc if excluded from the large non-communist
European bloc. He argued that "their association would dilute and
weaken the Community and even tend to destroy its institutions; that
association of a few would open the floodgates to similar demands by
many other states, including non-European ones."[21] But in 1961 the
mainstream position of the State Department favored a "growing
political, strategic, and economic monolith, clearly not neutral ..." and
did not want the neutrals' association to be used as an argument for the
major Commonwealth countries to apply for association, too.[22]
However, De Gaulle's veto of 1963 against the integration of Great
Britain more or less destroyed the real basis of Ball's European visions.
The dispute became obsolete, but was never solved in bilateral talks
between Austria and the U.S. From the written evidence one might even
draw the conclusion that the Kennedy administration wanted to reverse
this *Westernization* of Austria's neutrality policies, realizing that the
Soviet Union would never have accepted any form of institutional
integration of Austria into the EEC because it feared this would
strengthen the German capabilities within the Community. (This
argument blocked Austria's efforts after 1963 to become at least an

associate member of the EEC, since it has been taken over by French government under Pompidou. This enabled the Italians to block the negotiations in 1967 by just referring to the bombing in South Tyrol.) The more Germany tried to push the Austrian case (which they did from time to time), the stronger the French resistance grew. A 'special' association of the three neutrals (not full membership) might endanger the political and military integration of the EEC due to geopolitical pressure from the Soviet Union and alleged neutralization tendencies within the EEC (especially tendencies against tighter political and military coordination through supra-national institutions).

It should be mentioned here that to this day Austrian decision makers and journalists are not able to see that not only the Soviet Union hindered a closer affiliation to the European Economic Community in the 1960s, but that the EEC was also not prepared to accept Austria yet. Austria is and was no special case for European integration. Until 1963 the main and overall interest of the EEC was the British question, and all other issues—including the negotiations with the neutrals—were secondary. France was only the strongest force against an Austrian special agreement, and Italy the most outspoken one. The Soviet Union continued to stress the *Anschluß* issue. By mixing the provisions of the State Treaty (containing an annexation veto) with the Neutrality law, the Soviets argued in 1959 that Austria's economic integration—even under an association agreement—would incorporate Austria directly into NATO.[23]

This policy of *de-Westernization* of Austrian neutrality in the early 1960s continued in the economic sphere under President Johnson, who started to loosen the very tight economic blockade against the 'Soviet Bloc' by the Coordinating Committee (COCOM). The COCOM lists for export goods into Eastern Europe and the Soviet Union were considered to be of strategic importance in the cold war. Austria was strongly tied into this system, and Raab did not even succeed in lifting this embargo for specific projects such as the export of a steel mill to Czechoslovakia.[24] East-West trade should become an extremely important barometer for the intensity of détente (the Brandt-Scheel *Ostpolitik* was preceded by economic cooperation through joint ventures). But even in this area it was not the Austrian efforts towards more sovereignty in economic matters that prevailed, but the relaxation of international tension—especially in economic relations.

Despite some differences of opinion about the pragmatic approach towards détente in the 1960s the Austrian foreign policy course was accepted by U.S. decision makers and sometimes even used as a source of information and expertise on the U.S.S.R., the Berlin question, etc. (e.g., see the Austrian references in the Cuban missile crisis).[25] This specific Austrian *Ostpolitik* was developed by Chancellor Julius Raab on the basis of good bilateral relationships with the U.S.S.R. and was expanded by the policy of cultivating contacts with some neighboring 'satellite countries' such as Czechoslovakia (which turned out to be a failure even in the 1970s), Hungary, Yugoslavia, Poland and Romania. It was especially implemented by Foreign Minister Bruno Kreisky (1959-1965), sometimes heavily criticized in relation to Yugoslavia, and to some extent continued during the ÖVP one party government under Josef Klaus 1966-1970.[26] By increasing the level of the bilateral relations with Communist neighbors, the Austrian *Ostpolitik* should assist in reducing the tensions of the cold war and even work slowly towards a change within the bloc system and a more democratic structure. Especially Kreisky was always interested in sounding out the various groups in an allegedly monolithic cold war bloc (e.g. Rumanian opposition to certain policy aims of the Soviet Union, or Polish efforts for reduction of nuclear capabilities etc.). At the same time this policy should assist in coming to terms with disputes from the past (property and border issues), increase communication and tourism, as well as assist in family integration through the Iron Curtain. This policy worked very well with Hungary and Yugoslavia, but was not very effective with regard to the CSR.[27]

1968: Austria under the Nuclear Umbrella of NATO.
A Myth!

Whereas the Austrian government of 1956 had placed itself on the side of the 'West', the People's Party government of 1968 under Chancellor Josef Klaus was more cautious and reacted both in Austria and in the U.N. with moderate and restrained words. For some time Foreign Minister Kurt Waldheim even asked the Austrian ambassador to Prague, Rudolf Kirchschläger, to stop issuing visas for entry into Austria (due to alleged thefts of visa forms). The media reported rumors that the government would leave Vienna and try to find shelter in the Aussee region. In general the Austrian press and radio were much more aggressive in attacks against the Soviet Union than the government in Vienna. This was certainly the result of a very strong "Americanization" of media and journalists, in particular during the Allied occupation of

1945-1955. In September 1968 Klaus himself summarized that the "chancellor and foreign minister were too cautious," and that the press showed too little caution.[28] The Socialist opposition party reacted much more concerned, calling for condemnation of the intervention in CSR as well as a more bi-partisan foreign policy, which Klaus, in the long run, accepted by trying to obtain a three-party-statement of the parliament.

During this crisis of 1968 it again became quite obvious that the Austrian army had not reached the capabilities to defend the country if the Warsaw Pact decided to move ahead. Once more many people thought that the U.S. would protect Austria against such an intervention, and once more this turned out to be a myth due to the clear cut strategy of NATO and the U.S. excluding Eastern Austria as well as Czechoslovakia, which was considered an exclusive Soviet sphere of influence. The opposition leader Kreisky, though, had already considered a concept of *umfassende Landesverteidigung* (overall defense policy) with a strong international position as much more appropriate (somewhat similar to the Swedish concept, integrating the social partners and the workers in defense preparations).

Neutrality and Détente in the 1970s

The 1970s were clearly dominated by the Socialist government under Chancellor Bruno Kreisky, who directed the foreign policy not by authoritarian rule, but by a deeply rooted and permanent activism in international relations. He had always been a convinced anti-Communist fully backing the containment strategy of the Truman administration. At the same time, as foreign minister in the 1960s, he continued the special policy developed under Chancellor Julius Raab, trying to stabilize the East-West tension by good relations with the Soviet Union and the neighboring Communist countries. Already in 1959, still as secretary of state, Kreisky outlined the specific Austrian *Ostpolitik* when analyzing Adenauer's *Rußlandpolitik*: "In principle, the hard line of Adenauer corresponds to Austrian views, but German tactics were often wrong. The German chancellor tends to offend the sensibilities of the Russians and is much too inflexible and ideologically preoccupied when negotiating."[29]

Instead of accepting 'cold peace,' Kreisky quickly focused on increased economic cooperation between the bloc systems, without neglecting to continue a strict anti-Communist line in domestic policies. (In the Eisenstadt declaration of 1969, for example, Kreisky tried to cut all unauthorized contacts with Communist functionaries abroad as well as in Austria). In this he differed from Raab, who, after 1955, had developed a tendency in his neutrality policy referred to as *'Schaukelpolitik'*: When he offended one bloc by a decision (such as the permission to hold the Sudeten-German-Day in Austria), he agreed, as a compromise, to give in to the other bloc in another request (e.g. the Communist World Youth festival in 1959 advocated by the Soviet Union).

The main instrument for a broader and more coordinated approach of the neutrals (partly in cooperation with the non-aligned states) in the 1970s was the "Conference for Cooperation and Security in Europe" (CSCE). Originally a Soviet initiative from 1953, which allowed Europeans for the first time to negotiate directly with the superpowers, the CSCE, as Kreisky soon realized, gave small state groups like the neutrals or non-aligned countries the opportunity to be actors not just objects in superpower "geopolitics." Whereas the U.S. were still much more interested in direct superpower negotiations, and the crucial issue of nuclear armament reductions was excluded from the CSCE, the neutrals found their political niche. The four neutrals, Austria, Switzerland, Sweden, and Finland, coordinated their efforts, focusing on human contacts, information, education, and culture in order to increase the level of cooperation between East and West (including the discussion about democratic principles).[30] Concerning the conference agenda for military security, the four neutrals established a channel of coordination with Yugoslavia, Cyprus, Malta, and Liechtenstein and formed the N+N group (neutrals and non-aligned) on an informal but effective basis.

The role of the CSCE-process in increasing the opposition in the Communist bloc and assisting in peaceful transformation is still underestimated. Here, too, Chancellor Kreisky continued to stress the importance of peaceful cooperation without suppressing the ideological confrontation (e.g. in the human rights issue). In 1975 Kreisky was one of the very few signers of the Helsinki Treaty to stress this view (which was disliked by the Soviet Union): "We are prepared to continue the confrontation, and we welcome the Conference for Security and Cooperation in Europe since the main principle which we have agreed upon will allow a global confrontation with peaceful means. We interpret this part of the declaration of principles with regard to the right of each signatory state to choose and develop his political, social, and cultural system without any pressure."[31]

In practice that meant that Austria was prepared not only to assist political refugees from the CSR (Charta 77), but also to intervene permanently against the persecution of opposition activists like Václav Havel in the CSR or Alexander Sacharov in the U.S.S.R.—even when this implied that Austria did not act as a neutral state but intervened in domestic affairs. Both prominent opposition leaders as well as many other people were included in the various negotiation agendas.

With the decline of the cold war necessity to assist refugees from the East and Europe's first recession after the 'golden years' of the post-war boom, starting in the 1950s, the Austrian population began to resist the asylum function of Austria. Another political aspect concerning Kreisky's position correlated with the growing conflict between the superpowers, which arose because the Soviet Union had exchanged their rockets in Europe for more advanced missiles, and NATO had decided to close this gap with a new generation of missiles. Especially during the crisis years 1979/80 and 1981, the Austrian chancellor feared that the Soviet Union might end the détente completely, due to western overreactions to the Soviet Union's direct bloody intervention in Afghanistan and the establishment of local military rule in Poland. Thus, the process of stabilization in Europe, which resulted from the CSCE-process (including the acceptance of existing border lines), could potentially be reversed through an all out confrontation in Europe. Kreisky did not believe that, for example, the opposition movement in Poland (*Solidarnosc*) could transform the Communist government. He was convinced that the Soviets would suppress this movement with all means in order to stabilize their sphere of influence.

Since 1945 (and already after 1918) the Austrian population had resented the immigration of foreigners. The large solidarity with foreigners in 1956 had primarily been a result of mainstream cold war behavior, a broad pro-Hungarian media echo (except for the Communist press which used anti-foreigner prejudices), and the political message of the Austrian government that the U.S. and Canada would take most of the refugees and that only a few would stay in Austria. The same happened in 1968. Kreisky very well understood the resentment in Austrian society since he, too, was born into a minority. He was of Jewish origin, a minority which had not only experienced various forms of anti-Semitism but was persecuted on racist grounds by the Nazi regime and fellow Austrians between 1938-1945.

However, Kreisky tried to strengthen Austria's position vis-à-vis Switzerland, and according to international perceptions a neutral country had to include asylum competence. This position did not always correspond with great power politics. When Kreisky received an award from the "International Rescue Committee," a prominent philanthropic association of Jewish American intellectuals, the State Department and National Security Council objected to the participation of the president. This was not grounded in Kreisky's alleged anti-Jewish policies but in the fear that the Soviets might misunderstand this gesture since Austria continued to function as a transit country for Soviet Jewish emigrants even after the Schönau affair (in total 200,000 Jews left the Soviet Union through Austria since 1968).[32]

Whereas both the Nixon and the Ford administration, including Henry Kissinger, appreciated Austria's active role in the CSCE between 1973 - 1975, a policy shift by the Carter administration on the topic of the "3rd Basket" (exchange of information and culture to increase human contacts between East and West) caused major differences of opinion. Bruno Kreisky himself opposed Carter's all out human-rights foreign policy regarding the confidential communication with Eastern European countries.[33] He obviously feared that Austria's unique position as an East-West meeting place might be at risk. (The Carter policy already forecasted the early cold war tension of the Reagan administration). The Austrian government even hosted the Mutual and Balanced Force Reductions (MBFR) negotiations in October 1973. Nevertheless, U.S. observers did not regard the Austrian active neutrality policy of the 1970s as "appeasement," even through Austrian foreign policy officials "interpreted the Soviet invasion of Afghanistan as 'defensive' in character" and remarked "that the West should be wary of not 'losing its cool' over the invasion."[34]

Many Austrian observers still interpret the active Middle East policy in the Kreisky era as the basis of the Waldheim-debate and as an overexpansion of neutrality policy. A closer look at the U.S. perception, however, shows a quite different reaction. The Ford administration concurred with Austria's crisis management after the terror attack against the OPEC in December 1975—a management often criticized in the international media.[35] The same corresponds to the Carter administration—despite considerable differences of opinion on the question of human rights and détente (especially after the Soviet invasion of Afghanistan), or on the integration of the PLO in the Camp David agreement. Never before in international affairs have there been such intensive top-level exchanges of communication between the Austrian chancellor and leading White House representatives as during these years—although I do not want to minimize the differences of opinion. Due to massive lobbying by the Jews (who were traditionally in favor of the Democratic Party), Carter was not prepared to accept the PLO as a negotiating party.

The Soviet leadership fully accepted Austria's efforts to become a (permanent) meeting place of East-West negotiations on all levels. Especially in the late 1970s, however, the continuing political debates about human rights in Communist countries and Austria's open support of the dissidents' movements in the CSR and the U.S.S.R. lead to major bilateral tension. Once the Soviets even called back the organized elite back, who had been invited to participate in a 'public' lecture by Kreisky in Moscow, and canceled the event. As far as the Middle Eastern policies of Kreisky were concerned, he tried to get the Soviets more deeply involved, asking for U.N. missions and U.N. conflict solving efforts.

Side Riding in the 1980s? Back to 'Unmorality' in the Final Cold War

Whereas the U.S.-administrations from Carter to Reagan were very skeptical of Austria's and Kreisky's Middle East policies, Western European countries followed the political direction, trying to integrate the PLO by direct or indirect recognition of the political leadership under Arafat. France, Great Britain, and Germany reversed their anti-PLO policies and became, in the late 1970s and early 1980s, much more concerned of the Arab position in the Middle East conflict. This policy change had a strong economic background since Western Europe, after the two oil crises of 1973/74 and 1978, depended in the Arab oil. But starting in the late 1970s, and especially in 1980, it became clear that the European Union had become interested in joining Kreisky's views (as the mission led by EC Commission President Gaston Thorn indicated). EC-Europe now sought to back Palestinian interests, and, even though Western European states were still dragging their feet, they headed toward a step-by-step recognition of the PLO. But Kreisky was always 'ahead' of other European positions. He recognized the PLO as early as March 1980 and thus made an important contribution to the political and later diplomatic acceptance of Arafat as *the* representative of the Palestinian People. At that time Kreisky became—from the Israeli perception—a definitely one-sided, pro-Palestinian politician. Even the then head of the Israeli Labor Party, Shimon Peres, cut all contacts immediately.

It should be noted, however, that in the early 1970s Chancellor Kreisky tried to act—like in the détente process—as a neutral politician, trying to establish good relations with all partners in the Middle East conflict. During a visit of Foreign Minister Rudolf Kirchschläger the *Jerusalem Post's* headline read: "Austria-Israel. Relations best ever" (25 June 1972). This transfer of policies lasted until the 28 September 1973 when, during a terrorist attack by Palestinians against the transit camp of Schönau (which hosted mostly Jewish emigrants from the Soviet Union under the administration of the Jewish Agency), Kreisky promised to shut down this camp in order to safe the lives of the hostages taken in Schönau.

During this 'Schönau incident', which developed into an international debate in the U.S. and Israel, it became obvious that Kreisky was prepared to close the camp also because of the nearly exterritorial supervision by the Jewish Agency which was aiming for a direct transfer of the emigrants to Israel. Kreisky, for the first time, was fiercely attacked by international media and politicians like U.S. President Richard Nixon (in a mild manner) and the Israeli Prime Minister Golda Meir (in a very personal and aggressive way). The Austrian authority over the transit of Jewish emigrants was restored, and they could now independently choose the country of exile. In 1974 Golda Meir confirmed that the humanitarian role of Austria as the most important transit country for Russian Jews had not ceased. Between 1968 and 1986, 270,199 Jews could leave the Soviet Union via Vienna; only a small percentage chose to emigrate to countries other than Israel (e.g. in 1988 7.1 % went to the U.S.). Austria continued to act as a neutral asylum country in the cold war, especially for Russian Jews (after 1973 even more persons left through Austria than before the incident).

Despite his very unconventional and personal style of acting in the international arena, Kreisky trusted in the permanent international recognition and acceptance of Austria as a neutral country. He very well knew, as a result of his negative interwar experiences, that Austria was a small country, whose neutrality was not at all guaranteed by the Allies in 1955, and which was not—as far as eastern Austria and Vienna was concerned—a secret NATO area under the nuclear umbrella (as many politicians and diplomats still believe today).[36] Kreisky therefore continued and intensified the international trend, which started with the Allied Administration in 1945 and was indirectly confirmed by the

Austrian State Treaty. Even after 1966, during the People's Party government without the Socialists, this trend (including a very active U.N. policy) was continued and led to the principle decision to build an international center for the United Nations. Against broad domestic opposition, Kreisky carried out the establishment of the Vienna International Center, and in 1979 Vienna became the Third Headquarter of the United Nations. Kreisky kept his large and costly original building plans going—against the broadest public referendum in post war history[37]—since he thought that if the U.S. continued their anti-U.N. policies Vienna could also host the General Assembly of the United Nations.

Already in the late 1950s Kreisky, as foreign minister, realized that Austria would never match the strong military build up of the Swiss model since after 1945 for ten years Austria was completely demilitarized. The Austrian budget was already well established to support the economic recovery and a slowly growing social network with marginal military spending between 1955-1959 due to strong U.S. military assistance, which was cut in 1960. In an interview with the *Financial Times* (21 August 1979) Kreisky said that "International Organizations based in Austria are more important from a security and political point of view. They are as valuable as big stores of arms which might never be used."[38] Concerning military doctrine the Austrian army began to reorganize on the basis of guerrilla warfare, aiming for overall defense of Austrian society and the Austrian social partners in order to 'lengthen' an attack. It would cost the aggressor too much time and too many dead soldiers to break through Austrian territory (doctrine of deterrence). But the main component in the 1970s should be an active foreign policy to reduce tensions between the superpowers and within the region, as well to place Austria (like Switzerland) as an undisputed entity into the international diplomatic arena.

During the Reagan administration the relationship on 'cold war' matters became much more tense and for the first time after 1955, U.S. officials criticized Austria's neutrality position and policy. To this day research on the U.S.-Austrian relationship proclaims that the bilateral relations have declined to the lowest point since 1955 due to a speech for the political academy of the ÖVP, the Austrian People's Party (24 May 1982) by Ambassador H. Eugene Douglas (responsible for the Refugee Cooperation).[39] He very much criticized Austria's recognition of the PLO and the reception of Ghadafi and came to the conclusion that Austria had changed its foreign policy course considerably and violated the basis of her neutrality position (H. Eugene Douglas' criticism included Kreisky's attacks against U.S. Latin American policies and especially the Eastern trade policies of Austria). Certainly Ambassador Douglas overreacted to the change in the Austrian neutrality position, which was especially used by the People's Party, the major opposition party, to ask for a pro-transatlantic reversal of the neutrality policies of the late 1950s. The pro-Western status was—from their point of view—the correct 'neutrality' position. This 'transatlantic' reversal of neutrality policy was part of the general neo-liberal reorganization of conservative ideologies, trying to copy the examples of Margaret Thatcher in Great Britain and Ronald Reagan in the U.S. When the leader of the opposition party, Alois Mock, became vice-chancellor and foreign minister he was even prepared to eventually give up Austrian neutrality. It should be noted that the ongoing debates about NATO-membership and neutrality are still very much influenced by this policy shift of the ÖVP in the early 1980s. In my view the Austrian People's Party is still trying to adapt to the neo-liberal trend of the 1980s.

The conflict between Austria and the U.S. developed on different levels, and it took some time for it to explode in early 1982. Despite the general criticism of the Reagan administration concerning some policies of the Socialist International about Latin America and the cold war, Kreisky was seen as "one of the leaders of the Socialist International, who has been evidencing his anti-communism more loudly than anyone else."[40] Nevertheless, a consequence of President Reagan's obvious refusal to meet Willy Brandt, then president of the Socialist International, and due to the U.S. hard line policies after the establishment of military dictatorship in Poland, Kreisky started a series of attacks in January 1982. He asked for military balance, a more flexible policy towards the Jaruszelski government, and argued against U.S. support for dictatorships in Turkey and Latin American states.

Since the geopolitical framework had changed under President Reagan, the U.S. embassy in Vienna received orders to close the security risks of technology transfer in Austria and was asked to change the agreement of 1957, in which Austria merely "guaranteed the security of U.S. equipment, materials, or service furnished" by the U.S. government.[41] At that time the U.S. embassy asked for 'security surveys' conducted by U.S. experts in order to prevent any transfer of U.S. technology to the 'East' by the Austrian army. This technology debate was not only limited to secret negotiations but led to public debates about the Austrian technology leaks in 1982/1983.[42] Considerable U.S.

pressure on Austria transferred via the press into the domestic political debate (especially supported by the most important opposition party to the Kreisky-Government, the ÖVP), and the fear of major U.S. technology blockades resulted in the change of the Austrian Law for Foreign Trade to take into account the U.S. security limitations. This procedure was certainly a set back in the deregulation of Austria's Eastern trade. It just copied a procedure of the 1950s, but in the early 1980s not only alleged technology transfer, but Austrian machinery exports into the East in general, were considered contributions to the strategic strength of the Warsaw Pact (an accusation also directed against Switzerland).[43] Certainly Austria's interpretation of neutrality as an active status did not correspond with the general global aims of the Reagan administration and resulted, on a more concrete level, in a series of bilateral disputes along the lines of technology transfer into the 'Communist orbit'.

Despite these deep ideological confrontations, Kreisky was impressed by the Reagan administration's early Middle East approach in 1982—although nowadays we know that this plan was not very deeply established in an overall Middle East strategy. Reagan's 'hand-picked' ambassador earmarked for Vienna, Bruce Cummings (born in Vienna), had worked on the "Jews for Reagan" committee during the election campaign and fully agreed with Kreisky's views that peace in the Middle East required a solution of the Palestinian solution and a Palestinian state. Kreisky continued to back both the Reagan and Fez plan of the Arab League, and after two years of relative tension (especially in 1982) National Security Adviser Bill Clark paved the way for a meeting of President Reagan with Kreisky in early 1983. Even in 1984, after Kreisky had left office, he continued to keep the Reagan plan alive in the Middle East discussion.

Changes in the Magna Charter of Austria
in the 1980s and 1990s

When Kreisky left the government, after having formed a small coalition government between the Socialists and the Freedom Party (at that time under liberal leadership), it took only a few months that the neutrality policy became once more rather restrainted and took a slightly pro Western bias (e.g. Austria, for example, gave in on the issue of joining the economic war against the Communist block by applying for export licenses in the U.S. for exports into this area first.) At the same time the trend towards adjusting to the new round of economic integration in Europe increased in Austria, too, intensified by major economic structural problems within the nationalized industry and banking sector, as well as by social changes and new social movements (especially the Greens focusing on environmentalal issues). The new generation of Americans, Western Europeans, and Austrians also initiated a debate about the 'victim's theory' with regard to the Nazi past of Austria between 1938-1945. At the same time European integration was tightening, reacting to the large growth rates in Asia. The European Community decided to establish a Single Market by the early 1990s and to arrange for much closer political and military integration. Thus, Austria's global approach (represented by Kreisky being co-chair of the first North-South summit in Cancun in 1981) and active foreign policy were soon reduced to European matters.

Especially after 1986, when Franz Vranitzky took over the chancellorship from Fred Sinowatz, it became obvious that not only Austria's relation to Europe began to change dramatically, but also another component of post-war existence: the victim's theory. Since the first months of the provisional government of State Chancellor Karl Renner, all Austrian governments continued to stress the fact that Austria was not responsible for World War II and the Holocaust, but was a victim of German Nazi aggression. This certainly is correct as far as the state and institutions are concerned—parliament and political parties have already been dissolved under the authoritarian Dollfuß-regime in 1933/1934. At the same time responsibility for participating in the Nazi terror regime and for making profits from the expropriation and destruction of Austrian Jewry was evaded.

This important component of Austria's domestic affairs and international relations indirectly even supported the neutrality status and fitted into the newly established national identity (which excluded historical memories concerning the Nazi past). However, when in 1985 Minister of Defense Friedhelm Frischenschlager officially greeted the released war criminal Walter Reeder, a first wave of international and domestic debate broke out. When the ÖVP's candidate for the Austrian presidency of 1986, Kurt Waldheim, was confronted with his war-time past and his knowledge about war atrocities in Greece, which he had altogether omitted from his various biographies, the international debate made quite clear that the Austrian population could no longer stay 'neutral' in a new ware of discussion of the Nazi past and the Holocaust. Austria's international image was (on an elite level) damaged in the U.S.

and in Western Europe (not in the Middle East and the Arab World, nor in the 'East', which, however, tried to stay 'neutral' in this conflict).

Nevertheless, the general understanding that 'Austrian neutrality' might be a permanent status within Europe was asserted by the Soviet Union—even under Michael Gorbachev. The most experienced Soviet foreign policy expert and long time foreign minister, Andrej Gromyko, stated in his memoirs that Austria was *the* pillar of neutrality in Europe.[44] In meetings between 1987 and 1988 Chancellor Vranitzky tried to convince the Soviet leader that Austria's efforts to join the European Community would neither imply a revival of the 'Anschluß' nor an end of Austrian neutrality.[45] In January 1987, though, the Soviet ambassador in Vienna could not see a full membership of Austria acceptable for the Soviet Union. On 5 May 1987 the press spokesman of President Gorbachev backed this position, while the Austrian Foreign Minister Alois Mock supported the Austrian position and the right for different opinions. After a top level meeting of Vranitzky with Ruschkov in Moscow in October 1988, the Soviets accepted the Austrian decision that neutrality and EU-membership are compatible. This certainly constituted a major change in the Soviet perception of Austrian neutrality since 1955 and was primarily a result of the 'new look' of Soviet foreign policy in Europe. In retrospect one can see that this change forecasted the seachanges of 1989 and the new Soviet leadership, convinced that Germany, even if united, would not give up its Western integration and turn again 'eastwards'.

It is interesting to note that France had a similar fear of Austria joining the European Union to strengthen Germany and thus change the invisible power balance between the 'two'. President Mitterrand hesitated for three years to fully back the Austrian application to Brussels both because of the Austrian neutrality reservation (Austria applied, unlike Sweden and Finland, with a clear neutrality reservation formula in July 1989) and the old 'German' fears.[46]

In the long run neither the old Soviet reservations nor the French purist interpretation of European unity (repeated by Jacques Delors, the EU commission president, and many others during the diplomatic negotiations and in public events) were decisive in the final result. After the transformation of Europe in 1989 and the German unification in 1990, the EU policy perceptions soon became more concerned with the next round of integration—that of Eastern European countries—and a larger European concept (including opposition and prejudices against such a move). Austrian neutrality became more and more a matter of domestic politics—with no real interest in international debates and perceptions since Austria turned her concept of integral neutrality into a concept of 'differential' neutrality.[47] Austria accepted solidarity with U.N.-sanctions, and Austrian neutrality practise was several times overruled by U.N.-law (starting with the sanctions against the Iraq and transport of war material over Austrian territory). Austria has obtained observer status in the WEU and participates in NATO's Partnership for Peace as well as in the Euro-Atlantic Partnership Council.[48]

Conclusion

The international perception of Austria's neutrality today has widened, accepting not only the firm political, economic, and cultural integration in the 'Western European bloc' system (to use cold war categorizations) but also active military solidarity (short of joining NATO or another pro-Western European security and defense system). The ground for this different perception was already well prepared before 1955—e.g. Austria being able to join the Marshall-Plan—and in 1955—Austria joining the United Nations and, since the mid-1960s, participating in peacekeeping missions. The most important perception changes took place in the 1960s, when the U.S. accepted Austria's efforts towards 'bridge-building', and in the 1970s under Chancellor Bruno Kreisky and his globally oriented, active foreign policy—not withholding political critics (both towards the U.S. and the Soviet Union). The next historic perception change was on the side of the Soviet Union, which in late 1988—before the transformation of the Communist bloc and the unification of Germany—accepted that Austria joined the European Community. The Soviet Union hence realized that an Austrian EC membership did not automatically mean that Austria would join Germany and change the post-1945 power system in Europe in favor of German superiority. This change of perception did not only effect the Soviet but also the French leadership (comparable to the situation in the later 1960s). The Austrian domestic perception of neutrality has not been analyzed here, but it is quite obvious that especially the 1970s have broadened the 'feeling' of being neutral to mean at the same time being socially and economically secure. In the 1970s the active neutrality policy and the active economic policy fostered these views, which have certainly nothing to do with military security. Neutrality has become part of a small state identity, which is even more important then military security: In 1998 51% of the

Austrians think that neutrality does not offer military security against outside aggression, but still 40% vote against joining NATO, 54% vote against joining any military alliance. 68% interpret neutrality as integral part of Austrian state identity.[49]

Notes

1. The most sophisticated historical research and analysis of primary sources and secondary literature can be found in the impressive recent edition of Gerald Stourzh, *Um Einheit und Freiheit. Staatsvertrag, Neutralität und das Ende der Ost-West-Besetzung Österreichs, 1945-1955* (Wien: Böhlau Verlag, 1998). See also the "Historiography Forum" in this volume.

2. With regard to the ongoing debate compare the series of contributions in *Streitfall Neutralität*, ed. Andreas Weber (Wien: Czernin Verlag, 1999); concerning the broader European debate see *Beitreten oder Trittbrettfahren. Die Zukunft der Neutralität in Europa*, ed. Günther Bächler (Zürich: Verlag Rüegger, 1994).

3. *Foreign Relations of the United States (=FRUS) 1951*, vol. IV.2 (Washington, D.C.: US Government Printing Office, 1985),1034f. Oliver Rathkolb, "The Foreign Relations between the USA and Austria in the Late 1950s," *Contemporary Austrian Studies*, vol. 3, *Austria in the Nineteen Fifties* (New Brunswick: Transaction Publishers, 1995), 28.

4. Oliver Rathkolb, *Washington ruft Wien. U.S.-Großmachtpolitik und Österreich 1953-1963. Mit Exkursen zu CIA-Waffenlagern, NATO-Connection, Neutralitätsdebatte* (Wien: Böhlau Verlag, 1997), 68.

5. Willi Scholz, "Unveröffentlichter Diskussionsbeitrag für die Sitzung des Zentralkomitees der KPÖ," 13 March 1957 (a copy of this statement was given to the author by Dr. Viktor Matejka).

6. Concerning the power struggle within the post-Stalin Kremlin elite see Vladislav Zubok and Constantine Pleshakov, *Inside the Kremlin's Cold War. From Stalin to Khrushchev* (Cambridge: Harvard University Press, 1996), 157 ff.

7. Manfried Rauchensteiner, *Der Sonderfall: Die Besatzungszeit in Österreich 1945-1955* (Graz: Styria Verlag, 1979), 332.

8. Oliver Rathkolb, "Historische Fragmente und die 'unendliche Geschichte' von den sowjetischen Absichten in Österreich 1945," in *Österreich unter Alliierter Besatzung 1945-1955*, ed. Alfred Ableitinger et al. (Wien: Böhlau Verlag, 1998), 142-149.

9. Rathkolb, *Washington,* 120-127.

10. Oden to Commander in Chief, U.S. European Command, Military Aid, 1 March 1956, Record Group 59, 763.5-MSP/8-2456, National Archives, Washington D.C.

11. Rathkolb, *Washington,* 123.

12. FRUS 1955-57, vol. V, 181.

13. *Wiener Zeitung*, 5 June 1958.

14. Rathkolb, *Washington,* 136-138.

15. Wallinger to Selwyn Lloyd, Annual Report for 1955, 24 January 1956, copy from the Public Record Office in London, cited from an unpublished research project for the Ministry for Science and Research by the Bruno Kreisky Archives Foundation, Vienna ("Die österreichische Außenpolitik und der Beitrag Österreichs zur Entspannungspolitik

Europas 1953-1966," compiled by Stefan August Lütgenau, Vienna, 1991, 51).

16. Thomas O. Schlesinger, *Austrian Neutrality in Postwar Europe. The Domestic Roots of a Foreign Policy* (Wien: Wilhelm Braumüller, 1972), 35.

17. Ibid., 52.

18. Günter Schwaiger, *Österreichs Image im Ausland* (Wien: Service Fachverlag, 1988), 112.

19. See Michael R. Beschloss, *The Crisis Years, Kennedy and Khrushchev 1960-1963* (New York: Harper & Collins, 1991).

20. Oliver Rathkolb, "Austria and European Integration after World War II," *Contemporary Austrian Studies*, vol. 1, *Austria in the New Europe* (New Brunswick: Transaction Publisher, 1992), 51-52.

21. McGhee to Ball, 21 November 1961, NA, RG 59, Lot 250/5/18/3, Entry 3103, Box 4.

22. Tyler to the Acting Secretary, Association of Neutrals, 11 December 1961, ibid.

23. Rathkolb, "Austria and European Integration," 51.

24. For more details see Rathkolb, *Washington,* 133-136.

25. Oliver Rathkolb, "Bruno Kreisky: Perspectives of Top Level U.S. Foreign Policy Decision Makers, 1959-1983," *Contemporary Austrian Studies,* vol. 2, *The Kreisky Era in Austria* (New Brunswick: Transaction Publisher, 1994), 132-133.

26. Reinhard Meier-Walser, *Die Außenpolitik der monocoloren Regierung Klaus in Österreich 1966-1970* (München: Tuduv Verlag, 1988), 322-376.

27. For more details see Oliver Rathkolb, "Austria's 'Ostpolitik' in the 1950s and 1960s: Honest Broker or Double Agent?," *Austrian History Yearbook*, 26 (1995), 129-145.

28. Willi Sauber, "Die 'Kärntner Straße' zur Zeit der ÖVP-Alleinregierung," in *Die Ära Josef Klaus: Österreich in den 'kurzen' sechziger Jahren*, ed. Robert Kriechbaumer (Wien: Böhlau Verlag, 1998), 201. See also the Eisterer essay in this volume.

29. "Wiener Lob und Kritik der deutschen Außenpolitik," ref. 203, vol. 113, Politisches Archiv des Auswärtigen Amtes, Bonn.

30. Briefing Book, visit Kreisky in the U.S., 12/13 November 1974, Country File USA, Bruno Kreisky Archives Foundation, Vienna.

31. Bruno Kreisky, *Reden*, vol. 2 (Wien: Österreichische Staatsdruckerei, 1990), 756 (Rede über die Entspannungspolitik, 4 July 1978).

32. Rathkolb, "Kreisky," 139.

33. Rathkolb, "Kreisky," 134.

34. NATO and Western Security in the 1980s: The European Perception. Report of a Staff Study Mission to Seven NATO Countries and Austria to the Committee on Foreign Affairs. U.S. House of Representatives (Washington D.C.: Government Printing Office, 1980), 48. The Austrian counterpart was Ambassador Franz Ceska.

35. For a specific analysis of the terror - and partly different views concerning Kreisky's conflict management, see John Bunzl, *Gewalt ohne Grenzen. Nahost-Terror und Österreich,* (Wien Braumüller, 1991).

36. E.g. in *Die Presse*, 13 May 1995, former Ambassador Herbert Grubmayr stated that in 1956 U.S. Secretary John Foster Dulles had informed the Sovjets that crossing the Austrian border would mean World War III.

37. Information by Mr. Michael Auracher which in 1979 was in charge of the U.N. center in the cabinet of the then Finance Minister Hannes Androsch.

38. Helmut Kramer, "Austrian Foreign Policy from the State Treaty to European Union Membership (1955-1995)," in *Austria 1945-95. Fifty Years of the Second Republic*, ed. Kurt Richard Luther et. al. (Aldershot: Ashgate, 1998), 168.

39. John Michael Luchak, "Amerikanisch-Österreichische Beziehungen von 1955 bis 1985. Neutralität und der Ost-West Konflikt" (PhD. diss., University of Vienna, 1987), 426.

40. Arnold M. Silver, "The New Face of the Socialist International" (Paper of the Heritage Foundation, October 1981), research materials, Socialist International, Stiftung Bruno Kreisky Archiv, Wien.

41. Stiftung Bruno Kreisky Archiv, Wien, Country File USA, Copy from United Nations Treaty Series, vol. 288 (1958) and Enclosures from 1982.

42. Newspaper clippings (1982/1983/1984)—especially from the daily *Die Presse*—case in possession of the author. Compare also Linda Melvern, David Hebditch & Nick Anning, *Techno-Bandits. How the Soviets Are Stealing America's High-Tech Future* (Boston: Houghton, Mufflin, & Co., 1984), 142-157, unfortunately a book which seems to contain more fiction and fantasy than facts.

43. J. Michael Montia, "Aktuelle Tendenzen im Ost-West- Handel," *Europäische Rundschau* 1983.4, 47.

44. Andrej Gromyko, *Erinnerungen* (München: Econ, 1989), 317.

45. Ludmilla Lobova, "Österreich in der Außenpolitik der UdSSR und Rußlands. Die Rolle der Neutralität Ende der 80iger Jahre," *Europäische Rundschau* 27 (March 1999), 67-86.

46. Interview with Dr. Franz Vranitzky, 30 September 1998.

47. Kramer, Foreign Policy, 173.

48. Hanspeter Neuhold, "Austria in Search of its Place in a Changing World: From Between the Blocs to Full Western Integration," in *Austria 1945-95*, 217.

49. Österreichische Gesellschaft für Europapolitik, Pressekonferenz, 18 August 1999 (results of public opinion poll from 31 July 1998).

Sovereignty and the "Unnatural":
Fianna Fáil and Why the Anglo-Irish Agreement
Could Not Be a Neutral Act

David Irwin and John Wilson

Introduction

This paper focuses on the political nuances of Fianna Fáil's (the Republican Party's) oppositional response to the Anglo-Irish Agreement (1985); in particular, Fianna Fáil's deconstruction of the political structures of Northern Ireland to consolidate its hegemony of republican orthodoxy. The paper introduces Foucault's discourse of power/ knowledge to rationalize as "rightful" intervention by the Irish Republic in the governance of Northern Ireland. Central to this argument is the recognition that the Irish right to self-determination balanced by the principle of concurrent consent represents more the intellectual colla- boration of the party coalition than the triumph of moderation over the spirit of faction. Rather than evaluate the agreement for its normative themes, this paper endeavors to assess the contestation between the vertical discourse of the Fianna Fáil to achieve reunification de jure, and Foucault's horizontal reflexivity which facilitates the rhetorical disruption of wider continuities of power. This discrepancy between vertical/horizontal reflexivity reveals how political resolutions are actually subordinated by a shadow discourse that seeks to maintain the vertical reflexivity of dominance in order to perpetuate the concept of party political power.

Michel Foucault and Fianna Fáil's
Neo-Republican Politics

Michel Foucault's *The Archaeology of Knowledge* explores the relationship between knowledge as a general concept (*savoir*) and specific forms of knowledge (*connaissance*).[1] While the point of this differentiation is to locate *connaissance* within the domain of *savoir,* there is also the possibility of investigating the anterior/posterior space occupied by *savoir* and *connaissance* in reverse, i.e. the effect on *savoir* if *connaissance* precedes it. In choosing a strategy to explore the consequences this relationship has as an expression of power, we contend that Foucault's project identifies four operations. The first is concerned with plotting the boundaries of realism in order to locate power as tangible and not bound to idealistic conceptions of purpose, continuity, and freedom. Following from this is the elimination of diachronic traditions that privilege the history and continuity of ideas and, at the same time, hinder the possibilities of engaging in comparative analyses between different discourses. Linked to this is a third consideration, which seeks to remove restrictions that constrain discourse to expressions of specific metaphors of thought and expression. Finally, the fourth consideration of the archaeological project can be said to summarize the preceding three points because it questions the determinism of conventional discourse. In place of the often blind acceptance of repression as a mechanism of discourse, Foucault demands that concepts of freedom, meaning, and continuity are essential for progressive politics to be understood as discursive devices of power that seek to minimize potential contradictions between individuals and groups in society.

While these operations are designed to avoid mere descriptive detail of events within historical sequences, Foucault's own analysis is not so much a rejection of the grand scheme of history as an endeavor to plot likely instances that shape history. Foucault states that knowledge *(savoir)* is composed of statements which co-ordinate and subordinate concepts according to specific sites of reference and articulation, and provides perspectives and positions from which discursive practices may be adopted. He goes on to argue that "archaeology finds the point of balance of its analysis in *savoir*—that is, in a domain which the subject is necessarily situated and dependent, and can never figure as titular."[2] For Foucault, "*savoir* refers to the conditions that are necessary in a particular period for this or that type of object to be given to *connaissance* and for this or that enunciation to be formulated."[3] Yet this oversimplification, which relegates *connaissance* to occupy the role of subset in relation to *savoir,* ignores the complexity of the contribution of *connaissance* in its broadest connotative significance to *savoir.* If Foucault states a preference for *savoir* on the grounds that it is incapable of transcendent or empirical activity, while expressing a disdain of *connaissance* because it is open to this activity, he introduces a fundamental flaw into his analysis.

Broadly speaking, it is Foucault who confines *connaissance* to an epistemological site to reveal his preference for *savoir* as capable of transcendental and empirical activity. This is an important revelation as it severely challenges Foucault's consistency and leaves his method open to the allegation that it is sporting difference for its own sake and not because any epistemological justification merits this differentiation. While never explicitly acknowledging that such an inconsistency exits, he implicitly attempts to dissipate any suggestion to the contrary through a mild admission that *connaissance* plays an important role in *savoir* only when its status is articulated through the latter: i.e. archaeological analysis must show positively how a science functions in the element of knowledge. Foucault does not test his hypothesis in the area of politics-as-government. At best he merely suggests that politics "serves the interests of the bourgeois class ... and that it bears the mark of its origins even in its concepts and logical architecture."[4] His failure to test effectively the accuracy of his position cannot be valorized as a clever device to evade prescription. Clearly this begs the question as to whether Foucault's retreat from his thesis to explore new forms of knowledge justifies the simultaneous privilege that can be extended to both *savoir/connaissance* and *connaissance/savoir.* Since Foucault presents no practical application to support either position, we will argue that our examination of Fianna Fáil's supporting role in the events preceding the signing of the Anglo-Irish Agreement provides an implicit model of the *savoir/connaissance* paradigm.

Although the relationship and distinction between *savoir* and *connaissance* remains unclear in *The Archaeology of Knowledge,* it will be argued that some of Foucault's ideas presented in *Discipline and Punish* provide a more refined model to understand the validity and structure of the *connaissance/savoir* paradigm.[5] This can then be applied to explain Fianna Fáil's apparent refutation of the Anglo-Irish Agreement. The decision to consider reversion is not designed to present *savoir/connaissance* as the opposite of *connaissance/savoir.* Rather our intention is to demonstrate the cyclical process of power/knowledge where *connaissance/savoir* becomes a strategy for the processes of opposition to plot the parameters of what can be defined as legitimate political discourse. Although the relationship and distinction between *savoir* and *connaissance* remains unclear in the *Archaeology of*

Knowledge, it will be argued that some of his ideas presented in *Discipline and Punish*, Michel Foucault *Discipline and Punish* provides a more refined model to understand the validity and structure of the connaissance/savoir paradigm which can then be applied to explain Fianna Fáil's apparent refutation of the Anglo-Irish Agreement. The decision to consider reversion is not designed to present *savoir/connaissance* as the opposite of *connaissance/savoir*. Rather the intention is to demonstrate the cyclical process of power/knowledge where *connaissance/savoir* becomes a strategy for the processes of opposition to plot the parameters of what can be defined as legitimate political discourse.

The Background of the Anglo-Irish Agreement

The signing of the Anglo-Irish Agreement in November 1985 by Garret FitzGerald, Taoiseach (Prime Minister), and Margaret Thatcher, Prime Minister of Great Britain, and its subsequent deposition by the Irish government with the United Nations, concluded a process of meetings which began in 1980 and effectively ended the concept of nation-state as the norm for territorial organization. After a series of meetings with Thatcher, which took place during the second hunger strike at the Maze prison (March to October 1981), Charles Haughey (Taoiseach 1979-81) endeavored to situate the hunger strike within the context of his Republican government's mission to reunify the island of Ireland. A closer examination of events reveals the extent of the tightrope he had to tread between republican irredentism, the acknowledgement of the need to manage a frontier region, and the imperative to conserve Irish economic dependence on Britain. To satisfy traditional Irish republican ideology with a competing economic astuteness, Haughey sought to satisfy the expectations of a divided Fianna Fáil government and electorate by expressing a humanitarian concern for the hunger strikers who demanded an institutional and constitutional reform of the status of Northern Ireland. Such an approach was in keeping with the focus of discussions with Margaret Thatcher during their first summit meeting (May 1980). Moreover, Haughey's concentration on reforming prison bureaucracy held out the possibility of saving the political reputations of both British and Irish politicians seeking to disengage themselves from untenable obligations to the current and future status of Northern Ireland. For example, as far as the British Government was concerned, the communiqué issued after the second summit in December 1980 sought to locate the Northern Irish question within the broader policy frame of Britain's colonial legacies worldwide.

As the Lisbon Declaration on the future of Gibraltar (1980) pointed to Britain's eventual abandonment of sovereignty of this colony, the communiqué following the Dublin Summit indicated that the question of sovereignty regarding Northern Ireland was to be included in subsequent discussions with the Irish Republic. For Fianna Fáil issues of cross-border economic development represented progress so much that the totality of relationships to be explored at the summit meetings provided the basis for future progress in a tangible and acceptable manner. Thus, the argument presented by Haughey following the December communiqué, and during the Dáil (Irish Parliament) debate on the matter, sought a resolution of the hunger strike on humanitarian grounds in order to avoid any hint of legitimizing the Special Category Status (SCS) sought by the prisoners.

Mindful of the effective limits surrounding the broader socioeconomic discussions with Britain and of the increasingly narrow maneuverability this permitted the Irish Government in commenting on Britain's handling of the hunger strike, Haughey limited his comments in the Dáil to differentiating between the constitutional and institutional status of Northern Ireland. In practice this meant deliberately inviting the question on what 'the constitutional status of Northern Ireland' might signify in terms of its representational qualities rather than for its inferential possibilities: "The constitutional position of Northern Ireland is one matter. I do not deny that it is a matter of enormous importance and significance to me. I do not for one moment suggest that I do not avail of every opportunity of talking about the constitutional position of Northern Ireland. Every person in these islands in the political arena should be concerned with the constitutional position of Northern Ireland."[6]

On the issue of institutional relations Haughey was less circumspect in so far as the institutional structures, which could contribute to the economic objectives he had in mind, were unambiguous and not something "indeterminate ... Politics is concerned with political institutions. That is very important work."[7] Clearly, Haughey minimized the acute reality that the delights of economic benefit did not necessarily preface constitutional re-unification. In large part, the facility with which he recast the hunger strike in institutional rather than constitutional terms reflected the distance he sought to effect between northern and southern Irish republican ideologies. In addition, he sought to distance his party from its own perpetuating mythology of geographical unification. And so his unwillingness to engage the hunger strikers in constitutional arguments over Special Category Status (SCS) tacitly acknowledged Fianna Fáil's unwillingness to align rhetorical strategy directly with anything approaching deliberate intervention. Indeed, the reluctance of British and Irish governments to validate the hunger strikers' demands was based on a reluctance to acknowledge the sovereignty of prisoners and their right to confront the systemic faculty of government to discipline them for their actions in the first instance. A significant feature of this resistance lay in an analogous reticence by the British government to concede any ground to any pressure group. This resistance was a feature of the Conservative government policy in its handling of the miners' strike, the Falklands war, and its rigid policy of unilateral privatization.

Operating from within the paradigm of classical juridicism, both governments were acutely aware that the hunger strike could not be allowed to succeed since its success would vitiate the regulatory mechanisms of penology and dissolve the relationship between law and administration. In other words, the concern of both governments lay with the possible dissolution of criminalization within the wider administrating metaphor of normalization and not with the boundaries between the penal system and society. According to Thomas Dumma move from the apparatus of discipline to an apparatus of security efficiently removes the emphasis of control away from individual discipline and places it within the purview of "mass control of elements of behavior."[8] Such an emphasis on communitarian control is established upon a system of norms that regulates and fragments the actions of any individual in terms of their reference to a continuum of values and meaning. And it is precisely because the importance an individual places on the autonomy of their actions is registered against a continuum of meaning that integrity can be either conditionally guaranteed or accommodated. Thus any acquiescence from government to concede any level of reform, including penal reform, had to recognize that normalization was designed to establish norms through which mass control over society could be guaranteed. Consequently, it can be argued that normalization implicitly advanced the provision of a continuum of meaning that enabled government and citizens to register themselves against one another in a manner that permitted potential variance with the demographic and economic concerns it is designed to normalize. As a result of these possibilities the significant tensions between the "green" wing and the "party in government" wing within Fianna Fáil, and between the unionist and conservative ideologies of the British Conservative government, uncoupled the political from the historical imperative in order to simultaneously balance irredentism with the sovereign concerns of government.

When Garret FitzGerald replaced Haughey as Taoiseach in the summer of 1981, he enthusiastically embarked on a 'constitutional crusade' to "solve the Northern Ireland problem."[9] The communiqué that followed a meeting between FitzGerald and Thatcher in November 1981 stated that an affirmation to secure the unity of Ireland by agreement and in peace would only arise in the event of majority consent in Northern Ireland. It can be argued that this project to secure Irish reunification did not commence with this communiqué but represented another step in a gradual disintegration of Irish national identity which supposedly began with an abandonment of Keynesian models of economic nationalism in the 1950s. This cohesive retreat from autonomous nationalism was compounded by poor economic growth in the 1960s and 1970s in the Irish Republic and was further eroded by the conditional imperatives that made increasing external economic investment a consonant pattern in the Irish psyche. A similar pattern was evident in the North of Ireland where significant economic subvention from the British, and from Unionists grudging acceptance of their implicit political subjugation, exacerbated a nuanced view of how the future relationship between the North, the South, and Britain could proceed.

Following the publication of the New Ireland Forum *Report* the FitzGerald led coalition government—composed of Fine Gael (Christian Democrats) and Labour—which had won support from the principal constitutional nationalist parties, presented the British government with three possibilities to articulate the future governance of the island of Ireland. The first option proposed a united Ireland, the second a model that would precipitate a federal arrangement. The third option was a proposal that would give both Britain and Ireland joint sovereignty of Northern Ireland. Although Thatcher rejected each option, her government's subsequent dealings with the Irish government were characterized by a desire to super-ordinate the interests of Ulster with British interest without any direct reference to the concerns and opinions of Ulster unionism. W. Harvey Cox interprets the later appointment of Douglas Hurd, who was pro-Unionist and who had been moved from the

Foreign Office to become Home Secretary, as signifying the true extent and commitment of Britain's willingness to engage in progressive discussions with the Irish Republic.[10]

When the November communiqué was released, it advocated the promotion of political objectives to defeat paramilitarism. This proposal was designed to minimize the political credentials of Sinn Féin whose electoral success in the period after the hunger strikes had increased incrementally in spite of its associations with a renascent Irish Republican Army (IRA). In addition, the principal need to reduce nationalist alienation from the political and civil institutions operating in Northern Ireland was recast in terms of the need to accord communitarian integrity to both majority and minority interests. This strategy was designed to acknowledge the extent of southern Irish empathy with northern nationalism. The final issue articulated within the communiqué sought greater co-operation in conserving bi-partisan agreement on evolving a sustainable and credible security policy. Anthony Coughlan argues that Britain's desire for consensus in this area was predicated by her need to maintain a geo-strategic presence on the island as part of her defense strategy, and to allay American criticism of her abuses of civil rights in pursuit of her policy of law and order.[11] Equally important to resolving questions of territorial and sovereign integrity, the communiqué blithely focused on the need to arrive at a solution that would simultaneously satisfy the inter-government requirement to co-operate in a manner that avoided any intimation that such co-operation was repugnant to the constitutional principles of either state.

Fianna Fáil and the Limits of National Autonomy:
Savoir/Connaissance

Traditionally, Fianna Fáil's esprit critique has been constrained by an obligation to present reunification as the cornerstone of its constitutional discourse in the Dáil. Since Haughey's election as leader of Fianna Fáil (December 1979), his principal opponent, George Colley, demanded as tribute for his support in Cabinet that he have a veto on security and justice issues, and on the appointment of ministers to these portfolios. Haughey acceded to these requests and in the process created an effective coalition within Fianna Fáil. Ranged against Haughey were some of the cleverest and politically most moderate ministers in the parliamentary party, such as Desmond O'Malley, George Colley, James Gibbons, and Robert Molloy. Although supporters of Jack Lynch's civic republicanism, O'Malley and Gibbons were in favor of membership in a western defense alliance, while Colley and Molloy were against such a membership. Haughey's refusal to disclose to the Cabinet and Dáil the extent to which neutrality would be compromised in pursuit of a settlement on the North of Ireland was compounded by his opponents' division over neutrality. This situation finally led to such confusion within Fianna Fáil that it no longer knew what to represent. According to Bruce Arnold, Haughey prescribed the party line on Northern Ireland: In a reply to a traditional Republican deputy, Joe Farrell, T.D. (Teachta Dála, Member of Parliament) for the border constituency of Louth, Haughey stated that "Fianna Fáil had nothing in common with what is being done in the name of republicanism today in Northern Ireland."[12] While it can be argued that Haughey's strategy to divide and conquer minimized the ability of his opponents to unite and remove him from power, such a strategy had similar consequences for the level of support from among those who defined themselves as pro-Haughey within Fianna Fáil. Arnold states that Haughey's tactical game plan to stay in power at any price cost him the June '81 General Election because his enunciation of ephemeral proposals on northern and economic policies eluded the comprehension and support of deputies within Fianna Fáil and of the wider political support necessary to win an overall majority.

When Haughey endorsed the Social Democratic and Labour Party's (SDLP, NI) call for a forum to discuss ways to end violence in Northern Ireland, his opening address to the forum steering committee in May 1983 acknowledged that no progress could be made without a withdrawal of both British military and political presence in Northern Ireland. In his opening speech Haughey, who no longer felt constrained by the office of Taoiseach, attributed the cumulative British presence as the sole reason for the unworkable status quo. Curiously he went on to suggest that "no British Government will be able to provide any solution to the problem than in partnership with the Irish Government."[13] He argued for the principle of consent without jettisoning the ethos that had propelled the independence movement in the South. This view implicitly supported the maintenance of Articles Two and Three of the Irish Constitution (1937) on the grounds that their intent was not solely confined to claim jurisdiction of the remaining six counties but also to run the island independently on behalf of the whole Irish nation. This view ran counter to opinions expressed by FitzGerald and his minister for foreign affairs, Peter Barry, who had expressed views abhorring the impediment created in establishing a relationship with Unionists.

Nonetheless, his address did implicitly acknowledge the possibility that a new social contract might presuppose "a major revision of existing structures" to the extent that "a new constitution will be required for a new Ireland."[14] On the issue of neutrality Haughey argued that "Ireland would never allow her territory to be used as a base for attack on Britain and would be prepared to enter into a treaty arrangement needed for that purpose."[15] This speech was important because its concessionary ideology treated republican discourse as synchronous and not dependent on any sense of historical continuity. Moreover, it minimized any potential contradictions between individuals and groups in wider political society.

Fianna Fáil's continuing emphasis on territoriality resulted from an artificial mythology of dispossession, which occurred among the upper classes during the Cromwellian and Stuart Plantations of the seventeenth century. Thereafter the repossession and restoration of ancestral lands to the rightful claimants dictated the territoriality of republican thinking. Haughey's restatement of eighteenth century republican models, as signified by Grattan's parliament and declaration of independence in 1782, had much to do with the subordination of theoretical discourse by the discourse and infrastructure of governance as signaling the continuities that would be exhibited by his party upon its eventual return to government. Since its establishment Fianna Fáil has described itself both as a 'national movement' and 'organization.' As a movement it more easily engaged in a discourse whose a priori focus sought to effect national solidarity. The imperative to reflect and harness national solidarity during this period led to revisionism of its Republican paradigm so as to buttress its immediate political relevance and differentiate for its electorate the issues of individual probity from its collective responsibility as a party in government.

Thus Haughey's emphasis on republican communitarianism was an abandonment of *laissez-faire* policies of culture in favor of collectivism—which incorporated a presumption of difference from culture to culture. This approach permitted a *rapprochement* that allowed Ireland to perceive Britain as an ally in the process of change. Moreover, it permitted the Fianna Fáil organization to enter into a type of public life that was designed to strengthen "solidarity, public freedom, a willingness to talk and to listen, mutual debate, and a commitment to rational persuasion.[16] In many respects this movement enabled Fianna Fáil to broaden its discursive frames to engage more effectively in constructing practical institutions to promote civic/national participation and solidarity. Ronald Dworkin describes a type of republicanism which Fianna Fáil can be attributed to have engaged as proposing a sound conception of virtue to the extent that citizens believe to be their social and political responsibility to promote.[17]

This argument subordinates individual desires and interests—which is a characteristic of liberalism—in favor of the notion of 'public good.' The term 'public good' is not used in any teleological sense; rather it specifies a rhetorical use to engage the inherent fragility of political discourse in a world of historical change. Mindful of the transience of discourse, J.G.A. Pocock rejects the notion of universality on the grounds that human laws are not immanently universal but the products of "particular human situations ... in particular moments of time."[18] He elaborates on this idea by stressing the fact that republicanism is not an attempt to stamp its authority in a unilateral sense. To do otherwise presupposes that "it could achieve a distribution of authority such that every citizen's moral nature would be fulfilled."[19] Clearly, the failure of republicanism to recognize this would imply that it was aligning itself with the monarchical claim to temporally ape the cosmic order through the role and symbolic function of its sovereign.

What was significant about Haughey's contribution to the forum debate was his willingness to accommodate Fianna Fáil's republican formula within a wider context so as to explore the relationship between civil society and political community. Jeffrey Isaac argues that both aspects, civil society and political community, progress an argument for political emancipation insofar as each challenges the excessiveness and absolutism of ideology.[20] These aspects are cornerstones of republican argument insofar as each emphasizes the provision from the state of guarantees for the social behavior of minority groups without impoverishing such behavior by confining it to a rigorous assertion of individual rights. Far from limiting the scope of individual expression, republicanism articulates the participative value in collective decision-making, and the assimilation of individual citizens within the universality of citizenship of the *polis* or republic. Consequently, the period before the signing of the Anglo-Irish Agreement can be viewed as a fulcrum between Fianna Fáil's militant and progressive republican wings with the principal tension centering, to a large extent, in redefining its adherence to national autonomy while effectively shifting its ideology away from territoriality.

The traditional emphasis placed by Irish Republicans on land and territoriality reflects the residual influence of James Harrington, a seventeenth century English writer, and of John Stewart Mill, a nineteenth century English philosopher and economist. Harrington's argument on property ownership was "entirely subordinated to the idea of a transition from dependence to independence."[21] His reference to the ownership of property foregrounds the liberal/republican debate on property because it qualifies economic independence as a guarantor for political independence. The basis for such a guarantee lies in the acceptance of laws and institutions as positive elements, necessary for a state of civil society to function. Alternatively, ownership of property can equally be a debilitating form of social servility. In any event, Harrington's understanding of citizenship is located somewhere between republicanism and a valorization of liberalism as the independence and industriousness of the citizen. In this context 'liberalism' signifies private freedom, and 'republicanism' signifies the enactment of virtue as a public, and therefore civic, function.

If Harrington's ideas on republicanism center on the communal, independence and social stability, Adam Smith's contribution to republicanism focuses on substituting economic liberalism for mercantilist protection. This does not imply that the Smithsonian endorsement of market economics is exclusively liberal—where 'liberal' signifies the capability of the independent citizen who engages in politics, and of acts in the public interest. Isaac argues that Smith's understanding of economic liberty in this context is an expression of 'commercial republicanism,' which exalts industry and productivity and ridicules the artificial barriers to success sustained by the state's promotion and involvement in religious and economic privilege.[22] Nor does merging of liberalism and republicanism exclude the ideal of citizenship and of commitment to the public good. Rather the metaphors describe the operation of the citizen in terms of economic rather than civic obligation. This idea has been developed by William Galston, who argues that the practice of liberalism incorporates the public sphere of the state, where citizens operate "as full and equal citizens rather than as political subjects or social subordinates," and the private sphere of the state, where citizens are provided with "minimum decency, affluence, scope for personal development, approximate justice, openness to truth, and respect for privacy."[23] Clearly, Galston's defense of liberalism relies heavily upon the Aristotelian conception of civic obligation to "individual independence and patriotism."[24] The significance of Haughey's address to the forum lay in its ordination of liberal ideology. In other words, the centrality of any new understanding of self-realization to liberal democracy would be contingent on the substantial increase by foreign investors to buttress any new political settlement with a resilient economic infrastructure. By modifying the paradigm, Haughey de-centered the focus from the inviolability of Irish sovereignty on the grounds that the separatist economic policies of previous administrations had delineated Irish Republicanism from its broader republican spectrum of citizenship and individualism.

Fianna Fáil and the Limits of National Autonomy: Connaissance/Savoir

Throughout *Discipline and Punish* Foucault draws the distinction between disciplinary and contractual forms of power. The former classifies people in terms of a hierarchical relationship that allows one group of people to disqualify and invalidate another. Contractual forms of power are secondary, according to Foucault, even though they define individuals according to juridical systems based upon scales of universal norms. Working within a juridical metaphor, which nonetheless alludes to what Foucault intends for the *savoir/connaissance* paradigm, he suggests that juridicism is immense and universally widespread because of the finite ways through which power fixes the limits that are traced around the law.[25] While proposing the idea that power is axiomatic and is transported into social discourse by ideology, Foucault rejects it as incapable of independently responding intuitively to change in society. Since it cannot be understood outside such contexts as law, politics, and economics, Foucault's apparatus to investigate power-knowledge presents discourse as a palimpsest: presenting the discourse while simultaneously revealing structures that explain its conceptual and material genesis.

Foucault's purpose in writing *Discipline and Punish* was to explore how power is exercised in society. Unlike comments he made in an interview with Gilles Deleuze in 1972, in which he posed the question 'who exercises power,' his concern in *Discipline and Punish* is not with those principals whose function as decision-makers is to make decisions that enable citizens to articulate and orientate their lives. His concern is rather an understanding of those techniques "by which a decision is accepted and by which that decision could not but be taken in the way it was."[26] In the interview with Pierre Boncenne in which this statement was given, Foucault went on to state why his analysis could not merely be summarized by a universal application of power to understand society in the same way as Marxist analysis reduces most aspects of its rationality to economics. Alternatively, Foucault's concluding remarks in *Discipline and Punish* do provide a context to explore the normative apparatus of power. Although he does not specify how the apparatus functions, it is clear that he believes its control and power is hegemonic rather than oppositional. Nonetheless, we would contend that his critique of power is reductionist rather than normative by virtue of his exclusion of any scrupulous, whimsical, and humanist inflections that constitutes normative theories de facto. Foucault's effective re-articulation of economic Marxism means that power is only capable of operating as an oppositional critique insofar as it can be subsumed within its own dominance. Because of this particularly static reading given by Foucault to the working of power, his model appears reductionist and is as limiting as the theoretical Marxism his argument endeavors to supersede.

In *Liberal Government and Techniques of the Self* Graham Burchell argues that Foucault views government as a synonym for the use of power so as to establish a subjectification and, in effect, subjugation of the individual.[27] He states that Foucault perceives the classical liberalism of government as reconciling a "market freedom ... with the unlimited exercise of a political sovereignty."[28] This interpretation suggests that the State is cognizant of the realities of governance and derives its power from the legitimacy of its actions on behalf of the State. This can then extend liberal arguments to encompass the ability of the State to accommodate the demands of market freedom. Thus, the issue for Foucault becomes one of examining how liberalism can engage with the State on the basis of economics, and not how the State can provide the freedom for economics to operate within it. This distinction is important because it endeavors to align the liberal concern for individual rights with the classical republican paradigm that individuals only attain full expression through participating in self-government. In other words, the projects of both approaches to government optimize market relations and behavior in order to permit the incessant and rational intrusion of government. Thus, the various expressions of instrumentality that individuals are capable of exhibiting are actual encasements of government regulation.

Classical republican theory, as enunciated by Mark Tushnet, insists that individuals "draw their understandings of themselves and the meaning of their lives from their participation with others in a social world that they actively and jointly create."[29] This approach does not recognize the liberal distinction between the public and private understanding of rights on the grounds that "rights cannot be defined independently of ongoing political conversations about what is good for the individual and, equally if not more importantly, for the society."[30] However, the function of republicanism is severely constrained because the concept of liberalism it seeks to critique ranges from the "self-interested and acquisitive aspect of human personality" to the advocacy of the indivisibility and independence of moral right over personal preferences, to utilitarianism and situational ethics.[31] Faced with a situation where these interpretations of liberalism can operate singly and concurrently, the project of enunciating a republican homogeneity based on the original Aristotelian paradigm of *polis* is rendered more difficult.

Richard Fallon suggests that the interpretation of discourse in the liberal paradigm ignores the instrumentality of discourse as it is "constituted at any particular time by conventions, norms, and shared understandings—inarticulate as well as articulate—that are subject to change."[32] To counter this point, Tushnet proposes that liberalism operates outside of convention on the grounds that cultural neutrality and the liberal argument are mutually exclusive. To some extent this criticism is one which is echoed by Foucault in his critique of Kantian "pragmatic anthropology" in *The Order of Things*.[33]

Significantly, this argument also endorses a view that liberalism cannot adjudicate impartially because no policy cannot be based on the phenomenon of a non-neutral assumption. For Foucault, Kant's work represents the pursuit of limits within which points of transgression are identified but never crossed over. Faced with this fundamental limitation, Foucault suggests that criticism should be practiced as a historical investigation into the events that have led society to constitute itself by what is said, thought, and done on behalf of society. Similarly, Tushnet's model of republicanism is self-contradicting because it is constructed upon the belief that society is homogeneously communitarian. His argument rests on the assumption that there is no need for any theory of interpretation since republican society is structured on a common understanding of civic virtue and of the rightful subordination of a citizen's independent preferences. Clearly, Tushnet disregards the fact that his 'republican' model owes much of its inspiration to the liberal paradigm of moral right over personal preference.

Presented with conflicting evidence on the independent status of liberalism and republicanism, the primary characteristic of republicanism can be said to lie in its affirmation of government wherein the function of law-making reflects those laws under which individuals are willing to serve and be governed. This view contrasts with the liberal evolution from "'negative freedom' or 'freedom from' government intrusions into a protected domain of private right."[34] Foucault operates with a similar motive when he emphasizes the social contract of discourse as a device to organize and redistribute the powers and dangers of discourse, and to "evade its ponderous, formidable material- ity."[35] This means that discourse distributes its authority on the basis of exploring the unexpected and unintended possibilities between self- actualizing and escalatory speech acts. On the one hand, where power is distributed on the basis of self-actualization, it is performative since it redefines and restructures the conceptual universe wherein individuals locate themselves. On the other hand, where power is escalatory, discourse seeks to de-legitimize the relations between citizens in civil society by assigning and recasting their conceptual universe as an inevitably unconscious response to an environment which is not of their making. Both of these approaches are discernible in Haughey's speech to the New Ireland Forum in September 1983, where he dismisses Northern Ireland as an economic and political anachronism. In his analysis, economic activity in Northern Ireland is an incremental "reflection of the amount of resources, financial and economic, the British Government is prepared to make available from the British taxpayer."[36] His performative subtext is contained in the idea that a settlement would enable both economies to function as "a natural economic unit ... [by] ... eliminating unnecessary and wasteful duplication and competition."[37]

A significant development of escalatory discourse is its adoption of the positive aspects of self-government, where its constitutional character subordinates the liberal concept of individualism to the empathetic autonomy of self-government based on the rule by law of people. Such a version of republicanism is potentially open to the criticism that it was majoritarian and relied heavily on the empathetic and undominated goodwill of citizens to function. Clearly, this interpre- tation is appropriate when tested against a speech Haughey delivered to the forum in October 1983. In this speech he sought to prescribe the limits of the republican paradigm suggesting its success would only be contingent upon British withdrawal from Ireland. Even though the ensuing economic vacuum would need to rely heavily on external investment, his presentation hinged on the implicit belief that any new dependence was the inevitable result of agreement within the prescriptive system of government and of its accommodation of the principles of economics based on wealth and production.

Haughey's subsequent pronouncements on the normalization of Anglo-Irish relations (November 1983) and his conclusion at the forum (May 1984) reverses the textual primacy of Fianna Fáil's constitution in favor of the secondary text of Fianna Fáil's role as official opposition to the FitzGerald government. Nonetheless, the experience of how these statements apply to the dynamics of the republican/Republican debate does not concede the power to primary texts suggested by Foucault. Part of the reason lies in the situational focus that circulates the relevance of discourse in response to events *a posteriori*. Foucault elaborates on this point when he suggests that "discourses circulate without deriving their meaning or their efficacity from an author to whom they could be attributed."[38] Such a super-ordination of discourse operates outside the domain of attribution and thereby removes the necessity for any historical justification. On the basis that the Fianna Fáil leadership could only progress by loosening its ties with historical propositions considered to be true, it had to constitute an "anonymous system at the disposal of anyone who wants to or is able to use it, without their meaning or validity being linked to the one who happened to be their inventor."[39] Although liberated from the ideological bind of history, Haughey could now concentrate on ensuring that the rules governing the conduct of Fianna Fáil's stance during the forum debate reflected a degree of political consonance that re-actuated as permanent the symbols of territoriality and cultural homogeneity perpetuated in the party's original Constitution

Foucault presents two schemas to explain the workings of power.[40] The first schema is based on contract-oppression and is characterized by its reliance on jurisprudence; the second is a dominant-repression schema, which locates power on a struggle-submission continuum. Foucault argues that the former is essentially preoccupied with imposing mechanisms of repression aimed at constraining individual liberty and psychological sense of empowerment. However, his second model examines expressions of power as discoverable in terms of economic exchange. This second model, largely influenced by Karl von Clausewitz, is reductionist since it explains the function of power in historically specific terms. Included in these terms are essentially Marxist concerns like the establishment of civil and political institutions whose functions neutralize and sanction the effects of physical war and re-inscribe it in terms of unspoken warfare conducted through "the reign of peace in civil society."[41]

When Foucault contrasts both schemas, he argues that the contract-oppression is concerned with the establishment of a social contract for the legitimation of the sovereignty of government. Such a contract exists insofar as citizens willingly sublimate their rights of self determination in favor of autonomy defined for them by the government. Following this interpretation, Foucault asserts that the only occasion for power to become oppressive is when it transgresses its contract with civil society. Since he does not elaborate how a government can over-extend itself, it can be argued that government does not invalidate its contract with civil society. A more accurate interpretation might be that the exercise of government invalidates arguments in favor of the contract-oppression schema because the juridical principle, upon which it is based, aims to protect the rights of only those individuals who subscribe to the contractual paradigm of civil society. The dominant-repression schema, on the other hand, does not interpret oppression in terms of the social contract "but is, on the contrary, the mere effect and continuation of a relation of domination."[42] In other words, the enactment and analysis of power does not center on a juridical model of contract-oppression but on the dominant-repression schema of struggle and submission. Clearly, Haughey's opposition to FitzGerald's meeting with Thatcher in November 1983 was based on his recognition that British insistence on prioritizing issues of border security underlined a dominant-repression schema by copper-fastening Ireland's financial obligations to preserving the border, yet without exacting any British intent to withdraw from Northern Ireland.

When the Forum Report was published, Fianna Fáil was happy to denounce "the arbitrary division of Ireland" because British policy, which treated Northern Ireland as a security problem, had "contributed to the emergence in both sections of the community of elements prepared to resort to violence."[43] The central constitutional point of the party's commentary, which would become the single issue summarizing the party's opposition to the Anglo-Irish Agreement a year later, was that it disputed the fact that British sovereignty was without any territorial basis. Even though several pieces of British legislation, namely the Government of Ireland Act (1920) and subsequent Acts in 1949 and 1973, guaranteed the constitutional status of the north within the United Kingdom until the people declared otherwise, Fianna Fáil sought to distance itself implicitly from the Forum's commitment to unify through consent. This process of exerting some constraint on the outcome of the negotiations that would be consonant with Fianna Fáil ideology was underpinned by the Foucaultian rhetorical use of *vraisemblable*, a term Foucault employs to describe the inevitability of something as natural. This theme, supporting all pronouncements on 'the right' solution, was echoed by Haughey in his annual Wolfe Tone Commemoration address: "We must all recognise that nothing will work whether in the short or long term except the establishment by agreement of an Irish unitary state and the withdrawal of Britain with honour and dignity from a new peaceful and reconciled Ireland."[44]

A significant development in the doctrinaire assumption that political process could have only one realistic outcome was developed by the Republic's Minister for Foreign Affairs, Gerard Collins in a debate on the motion "That this House demands the unity of Ireland" at the Oxford Union in October 1984. Collins argued the only solution was to reverse the gerrymandered institutions that had been created against the wishes of the electorate in the last all-Ireland election in 1918.

Thatcher's initial 'out, out, out' rejection of the proposals from the Forum Report placed FitzGerald in an invidious position because this meant that any form of joint-authority over Northern Ireland could only evolve to the limit that would not alter British sovereignty. During various meetings between Thatcher and FitzGerald, and between Geoffrey Howe and Peter Barry, the British Foreign Secretary and the Irish Minister for Foreign Affairs respectively, security issues and foreign investment became dominating themes subordinating as inviolate the issue of sovereignty. Arwel Owen presents a vivid account of the convergence of interest groups whose common focus was to oppose any Anglo-Irish settlement.[45] Unionist opposition reached its ideological zenith in a reply from James Molyneaux and Ian Paisley, leaders of the Ulster Unionist Party and the Democratic Unionist Party respectively, wherein they refuted any diminution in sovereignty.[46] In their letter they also sought to assert the "right of the people of Northern Ireland to self-determination a condition precedent to consideration of Irish demands." Speaking in Brussels FitzGerald stated that unification had to take second place to "securing ... a better deal now for both communities in Northern Ireland."[47]

Signing the Agreement would entail the acceptance of its provision for an Intergovernmental Conference of Ministers to deal with political, legal, and security issues. The Agreement would also promote the idea of cross-border cooperation but would not carry any operational responsibility for security policy, relationships between security and community, or penal policy. The principal policy issues contained in the Agreement required the Republic to sign the European Convention on the Suppression of Terrorism settlement and to agree to the Royal Ulster Constabulary's "primacy over the armed forces in security matters."[48] In spite of Fianna Fáil's opposition to the Agreement on the grounds that it enshrined partition, a sizable majority of the Irish people (59%) was in favor of it, as an Irish Times/MRBC poll showed. At the same time, a Sunday Times/MORI poll conducted in Northern Ireland revealed that 75% of Protestants were opposed to the Agreement while 65% of Catholics were in favor of it. In the days after the signing there appeared to be a general consensus that the Agreement would make a substantial contribution to defeating paramilitarism.

Cox has argued that the Agreement was a best attempt by two governments to "provide for the management of a mutual frontier territory on the basis which is intended to accommodate conflicting 'legitimate' claims on both sides."[49] Certainly realities of implementing the Agreement seemed to give the Irish Republic moral co-sovereignty because of their empathic relationship with northern nationalism and the SDLP. Moreover, the manner in which inter-governmental activity is subject to neither Dáil nor Parliament actually compounds the semblance of a democratic tyranny to the extent that Anglo-Irish ministers can continue to discharge their duties and discussions even if devolution is granted. In other words, devolution as intrinsically provided for within the terms of the Agreement renders the ambiguities of ideology away from historically identifiable forms of either British or Irish concepts of nationalism.

Haughey's rejection of the Agreement was based on an interpretation that political, legal, and constitutional realities precluded the Irish Republic from critically appraising the extent of British administration of Northern Ireland once they agreed to engage in joint-sovereignty. Speaking in the Dáil he said that the Agreement bolstered the "legitimacy of the Unionist position ... the Irish Government is saying to the world, that Northern Ireland is legitimately part of the British State."[50]

Conclusion

Foucault addresses particular choices open to the bridging (*apport*) between thinking and speaking in the context of discourse. By defining *apport* as the structure that puts language into action to produce a "meaning effect," Foucault compares discourse to nothing more than a utility to annul itself against the intentions of individuals and institutions that dispose of it as signs in the pursuit of power.[51]) This observation is particularly appropriate in the context of Haughey's iteration that the non-executive nature of the Inter-Governmental Conference could not achieve any meaningful level of agency. To argue otherwise would ultimately have cast the entire Agreement not only as an ephemerally rhetorical event but as an endorsement of something which would actually have invalidated the realities of the Irish Republic's constitutional claims for Fianna Fáil. In other words, an "alternative" conception of a republic could not be imposed through a paradigm of social existence—in the wider republican sense—if there could be no implicit agreement that it was consistent with the continuities and rigor of international law. This is an important observation because it ultimately questions the *raison d'être* of Articles 2 and 3 of the Constitution. Finally, Fianna Fáil's rejection of the Agreement meant an exclusive abandonment of republican sovereignty because of a persistent superordination of the principal of cultural consent over issues of regional mobilization in promoting "economic strength and access to loci of decision-making."[52] Indeed, the idea of monocephality, where politico-economic and cultural dimensions are influenced by one principal area of power, precluded the possibility of Fianna Fáil's acceptance of the Agreement. This argument can be made because the locus of control still resided in London. Therefore, Haughey's resistance to the Agreement represented a persistent commitment and defense of national identity that involved a commitment to the idea of national territory. What Haughey actually refused to acknowledge was the very idea of nation-state and territorial unification being liquidated by the aleatory inevitability of neo-liberal and republican thinking that permeated the organic federalism underscoring Irish sociopolitical membership of the European Union.

Notes

1. Michel Foucault, *The Archaeology of Knowledge* (London: Routledge, 1994).

2. Ibid., 183.

3. Ibid., 15.

4. Ibid., 185.

5. Michel Foucault, *Discipline and Punish* (London: Penguin, 1991).

6. Charles Haughey, *The Spirit of the Nation: The Speeches of Charles Haughey,* ed. Martin Mansergh (Cork: Mercier, 1986), 413.

7. Ibid.

8. Thomas Dumm, *Michel Foucault and the Politics of Freedom* (London: Sage, 1996), 131.

9. Raymond Smith, *Garret the Enigma* (Dublin: Aberlow, 1985), 445.

10. Harvey W. Cox, "Managing Northern Ireland Intergovernmentally," *Journal of Parliamentary Affairs* 40 (1987): 80-97.

11. Anthony Coughlan, *Fooled Again? The Anglo Irish Agreement and After* (Cork: Mercier, 1986).

12. Bruce Arnold, *Haughey: His Life and Unlucky Deeds* (London: Harper Collins, 1993), 179.

13. Haughey, *The Spirit of the Nation*, 753.

14. Ibid., 755.

15. Ibid., 756.

16. Richard J. Bernstein, *Beyond Objectivism and Relativism* (Philadelphia: University of Pennsylvania Press, 1983), 226.

17. Ronald Dworkin, *Law's Empire* (New York: Fontana, 1986).

18. J.G.A. Pocock, *The Machiavellian Moment* (Princeton: Princeton UP, 1975), 66.

19. Ibid.

20. Jeffrey C. Isaac, "Republicanism vs. Liberalism? A Reconsideration," *History of Political Thought* 9 (1988): 349-77.

21. J.G.A. Pocock, ed. *The Political Works of James Harrington* (Cambridge: Cambridge UP, 1977), 57.

22. Isaac, "Republicanism vs. Liberalism."

23. William Galston, "Defending Liberalism," *American Political Science Review* 76 (September 1982): 627-9.

24. Isaac, "Republicanism vs. Liberalism," 375.

25. Michel Foucault, *Discipline and Punish*, 223.

26. Michel Foucault, *Politics, Philosophy, Culture: Interviews and Other Writings 1977-1984* (London: Routledge, 1988),104.

27. Graham Burchell, "Liberal Government and Techniques of Self," in *Foucault and Political Reason,* ed. Andrew Barry et al. (London: University College London, 1996), 19-36.

28. Ibid., 21.

29. Mark Tushnet, *Red, White, and Blue: A Critical Analysis of Constitutional Law* (Cambridge, Mass.: Harvard University Press, 1988),10.

30. Richard H. Fallon, "What is Republicanism and Is It Worth Reviving?," *Harvard Law Review* 102 (1989): 1701.

31. Ibid., 1705.

32. Ibid., 1712.

33. Michel Foucault, *The Order of Things* (London: Routledge, 1994).

34. Fallon, "What is Republicanism," 1721.

35. Michel Foucault, "The Order of Discourse," in *Language and Politics*, ed. Michael Shapiro (Oxford: Blackwell, 1984), 109.

36. Charles Haughey, Speech to the New Ireland Forum, 773.

37. Ibid.

38. Foucault, "The Order of Discourse," 116.

39. Ibid., 118.

40. Michel Foucault, "Two Lectures," in *Power/Knowledge* (Hemel Hempstead: Harvester Press, 1980), 78-108.

41. Ibid., 90.

42. Ibid., 92.

43. Fianna Fail, *Why Fianna Fail is Fully Satisfied with The Forum Report* (Dublin, Party Political Statement, 1985).

44. Charles Haughey, "Annual Wolfe Tone Commemoration," Speech, September 1984, Fianna Fáil Archive, Dublin.

45. Arwel Owen, *Political Concepts: A Reconstruction* (Oxford: Blackwell, 1994).

46. *Newsletter*, 2 October 1988.

47. *Irish Times*, 9 November 1985.

48. Owen, *Political Concepts*, 35.

49. Harvey W. Cox, "Managing Northern Ireland Intergovernmentally," *Journal of Parliamentary Affairs* 40 (1987): 93.

50. Charles Haughey, "The Anglo Irish Agreement," Speech, November 1985, Fianna Fáil Archive, Dublin, p. 4-5.

51. Foucault, "The Order of Discourse," 124.

52. Stein Rokkan and Derek Urwin, *The Politics of Territorial Identity: Studies in European Regionalism* (London: Sage, 1982), 2.

Neutrality Must Change

Heinz Gärtner

While the dramatic events of 1989/90 indelibly transformed the entire, global political landscape, it was still in Europe that the greatest changes occured. During the cold war, European defense planning was mostly based on one, main threat. This threat has now faded away, and global as well as European security requirements are currently undergoing profound changes as a consequence. Today there is no major threat to deter, and many of the new dangers tend to be smaller in scale, regional in nature, and located on the periphery or outside of Europe. The very nature of the security threat has changed. A single, overriding threat originating from a monolithic source has been replaced by a multitude of different threats, including the resurgence of centuries-old ethnic conflicts frozen by the cold war.

Security institutions are forced to adapt as, from Portugal to Poland and beyond, the dissolution of the unique political and strategic milieu of the cold war compels a reappraisal of national security policies. European countries are seeking security for a continent that has undergone a major structural transformation. Crisis management is the paradigm that forms the cornerstone of a new system of international security which, in turn, faces a far wider array of threats than during the cold war. By far the greatest portion of the operational efforts of the North Atlantic Treaty Organization (NATO) and the Western European Union (WEU) has already shifted away from collective defense toward crisis management activities.

Military alliances and neutral states alike have to reconsider their cold war strategies and resist the natural tendency towards inertia. NATO wants to keep its collective defense commitments that have their roots in the cold war and so does the WEU. Neutral states are often loath to relinquish their cold war image of themselves despite the changing times. Conversely, critics of neutrality still use John Foster Dulles' arguments of the cold war[1]: In 1956 he called "the principle of neutrality … an obsolete conception, and, except under very special circumstances, it is an immoral and shortsighted conception."[2]

Neutral Austria has to reconsider its strategic options in post-cold war Europe. This article deals with the concept of neutrality in future European security systems. For neutral states who recently joined the EU, it remains unclear what this entails in terms of other memberships. Do these states now have to become members of the WEU and NATO as well? If so, this would have significantly different implications for their domestic debate on neutrality. Were the EU to develop a stronger common defense policy, neutrality would come under growing criticism and face an increasing legitimacy problem, internationally and domestically. How much security would neutral states gain by joining an alliance?

This article discusses whether neutrality, defined as non-membership in military alliances and non-participation in wars, has a future in a European security system. It looks at small states' past experiences with their attempts to be allied or remain neutral, and explores the incentives for states to come to each other's defense. Does a formal alliance provide more security than a non-allied status in the post cold war era?

The Cold War System

The old system was based on the concept of 'balance of power'. For Hans Morgenthau alliances are the "most important manifestation of the balance of power."[3] In this observation members of alliances have common interests based on the fear of other states. Stephen Walt has since modified this concept, viewing alliances as the result of a "balance of threat."[4] He shows that the overwhelming coalition led by the United States against the U.S.S.R. and its allies was a result not of the power of the U.S.S.R. but of its perceived threat. This traditional model, where the existence of alliances and a potential threat were inseparable, is consistent with the bipolarity of the cold war.

It was in this context that neutrality arose as an instrument to avoid bandwagoning and accommodating with great powers—at least in military terms. When the major powers could not include certain states into their own sphere of influence, they often accepted their status of neutrality in order to prevent these states from becoming part of a rival sphere. Austrian and Finnish neutrality are prime examples. The end of the bipolar conflict has brought about the demise of this rationale, and with it this function of neutrality.

NATO

Based on the assumption that alliances can hardly survive without a sufficient threat, some analysts concluded after the end of the East-West conflict that "NATO's days are not numbered but its years are."[5] No alliance in history survived its enemy for very long. This is true for the coalition against Napoleon, the First World War Entente against Germany and the anti-Hitler coalition. Nine years after the end of the cold war, however, NATO shows no signs of its demise. The prediction that alliances would weaken without threat appears to be wrong. NATO looks like it will be an exception to these rules and to the fundamental logic of alliance theory. How can NATO endure in the absence of a serious opponent?

The reason lies in NATO's capacity for change. NATO is redeveloping its basic structure: Preparing for a coalition war is no longer the only or even primary item on its agenda and its focus now includes crisis management, peacekeeping, humanitarian action, as well as peace enforcement. The 'new NATO' looks and acts in part quite differently from the old NATO. Simultaneously, the definition of the NATO area (Article VI) is losing relevance—the NATO-led operation in Bosnia and NATO's preparation for an intervention in Kosovo/Yugoslavia are a case in point. NATO will be focusing on new areas in the time to come. It will and can no longer focus on a single mission of collective defense as during the cold war, for if NATO remains a traditional alliance of collective defense as enshrined in Article V of the Washington Treaty, it is likely to die out or deteriorate. The new NATO's challenges lie beyond its territory in international terrorism, the proliferation of weapons of mass destruction, the disruption of Gulf oil supplies, and the control of instability along NATO's southern and eastern flanks. Since these challenges do not represent a direct threat to NATO territory, the real issue for NATO's future is not territorial defense but rather its structural transformation into a crisis management alliance.

The older rationale will not disappear altogether, though. The core of cold war NATO, (nuclear) deterrence and collective defense (enshrined in Article V of the Washington Treaty), still remains, although it is of decreasing importance. This concept long defined the primary purpose of the alliance, i. e. the defense of NATO territory against a major attack. Even though NATO's activities are now less concentrated on collective defense, this concept has become part of NATO's identity.

NATO's transformation is marked by a bifurcation, in which the collective defense now coexists with the more important concept of crisis management. It remains to be seen which of these elements most influences the NATO of the future: the old-style NATO based on collective defense and balance of power, or a new NATO based on the emerging principles and tasks? The old concept is not likely to be completely overcome. More likely, both will endure, as the Strategic Concept of April 1999 shows. However, the two concepts tend to be mutually exclusive, and herein lies a source of profound tension.

The European Union (EU) and the
Western European Union (WEU)

The WEU is characterized by a similar bifurcation. The origins of Article V of the Brussels Treaty of 1948 can also be located in the cold war.[6] Since the so-called 'Petersberg declaration' of 1992, the WEU will also focus on missions that include crisis management, peacekeeping, humanitarian action, and peacemaking. If the above observation of shifting challenges and tasks is correct, the 'Petersberg missions' will become more important than Article V. José Cutileiro, secretary general of the WEU, acknowledges: "Today the WEU is a politico-military tool for crisis management. It will run operations that Europeans decide to undertake and in which North Americans do not wish to participate directly."[7]

The EU Treaty of Amsterdam of June 1997 includes the 'Petersberg Tasks'. Article 17 states that "the Union can avail itself of the WEU to elaborate and implement decisions of the EU on the tasks referred to …" These are "humanitarian and rescue tasks, peacekeeping tasks and tasks of combat forces in crisis management, including peacemaking." The Treaty does not merge the WEU and EU. It simply states that "the WEU is an integral part of the development of the EU … The EU shall … foster closer institutional relations with the WEU with a view to the possibility of the integration of the WEU into the Union …" The precondition is a European Council decision and adoptation of such a decision by the Member States only "in accordance with their respective constitutional requirements."[8]

The Common Foreign and Security Policy (CFSP) of the EU shall, according to the treaty, "include all questions relating to the security of the Union, including the progressive framing of a common defense policy ... which might in time lead to a common defense, should the European Council so decide." Such a decision has to be "in accordance with [the Member States'] respective constitutional requirements." Based originally on a Swedish-Finish proposal, the Treaty allows "all (EU) Member States contributing to the tasks in question to participate fully on an equal footing in planning and decision-taking in the WEU." Membership in the WEU, therefore, is not necessary to participate in the 'Petersberg Tasks'.[9] For the time being, the CFSP will emphasize "common defense policy" (e.g. crisis management measures) rather than collective defense. "Common defense" remains undefined and requires further debates. The federal approach still aims to merge the EU and WEU, and Article V (collective defense and binding security guarantees of the WEU treaty) should be incorporated into the EU. This would lead to the creation of a new military alliance.[10] Such a radical development is very unlikely and not an option for a very long time. It is also conceivable that the WEU changes dramatically and abandons Article V, or that the WEU dissolves entirely and the main European defense role remains with NATO.

The EU after Amsterdam focused on the 'Petersberg Missions', including crisis management, peace-keeping, humanitarian action, and peace-enforcement, rather than Art. V operations (collective defence and security guarantees).

- According to the declaration of the European Council[11] in Cologne in June 1999, which is based on a proposal by the German EU-presidency,[12] a common European policy on security and defence requires "a capacity for action backed up by credible military capabilities and appropriate decision-making bodies and proce-dures." The focus therefore should be to assure that the EU possesses the necessary capabilities (including military capabilities) to conduct crisis management operations in the scope of the 'Petersberg Tasks'. The main characteristics include: deployability, sustainability, inter-operability, flexibility, and mobility. Further arrangements to enhance the capacity of European multinational and national forces to respond to crisis situations will be needed. NATO remains the foundation for collective defence (Article 5). In the case of integration of the WEU into the EU the commitment of this Article and of Article V of the Brussels Treaty will be preserved for the member states already party to these treaties. The document stresses that the policy of the EU shall not influence the specific character of the security and defense policies of certain member states: "States will retain in all circumstances the right to decide if and when their national forces are deployed." There should be the possibility of all EU member states (NATO members, neutral and non-aligned states) to participate fully and on equal footing in European operations drawing on NATO assets and capabilities; and there should be satisfactory arrangements for European NATO members who are not EU member states. Both EU-led operations using NATO assets and capabilities and EU-led operations without recourse to NATO assets and capabilities should be possible, and unnecessary duplication should be avoided. Regular meetings of defense ministers, i.e. a permanent body of representatives with political and military expertise, are planned. This declaration includes many changes proposed by European neutral and non-aligned states, explicitly excluding Article V commitments. The equal role of these states is underlined.

The European Council in Helsinki in December 1999 adopted the two presidency progress reports on developing the Union's military and non-military crisis management capability as part of a strengthened common European policy on security and defense. The Finish presidency[13] of the EU has set priority to the mandate given by the Cologne European Council to strengthen the common European policy on security and defense by taking the work forward in military and non-military aspects of crisis management. The document stresses that the Atlantic Alliance remains the foundation of the collective defense of its members. The common European headline goal has been adopted for deployable military capabilities based on a British and French proposal that called for a European rapid reaction force of up to 60,000 troops, capable of deployment within 60 days, which should tackle military crises without outside help. The European Council underlines its determination to develop an autonomous capacity to take decisions and, where NATO "as a whole is not engaged," to launch and conduct EU-led military operations in response to international crises. (It is not clear whether the EU first has to ask NATO before it conducts an EU-led operation, however). This process will avoid unnecessary duplication and does not imply the creation of a European army.

- A standing Political and Security Committee (PSC) has been established that deals with all aspects of the CFSP including the common European security and defense policy. The Military Committee (MC) will provide for consultation and cooperation between the member states, give advice and make recommendations though the PSC. The report stresses that the European Union will contribute to international peace and security in accordance with the principles of the United Nations Charter. The Union recognizes the primary responsibility of the United Nations Security Council for the maintenance of international peace and security. Also, a non-military crisis management mechanism will be established to coordinate and make more effective the various civilian means and resources, along with the military ones, at the disposal of the Union and the member states. The Portugese EU-presidency established a Commitee for Non-military Crisis Management.

Neutrality

Politically, the adoption of a permanently neutral status was the price Austria had to pay the Soviet Union for the latter's agreement to restore full Austrian independence in the Austrian State Treaty of 1955. In the Moscow Memorandum of 15 April 1955, the U.S.S.R. agreed to sign the State Treaty in exchange for the declaration of permanent neutrality by Austria. The Memorandum was legally non-binding, however. Even though neutrality was not really a free choice, it was the best deal Austria could get.

On the legal level, however, Austria tried to avoid the image of a neutralized state. It was felt that permanent neutrality imposed on the country in a treaty, especially in an agreement with the Great Powers, would make this status less respectable. Hence, the Austrian Parliament adopted the Federal Constitutional Law not before it regained full independence (it waited until the last soldier of the occupation forces had left its territory).[14] Article I (1) emphasizes, therefore, that: "For the purpose of the permanent maintenance of its external independence and for the purpose of the inviolability of its territory, Austria, of *its own free will,* declares herewith its permanent neutrality which it is resolved to maintain and defend with all the means at its disposal." The neutrality law in Article I (2) only prohibits Austria from joining a military alliance and the deployment of foreign troops on its soil: "In order to secure these purposes Austria will never in the future accede to any military alliances nor permit the establishment of military bases by foreign States on its territory."[15]

According to the Hague Convention of 1907 on sea and land war, neutral states are required to refrain from all direct or indirect participation in wars. For Europe after 1990, however, this legal tradition has become fairly outdated.[16] Within the borders of the EU and among the OECD (Organisation for Economic Co-operation and Development) countries war is no longer an issue. Furthermore, wars between states have become increasingly rare. War within states, however, are not covered by this trend.

Austria's concept of neutrality is historically and globally unique. Its form of neutrality cannot be put on a level with other concepts of neutrality. Certainly, it followed the legal structure of the Swiss example, but it was born in the East-West conflict. Finland has similar cold war historical roots, but a different legal basis. Presumably, Austria's understanding of neutrality belongs to a model of the past. The question remains whether the idea of neutrality will survive in a different form. This does not mean a return to the 'policy of active neutrality' of the Kreisky era (chancellor between 1970 and 1983), which was less a neutrality policy than an active foreign policy. The privileged role of *mediation* associated mainly with neutral states has become a remnant of the East-West Conflict.[17] This does not mean that neutral states will henceforth be avoided as meeting and mediating places. Austrian territory is home to one of the seats of the U.N. and the headquarters of the International Atomic Energy Agency (IAEA), the United Nations Industrial Development Organization (UNIDO), the Comprehensive Test Ban Treaty Preparatory Commission (CTBTO), and the Organization for Petroleum Exporting Countries (OPEC). The Organization for Security and Co-operation in Europe (OSCE) is also based in Vienna.

Permanent neutrality between East and West was a more or less effective means to protect Austria from the military blocs during the cold war. Yet, the concept of neutrality has to change along with the concept of alliances. This does not necessarily mean the converse, however—that neutral states will now have to join an alliance. It means only that the status of neutrality must take on a new meaning. Austria's neutrality has already de facto adapted several times to changing situations: membership in the U.N. was a move away from the Swiss model; the permission for the aircraft of the anti-Iraq coalition to overfly

Austrian airspace in the second Gulf war (1990/91) was compatible only with a broad interpretation of the legal concept of neutrality; membership in the EU with its CFSP and Amsterdam Treaty (that includes peacemaking) has little to do with traditional understandings of neutrality. Neutrality has become a function that does not extend beyond the negative definition of non-membership in NATO.[18] This is not to say that little remains of neutrality, but that these changes demonstrate the flexibility of the concept even within its existing legal framework.

Both NATO's and the WEU's old core concepts are incompatible with a traditional understanding of neutrality. But is there potential for a new conception of neutrality within NATO and the WEU's new elements? Both have created instruments for crisis management and peacekeeping, and NATO's enhanced Partnership for Peace (PfP) also includes non-members for such missions. All EU members can also participate in the so called 'Petersberg Tasks' of the WEU. Let us now look at these new developments more closely.

Cooperation with NATO

The Partnership for Peace (PfP) program has already been designed according to the new requirements. Cooperation of the Partners with NATO can be organized on an individual level through peacekeeping exercises, military-to-military contacts, and similar activities. The Implementation Force (IFOR) and the Stabilisation Force (SFOR) in Bosnia was NATO's first joint operation with PfP and other non-NATO states. In Madrid in July 1997, NATO formally launched an enhanced form of PfP which widened the range of participation. Military exercises now can cover the whole spectrum of possible crisis interventions. Building on the success of the common experience in Bosnia, Partners will be involved in planning and preparing for contingency operations. The Partnership for Peace will be more operational, and military exercises will be more complex and robust. Partners will have a stronger presence at NATO Headquarters and will be involved more deeply in decision-making and planning. All in all, the Partnership for Peace will facilitate NATO's ability to integrate Partner forces in future operations. The experience in Bosnia, where sixteen NATO countries cooperate in the NATO-led peacekeeping force SFOR with no less than twenty non-NATO countries, is the model for the future. Without the Partnership for Peace, such a broad yet highly effective military coalition would not have been possible. In February 1998 PfP-Partners participated for the first time in a crisis management exercise (CMX). The scenario focused mainly on actions that NATO might have to take to implement a U.N.-mandated peace support operation.

The new Euro-Atlantic Partnership Council (EAPC) provides a mechanism for productive consultation and more meaningful communication among Partners as well as a framework in which the enhanced PfP can develop. There will also be possibilities for closer political dialogue and consultations, and greater scope for joint decision-making and coordination. With the creation of the EAPC, NATO carries forward its transformation on the basis of a broad, cooperative approach to security. Partners will have new opportunities to consult with the Alliance more regularly and more substantively. The EAPC is thus the logical political complement to a stronger, more operational Partnership for Peace. As the Basic Document of the Euro-Atlantic Partnership Council of 30 May 1997 states: "In addition, the Council will provide the framework to afford Partner countries, to the maximum extent possible, increased decision-making opportunities relating to activities in which they participate."[19]

The specific subject areas in which Allies and Partners would consult within the framework of the EAPC might include, but are not limited to: political and security related matters; crisis management; regional matters; arms control issues; nuclear, biological and chemical (NBC) proliferation and defense issues; international terrorism; defense planning and budgets; defense policy and strategy; and security impacts of economic developments. EAPC's scope will include consultations and cooperation on issues such as: civil emergency and disaster preparedness; armaments cooperation under the aegis of the Conference of National Armaments Directors (CNAD); nuclear safety; defense related environmental issues; civil-military coordination of air traffic management and control; scientific cooperation; and issues related to peace support operations.

This new array of options and cooperation provides for an innovative capacity in the face of new challenges not requiring an Article V (collective defense) response. The broad security approach encompasses not only military, but also economic, political, societal, and environmental concerns. These occur simultaneously at global, regional and local levels. As non-Article V contingencies they will be addressed by 'coalitions of the willing' which include, as in Bosnia (IFOR/SFOR) and Kosovo (KFOR), both NATO and non-NATO members.

More than merely a new form of cooperation, NATO's new instruments and tasks will blur the differences between members and non-members (i.e. partners). PfP/EAPC offers almost all the benefits of NATO except the collective security guarantee articulated in Article V of the Washington Treaty. As the former U. S. Defense Minister Perry foresaw in December 1996 during a meeting of NATO Defense Ministers in Bergen: "The difference between membership and non-membership in NATO would be paper-thin." Indeed, in some cases non-NATO members may play an even more important role in the new operations than NATO members as NATO's focus gradually shifts away from Article V missions (territorial defense) to non-Article V missions (crisis management).[20]

The innovative Combined Joint Tasks Forces (CJTFs) are specifically designed to include the participation of non-NATO countries for both non-Article V contingencies outside Alliance territory and Article V tasks. The concept builds on NATO's practice of multinational, multiservice operations and, therefore, could involve humanitarian relief, peacekeeping, or peace enforcement. The CJTF concept would also facilitate the use of NATO's collective assets by the WEU, as well as provide a mechanism for involving non-NATO PfP-Partners in NATO-led operations. Finally, as not all allies may be engaged in every non-Article V contingency, the CJTF concept is designed to deal flexibly with the ad hoc nature of participation without sacrificing cohesion, effectiveness, and reaction time.[21]

Neutrality and the European Union

So far, there is no reason to think that neutrality would be absorbed by an integrated European defense system. CFSP decisions will be taken with unanimity. For the adoption of joint actions or common positions on the basis of a common strategy or their implementation, decisions with qualified majority are possible. Common strategies have to be decided unanimously, however. A member state can oppose the adoption of a decision to be taken by qualified majority for "important … reasons of national policy." The "constructive abstention" gives each member state the option of not participating in the implementation of a unanimously adopted decision. Such an abstention will not prevent the adoption of such decisions, however. Decisions having military or defense implications are not decided with qualified majority (Article 23 of the Treaty of Amsterdam).

As mentioned above, the EU after Amsterdam will focus on the 'Petersberg Missions', including crisis management, peacekeeping, humanitarian action, and peace enforcement, rather than Article V operations (collective defense and security guarantees). Based originally on a Swedish-Finnish proposal, the Treaty allows "all (EU) Member States contributing to the tasks in question to participate fully on an equal footing in planning and decision-taking in the WEU." Membership in the WEU, therefore, is not necessary to participate in the 'Petersberg Tasks'.[22] This was confirmed at the meetings of the European Council in Cologne and Helsinki.

Austria's Formula: 'PfP and Petersberg'

Today's European security system has moved far beyond the structures (and strictures) of the cold war to a bifurcation within NATO and EU (WEU), between collective defense and crisis management. The latter offers a wide scope of options for new missions. We have today a European Union which adopted the Amsterdam Treaty with its 'Petersberg Tasks' and a new NATO with PfP and EAPC. All of these are non-Article V initiatives. Since only Article V's security commitments are incompatible with Austria's neutrality law, why should Austria not concentrate on these new elements encompassed within the formula *'Petersberg plus PfP'*?[23]

Austria could participate in crisis management, peacekeeping, humanitarian action, and even peace enforcement operations within the framework of the Partnership for Peace (PfP). The new Euro-Atlantic Partnership Council (EAPC) provides the opportunity for Austria, as a non-member, to take part in NATO's consultative and decision-making processes. Austria already participates in IFOR and SFOR in Bosnia and KFOR in Kosovo. Currently there are more than 1,000 Austrian troops active in thirteen peacekeeping operations. This demonstrates that Austria, while maintaining a form of neutrality, is not a 'free rider'.

Austria does not need security guarantees along the lines of Article V because no major attack on Austrian territory is likely. Therefore, membership in a collective defense system does not automatically increase Austria's security. The concept of neutrality is flexible enough to allow Austria's participation in the 'Petersberg Tasks' or PfP without necessitating formal membership in NATO or the WEU.

Sweden, a country with a long neutral tradition, also sees changes in the nature of neutrality. The 1998 report on Swedish security states clearly: "Our policy of non-participation in military alliances precludes our participation in operations that concern the defense of our territory and security guarantees. But it presents no obstacle to Sweden's participating in other ways in the emerging, multi-faceted European security cooperation where the focus is on cooperation based on trust, conflict-prevention and crisis management."[24]

For the future Sweden wishes to stress the following points: The real security challenges for Europe today and in the foreseeable future lie in the area of crisis prevention and crisis management, not territorial defense and mutual defense commitments. Precisely for this reason, the Amsterdam Treaty brought the 'Petersberg Tasks' to the forefront, which should remain the guiding principle. In this context, the primary responsibility of the U.N. Security Council for the maintenance of international peace and security should be reaffirmed. All EU action must be in accordance with the U.N. Charter, including a Security Council mandate for enforcement action. Through the Amsterdam Treaty, the 'Petersberg Tasks' became central elements of the CFSP. An integrated civilian and military approach to conflict prevention and crisis management should be established. Particular emphasis should be placed on preventing the escalation of emerging conflicts, in order to avoid having to resort to military means.

Notes

1. E.g. Peter Michael Lingens on Austrian neutrality in *Der Standard,* 3 March 1994; 22 May 1995; *Die Presse,* 11 June 1997.

2. John Foster Dulles, in a speech on June 9, 1956; U.S. Department of State *Bulletin,* June 18, 1956, pp. 999-1004, quoted in Paul W. Blackstock, *The Strategy of Subversion: Manipulating the Politics of Other Nations* (Chicago, 1964): p. 31.

3. Hans Morgenthau, *Politics among Nations,* 6th ed. (New York: Alfred A. Knopf, 1985): 205–206.

4. Stephen M. Walt, *The Origins of Alliances* (Ithaca: Cornell Univesity Press, 1987).

5. Kenneth N. Waltz, "The Emerging Structure of International Politics," *International Security* 18 (Fall 1993): 75-76. See also John J. Mearsheimer, "Back to the Future," *International Security* 15 (Summer 1990): 52.

6. Article V of the 1948 Brussels Treaty states: "If any of the High Contracting Parties should be object of an armed attack in Europe ... the other High Contracting Parties will ... afford the Party so attacked all the military and other aid and assistance in their power." The Brussels Treaty and Protocols, quoted. in Alfred Cohen, ed., *The Western European Union and NATO* (London: Bassey's 1989): 71.

7. *International Herald Tribune,* 17 December 1998. *NATO-Review,* no. 1(Spring 1998): 18.

8. The Treaty of Amsterdam, Article 17.

9. Austria presently occupies observer status in the WEU.

10. The WEU-Treaty prohibits such a development, however. Article IV states that "recognizing the undesirability of duplicating the military staffs of NATO, the Council and its Agency will rely on the appropriate military authorities of NATO for information and advice on military matters." The Brussels Treaty and Protocols, quoted. in Cohen, ed., *The Western European Union*, 71.

11. Declaration of the European Council on Strengthening the Common European Policy on Security and Defence, 3 June 1999.

12. Draft Presidency Reaction: Strengthening the Common European Policy on Security and Defence, 7 May 1999.

13. The Finish Presidency, Presidency Report to the Helsinki European Council Strengthening of the Common European Policy on Security and Defence: Crisis Management, Helsinki, 11-12 December 1999.

14. Hanspeter Neuhold, "Austria's Security Policies in a Changing Europe," (Paper delivered at the Conference on Small States and Security, Vancouver, Can., 1994).

15. English translation in Alfred Verdross, *The Permanent Neutrality of Austria* (Vienna: Verlag für Geschichte und Politik, 1978), 28.

16. Laurent Goetschel, "Neutrality, a really dead concept?" (Paper delivered at the third pan-European International Relations Conference and Joint Meeting with the International Studies Association in Vienna, 16-19 September 1998).

17. For example, the main mediator in the conflict in the Yugoslav province Kosovo was the U.S. envoy Richard Holbrooke. The host of the Oslo accords between Israel and the PLO is a NATO member. The Hague was chosen as headquarters of the agency charged with monitoring compliance with the 1993 chemical weapons ban. See also Anton Pelinka, "Austria's Future Is in Europe," *Europäische Rundschau*, Austria and the European Union, no. 17 (Special Edition, 1998), 78; Hanspeter Neuhold, "Austria and European Security: the Question of Neutrality," in *Managing Security in Europe: The European Union and the challenge of enlargement*, ed. Franco Algieri, Josef Janning, Dirk Rumberg (Gütersloh: Bertelsmann, 1996), 24.

18. Pelinka, "Austria's Future," 78.

19. Basic Document of the Euro-Atlantic Partnership Council of 30 May 1997, in *NATO-Review*, no. 4 (July-August 1997): 11-12.

20. F. Stephen Larrabee, *NATO Enlargement and the Post-Madrid Agenda* (RAND, Santa Monica: Cambridge University Press, 1997).

21. John Barrett, "NATO Reform: Alliance Policy and Cooperative Security," in *New Security Challenges: The Adaptation of International Institutions, Reforming the U.N., NATO, EU and CSCE since 1989*, ed. Ingo Peters (New York: St.Martin's Press, 1996) 123-152, here 136.

22. Austria presently occupies observer status in the WEU.

23. Helmut Türk argues that Austria's neutrality is not an obstacle to NATO membership because NATO changed and Article V is unlikely to be applied. Helmut Türk, *Österreich im Spannungsfeld von Neutralität und Kollektiver Sicherheit* (Wien: Verlag Österreich, 1997).

24. Ministry of Defense, Sweden, "Swedish Security Policy in the Light of International Change," 20 February 1998, 22.

Austria's Permanent Neutrality—Its Origins, Development, and Demise[1]

Paul Luif

1. Introduction

For a long time, Austria's permanent neutrality was seen as an element of the country's identity, one that would last, if not forever, at least for a very long time. Its usefulness was self-evident and rarely questioned. When in September 1990 Jörg Haider, the populist leader of the Freedom Party (FPÖ), started to demand, in view of the changes in Eastern Europe, a debate about neutrality and the closely connected State Treaty, his attempt was greeted as foreign policy "nonsense."[2]

This article starts with a short analysis of the meaning of neutrality in international relations. It then examines why Austria chose neutrality in 1955, and what kind of neutrality it settled for. The development as well as the features and functions of 'active neutrality' will then be analyzed. Finally, the article describes the changes of Austrian neutrality and the background to the conceivable abandonment by Austria of this foreign policy status.

2. Types of 'Neutrality'

In the Westphalian system of independent nation-states, and according to its theoretical counterpart, the position of each member toward the other members of the system has important implications for the security of the individual nation-state. At the same time, its position also effects the whole system. The most significant consequences of the Westphalian system have been the formation of alliances and the balance of power. The complement to alliance membership has been neutrality. In state practice, several kinds of 'neutrality' did in fact develop:

1. *Occasional (temporary, ordinary, simple,* ad hoc) *neutrality,* or a state's neutrality in a particular war between other states. This original form of neutrality emerged from the interaction of state practice, scholarly thought, and international treaties already at the end of the Middle Ages. The customary law of neutrality was codified only in 1907 at the second Hague Peace Conference in the Hague Conventions V (neutrality in the case of war on land) and XIII (neutrality in naval war). The international law of occasional neutrality applies only to states that remain neutral in a war, regardless of their prior policies. Occasional neutrality in a war does not commit a state to neutrality in another war or to any rules of conduct in peacetime.[3]

2. *Permanent ('eternal', perpetual,* de jure) *neutrality* under international law commits a state to neutrality in all future wars and obliges it to avoid such peacetime ties and policies as would make its neutrality in war impossible. The institution of permanent neutrality under international law began to take shape in the early nineteenth century. It particularly reflected the case of Switzerland. However, the peacetime duties and rights of permanently neutral states have not been codified. They are part of customary international law and have remained a matter of political and scholarly debate. During wars, the rules of occasional neutrality apply also for the permanent neutrals.

3. *Conventional (continuous,* de facto) *neutrality* without an international legal basis began to emerge from instances of repeated occasional neutrality even before the legal institution of permanent neutrality took shape. Typically, the states that follow this line tend to call their policies neutral (or non-allied). They follow a more or less neutral course in practice, but fail to commit themselves to permanent neutrality under international law. Swedish foreign policy from the early to mid-nineteenth century onwards is perhaps the best example of this variant. In the case of Switzerland, one may discern a sequential move from occasional to continuous and finally to permanent neutrality.

4. *Nonalignment*: After World War II, many of the colonies that had gained independence wanted to keep out of the alliances created during the early phases of the cold war. In Europe, Communist Yugoslavia left the Eastern bloc without joining the Western system of alliances. Together with India and Egypt it was among the leading nations of the Nonaligned Movement, founded in the late

1950s. Without any legal obligations and lacking a clear definition of their status, these countries wanted to reduce the tensions between East and West and change the international system in a way that would improve the situation of the weaker and poorer countries, in particular in the Third World. In doing so, many of the statesmen in the nonaligned countries were rather critical of the West and less so of the Communist states. A few of these countries, in particular Castro's Cuba, even regarded the East as 'natural ally'.

3. Austria's Choice in 1955

The liberation of Austria from Nazi rule in 1945 quickly turned into an 'occupation' by the four victorious Allies (France, Soviet Union, United Kingdom, United States). They were in no hurry to end the four-zone division of Austria. The circumstances were similar to those of Germany, with one big difference: after the general elections of November 1945, there existed a democratically legitimized government for all of Austria. But its room to maneuver was limited since the representatives of the Allies closely controlled its conduct. Before long, the beginning of the cold war made this situation almost hopeless, with no quick solution in sight. None of the four Allies wanted to surrender the strategically rather important Austrian territory to the other side. The Austrian politicians from the two main parties, the conservative ÖVP (People's Party) and the socialist SPÖ (Socialist Party, since 1991 Social Democratic Party), constituted a grand coalition government (which up to 1947 included a member of the tiny Communist Party). Some politicians espoused 'neutrality' as a way to keep the country out of the unfolding East-West tensions. With this approach they wanted to expedite and simplify an agreement among the four Allies on the 'State Treaty', the legal instrument for the withdrawal of the Allied troops.[4]

In the early 1950s, as there was no end of the negotiations in sight, both government parties sought the support of the West, in particular the United States, to get rid of the Soviet Union's occupation of eastern Austria. The Soviet rule impeded the economic development and constantly threatened personal freedom in the eastern provinces. It was about to lead to a *de facto* division of the country. However, the close contacts with the West turned out to be not very successful, with the Soviet Union stalling and the Western powers not ready to risk any major crises for Austria's freedom.

The death of Stalin gave occasion to expect a more amendable attitude of the Soviet Union. The Soviet position had held two rather troublesome elements for Austria: the stationing of troops (even if reduced to only a small contingent) on Austrian soil as long as the German question was not solved, and the inclusion of a 'neutrality clause' into the State Treaty. Both points were unacceptable to the Austrians. First, the link to the solution of the German problem promised to set the date of the final troop withdrawal *ad calendas graecas*. Second, a State Treaty with a neutrality obligation would give the four Allies, in particular the Soviet Union, a *droit de regard* on the implementation of this duty.

In February 1955, the Soviet Union hinted that it might drop the connection of the Austrian problem with the German question. But it firmly insisted on a guarantee that Austria would not become part of the Western system of alliances.

The solution was an 'operational calendar': Step by step the Allies would pledge to leave Austria, the Austrians would promise to adopt a neutrality status, and both sides would then implement these proclamations. Neutrality was not included in the State Treaty, signed in May 1955 in Vienna by the foreign ministers of France, the Soviet Union, the United Kingdom, the United States, and Austria. To ensure Austrian compliance, its politicians promised a constitutional law establishing Austria's permanent neutrality. This law was passed on the first day after the last foreign soldier had left Austria (26 October 1955):

1. For the purpose of the lasting maintenance of her independence externally, and for the purpose of the inviolability of her territory, Austria declares of her own *free will* her perpetual neutrality. Austria will maintain and defend this with all means at her disposal.
2. For the securing of this purpose *in all future times* Austria will not join any military alliances and will not permit the establishment of any foreign military bases on her territory.[5]

By stressing the "free will," the Austrians wanted to maintain that their country was not 'neutralized', not pushed by the Allies (in particular by the Soviet Union) to adopt that status, but that it was their own choice. In fact, it was their decision, but the alternative would have been the further stationing of foreign troops in the country.[6] Looking with today's knowledge on the (economic and social) gap between West Germany and (former) East Germany, one has, besides independence, an additional reason to understand why the Austrians were only too happy to end the four-power occupation with the means of neutrality.

There were nuances in the attitudes concerning 'neutrality'. The Socialists were eager to have a clear definition of the obligations the Austrians would have to accept, since they regarded the notion of 'neutrality' as too vague and open to interpretations. They also wanted to heed the skeptical attitudes of the Western powers, in particular the United States. The Conservatives on the other hand, and here especially Federal Chancellor Julius Raab, were determined to get rid of the Soviet occupation and were more accommodating.

The common denominator was neutrality "of the type maintained by Switzerland". This was agreed to in the so-called Moscow (or Austro-Soviet) Memorandum, initialed by the delegation of the Austrian government in Moscow, 15 April 1955.[7] With this formula the apprehensions of the United States[8] and the concerns on part of the Austrians could be eliminated.

The Swiss understanding of neutrality was compiled in 1954 by Rudolf Bindschedler, a scholar with close ties to the Swiss foreign ministry. The legal department of the Swiss foreign ministry recapitulated this compilation in a briefer version a few years later. It has often been designated as the *conception officielle suisse de la neutralité*.[9] It enumerated three basic duties of a permanent neutral in peacetime:

1) an obligation to begin no war;
2) an obligation to defend its neutrality and/or independence;
3) the so-called secondary duties or *Vorwirkungen* (antecedent effects) of permanent neutrality. These can be summarized as the obligation of a permanently neutral country to do everything so as not to be drawn into a war and to abstain from all that could draw it into a war.[10]

This last set of peacetime neutrality obligations, the *Vorwirkungen*, have been the most debated aspects of permanent neutrality. The Swiss *conception officielle* noted three elements among these obligations: First, the obligation of the neutral country to arrange its foreign policy so that it will not be drawn into any war (the *conception officielle* describes this as "political neutrality"). In particular it must not conclude any treaties which oblige it to wage war (e.g. offensive or defensive alliances or agreements on collective security). But there is no obligation to maintain any so-called moral or ideological neutrality.[11]

Second, a neutral country may generally not conclude any military agreements with other countries ("military neutrality"). Third, "economic neutrality" exists in so far as the permanently neutral country may not conclude any customs agreements or economic unions with any other country because it would thereby, to a certain degree, relinquish its independence in a political respect as well. In such a case, "even the legal possibility of the union treaty's denunciation or a special clause relating to hostilities would not alter anything in the existent situation." For the rest, "economic neutrality" does not exist except in so far as the neutral country expressly or intentionally supports "the rearmament or politically motivated economic measures of other countries directed against their opponents."[12]

However, in 1955 the Austrian politicians had apparently no intention to understand neutrality in such a broad way. The limited extent of Austria's neutrality was stressed by Chancellor Raab when he introduced the bill in the Austrian Parliament. He called Austria's neutrality a "military neutrality" which would include "no obligations and commitments whatsoever in the economic or cultural field."[13] The narrow interpretation of neutrality as "military neutrality" is also reflected in the constitutional law quoted above ("Austria will not join any military alliances and will not permit the establishment of any foreign military bases"). In contrast to Switzerland, Austria joined the United Nations already in December 1955 and then, in April 1956, became a member of the Council of Europe, which comprised only 'Western' countries. At the same time politicians started to talk about Austria joining the European Coal and Steel Community, the initial element of European integration. Austria could have been well on the way to becoming one of the founding members of the European Union.

It thus appears that in the early phase of the neutrality status Austrian statesmen did not take 'neutrality' very seriously. In 1955 neutrality was simply the magic shibboleth: "you could get everything [from the Soviets] if you would only use the word 'neutrality'," argued the Austrian ambassador in Moscow at that time, Norbert Bischoff,[14] to convince his wavering government. Overcoming the reluctance of his Socialist coalition partners, Chancellor Raab used the word in Moscow, and, indeed, it provided the means for the conclusion of the State Treaty and the withdrawal of the Allied troops. After this 'liberation' one would decide on the next steps ... In this respect one has to keep in mind, that Switzerland as well as Sweden, in spite of their 'neutral' rhetoric, had close military contacts with NATO. In case of East-West hostilities they could almost count on help from the Western Alliance. In Austria's provinces occupied by the Western allies, provisions for military assistance in an East-West conflagration had been made as well.[15]

The Soviet Union had at least three objectives with a *neutral* Austria in mind: to keep it independent and make a renewed 'Anschluss' impossible, to keep Austria out of NATO, and to set an example for (West) Germany.[16] The third intention clearly backfired. The Hungarian uprising in October/November 1956 would probably not have been possible without the Austrian example; the revolutionaries did declare the neutrality of Hungary. This seems to have been the main reason for the Soviet military intervention.

However, the Hungarian uprising had repercussions on Austrian foreign policy. The Austrian politicians, strong in their verbal disapproval of the Soviet conduct, were in turn heavily criticized by Soviet media and statesmen for their pro-Hungarian attitudes. This induced the Austrians to be more cautious in their foreign policy behavior. They were now conscious of the importance of friendly relations with the Soviet Union, which had militarily intervened just sixty kilometers east of Vienna, without the West giving the (widely expected) military support to the insurgents.

In view of the Soviet opposition, the move toward joining the European Economic Community (EEC, founded in 1957) slowly disappeared from the political agenda. But there were also domestic reasons for such a development. Representatives of the SPÖ's left-wing, such as Transport Minister Karl Waldbrunner, became critical of closer relations with the Common Market. In June 1959 even the chairman of the SPÖ, Bruno Pittermann, denounced the EEC as a 'bourgeois bloc' and excluded EEC membership. This refusal coincided with a strict neutrality interpretation among ÖVP politicians, who asserted that neutrality would also imply "certain requirements" in the economic field.[17] Most of the specialists in international law started to maintain—as the Swiss *conception officielle* postulated—that a neutral country could not join the EEC, even if it would be admitted with a neutrality clause. The economic dependence on the other EEC members would be so strong that the promise of a neutral member to freeze relations or leave the organization during a war involving other EEC members would not be credible.[18]

International law scholars introduced another element into the legal interpretation of Austria's international status when they assumed a special relationship between Austria and the community of states. The neutrality declaration was in fact a *unilateral* Austrian act. This act—the Federal Constitutional Law of 26 October 1955—was issued to the states with which Austria had diplomatic relations at that time. The explicit or implicit recognition of this notification had created 'quasi-treaty' relations between Austria and these states. All states would have to heed Austria's status. A unilateral renunciation of the status (by other states as well as Austria) would not be possible. In practice, this requirement could bind the further adherence to neutrality to the opinion of the important states in the world, especially to that of the Soviet Union/Russia. This extension of Austria's legal obligations was strongly criticized, among others, by Günther Nenning, a prominent journalist from (at that time) the right wing of the Socialist Party. For him Austria had no obligation under international law to maintain its neutrality in perpetuity or to abandon it only with the consent of the Soviet Union. On the contrary, Austria's status could "be ended at any time by a constitutional law."[19] Nenning's criticism notwithstanding, the 'quasi-treaty' concept was finally embraced by the government. It was only discarded in 1995, when a Russian representative formally accepted the possibility of Austria's unilateral abandonment of neutrality.[20]

4. 'Active Neutrality'

After some debate the large majority of the ÖVP as well as most representatives of the SPÖ opted for membership in the European Free Trade Association (EFTA). This rather loose organization created a free trade area (excluding agricultural goods), its members preserving their own import tariffs and other trade restrictions toward non-member countries. Not only the Socialists saw advantages in an EFTA membership. According to Chancellor Raab, joining EFTA benefited the ÖVP's supporters among small businesses and farmers. In contrast, the EEC was assumed by the ÖVP-SPÖ government to pay little attention to Austria's special situation and not to grant any exceptions for the weaker Austrian competitors.[21]

When the United Kingdom, the most important member of EFTA, applied for EEC membership in mid-1961, Austria, together with Sweden and Switzerland, tried to reach an association agreement with the EEC and thus bridge the economic 'gap' that had developed in Western Europe. The moment President Charles de Gaulle rejected Britain's request for EEC membership in early 1963, the negotiations with the neutrals were stopped as well. Only Austria continued to try and reach an agreement on a tight association (resembling full membership) with the EEC. The background to these attempts was the strengthening of the 'reformers' in the ÖVP, who demanded close relations with Western Europe and consequently stressed the narrow definition of neutrality as being only a 'military neutrality'. The 'reformers' and many economists emphasized the importance of Austrian participation in the more dynamic market of the EEC, but a 'hidden agenda' existed as well.[22] Close association with the EEC would help liberalize Austria's society and economy. A permanent exclusion of Austria from the EEC would bring the country closer to the East and a socialist planned economy. Some important power positions of the SPÖ would be weakened by close association with the EEC: the control of the nationalized industries and the labor market. The *rapprochement* to the Common Market would "bring an impetus toward a market economy that would not have been possible in direct [domestic] political competition."[23]

Attempts to reach a special relationship with the EEC were even intensified under the new ÖVP government in 1966, but failed in mid-1967. After the invasion of Czechoslovakia by Warsaw Pact troops in August 1968, the notion of a specific, limited 'military neutrality' was finally rejected by Kurt Waldheim, the foreign minister of the ÖVP government. The obligations of a neutral country would go beyond the obligations of not joining military alliances and not permitting the establishment of foreign military bases. The neutral "has even during peacetime to conduct a foreign policy that will keep it from getting involved in future armed conflicts and in political struggles which could lead to such conflicts." At the same time, Waldheim stressed the importance of an "active participation in international cooperation" for a neutral country.[24]

These words were early signs of a profound change in Austrian external relations. Bruno Kreisky, chancellor of an SPÖ government from 1970 to 1983, went much further with a foreign policy focusing less on (Western) Europe and more on 'global' aspects.[25] Kreisky's 'active neutrality' can be characterized by the following points:

- Intensified *contacts with other countries*, travel diplomacy.
- Emphasizing the *global aspects* of foreign policy in contrast to a concentration on the neighboring countries and (Western) Europe; this included:
  - stressing the importance of development aid;

- strengthening the relations with the nonaligned countries, especially in the Third World;
- cooperation with the so-called "like-minded countries" to reduce the friction between the rich North and the poor South.
- Increased support for *disarmament*, offering neutral surveillance etc.
- Giving emphasis to the *United Nations* through, e.g.:
  - setting up contingents for peacekeeping operations of the U.N.;
  - providing a candidate for the position of the U.N. secretary general (Kurt Waldheim);
  - locating new U.N. organizations on Austrian territory.
- *Good offices and mediation* during international conflicts and crises, especially to promote détente or reduce the tensions between East and West.
- *Criticism of both superpowers*, in particular of the United States.
- Support for a *pan-European security policy*; active cooperation in the N+N Group (Group of the neutrals and nonaligned countries in Europe) as part of the Conference on Security and Cooperation in Europe (CSCE).
- Emphasis on *foreign policy* and downgrading military defense as an element of security policy.[26]

This emphasis on an 'active' policy from the late 1960s to the early 1980s was actually not an entirely new development. Sweden initiated a similar position already in the early 1960s. Immediately after World War II, Swiss Foreign Minister Max Petitpierre talked about neutrality *and* solidarity, to counter the accusations against Swiss behavior during the war. Petitpierre's term of office (1945–1961) was later labeled as "16 years of active neutrality."[27]

Kreisky's foreign policy advanced due to the solution of two problems which had hampered Austrian external relations in the 1960s: the end of the conflict between South Tyrol and Italy in 1969, and the free trade agreements with the European Community (EC), signed in 1972. Domestically, the great popularity of Kreisky, and the fact that he governed with absolute majorities from 1971 on, gave him quite some leeway for external matters. In addition, the détente, the reduced tensions between East and West in the 1970s, also had a positive effect on Austria's room of maneuver.

5. Functions of Neutrality[28]

What were now the functions of this 'active' neutrality for Austria?[29] First, one has to mention the achievement of *freedom and independence* through the withdrawal of foreign troops from Austrian territory. Neutrality was the 'price' for this freedom, but most Austrians were ready to pay it.

The withdrawal of the troops had some costs for the Western Allies, since Austria, together with Switzerland, became a neutral 'wedge' between the Central and Southern Command of NATO. As we have seen, the Soviet Union wanted Austria's neutrality to be a 'bait' for West Germany, but this backfired since the bait was actually taken up by Hungary. Nevertheless, the neutral status made it easier for Austria to have *good relations with countries of the Eastern bloc*. But there were exceptions, like the often strained relations with Czechoslovakia.

Neutrality reinforced the *prohibition of the 'Anschluss'* in the State Treaty, as mentioned above. At the same time, it made a clear distinction between Austria and (West) Germany. This difference was instrumental for the Austrians to develop their own *identity*. The 'differentiation' between neutral Austria and NATO member West Germany helped Austrian statesmen and politicians gain an amount of *prestige and influence* in international politics, which was not warranted by its rather small size.

The importance of 'active neutrality' for Austria's *security* was often in the center of political debate. Politicians, in particular from the Socialist camp, gave it greater weight than military defense. In a rather extensive interpretation of the constitutional law on neutrality, where neutrality, was designated as the 'purpose', the means to maintain Austria's external independence, neutrality was now regarded by some as a *fundamental principle* of the constitution itself.

A particular and rarely debated function of Austria's permanent neutrality can be seen in the protection against encroachment by the outside world. Permanent neutrality called for 'qualified independence'. Ideally, the permanently neutral state should be prepared to remain politically and economically self-sufficient during wars, to avoid any involvement in military conflicts. This quest for 'autarchy' called for various measures, already in peace-time. Therefore, Austria did not open its agricultural markets to foreign competitors. It had to ensure a full supply of foodstuff by its own farmers. Another more curious example is the prohibition of the import of antibiotics in the free trade agreements with the EC. In general, protecting the interests of farmers, small business people, the large nationalized industry, and the trade unions on the labor market against foreign competitors in negotiations with the EC or GATT was much easier when waving the neutrality flag than being forced to use economic arguments. One probably cannot explain and understand the development of the Austrian social partnership, the exceptionally strong 'corporatist' structure of its economy and its political system without giving due weight to Austria's permanent neutrality. Similar to other neutrals a large and growing 'sheltered sector' existed as part of the economy. In domestic politics, permanent neutrality and its firm anchoring in a constitutional law made it rather easy to reject any demands by political groups for opening up the markets to increase competition and to oppose any political and economic 'liberalization' through, for example, EC membership. This *protection of the corporatist system* was an important, but in the scholarly debate rarely mentioned, function of permanent neutrality.[30]

6. Modification of Neutrality in the 1980s and 1990s

In the late 1970s and the early 1980s, in particular after the Soviet invasion of Afghanistan, tensions rose again in the relations between East and West. In this new ('second') cold war the United States (under President Ronald Reagan) and its somehow reluctant Allies renewed and reinforced the controls for high technology exports (especially computers) to the East. The neutrals, in particular Austria and Sweden, came under strong pressure by U.S. officials to introduce and/or strengthen such controls.

As a first reaction, Bruno Kreisky and the Austrian government rejected the demands by the Western Allies.[31] Austria would not participate in a politically motivated embargo. But its industry required secure access to Western, especially U.S., high technology. This was particularly true for the nationalized industry which at that time wanted to modernize in an effort to improve its competitiveness. The United States threatened to reduce or even stop the exports of high technology to countries not complying with COCOM (Coordinating Committee for Multilateral Strategic Export Controls), the control regime established by the Western powers during the 'first' cold war. After some hesitation, Austria signed a U.S.-Austrian Customs Mutual Assistance Agreement in 1986. A year later it made the COCOM lists part of the Foreign Trade Act.[32] The renewed tensions between East and West had reduced the leeway of the neutrals, the 'active' foreign policy gave way to a more cautious behavior.

The fall of the Berlin Wall on 9 November 1989 and the subsequent end of the East-West divide in Europe had again different effects on the concept and practice of neutrality. The COCOM regulations ceased to be relevant; on 31 March 1994, COCOM was dissolved. In the meantime, the neutrals joined control regimes that prevented the proliferation of nuclear, chemical, and biological weapons, and of their delivery systems. In December 1995, 28 countries (including the 15 EU member states, Switzerland, Norway, the US, Canada, the Visegrad countries, and Russia) agreed to establish the "Wassenaar Arrangement on Export Controls for Conventional Arms and Dual-Use Goods and Technologies." In a somewhat historical irony, the countries agreed to locate the secretariat of the Wassenaar Arrangement in Vienna, Austria.

Another step in 'reinterpreting' permanent neutrality was brought about by the events after the Iraqi invasion of Kuwait on 2 August 1990. The U.N. Security Council's decision to take action against Iraq (first economic sanctions, then authorizing military measures) made it necessary to bring Austria's constitutional position into line with the country's membership in the U.N. The Penal Code's article punishing actions that could endanger Austria's neutrality had to be quickly modified so that it no longer applied in circumstances where the Security Council had authorized military action under Chapter VII of the U.N. Charter. The Austrian regulations for approving the import, export, and transit of war material were similarly modified.

Austrian policy now started from the premise that the actions in question were steps taken by the United Nations against an aggressor under the international system of collective security. They did not constitute a 'war' according to the meaning of the term in international law, and for that reason did not call for the application of neutrality law.[33]

Just when EC integration became more dynamic (Jacques Delors becoming President of the Commission in January 1985, the Commission White Paper on Completing the Internal Market, June 1985, and the signing of the Single European Act, February 1986), Austrian industry, in particular its nationalized section, got into trouble. For all its efforts to modernize, the financial difficulties of Austria's nationalized industry in November 1985 heralded a deep crisis of the Austrian corporatist model.

The general elections of 23 November 1986 brought a significant change in government, after the end of the SPÖ rule in 1983 and a short spell of a small coalition government of the SPÖ/FPÖ. A new version of the grand coalition, this time under the leadership of the Socialists, came to power. In its statement of policy of January 1987, the new government declared that intensifying Austria's relations with the EC was a "central objective" of its foreign policy.[34] In May 1987, the Federation of Austrian Industrialists, an association of the bigger Austrian companies and one of the most important economic organizations, formally demanded EC membership. It would be the only possible way to fully participate in the emerging internal market.[35] A study by two specialists in international law, commissioned by the Federation of Austrian Industrialists, claimed at the same time that membership in the EC would be compatible with Austria's neutrality.[36] In December 1987, in a surprising *volte-face* abandoning the long-standing tradition of its 'founding father' Chancellor Raab, the Federal Chamber of Commerce (which represents small and medium-sized enterprises) also opted for Austria to join the EC. Subsequently, in January 1988, the ÖVP, the party with close links to business groups, as well as junior partner of the grand coalition government, decided to request full membership in the EC.

More than a year later, in April 1989, the SPÖ finally accepted the idea of applying for EC membership. It specified several conditions for the forthcoming negotiations with the EC, such as keeping the social welfare standards in Austria and upholding the strict environmental protection laws. In particular it stressed the necessity to preserve Austria's permanent neutrality. For that reason, and also because of the continuing opposition from the Soviet Union (the fall of the Berlin Wall would occur only months later), Austria applied for EC membership on 17 July 1989 with an extensive neutrality 'clause' with clear references to the tradition of 'active neutrality':

> Austria submits this application on the understanding that its internationally recognized status of permanent neutrality, based on the Federal and Constitutional Law of 26 October 1955, will be maintained and that, as a member of the European Communities by virtue of the Treaty of Accession, it will be able to fulfill its legal obligations arising out of its status as a permanently neutral State and to continue its policy of neutrality as a specific contribution towards the maintenance of peace and security in Europe.[37]

But when Austria, together with Finland and Sweden, joined the European Union (EU, as the EC has been called since the Maastricht

Treaty) on 1 January 1995, no exception for any of the new members' neutrality was made. On the contrary, they had to sign a Joint Declaration (added to the Final Act of the Accession Treaty), in which they promised that they would be "ready and able to participate fully and actively" in the Common Foreign and Security Policy (CFSP) of the EU and that their "legal framework" would be "compatible" with the rules and traditions of the CFSP.[38]

In two steps Austria made good on these demands. First, the government defined neutrality in a narrow way, finally and officially abandoning the 'active neutrality' concept. In a declaration on neutrality, added to the minutes of its meeting of 9 November 1993, the cabinet declared that "... the Federal Government proceeds from the assumption that Austria is not obliged to participate militarily in wars, not obliged to accede to military alliances and to establish military bases of foreign states on its territory."[39] Thus, the circle was closed since this definition of permanent neutrality went back to the narrow wording of the constitutional law from October 1955.[40]

The second step Austria took to meet the EU demands was a new article introduced into the Federal Constitution (Article 23f). It simply stated that Austria would "participate" in the CFSP, but also added that this would include participation in "economic" embargoes. The Maastricht Treaty, which went into effect during the accession negotiations on 1 November 1993, stated in its Title V that the CFSP covered "all areas of foreign and security policy." This applied to "all questions related to the security of the Union, including the eventual framing of a common defense policy, which might in time lead to a common defense." The rules concerning the "common defense policy" and the "common defense" had not yet been implemented when the three new members joined the EU on 1 January 1995. But it was already clear at that time that the CFSP would probably not be confined to 'economic' security matters.

7. Austria as a Member of the EU
7.1. Adjusting to EU membership

After joining, Austria, like the other new EU members (Finland and Sweden), became an observer in the Western European Union (WEU), which was to develop into the 'defense arm' of the EU. At the Intergovernmental Conference (IGC) of 1996/97, Austria was actually among the countries opting for a stronger integration. Concerning CFSP matters, the Austrian government was generally for a supranational structure of the EU's second pillar: In the framework of a general, further development of the Union even a *"step-by-step transition to a communitarian approach in foreign policy questions"* would correspond to the logic of the integration process.[41] Since this would probably not be possible at the IGC, Austria would pragmatically support reforms that would strengthen the efficiency of the CFSP without changing its intergovernmental decision-making. In this vein, the government proposed a *"cautious transition to majority voting"* in the CFSP with various safeguards in areas of "vital national interests."[42]

The capacity of the EU in areas like conflict prevention and crisis management, peacekeeping operations, disaster relief and humanitarian actions should be enhanced by the IGC. Here, the Austrian government anticipated the Finnish-Swedish proposal, which led to the inclusion of the so-called Petersberg tasks into the Amsterdam Treaty.[43] This Treaty, the final outcome of the IGC, included "humanitarian and rescue tasks, peacekeeping tasks and tasks of combat forces in crisis management, including peacemaking" (Article 17 (ex Article J.7) of the Amsterdam Treaty).

According to the Austrian government's position in the IGC, these Petersberg operations should "not prejudice the specific character of the security and defense policy of certain member states—also Austria's policy." This wording was a compromise between the two government parties. The Social Democrats wanted to use the word "neutrality" in this context, but the ÖVP rejected this demand. The government would be against a fusion of EU and WEU but would support an intensified cooperation between both organizations.[44]

During the ratification process of the Amsterdam Treaty in Austria, a debate on neutrality took place inside the SPÖ. Science Minister Caspar Einem from the party's left wing warned that the treaty would not be compatible with Austria's neutrality. In particular he criticized that the Amsterdam Treaty allowed peacemaking with combat forces—i.e. 'making war', in his view—without an explicit authorization by the U.N. Security Council. He did not want any blood to be shed, expecially not Austrian blood.[45]

To ratify the Amsterdam Treaty, Article 23f of the Federal Constitution had to be amended after only two and a half years in force. It was extended to four paragraphs and extremely complicated rules were included for Austrian decision-making on CFSP matters. Both the chancellor and the foreign minister have to cast the same vote in the EU

Council concerning e.g. the Petersberg tasks, which thus demands a consensus among the two grand coalition parties. On 18 June 1998, the members of the SPÖ, the ÖVP, and the Liberal Forum voted for the ratification of the Amsterdam Treaty and the amended Article 23f (thus providing the necessary two-thirds majority), while the populist FPÖ and the Greens voted against it. Some Social Democratic members of parliament wanted to protest against the ratification because of the "dangerous erosion" of Austria's neutrality, but they were confused and missed the opportunity to show their opposition.[46]

Austria's relations with NATO have been another bone of contention in this country's political debate. The Atlantic Alliance offered participation in the Partnership for Peace (PfP) program to all European countries at the Summit Meeting in Brussels, January 1994. The governments of Finland and Sweden were quick to accept this offer and signed the "Framework Document" in May 1994. The decision on PfP took longer in Austria. Here, the Social Democrats opposed participation for several months, whereas the ÖVP strongly pushed for participation. Only in February 1995 did Austria sign the "Framework Document." The same scenario could be discerned with "enhanced PfP," a program launched by the Allied Foreign and Defense Ministers in spring 1997, when once again Finland and Sweden reacted much earlier than the Austrian authorities.

The debates on the ratification of the Amsterdam Treaty and the attitudes toward PfP are only a reflection of the general attitudes of Austria's then ruling parties concerning security and defense cooperation.[47] Already in June 1994 Defense Minister Werner Fasslabend (ÖVP) wanted Austria to join the WEU. Later the ÖVP started to push for NATO membership as well, since WEU membership alone would not be feasible. These advances met with strong opposition from the SPÖ. But there were some dissenting voices in the SPÖ and the ÖVP concerning NATO membership. Some regional governors (*Landeshauptleute*) of the ÖVP were reluctant to support the push toward NATO, and a few representatives from the SPÖ opted for NATO membership. In July 1997, the ÖVP officially demanded Austrian NATO and WEU membership.[48] To avoid any quarrels inside the government during Austria's EU Presidency (July till December 1998), it was decided in the "Coalition Agreement" after the December 1996 elections to submit to Parliament a report on Austria's security options. This "Options Report" would examine all possible alternatives, "including the question of Austria's full membership in WEU."[49]

At the end of March 1998, the two government parties could not find an agreement on this "Options Report," with NATO membership being the bone of contention. The ÖVP pushed hard for Austria to join the Atlantic Alliance, seeing a window of opportunity when other countries of Central Europe were just accepted as new members. Participation in the Euro-Atlantic Partnership Council would not be sufficient. The SPÖ rejected that argument, seeing no security threats for Austria which would require the abandonment of its established foreign policy status, neutrality. Eastern enlargement of NATO would even enhance Austria's security situation.[50] The alternative proposed by the Social Democrats was "the creation of a European defense under European command with purely defensive character and without the United States."[51] The SPÖ's option for a "European defense" could also be seen as a latent anti-Americanism among a number of Social Democrats. It could even seem to express the hope that this "European defense" will never (or only in the very long term) be realized, which would make any debate about the end of neutrality pointless.

7.2. The new dynamics of the EU's security and defense policy

However, it was exactly during Austria's EU presidency that the debate on European defense identity gained momentum. Just before the Informal Meeting of the Heads of State and Government of the EU member states in Pörtschach (Carinthia, 24-25 October 1998), Prime Minister Tony Blair made plain that he was ready to drop Britain's longstanding objections to an EU defense capability. If necessary, the EU would proceed without the United States, but it would always be under NATO's authority.[52] In spite of negative comments by his coalition partners, Austrian Defense Minister Werner Fasslabend (ÖVP) organized the first ever (informal) meeting of EU defense ministers in Vienna, 3 - 4 November 1998. Finally, in Saint-Malo, 4 December 1998, the heads of state and government of France and the United Kingdom agreed that the EU "needs to be in a position to play its full role on the international stage." To this end, the EU "must have the capacity for autonomous action, backed up by credible military forces, the means to decide to use them and a readiness to do so, in order to respond to international crises."[53]

The Cologne European Council, 3-4 June 1999, and the Helsinki European Council, 10-11 December 1999, implemented these ideas. The goals the EU member states set themselves were to establish, by the year

2003, the ability to deploy rapidly, and then to sustain forces capable of the full range of the Petersberg tasks as set out in the Amsterdam Treaty. This would even include the most demanding tasks and operations involving a troop level up to 50,000 – 60,000 persons. These forces should be militarily self-sustaining with the necessary command, control, and intelligence capabilities, logistics, other combat support services, and, as appropriate, air and naval elements.[54] It is clear that the EU decision-makers did embrace here the lessons of the Kosovo conflict. The 78-day air war (March to June 1999) that culminated with the occupation of Kosovo by NATO-led peacekeepers, clearly showed that the Europeans were unable to act alone and heavily dependent on U.S. forces.

The Presidency Conclusions of the Cologne Summit mentioned that in EU-led crisis management "NATO members, as well as *neutral and non-allied* members, of the EU can participate fully and on an equal footing."[55] According to newspaper reports, the word "neutral" was included at the insistence of Austrian Chancellor Viktor Klima in contacts with his party friend Chancellor Gerhard Schröder from Germany. The SPÖ was just waging a campaign for the European Parliament elections (13 June 1999). Public opinion polls showed that during the Kosovo crisis, neutrality became more popular than ever in Austria. The SPÖ (and the Greens as well) strongly pushed neutrality with the slogan "safeguard neutrality, ensure employment"[56], while the ÖVP and the FPÖ attenuated their wish to abolish neutrality. The SPÖ even changed the poster which, at the beginning of the campaign, showed Viktor Klima with Tony Blair and Gerhard Schröder. During the bombing of Kosovo by NATO it was changed to Klima with prime ministers Göran Persson of Sweden and Paavo Lipponen of Finland—two little known politicians in Austria. This should prove that Austria would work together with other neutrals and not with NATO countries. The SPÖ gained some 2.6 percentage points and surpassed the ÖVP in the elections for the European Parliament. Neutrality seems to have played only a minor role in the voting decisions. This could be a reason why, during the election campaign for the *Nationalrat* (elections on 3 October 1999), the SPÖ only sporadically used neutrality as a campaign slogan. The Presidency Conclusions of the EU Helsinki Summit did not explicitly mention the neutrals and non-allied countries.

In addition to the push by France and Germany, there were other dynamic developments which had a 'spillover' effect on EU security integration. The consolidation of the U.S. defense industry into four or five large companies forced the European competitors to abandon the 'national champion' approach and to merge across national boundaries.[57] To attain the gains of such a consolidation, the EU member states have started to coordinate their weapons procurement. But such a coordination and standardization requires joint development of military strategies—and this would call again for a stronger common defense policy.

7.3. Misinterpreting the EU's dynamics

These unfolding events also show that an analysis of the EU along the lines of 'realism' with the notions of a traditional alliance theory misses some important points in the dynamics of EU development: the strong interdependence of the various sectors of EU integration, the learning processes going on, and the 'spillover' effects that the 'neofunctionalists' already elucidated in the late 1950s and early 1960s.[58] For a long time realists rightly maintained that spillovers would not occur in 'high politics' areas like security policy,[59] but the end of the cold war, the events mentioned above, as well as the introduction of the Euro among eleven EU members warrant some modification of this assertion.[60]

A similar 'insensibility' toward Europe's dynamic development in security matters can be found among Austrian politicians. Party officials, especially from the SPÖ and the Greens, which rather late and only reluctantly had accepted EU membership for Austria, did not realize that the EU could not be regarded as an 'ordinary' international organization where each member state can control the agenda and the organization's evolution. Since the mid-1980s, with the White Paper on the completion of the internal market and the Single European Act, the EU has displayed again a dynamics, which reluctant member states have found hard to contain--the most obvious example being the United Kingdom under Margret Thatcher and John Major.

The Common European Security and Defense Policy (CESDP) of the EU has thus developed after the establishment of the Maastricht Treaty in 1993—at first slowly, but between 1998-1999 at an accelerated pace. In spite of this development, the main argument of neutral and non-allied EU member states for maintaining their status has been that crisis management, according to the Petersberg tasks of the EU Treaty, is fully compatible with neutrality, since the EU Treaty does not include a military assistance clause like the Washington Treaty's

Article 5 (or Article V of the WEU Treaty). Such an article would not be needed even for robust crisis management, including military peace-enforcement. In addition, collective defense, based on Article 5, has been regarded as quite irrelevant for the new strategy of NATO, which basically concerns only crisis management[61], and is therefore expendable for the EU's CESDP.

This assertion has been challenged. Article 5 tasks of NATO remain in order, not only for classic defense, but also for possible crises which could escalate in or around Europe. "NATO would then have to make clear that it could resist major armed action, including action against its own treaty area."[62] That is more or less what happened in and around Kosovo from March till June 1999. As already indicated during the Bosnia crisis, it was neither the EU, nor the OSCE, nor the United Nations, but NATO which put an end to the vicious policy of ethnic cleansing by Serbia's Slobodan Milosevic in Kosovo. The Kosovo crisis also showed how easily such a conflict could escalate when the massive flow of refugees threatened to destabilize Albania and Macedonia, directly menacing Greece and Italy, two NATO members.

The behavior of Austria during the Kosovo crisis was a clear indication of the difficulties and inconsistencies of neutral and non-allied behavior during a crisis in which massive military means had to be used to enforce peace or at least to stop indiscriminate killing and ethnic cleansing. NATO started bombing Serbian forces in Kosovo and Serbia proper without a mandate by the Security Council under Chapter VII of the U.N. Charter. Therefore, the Austrian government did not allow transit flights of NATO planes across Austrian territory, thus forcing NATO aircraft to make rather big detours around Austria (and Switzerland as well). Thus, Austria was not a neutral sitting passively 'on the fence', but in fact hampered NATO's military actions.[63] At the same time in the EU context, however, Austrian Chancellor Viktor Klima supported the statement of the EU's informal Summit in Brussels, April 1999: "The Heads of State and Government reiterate their determination not to tolerate the killings and deportations in Kosovo and believe that the use of severest measures, including *military action*, has been both *necessary* and *warranted*."[64]

The Kosovo crisis not only exposed contradictory behavior of Austrian officials, but also clearly showed the importance of Article 5. Hungary, Austria's neighbor, had been less than two weeks member of NATO when the bombing in Yugoslavia started. In contrast to Austria and in spite of its difficult situation concerning the Hungarian minority in Yugoslavia, it opened its airspace for NATO military aircraft.

Another problematic aspect of neutral behavior was displayed at the June 1999 Cologne Summit. Against their wish, or at least without great enthusiasm from the neutral and non-allied members, the EU countries designated Javier Solana as High Representative of the CFSP. Solana, as secretary general, had just led the successful NATO campaign against Slobodan Milosevic in Kosovo. His designation was another clear sign that the majority of the member states wanted the further evolution of the CESDP.

The interdiction of NATO transit across Austria during the Kosovo crisis was only the 'highlight' of similar incidents during 1998-1999. In September 1998, France asked Austria for permission to transport war material (tanks) on the Danube to Slovakia for military exercises there. Expecting an unproblematic go-ahead, the French had already chartered (and paid for) the necessary transport capacities on ships. When the Austrian authorities did not grant permission, France had to organize a transport (and pay a second time) via Poland. This 'unfriendly' behavior toward a fellow EU member state (and in addition the strongest supporter of a more independent European security policy) gave rise to hostile comments (see below).[65]

From 9 to 20 March 1999, NATO held in the Friuli-Venezia-Giulia region of north-eastern Italy a military exercise, "Adventure Exchange 99," and invited the Czech Republic, Hungary, and Poland (all about to become NATO members) to participate. The easiest and quickest route from these countries to Northern Italy would have been through Austria, but the Austrian government did not allow transit of their military. The Social Democratic interior minister, in charge of transit authorization, forbid the transit. He was criticized by the ÖVP ministers, who would have opened Austria's transit routes.[66]

During the Kosovo crisis in spring 1999, Macedonia participated in a NATO-PfP (communication) exercise in Germany and was allowed by the Austrian interior ministry to send radio transmitters across Austria for that purpose. But the return trip was not permitted, since the 'war material' would go from Austria to a crisis zone—Austrian law does not allow transport of military goods to such areas. Finally, the radio transmitters were regarded as belonging to the Macedonian postal services and could cross Austria again.[67]

This behavior of Austria, which in most cases had very little to do with the legal obligations of permanent neutrality, was strongly criticized by other countries, but usually not in public, since normal 'diplomatic protocol' does not allow rude language between friendly nations. In particular officials from the same party family avoid criticism of their colleagues in other countries. But one testimony from Martin Walker, European correspondent of the liberal *Guardian*, can give an idea of the negative views held by officials from other countries: "The French were very, very cross back in October [1998] when Austria decided that the French could not use Austrian territory to send some of their troops across to take part in peacekeeping exercises and Austria has been called in my presence 'a free rider' by other NATO members."[68]

Critical comments could be read in international newspapers, like the *Financial Times*. The idea of the EU's absorption of WEU could leave loyal NATO allies such as Turkey out in the cold, while "giving awkward neutrals like Austria—which has kept NATO warplanes out of its airspace—an effective veto on European security policy."[69] Other commentators wrote about *"la frilosité des pays neutres qui redoutent une militarisation de l'Europe"* and which could endanger the "great leap forward" in European defense.[70]

8. Conclusions

In spite of these experiences and commentaries, Chancellor Viktor Klima had a rather positive view of neutrality at the beginning of the new millennium: "The concept of neutrality still is a good security policy course for Austria. Neutrality never means an aloof position or being indifferent toward victims and culprits. Neutrality and solidarity were and are no opposites. We have proved this during almost 40 years of peacekeeping missions."[71]

How realistic are these claims? Neutrality has lost most of the functions that were mentioned above; only a few, somewhat peculiar *external functions* remain. Neutral Switzerland and Austria, together with Slovakia and the Ukraine, could still form (and almost did so during the Kosovo crisis) some kind of *neutral 'wedge'* inside NATO territory, especially in view of Hungarian NATO membership. The *'defense' of the corporatist system* against external as well as domestic critics could be another remaining function. But EU membership brought an opening up of Austria's economy and reduced its 'sheltered' sectors, making the above function rather irrelevant. A third function could be found in the *justification of the very low defense expenditure* of the Austrians. With only about 0.8 percent of GDP, Austria spends less than half of the average of the NATO countries for defense, less also than the other neutrals and its much poorer neighbors.

Austria does not compensate this 'free-riding', this low share of defense expenditure, with other outlays. Admittedly, Austria contributes one of the largest numbers of troops to U.N. peacekeeping operations. But it is also (partly) compensated by the U.N. for these costs. In addition, Austria has participated in the less risky missions, like on the Golan heights and in Cyprus. When Austria sent troops to more dangerous and costly assignments (i.e. without compensation), like Bosnia and Kosovo, they came later and in lower numbers than those of comparable (NATO) countries. Austria's development aid is far below the average of industrialized nations. Its support for Eastern Europe, at the beginning of the 1990s higher than that of the other West European countries, has declined.[72] The often mentioned ten billion Schillings that the country spent during the last forty years on U.N. peacekeeping pales in view of the fact that a doubling of the Austrian defense budget (to come closer to the average defense spending of its EU partners) would cost Austria more than 20 billion Schillings in one year! The pressure on Austria to increase it defense budget will be strong in case the EU starts to set criteria for improved and strengthened European defense capabilities.

It is in *domestic politics* where neutrality still has had an important function. Neutrality is rather popular, even more so after the Kosovo crisis. In early December 1999, people were asked in a public opinion poll if they would want to replace neutrality with an "active peace policy" (as ÖVP leader Wolfgang Schüssel had proposed). Only 30 percent of the population at large thought that it would be a "good idea," 61 percent regarded such a change as "not such a good idea." Opinion leaders, when asked the same question, had a completely different view: 59 percent thought it would be a "good idea," and only 38 percent "not such a good idea."[73]

Although the FPÖ is regarded as a typical example of a (right-wing) 'populist' party, in security matters it has 'ignored' popular will. Already in the early 1990s, its leader, Jörg Haider, pushed for an abandonment of neutrality and for NATO membership (see above). At the same time he rejected accession to the EU. In its Party Program from October 1997, the FPÖ has accepted the EU, but only as a loose confederation. The Program demands full membership in NATO and the WEU.[74] One explanation for the position of the FPÖ could be the critique of neutrality by its forerunner, the VdU, in 1955. The VdU regarded neutrality as imposed by the Soviets.

In contrast to the FPÖ, the SPÖ has widely used the popularity of neutrality for electoral purposes, as the elections for the European Parliament showed in June 1999. In addition, as long as neutrality is part of Austria's constitution and the SPÖ holds at least one third of the members of parliament, neutrality cannot be changed without the consent of the SPÖ. Therefore, the SPÖ can influence Austrian foreign policy even without an SPÖ foreign minister and, indeed, even from outside the government. Neutrality in its strict meaning sets limits to Austria's foreign and security policy. Therefore, it must be regarded as an instrument of *domestic power politics*.[75]

But can neutrality still deliver this function? As was indicated above, Austrian neutrality has been based on international law, thus giving the specialists in international law an important say in its interpretation. In view of the many changes to neutrality in the 1990s, a growing part of Austria's specialists has lost its interest in interpreting neutrality in an extensive manner, some even started to strongly oppose neutrality.[76] The mainstream (*herrschende Meinung*) of Austrian lawyers asserts that the various (direct and indirect) amendments to Austria's neutrality, in particular through the EU's Maastricht and Amsterdam Treaties, have emptied its content. Neutrality is therefore "not any more a legally correct label for Austria's status in the international community of states." It would be more correct to speak about mere "non-alliance" (*Bündnislosigkeit*).[77] Journalists and political scientists have written about the "death" of neutrality.[78] Yet most Austrians still have not realized "how dead neutrality already is."[79] Neutrality has changed its contents in the past, but now "neutrality has itself changed to death."[80]

During the negotiations for a new government after the general elections of October 1999, the SPÖ, apparently disregarding the view of Viktor Klima of a few weeks before, acknowledged the 'end' of neutrality—at least in the context of the EU. It accepted the inclusion of a military assistance clause into the EU Treaty (integrating Article V WEU Treaty into the EU Treaty) and a corresponding amendment of Austria's neutrality law, but insisted on a referendum.[81] Still, the question of NATO membership remained, since the military security of Europe will for a long time rest with NATO. The EU's military elements will cooperate closely with and inside NATO. Europe will not be a completely independent military power in the short and medium term.

An EU country that wants to fully participate in European security and defense policies will have to join NATO; neutral and non-allied EU members will thus remain somewhat 'awkward partners'.

According to an Austrian proverb, "The presumed dead live longer" (*Totgesagte leben länger*). Future will tell if the negative effects of neutrality for Austria on the international stage will outweigh the positive connotations neutrality still has among the general public. In 1955, politicians had to convince the public about the importance of neutrality. Since then, every child in school has learned about the significance of neutrality for Austria's well-being. The events of the 1990s made many officials aware of the problematic effects neutrality started to have on Austria's international capacity to act. Yet the general public still has to be convinced about the 'end of neutrality'.

Notes

1. The article was written in February 1999 and updated in January 2000. It is based on two publications of the author: Paul Luif, *Der Wandel der österreichischen Neutralität. Ist Österreich ein sicherheitspolitischer "Trittbrettfahrer"?*, 2nd, amended version (Laxenburg: Austrian Institute for International Affairs, April 1998, Working Paper of the Austrian Institute for International Affairs, AP 18) and Paul Luif, *On the Road to Brussels: The Political Dimension of Austria's, Finland's and Sweden's Accession to the European Union* (Vienna: Braumüller, 1995, Laxenburg Papers, No. 11).

2. "Kontroverse um Haider-Vorstoß gegen Staatsvertrag," *Die Presse*, 14 September 1990.

3. Classical international law allowed neutrality only as an alternative to participation in wars, while an intermediate form between belligerency and neutrality was not recognized. For the developments after 1945 concerning "benevolent neutrality" and "non-belligerency" see Dietrich Schindler, "Transformations in the Law of Neutrality Since 1945," in *Humanitarian Law of Armed Conflict: Challenges Ahead. Essays in Honour of Frits Kalshoven,* ed. Astrid J.M. Delissen and Gerard J. Tanja. (Dordrecht–Boston–London: Martinus Nijhoff, 1991) 367–386, here 373.

4. The most extensive analysis of Austria's striving for full independence from 1945 to 1955 is to be found in Gerald Stourzh, *Um Einheit und Freiheit. Staatsvertrag, Neutralität und das Ende der Ost-West-Besetzung Österreichs 1945-1955*, 4th edition (Vienna–Cologne–Graz: Böhlau, 1998). See also the "Historiography Roundtable" in this volume.

5. This quasi-official English translation of the Article 1 is taken from Gerald Stourzh, *Geschichte des Staatsvertrages 1945-1955. Österreichs Weg zur Neutralität. Studienausgabe*, 3rd edition (Graz–Vienna–Cologne: Styria, 1985), 239, emphases Paul Luif. The text was not reproduced in the 4th edition, see note 4.

6. The only party in parliament that voted against the neutrality law was the VdU (League of Independents, the precursor of the FPÖ) because it opposed the "own free will" clause; see Stourzh, *Um Einheit und Freiheit*, 556–558.

7. For the text of the Moscow Memorandum see Alfred Verdross, *The Permanent Neutrality of Austria* (Vienna: Verlag für Geschichte und Politik, 1978), 26. For a detailed analysis of the 'Swiss model' see Christian Jenny, *Konsensformel oder Vorbild? Die Entstehung der österreichischen Neutralität und ihr Schweizer Muster* (Bern: Paul Haupt, 1995).

8. At the (unsuccessful) Berlin Conference, February 1954, Secretary of State John Foster Dulles maintained *"if Austria wants to be a Switzerland, U.S. will not stand in the way, but this should not be imposed"* and "… it is one thing for a nation to choose to be neutral and it is another thing to have neutrality forcibly imposed on it …" From Stourzh, *Um Einheit und Freiheit,* 310-311, emphasis in the original.

9. See Verdross, *The Permanent Neutrality of Austria,* 35–38.

10. Ibid., 36.

11. According to the *conception officielle,* the "onus of neutrality duties under international law does not rest on the individual." Therefore, permanent neutrality does not require a restriction on the freedom of the press. Ibid., 37.

12. Ibid., 38.

13. Policy declaration of Chancellor Raab, 26 October 1955, quoted from Hans Mayrzedt and Waldemar Hummer, *20 Jahre österreichische Neutralitäts- und Europapolitik (1955–1975). Dokumentation,* Part I (Vienna: Braumüller, 1976), 90, translation Paul Luif.

14. Quoted from Stourzh, *Um Einheit und Freiheit,* 423, translation Paul Luif.

15. Ibid., 393.

16. Particularly on the last point see Michael Gehler, "The Austrian Solution in 1955 as a 'Model' for Germany?," *Contemporary Austrian Studies,* vol. 3, *Austria in the Nineteen Fifties* (New Brunswick: Transaction Publishers, 1995), 39–78.

17. Thus the state secretary in the interior ministry, Franz Grubhofer, "Neutralität und Staatsschutzgesetz," in *Die Furche* 51/52, 21 December 1957, pp. 3-4.

18. The *locus classicus* of this argument is Karl Zemanek, "Wirtschaftliche Neutralität," in *Juristische Blätter 81,* no. 10/11 (1959): 249–251. One can surmise that most of the specialists in international law were ideologically closer to the ÖVP than to the SPÖ.

19. This critique of an Austrian "self-restraint" was expressed in a series of articles in the socialist weekly *Heute* (between 31 October and 21 November 1959), translation Paul Luif.

20. See Andreas Unterberger, "Moskau gibt Österreich grünes Licht: 'Neutralität entscheidet Wien allein'," in *Die Presse,* 17 October 1995, p. 4.

21. This was the argument of Raab in the government's policy declaration on 23 March 1960; see Mayrzedt and Hummer, *20 Jahre,* 337–349.

22. For a discussion of the economic problems regarding an agreement with the EEC in the 1960s see Paul Luif, *Neutrale in die EG? Die westeuropäische Integration und die neutralen Staaten* (Vienna: Braumüller, 1988), 104–111.

23. The quotation is from the conservative journalist Alexander Vodopivec, *Die Balkanisierung Österreichs. Die große Koalition und ihr Ende,* 2nd edition (Vienna–Munich: Molden, 1966), 233, translation Paul Luif.

24. Austrian Foreign Minister Kurt Waldheim on 7 November 1968, quoted from Mayrzedt and Hummer, *20 Jahre,* 145-146, translation Paul Luif.

25. On Kreisky's foreign policy see Erich Bielka, Peter Jankowitsch, and Hans Thalberg, eds., *Die Ära Kreisky. Schwerpunkte der österreichischen Außenpolitik* (Vienna–Munich–Zurich: Europaverlag, 1983); Otmar Höll, "The Foreign Policy of the Kreisky Era," *Contemporary Austrian Studies,* vol. 2, *The Kreisky Era in Austria* (New Brunswick–London: Transaction Publishers, 1994), 32–77.

26. For similar policies developed in the other neutral countries, in particular Sweden, see Paul Luif, "Neutralität und Frieden. Grundlegende Bemerkungen zu Geschichte und Gegenwart," in *Dialog-Beiträge zur Friedensforschung 6, Österreichische Neutralität und Friedenspolitik I* (1986): 17–76, here 56-57.

27. Max Petitpierre, *Seize ans de neutralité active. Aspects de la politique étrangère de la Suisse (1945–1961)* (Neuchâtel: Éditions de la Baconnière, 1980).

28. See Luif, *Der Wandel,* 17–24.

29. Compare also the intentions of the Soviet Union as discussed above.

30. For more details see Luif, *On the Road to Brussels,* 139-142.

31. Parts of this section are taken from Luif, *On the Road to Brussels,* 143-144. For an early account see Paul Luif, "Strategic Embargoes and European Neutrals: The Cases of Austria and Sweden," in *Challenges and Responses in European Security. TAPRI Yearbook 1986,* ed. Vilho Harle (Aldershot: Avebury, 1987), 174–188.

32. Hendrik Roodbeen, *Trading the Jewel of Great Value. The Participation of The Netherlands, Belgium, Switzerland and Austria in the Western Strategic Embargo* (Leiden: Proefschrift, 1992), 313.

33. *Austrian Foreign Policy Yearbook 1990,* 64-65.

34. Erklärung der Bundesregierung vor dem Nationalrat von Bundeskanzler Dr. Franz Vranitzky, 28 January 1987, Vienna: Bundespressedienst, 1987, 32-33

35. *Europa—unsere Zukunft. Eine Stellungnahme der Vereinigung Österreichischer Industrieller zur Europäischen Integration* (Vienna: Vereinigung Österreichischer Industrieller, 1987)

36. Waldemar Hummer and Michael Schweitzer, *Österreich und die EWG. Neutralitätsrechtliche Beurteilung der Möglichkeit der Dynamisierung des Verhältnisses zur EWG* (Vienna: Signum Verlag, 1987). At that time, most other international lawyers opposed this thesis. See e.g. Heribert Franz Köck, *Ist ein EWG-Beitritt Österreichs zulässig? Die völkerrechtliche und verfassungsrechtliche Zulässigkeit eines Beitritts Österreichs zur Europäischen Wirtschaftsgemeinschaft* (Vienna: Orac, 1987)

37. Translation taken from: The challenge of enlargement. Commission opinion on Austria's application for membership. Document drawn up on the basis of SEC(91) 1590 final. *Bulletin of the European Communities,* Supplement 4 (1992), 6; for details see Luif, *On the Road to Brussels,* 196–199.

38. See documents concerning the accession of the Republic of Austria, the Kingdom of Sweden, the Republic of Finland, and the Kingdom of Norway to the European Union, *Official Journal of the European Communities,* C 241 (29 August 1994): 381.

39. "Das interne Protokoll zur Neutralität, das gestern, Dienstag, vom Ministerrat in Wien beschlossen wurde (es wird in Brüssel nicht vorgelegt)," *Die Presse,* 10 November 1993, p. 4, translation Paul Luif.

40. The text of this law is quoted above; see endnote 5.

41. "Österreichische Leitlinien zu den voraussichtlichen Themen der Regierungs-konferenz 1996, Wien, im Mai 1995," *Österreichische außenpolitische Dokumentation. Texte und Dokumente*, no. 4 (August 1995): 7–50, here 31, emphasis in the original, translation Paul Luif.

42. Ibid., 34-35, emphasis in the original, translation Paul Luif.

43. See text of the joint Finnish-Swedish memorandum (25 April 1996) regarding the tasks of the European Union in military crisis management and the arrangement of the EU-WEU relationship in that area, mimeo.

44. "Österreichische Leitlinien," 39.

45. "Einems Warnung. 'Blut von Österreichern'," *Falter* no. 25, 19–25 June 1998, p. 13.

46. "Ein Brief und eine Abstimmungspanne ohne Folgen," *Die Presse*, 19 June 1998.

47. For a detailed analysis see Luif, *Der Wandel.*

48. "ÖVP-Parteivorstand legt sich fest: Für Vollbeitritt Österreichs zu Nato und WEU," *Die Presse*, 15 July 1997.

49. Koalitionsübereinkommen zwischen der Sozialdemokratischen Partei Österreichs und der Österreichischen Volkspartei, Vienna, 11 March 1996, mimeo, 18, translation Paul Luif.

50. This argument, like the attitude of Minister Einem on shedding Austrian blood (see note 44), comes very close to accepting "free riding" as a valid foreign policy doctrine, bolstered by the fact that Austria spends much less than most European countries on military defense; see below.

51. So the head of the SPÖ parliamentary group, Peter Kostelka; see "'Schüssel, kalter Krieger'. SPÖ-Klubobmann Peter Kostelka über die Neutralitätsdebatte und das 'immerwährende Nein' der Sozialdemokraten zur NATO. Interview mit Martin Staudinger und Klaus Zellhofer," *Falter*, no. 29, 17–23 July 1998, p. 10, translation Paul Luif.

52. Philip Webster, "Britain to back defence role for Europe," *The Times*, 21 October 1998.

53. Franco-British summit—Joint declaration on European defense, 4 December 1998, Saint-Malo (French Embassy in the United Kingdom).

54. Helsinki European Council, 10-11 December 1999, Presidency Conclusions, Points 25–29; see also Annex 1 to Annex IV: Presidency Progress Report to the Helsinki European Council on Strengthening the Common European Policy on Security and Defence.

55. Cologne European Council, Presidency Conclusions, 3-4 June 1999, Annex III: European Council Declaration on Strengthening the Common European Policy on Security and Defence, Point 3, emphasis Paul Luif.

56. See Andreas Weber, "Einleitung," in *Streitfall Neutralität. Geschichten—Legenden —Fakten,* ed. Andreas Weber (Vienna: Czernin Verlag, 1999), 11–21, here 16.

57. Weapons are the only goods that are not freely traded across borders in the EU, see Article 296 EC Treaty: "any Member State may take such measures as it considers necessary for the protection of the essential interests of its security which are connected with the production of or trade in arms, munitions and war material."

58. The *locus classicus* of neofunctionalism is Ernst B. Haas, *The Uniting of Europe. Political, Social and Economic Forces 1950-1957* (London–Stanford, CA: Stevens & Sons–Stanford University Press, 1958).

59. The most clear and concise explication of this assertion is found in Stanley Hoffmann, "The European Process at Atlantic Crosspurposes," *Journal of Common Market Studies*, vol. 3, no. 2 (December 1964): 85–101.

60. For an example of this realist approach in the context of the Austrian debate see Heinz Gärtner "Konzepte zur europäischen Sicherheit—ein Theorievergleich," *Österreichisches Jahrbuch für internationale Sicherheitspolitik,* ed. Erich Reiter (Graz–Vienna–Cologne: Styria, 1997), 107–134. Gärtner mentions neofunctionalist theories but does not use them in explaining the dynamics of EU security integration, still viewing it as "alliance politics."

61. See e.g. Gärtner, "Konzepte," 130.

62. Paul J. Teunissen, "Strengthening the Defence Dimension of the EU: An Evaluation of Concepts, Recent Initiatives and Developments," *European Foreign Affairs Review*, vol. 4, no. 3 (Autumn 1999): 327–352, here 350.

63. NATO was lucky insofar as Vladimir Meciar, Slovakian prime minister with close relations to Russia, had been voted out of office in the September 1998 and also did not succeed in the presidential elections of May 1999. NATO could use Slovakia's air space, otherwise the detours would have been even bigger.

64. Chairman's Summary of the Deliberations on Kosovo at the Informal Meeting of the Heads of State and Government of the European Union in Brussels on 14 April 1999. Press release 14 April 1999 (German Presidency), Point 2, emphasis Paul Luif.

65. "Sicherheitspolitischer Rückwärtsgang Wiens. Kanzler Klima verbietet Transit französischer Panzer," *Neue Zürcher Zeitung*, 30 September 1998, No. 226, p. 3.

66. See Andreas Weber, "Einleitung," 11; "Nato-Transitland Österreich," *Der Standard*, 16 February 1999, p. 4.

67. Weber, "Einleitung," 12.

68. Martin Walker, European Correspondent of The Guardian, on Blue Danube Radio, Vienna, 12 December 1998.

69. David Buchan, "WEU: Solana prepares for tough balancing act on defence," *Financial Times*, 2 June 1999.

70. Laurent Zecchini, "Le grand bond en avant de la défense européenne," *Le Monde*, 10 December 1999.

71. "Ist unsere Erde noch zu retten? ... und noch vier wichtige internationale Trends 2000," *Welt am Sonntag*, 2 January 2000, no. 1, p. 16, translation Paul Luif.

72. For details see Luif, *Der Wandel,* 59–76.

73. "Die Neutralität steht weiter hoch im Kurs," *Format*, 6 December 1999, no. 50, p. 5; poll by OGM, n=500 for the population at large, n=200 for opinion leaders.

74. Christoph Kontanko, ed., *Die Qual der Wahl. Die Programme der Parteien im Vergleich* (Vienna: Czernin Verlag, 1999), 118.

75. See Patrik Volf, "Immer wieder Königgrätz," *Falter*, no. 51–52, 24 December 1999–13 January 2000, pp. 8-9.

76. See e.g. Heribert Franz Köck, "Österreichs 'immerwährende' Neutralität: Mythos geht zu Ende," *Journal für Rechtspolitik*, vol. 1, no. 4 (1993): 210–239, and compare it to his booklet from 1987, note 36.

77. Theo Öhlinger, "BVG Neutralität," in *Bundesverfassungsrecht. Loseblattausgabe*, ed. Karl Korinek and Michael Holoubek (Wien: Springer, 1999).

78. Eric Frey, "Die Neutralität ist tot—aber keiner will ihr den Totenschein ausstellen. Die 'Immerwährende' auf Abruf," *Der Standard*, 29 January 1993, p. 19.

79. Anton Pelinka, *Austria. Out of the Shadow of the Past* (Boulder, CO–Oxford: Westview Press, 1998), 169.

80. Margaretha Kopeinig, "'Die Neutralität ist tot'. Der Politologe Paul Luif wirft der Regierung eine 'schizophrene Sicherheitspolitik' und Unglaubwürdigkeit vor," *Kurier*, 27 April 1999, p. 3.

81. "Das Regierungsprogramm im Wortlaut," *Die Presse*, 20 January 2000.

NONTOPICAL ESSAYS

Cold War Crises on Austria's Borders

The Hungarian Crisis and Austria 1953-58:
A Foiled Model Case?

Michael Gehler

I. Introduction: The Bigger Picture

Since the fall of the Iron Curtain in 1989, the political crisis in Hungary in the 1950s, culminating in the outbreak of revolution in the autumn of 1956, has increasingly become a focus of research in the fields of contemporary Central European, Eastern European and international history.[1]

After the spontaneous uprising in the GDR on 17 June 1953,[2] the Hungarian rebellion of October and November 1956[3] was the second desperate attempt within the satellite system to fight against the military and political might of the Soviet Union, an attempt which from the very start had little chance of success. Just like the protesters on the streets of East Berlin and other cities in the GDR more than three years before, the rebels in Budapest and throughout the country were brutally steamrolled and silenced. They were stimulated by a dubious phraseology of liberation from the West, primarily by the 'roll-back' rhetoric from the Eisenhower-Dulles administration, but at the decisive political moment they were left alone. How and why was the United States supposed to intervene? Such an intervention would in all probability have led to war.

One of the roots of the Hungarian revolution dated back to 1953 when, after the death of Stalin (5 March 1953), the first signs of erosion became evident in the system of satellite states. In a speech before the Central Committee on 3 July 1953, Imre Nagy, at the time president of the Parliament, criticized the mistakes of the past and admitted that crimes had been committed. He went too far trying to settle scores, and in 1955 he was relieved of his duties as prime minister. That same year did also not bring about the change on the international level that the reform Communists and critics of the regime in Hungary had hoped for. Even though the Western neighbor, Austria, was freed from Soviet troops through the State Treaty (15 May 1955) and declared itself neutral (26 October)—a model effect which should not be underestimated—the summit meeting (18 to 23 July) and the foreign ministers' conference (27 October to 16 November) in Geneva did not bring about a decisive breakthrough in the East-West confrontation.[4] It was rather the year 1956 that was to be decisive.

Beginning with the memorable 20th party congress of the Communist Party of the Soviet Union, when Nikita S. Khrushchev, in his secret speech of 25 February, closed the book on Stalin's regime of terror, things began to bubble in Hungary more actively than before. A corps of the Soviet army was stationed there for special use, which included four divisions, that is 40,000 members of the Red Army. Yuri Andropov, ambassador of the U.S.S.R., acting as more than just the head of a legation, had already advised the head of the KGB, Lieutenant General Ivan Serov, about the situation in the country, since there was no Soviet garrison in the capital. In the spring of 1956, large-scale Soviet military maneuvers took place near Lvov. On 30 June, unrest had already begun in the Polish trade city of Poznan. Workers and students rebelled against the government. The People's Army and State Security Service succeeded in restoring order only with brutal violence. There was a loss of over fourty lives. The situation only calmed down in mid-October with the confirmation of Wladislaw Gomulka as head of the Communist Party and the withdrawal of the Soviet divisions to their garrisons.

In addition to the crisis situation in Warsaw, the appropriation of the Suez Canal by President Nasser, an ally of the U.S.S.R., threatened to lead to war in the Middle East. On 24 October 1956 a secret summit took place in Moscow of all East bloc country party chiefs. However, the head of the Hungarian Communist Party, Ernö Gerö, did not want to leave Hungary because of the tense situation in Budapest. The evening before, on 23 October, a student demonstration, which had begun peacefully, had developed into an armed uprising against the Communist regime. Gerö called on the Soviet military attaché for Moscow to restore peace and order. Defense Minister Shukov spoke with Party Head Khrushchev, who at first hesitated to give the order to intervene. When Andropov also raised the alarm, Khrushchev was ready to fulfill Gerö's request. As desired, the Hungarian government issued a written request for Soviet intervention, whereby the Soviet army marched into Budapest in the morning hours of 24 October.

The idea that the situation in Hungary could be solved by a full-class demonstration of military might was a completely erroneous assessment. The demonstrators were not discouraged by the intervention of Soviet troops, and the turmoil escalated into a people's uprising and a battle for freedom. On 28 October the Soviet leaders Mikoyan and Suslov gave Imre Nagy a 'free hand' as new premier. In the firm belief that Moscow would not renounce him, he reached an understanding with the rebels, and on 1 November he proclaimed an independent Hungary that was neutral according to the Austrian model, only socialist. Nagy obviously thought of an adaptation of ways and means according to the 1955 'Austrian solution'. Austria's legation in Budapest reported in a telegram to the *Ballhausplatz* (office of the chancellor): "Nagy sucht Bereinigung Verhältnisses auf österreichische Art – Verhandlungen schon weit gediehen" (Nagy seeks to resolve situation the Austrian way—negotiations well advanced).[5] But in reality the U.S.S.R. played a machiavellian double game—it used Nagy's popularity with the masses to win time in order to test the waters of foreign reaction regarding an intervention and to take further military precautions which they considered necessary.[6]

While the revolutionary and freedom-oriented Hungarians believed that they had successfully asserted themselves, 'Comrade Koniev' was ordered to Budapest on 30 October. Marshall Ivan Koniev was commander-in-chief of the Warsaw Pact. The war in the Middle East, which had broken out the day before, and the political disinterest of the United States provided the impetus to the Soviet leaders for a second intervention on 4 November. Imre Nagy and his reform Communist government were deliberately deceived by the U.S.S.R. Khrushchev and Tito had already agreed at the beginning of November to fight the Hungarian 'counterrevolution' and to dispose of Nagy. Belgrade suggested János Kádár as the new head of the government and declared itself ready to lure Nagy into the Yugoslavian embassy and to isolate him there until the Red Army had Budapest under its control. By the middle of November, the military uprising in Hungary was quashed.

On 16 June 1958 Nagy and his cohorts were executed in Budapest. Between 1956 and 1961 over 400 people were executed, while approximately 20,000 men and women received heavy prison sentences. The Hungarian dream for freedom through neutrality lasted only two weeks in autumn 1956. Sixteen Soviet divisions now controlled the country.

The application of the Austrian model lay in the interest of neither the West nor the East, nor was Austria's neutrality mature enough to be recommended.

The Hungarian revolution of 1956 can also be seen in the context of the country's changing relationship with Austria beginning in 1953. The end of the occupation of Austria was closely associated with the withdrawal of Soviet troops from Hungary. Austria, therefore, functioned after 1955 as a 'model case' (although the two cases were incomparable). Austria's State Treaty and neutrality were decisive in triggering revolution in its Eastern neighbor.

But John Foster Dulles' statements were also closely listened to in Budapest. When he came back from Vienna after signing the State Treaty in May 1955, he gave an address on national television with 'Ike' Dwight D. Eisenhower sitting next to him. In this speech entitled "An Historic Week" Dulles also mentioned that he hoped Austrian neutrality would have an effect on its Eastern neighbors. According to Günter Bischof, Dulles definitely had a strong sense of the "Trojan Horse" opportunities of the Austrian neutrality.[7]

Since Austria was one of the neighboring countries most affected by the immediate consequences of the Hungarian revolution, it played an essential role in the further development of events. Battles sometimes took place along the border. For Hungarian refugees, Austria was the gate to the Western world. The Hungarian government had declared its withdrawal from the Warsaw Pact and its neutrality. The world's gaze focused even more on Austria and its behavior. The country which had just been granted freedom by the occupying powers stood before its first trial, which, above all else, reviewed its declaration of neutrality of October 1955.

In the following paper, based on systematic primary source research in the Austrian state archives:

a)   aspects of the bilateral relationship from 1953 to 1958 will be illustrated;

b)   political perspectives of the Austrian diplomatic representatives in Hungary, Poland, and Yugoslavia will be presented;

c)   revolutionary events will be analyzed, examining both the possibility of Hungary becoming neutral, as well as Austria's self-image regarding its own policy of neutrality; and

d)   the question of the applicability of the 'model case' 1955-58 shall be discussed.[8]

II. The Beginning of a Normalization Process 1953-54, the Bloody Autumn of 1956, and the Consequences 1957-58

1. The initial reduction of tensions in relations between Austria and Hungary from 1953-54

The signing of the State Treaty, the withdrawal of Allied troops, and the declaration of permanent neutrality[9] brought about an 'Austria euphoria' in Hungary, which had not been seen since 1945. Austria's policy was admired by the Hungarian neighbor. There was also increasing rapprochement in political circles, the specific background of which the Austrian envoy Karl Braunias located in the attitude of the Kremlin. The original inter-Allied agreements, which had been reached in the context of the peace treaties of 1947,[10] provided that the Soviet troop withdrawal from Austria would be followed by a similar withdrawal from Hungary. But with the conclusion of the Warsaw Pact on 14 May 1955, a new reality came into affect. As a diplomat, Braunias had certain experiences with the Eastern and South-Eastern European regions. He served as Austrian legation counselor in Moscow between 1949-50 and as Austrian envoy in Belgrade between 1951-52. In January 1956 he referred to the unchanged power structure between the Kremlin and Budapest:

> In Moscow, the 'well-intentioned policy toward Yugoslavia and Austria' button is pushed, and immediately the Hungarian politicians hurry to implement these instructions in word and deed, especially if it doesn't cost anything.
>
> In the military arena, the Soviet Union remains the master in Hungary and doesn't need the Hungarian armed forces to carry out its orders. The Soviet Union is withdrawing its troops from Hungary, and its specialists as well. However, those troops which are 'connected' to Soviet units in Austria remain in Hungary. The Warsaw Agreement gives the Soviet Union the possibility to station troops in Hungary, just as it gives Hungary the possibility to send troops to the Soviet Union. (However, two similar actions don't always have equal reactions.)[11]

The normalization of relations with Yugoslavia, with which Communist Hungary had lived in cold war since 1949, and the openness toward Austria in the political arena went hand in hand with a clearly increasing anti-Soviet tendency in the Hungarian population. Although the U.S.S.R. made the effort to give way and to make positive gestures, these had only a limited effect:

> Even though the Soviet Union is sending various messengers of peace to Hungary in the form of artists and scientists of various types, and even though in the last year they released the last Hungarian prisoners of war and civilian internees, the majority of the Hungarian people rejects Soviet rule and this attitude expresses itself wherever it can. It is expressed on the playing fields, where, during international matches, support is shown for the respective opponents of Soviet teams. And if the Hungarian team is the opponent of the Soviets and the Hungarian players have received the order not to win, then they are so cheered on by the fans that they really have to win even if that was not in the plan of the organizer.[12]

Already in March 1955 Austria's envoy reported about a government crisis in Hungary that had been going on for some time. Prime Minister Nagy, who was presented as conservative, "opportunist," "nationalist," and "Public Enemy Number One," gained ever more popularity and respect with the people, whereas "the unpopular" Rákosi became "more and more unpopular."[13] Not only had the Communist regime in Hungary lost all credit with the people, but every day it became more and more hated: "The people are apathetic or they dream of a quick liberation. The danger of war," of which the government always spoke, was taken seriously inasmuch as war was seen as "the beginning of the end of the Russian Communist oppression and thus was almost longed for." The Austrian legation concluded in December 1954 that the U.S.S.R. could not withdraw their troops from Austria "without giving the opposition in Hungary new impetus." A "danger of Anschluss" was constantly spoken of in official statements: "the maintenance of their position of power in Hungary is one of the reasons that caused the Soviet Union to deny U.S. our well-earned right to have a State Treaty and their withdrawal from our country using the most flimsy of pretexts. The Hungarian government has to provide support in this matter since Rákosi and his comrades request protection from the danger of Anschluss."[14] After the conclusion of the State Treaty and Austria's declaration of neutrality, the "danger of Anschluss" ought to have been done away with. A thaw in the Austrian and Hungarian relations seemed to begin. The country that was geographically located in the West now served as a positive example to many, even to Communists.

At every possible turn and even on the most disparate occasions, Hungary's political representatives attempted, in discussions with their Austrian counterparts, to establish a relationship with the country which had been freed of the four occupation powers. Rákosi, the first secretary of the Central Committee of the Communist Party, repeatedly emphasized the establishment of good neighborly relationships with Austria.[15] The acceptance of the Austrian neutrality law, Raab's remarks in Parliament, and his hints regarding good neighborly relations caused a sensation among Hungarian politicians and pleased them. Many functionaries who had genuine sympathies for Austria were glad about the fact that these sympathies were not meant for a Western country, but a neutral one, making it considerably easier to make their position known.[16] Neutral Austria, which had been freed with the approval of the U.S.S.R., had to appear absolutely legitimate as a point of attraction and as an example for Communist functionaries. The First Vice President Daniel Nagy reported to Braunias about the success of Hungarian swine breeding—there were nine million hogs in the country, thus close to one pig for every Hungarian—in order to build a bridge to the Western neighbor: Nagy paid tribute to the friendly bonds between the two nations "which are both pork eaters." Prime Minister Andreas Hegedüs then spoke of political matters and expressed his happiness about the reduction of tensions in the international area and Hungary's admission to the United Nations.[17] He was satisfied and proud to have become a member of the world organization along with Austria (15 December 1955).

The initial reduction of tensions in bilateral relations had already begun *before* Austria's "annus mirabilis" (Gerald Stourzh) of 1955. Negotiations on assets had already been initiated between Vienna and Budapest in 1953 but had to be broken off in the autumn of the same year. These negotiations dealt with the compensation for Austrian assets that had been confiscated.[18]

After Deputy Prime Minister Andreas Hegedüs made known the desire to establish good neighborly relations in December 1954, Hungarian politicians repeated this formula on different occasions: for example, the First Party Secretary Mátyás Rákosi expressed it at a banquet on the occasion of the ten year anniversary celebration of "Hungarian Independence" in April 1955, and in the same month, the newly designated Prime Minister Hegedüs and Foreign Minister János

Boldoczky stated it again in the National Assembly; on 17 November, on the occasion of the anniversary of the October Revolution, Secretary of the Party Central Committee Istvan Kovacs followed at a banquet with a similarly formulated statement. Braunias made clear that such declarations were welcome in Austria, but that they would only be believed if they were followed by action. He cited, among other cases, the treatment of Austrian citizens and their assets in Hungary. Braunias enumerated the most important unresolved points, which would have to be resolved in reference to such a worthwhile normalization. He had coordinated the concept with the Hungarian foreign minister and was able to register as his first success that Budapest already made concessions on three points the next day. Braunias mentioned a *relaxation in both directions*, including:

first, the possibility for Austrian citizens and holders of dual citizenship in Hungary to cross the border—a great number of cases had already been approved on the part of the Hungarians;

second, a more generous distribution of entrance visas to Austrian citizens—in 1955 4,000 visas were given to Austrians, the majority for sporting events and weekend bus excursions;

third, the abolition of visa fees for athletes, artists, and scientists;

fourth, the abolition of the mandatory Hungarian police escort for Danube Steam Ship Company ships, which was approved by Budapest; and

fifth, the facilitation of free movement and the improvement of accommodations for Austrian railway, police, and customs personnel at the border train station at Hegyeshalom.

The negotiations on assets, which were interrupted in the autumn of 1953, were supposed to resume in January 1956. Also planned were the facilitation of cross-border traffic, the re-activation of existing road border crossing points at Klingenbach-Sopron, Rattersdorf-Köszeg, Heiligenkreuz-Rabafüzes, and Mogersdorf-St. Gotthard, as well as the opening of nine additional border crossing points for smaller border traffic. In addition, measures were taken for the normalization of traffic and the preparation for its increase. In the course of economic negotiations in September and November 1955, after the "anomaly of Soviet economic administration in Austria" had been removed, an increase in trade volume of up to 40 percent was agreed upon. The national banks of both countries had agreed upon capital transfer in the event of the sale of assets, which was without limit. In Austria this meant practically everything, and in Hungary it meant, for example, land.[19]

If one compares the trade data from 1937 with those of 1946, a tremendous decrease can be observed from 15 percent to 2.7 percent (Austrian exports) and from 16 percent to 3.2 percent (imports). But in September 1948 a first trade treaty between Budapest and Vienna was signed, and the traffic of goods increased remarkably from 70.7 million Austrian Schilling in 1947 to 894.4 million Austrian Schilling in 1955. In 1956 the extent of trade expansion reached over one billion Schilling.[20]

What was especially noticeable in the area of political relations was the recognition of neutrality that occurred in an "extremely rapid and especially festive form." Hungary was the fifth country that felt obliged to take this step, and, before the U.S.S.R., it was the first of the so-called 'Eastern Bloc' to do so. It took place in the form of a declaration by the head of state and the presidium of the People's Republic, which was published in the national law gazette.[21] Did this already suggest that Budapest saw a model for Hungary in the Austria solution of 1955?

2. Neutralizing Hungary in 1955?

Soon after the perfecting of the Austria solution, deliberations arose in Western diplomacy about the possibility of a neutralization not only of Germany,[22] but also of Central Europe in general. In the opinion of the Italian envoy in Budapest, a neutralization of Czechoslovakia and Hungary would be an important point to discuss by the heads of government in Geneva. As opposed to the U.S. envoy, who did not consider the inclusion of 'East Bloc countries' in a European ring of security as being worthy of pursuit, Giardini, the Italian envoy to Budapest, was of the opinion that U.S. diplomacy would vigorously demand it, whereby it would not be a cheap attack but rather a serious initiative and a contribution to the reduction of tensions. The Soviet Union wanted to achieve this reduction of tensions because, in the long run, they would always be on the weaker side. Giardini was a realist when he pointed out that such an American initiative, for whatever reasons, would not be successful, and that the Geneva conference would be a failure.[23]

In 1955, the Stalinist Rákosi managed, with great effort, to eliminate the internal political resistance to his course of policy, although he was not able to deal with his foreign policy opponent, the reform-minded Communist Tito. Braunias succinctly summed up the situation—if Soviet policy were to return to Stalinism, then Rákosi would be saved: "After all, after Imre Nagy is eliminated, [Rákosi] is the only personality with any stature in the midst of a great number of faceless functionaries."[24]

What was to happen to Rákosi in the event that Soviet policy did not stick to Stalinism was not openly mentioned by Braunias. However, he did not leave his headquarters in the dark about the conditions in Hungary:

> Out of all the Eastern Bloc states, Hungary may be the country in which the people are allowed to be the most active. There is not only the existing 'jus murmurandi', it is also possible to express one's misgivings more loudly about the regime without police intervention. Contact between Hungarians and the offices of foreign representatives in the capital is not hindered; visitors are generally not under surveillance, the representatives are not controlled. Where religious life is involved, freedom of worship in the narrow sense had not been touched. Up to this point, Communism has not been able to leave its mark on cultural life. Many more foreigners are coming to Hungary than to other Eastern Bloc countries. Listening to foreign broadcasts is not forbidden, although it is made difficult by jamming. All of this goes to show that in Hungary, the Communist regime is the most frail. Perhaps it can count on the support of 10 percent of the people, amongst the youth perhaps 20 percent. It can, therefore, not see as its goal rallying the support of masses of the population. Even in the most ideal case it can only expect to create apathy, an indifference toward all political events.[25]

It was implicitly stated what would befall the Rákosi regime if de-Stalinization came about. But this was still not recognizable as 1956 dawned. The previous year, in which the hopes of the people for a reduction of tension had been high, did not bring the desired success. The circles which were dissatisfied with Rákosi set more and more deadlines by which the hopes of freeing the country ought to have been fulfilled. Braunias reported that a neutralization would already be satisfactory. With the failure of the Geneva summit in the summer and the Geneva conference of foreign ministers in the autumn of 1955, deep disappointment about the absence of further progress regarding the reduction of tensions in central Europe was observed: "Another soap bubble of hope has popped," Braunias let Vienna know, "and no other glimmer of hope is visible on the horizon." In its place a deep hopeless-ness set in, since the 'roll back' of the Eisenhower-Dulles administration turned out to be substanceless propaganda. It was felt that "the West had given up Hungary, the Occident had written off the outpost of humanis-tic civilization. In the dark days of December, desperation reigned, as in the times of Turkish rule when hopes had been placed on France, which then formed an alliance with Turkey. 'We are alone': this old saying once again became reality." As soon as new messages from Eisenhower and Dulles about Eastern Europe had been heard at Christmas 1955, new hopes were once again awakened. Hegedüs' New Year's address and meetings in industrial plants, in which protests against "this interference in Hungarian matters" were raised, illustrated the high degree of reaction.[26]

In spite of all the new indications and friendly demonstrations of good will, the bilateral relations between Austria and Hungary were still far from conflict-free. The Hungarians asked repeatedly for an Austrian Parliament delegation, from which they expected "a warming in the atmosphere which, in spite of all the mutual declarations, they perceived as frosty," primarily because it "has been adversely affected by the up to now one-sidedness—the Slavic grip—of the conditions." They claimed that they would "use any opportunity to establish a dialogue with the West and, above all, with the neighbor to the West." The non-acceptance of the invitation would, as Austria's new representative Walter Peinsipp made clear in Vienna, negatively affect Hungary's prestige.[27] As a diplomat, Peinsipp did not have special knowledge about the Middle and Eastern European regions. He served as consul at the *Berufskonsularamt* (consulate) in Zurich between 1949-51, as legation counselor in the *Wirtschaftspolitischen Abteilung* (section for economic policies) at the *Ballhausplatz*, and as envoy in Ottawa afterwards.

As the Hungarian invitation dated back to 1955, Foreign Minister Figl welcomed the initiative, since he believed that the Hungarians could be taken seriously about their efforts to establish a good relationship. Hungary had removed the technical barriers and in addition, negotia-tions about compensation for confiscated Austrian assets were in progress. He asked the president of the Parliament, Felix Hurdes, to deal with this matter as soon as possible.[28] In the course of the revolutionary events in Hungary, however, the response was consciously delayed and finally dropped altogether. Undersecretary Kreisky was, in principle, against a visit by a parliament which had not been freely elected. Figl agreed, upon which it was decided "to cancel the visit, if possible."[29]

3. Austria as the priority

After the 20th Party Congress of the Soviet Communist Party in the beginning of 1956 and the announcement of 'democratization', Rákosi's expected loss of power began in the course of de-Stalinization, finally leading to his resignation at the end of June 1956.[30] Austria's representation in Budapest attempted to put straight the image portrayed in foreign media that this was an action against the Hungarian government. It was only "an explosion of nationalist circles [sic!] within the party against the Rákosi regime." The event was also "in no way whatsoever related to the events in Poznan [sic!]." In this Polish business center, a worker and student rebellion against the Polish government had taken place on 30 June 1956, which had in fact a considerable influence on later unrest in Hungary. The Austrian observer pointed out the specific situation in Hungary and the differences with the unrest in Poland. The development showed

> what explosive material there is in Hungary and that the opposition is mustering and risking something. The biggest mistake, however, would be—as already pointed out—to interpret the events of 29 June as an explosion against the regime. The question arises, though, how it could have come to these demonstrations, even more so since the earlier evenings of debate of the [Petöfi] circle [an intellectual discussion circle within the framework of the Communist Youth League which opposed Rákosi] left the expectation that such a point of culmination would happen soon.
> That it was writers and intellectuals who led the opposition and not the workers, despite general dissatisfaction, had its basis in the particular circumstances of the country, that is, that this regime followed feudalism, in which the bourgeois class was too tiny, too insignificant, and too intimidated to be able to act as the opposition, and in which the working class was not brought up with an active fighting spirit, as was the case in Poland, where its effect is felt today."[31]

The appointment of Imre Horváth as the new Hungarian foreign minister was interpreted as "a step toward the West," because he "distinguished himself considerably from his Hungarian colleagues, not only because of his pleasant and conciliatory manner, but also through the moderation of ideology."[32]

When Julius Raab gave an interview in September 1956 to *Radio Budapest* and the central organ of the Hungarian Communist party, *Szabad Nép*, in which he spoke in favor of good neighborly relations, this was received by leading Hungarian figures "with great satisfaction." Peinsipp noted the widespread, pro-Austrian sentiment in the country that went beyond the political elite: "It is no wonder that it is the topic of the day amongst the people, because it is Austria that is in fashion now and every good word from the other side of the border is understood by the population as friendliness toward the Hungarian people." Peinsipp was surprised about "the positive and honest resonance" that Raab's reference to the "common past" of the two countries had received. Deputy Foreign Minister Sebes, according to Peinsipp a cynic, Stalinist, and planner,[33] immediately pushed for an invitation for the chancellor to visit Budapest. Peinsipp, however, attempted to dampen the Hungarian euphoria and to confront it with reality. With regards to foreign visits, a head of government in Austria had to act in concordance with the opinion and sentiments of the people. The normalization of relations had not yet progressed far enough "for it to be advisable to approach this question." The diplomat expressed that "first and foremost, a lasting peace on the border had to be achieved," the negotiations on assets had to be concluded, and the question of dual citizenship and reunification of families had to be resolved. As uncomfortable and unwelcome as these clarifications were to Peinsipp, they appeared to be very necessary as indications of reduction of tension in relations and to make clear "that what has happened up to now was still perceived by the Austrian people as a breaking down of barriers, which had not been put up by the Austrians." At the same time, Peinsipp made clear to the *Ballhausplatz* that Hungary would surely come back to the topic of the chancellor's visit, since for them it was a matter of "safeguarding the priority":

> They were really plagued by the fear that another Eastern Bloc country would beat them to it and muscle them out of the leading role. It is not saying too much, if I may point out, that they regard every step by their bloc partners toward Austria almost with jealousy. Various desires where Austria was concerned, such as the visit of a Parliament delegation, a ministerial visit, or a visit by the chancellor, are primarily

based upon making sure not to be left behind anyone else in the Eastern Bloc and in some way to be in the lead.[34]

4. Background and immediate, long-term causes of the uprising of 1956 from the Austrian vantage point

Rákosi's forced resignation in July, which took place under pressure from the Soviet emissary, and the readmission of Imre Nagy to the Communist Party in October—all of which were events which took place in the course of the 20th Party Congress of the Communist Party of the Soviet Union—marked a political change in Hungary,[35] which Peinsipp attempted to place in the proper context of the normalization of relations between Moscow and Belgrade:

> The resolution in the case of Nagy shows more than anything else what has been happening here lately, in what a far-reaching manner things have begun to move, and how far the pendulum is about to swing to the opposite extreme. The fact that the resolution of the case occurred before the party pilgrimage to Belgrade plays less of a role . . . in the evaluation . . . than the fact that this resolution matched the position of the opposition and, above all, of Nagy himself and that it occurred immediately after the return of [Ernö] Gerö and [János] Kádár from the meetings with [Mikhail] Suslov. It was through the latter that Rákosi had brought about the fall of Nagy and who in the spring was still trying to prop up Rákosi in his opposition to Nagy . . .
>
> The timing of Nagy's readmission to the party is related to the pilgrimage to Belgrade, not in the way that the Western press suspects, but only insofar as, after Gerö and Kádár had brought the approval or *nihil obstat* with them from Moscow, the Politburo took the opportunity to do what was inevitable as fast as possible and to rehabilitate Nagy while leaving some questions open, in order to be able to embellish the bouquet to Tito with his favorite Hungarian flower at the last possible moment, while the train was waiting in the station, so to speak.[36]

The friendliness of the Hungarian representatives toward their Austrian counterparts increased noticeably. The envoy Kovacs in Brussels went to the ambassador Martin Fuchs and reaffirmed, against the background of the beginning 'democratization' in his country, the closeness "of a centuries-old commonality of interests and destiny within the framework of the monarchy." He expressed his conviction that a rapprochement between Vienna and Budapest, especially in economic and cultural areas, could "only be an advantage" for both countries.[37]

Because of the recent internal political openness and liberalization, Hungarian youth and students at the Technical University, who had also turned toward Austria as an example, organized a demonstration of sympathy on 22 – 23 October 1956 for rebelling Polish students and worked toward their general goal through other mass demonstrations.[38] This was *the immediate cause* for the uprising. A provocative speech by the first secretary of the party, Ernö Gerö, was like pouring gasoline in the fire. After the youths occupied a weapons factory, armed revolt followed. The hunt for officials of the state security police began, broadcasting buildings and the House of Parliament were stormed, and clashes with the police followed. The government of Hegedüs was finally dissolved by the government of Nagy, in whose cabinet non-party members were now included.[39]

As long-term causes for the uprising, nine reasons were listed in a situation report for the Austrian foreign ministry: *first*, the extremely low standard of living; *second*, terror by the state police that had been going on for years; *third*, the exploitation of the working class by a virtual slave driver system; *fourth*, the economic exploitation of the country by the Soviet Union; *fifth*, the stationing of Soviet troops on Hungarian territory for an indefinite period of time; *sixth*, the systematic pillaging of farmers; *seventh*, the reckless class struggle; *eighth*, the relaxed access to publicity of the Hungarian intelligentsia since the beginning of de-Stalinization in March 1956; and *ninth*, the replacement of Rákosi by "the hated and feared left-extremist, Gerö."[40]

A look at *the composition of the insurgents* throws light on the attitude of the classes toward Communism: the protest movement was dominated by university and high school students and the working class youth of state artisan, trade, and industry institutions, who had been thought of by the party as the 'elite school'. Workers joined in only hesitatingly in the course of the battle. Hungarian troops supplied the fighters with weapons and ammunition, but they themselves remained passive. Only individual *Honveds* (members of the Hungarian militia reserve) joined the insurgents. The participation of the bourgeois circles was close to nothing. The majority of the masses filled the streets and demonstrated, but they did not actively get involved in the battles.

With regard to *the character of the events*, informative details were provided. The report, which dated, however, from the end of October, only spoke of a "revolt." The outbreak, the course of events, and the degree did not seem to indicate a *'levée en masse'*. Thus it was in no way an action which was planned or one which had been prepared for a long time, but rather a spontaneous outbreak by the embittered people. This would explain their taking the law into their own hands and the lynching of party functionaries and officials of the state security apparatus.[41] Under "Significance for Austria," the situation report listed:

> The sound of the words 'Austria', 'Austrian', and 'Vienna' triggers spontaneous, enthusiastic declarations of sympathy and gratefulness. This sad occasion offers Austria the unique chance to be the active initiator of an honest friendship between the two peoples.
>
> Furthermore, the following can be stated: The threatening military grip on the Eastern part of Austria by three countries with Communist regimes no longer exists. The gap between the Hungarian people and the Soviet dictators has been widened through these events to such an extent that Hungary will be ruled out as a military ally of the Soviet Union for a long time.[42]

The situation, though, remained in flux. In the second paragraph of the quote, Peinsipp made an annotation by underlining the words "no longer exists," and he added "for the time being."[43]

5. Our protection lies in our neutrality: Austria's immediate reactions and actions[44]

Judging from the obvious relationship between the Austrian solution of 1955 and the revolutionary events in Hungary of 1956,[45] the thesis of the French diplomatic representative to Vienna, François Seydoux sounds very likely: according to Seydoux the neutral Alpine Republic, even though it could not serve as a model for Germany, could be a Trojan horse regarding Central and Eastern Europe.[46] This thesis seems to have found a very swift confirmation, almost representing a threat to the existence of the U.S.S.R. and its satellite system. If the Austrian chancellor—independent of what he really wanted and thought[47]—officially *had to be reserved* in the case of Germany regarding the recommendation of a 'model case', then he found himself in an even more difficult situation with respect to the revolutionary events in Hungary, regarding both the execution of Austrian neutrality and the question of its transferability to Hungary. Julius Raab hoped that the efforts of the Hungarian freedom fighters would lead to the liberation of their country.[48]

After the outbreak of the uprising and the first intervention by Soviet units (on 23-24 October), Raab, following an extraordinary session of the government on Sunday, 28 October, felt compelled to issue an unequivocal appeal to the U.S.S.R. The courageous call was:

> The Austrian government has been painfully and with sympathy following the five day old bloody events with heavy losses in neighboring Hungary. It requests the government of the U.S.S.R. to cooperate so that the military clashes are broken off and the flow of blood stops.
>
> Based upon Austria's freedom and independence which are ensured by its neutrality, the Austrian government favors a normalization of conditions in Hungary with the goal that through the reestablishment of liberty in accordance with human rights, European peace will be strengthened and ensured.[49]

The ambassadors of the USA, Great Britain, and France were informed about this resolution with a note and they were told that a copy would be sent to the United Nations Security Council. The Hungarian envoy was informed by Foreign Minister Leopold Figl of the measures taken by Austria in order to protect its borders and to defend its neutrality. In similar telegrams, Vienna immediately informed its representatives in Paris, London, and Washington in order to make clear the extremely difficult situation in which Austria found itself:

> If the uprising in Hungary is brought to an end through a massive Soviet military operation, as it now appears will happen, it is likely that larger units of Hungarian freedom troops will make it to Austria. As far as is possible, all provisions have been made on the Austrian side to immediately accept those groups which lay down their arms, and to grant them asylum.

A longer stay of these units on Austrian soil would not only exceed Austria's financial and economic capacity, but would also signify a serious political and military threat.

Please bring this to the attention of the government of the country where you are stationed and propose that they take whatever action is necessary in order to move these groups to other Western countries without delay.[50]

The federal government immediately ordered *seven measures*, to which it also referred during the following period, when the Soviets accused Austria of an alleged violation of neutrality. These measures were: *first*, the establishment of a prohibited zone by the Austrian military (denial of entry for unauthorized); *second*, inspection of the prohibited zone by the Austrian minister of defense and the military attachés of the Great Powers; *third*, requiring Ferenc Nagy to leave Austria; *fourth*, a moratorium on the issuing of visas to foreign passport holders (emigrants); *fifth*, increased control of the Western border; *sixth*, the prohibition of political activity among refugees and exiles; and *seventh*, the disarming and interning of those who are armed.[51]

Foreign Minister Leopold Figl and the envoys Heinrich von Haymerle and Wilfried Platzer received the newly appointed Soviet ambassador Sergei Lapin and the envoy Timoshenko on 28 October. Figl pointed out that Austria, as a neutral country and a neighbor of Hungary, felt obliged to urgently appeal to the U.S.S.R. to reestablish normal conditions and to promote peace in Europe. Lapin replied that the measures that the Austrian government took on the border were understandable, but the appeal had a "strange tone" to it. According to Lapin, the Hungarian government had "asked the U.S.S.R. for help," the government of Nagy existed, and it had already begun its work. Agreements would be reached. This matter was purely between the Hungarians and the Soviets. Figl replied that Austria was greatly worried that the fighting would go on and that Hungarian units would flee to Austrian territory. Because of that, Austria's security would be threatened. If Soviet units were to come across the border, Austria would have to insist that they would also have to lay down their weapons. The Soviet government would have to order its troops to respect neutral ground. Lapin answered that the U.S.S.R. "has no intention of jeopardizing Austrian neutrality in whose creation they themselves have participated." However, he continued, no one could doubt that the Soviet troops, participating "in the steps taken in

Hungary," acted in accordance with the Warsaw Pact and at the request of the legal Hungarian government. He assured them that the situation would "already become normal again today," which, however, proved to be a pious wish and too optimistic.

The former Hungarian Prime Minister Ferenc Nagy had actually arrived by plane in Vienna. After the federal government, through the envoy Heinrich von Haymerle, had called upon him not to cause Austria any difficulties, not to cast a bad light upon the Hungarian Aid Program through his visit, and to leave the country, Nagy demonstrated little understanding in the beginning. He countered that Austria's attitude would not be understood by the West and that it would disappoint Hungarian emigrants. After relevant clarifications, however, he relented when he was told by an intermediary that the decision of the federal government was not directed against him personally. He was assured that there would be the possibility of a visit after the normalization of relations.[52]

The federal government made an effort to keep this event under wraps. But because of a misunderstanding—caused by a *Reuters* report—a news bulletin was published by the Austrian Press Agency (APA), which the government would have wanted to avoid with regard to the Western Powers: "In consideration of the maintenance of neutrality, Nagy was informed on the part of Austria that his departure should take place at once in order to avoid difficulties regarding this situation. Nagy then left Austria by train."[53]

Vienna continued to react prudently and cautiously in order not to provoke the U.S.S.R. at all. A planned Hungary debate in the Parliament did not seem to be opportune, although Raab's declaration was supposed to be repeated. Because of the Suez crisis, which had escalated with the outbreak of the Middle East war on 29 October, the international situation was complicated even further.[54] The political department of the foreign ministry recommended:

> Our protection lies in our neutrality. The political department takes the liberty to once again warn against declarations by Parliament which could arouse the impression in Moscow that, with the uprising in Hungary, our neutrality had been swept away. In contrast to this, the political department would consider it extremely valuable if the chancellor were to make the intended declaration to Parliament today, since it would again clearly emphasize the position of the Austrian government.

Up till now, Austria has clearly done more than the entire Western World put together. Our task now will be to continue this assistance, but silently.[55]

6. *International and intra-bloc reactions in the context of Nagy's declaration of neutrality and the second Soviet intervention*

For Vienna, it was decisive how Washington would react. On 3 November Ambassador Karl Gruber reported that the United States was not prepared for the events in Budapest, "even though their publicly declared foreign policy was oriented toward the liberation of these peoples." John Foster Dulles confessed that things had developed much too fast. The planning board of the State Department had worked out a "comfortable theory" according to which the Eastern European countries would gradually break away from Russia without war or any explosion, and the countries involved would return to normal conditions. Gruber, the former Austrian secretary of state for foreign affairs (1945-1953), responded to this laconically: "As happens so often, the facts do not follow the theories," and added, "Washington does not know what it should do." Different alternatives were considered: "Military attack: not possible at this time. Covert support: insufficient. What is missing is both the apparatus and, above all, certain geographical preconditions (if only Hungary had a sea coast). What essentially remains, therefore, is making moral appeals and lodging legal actions." Gruber's slightly ironic and pragmatic comments culminated in the statement that this time, at least, the refugees were being helped "in a generous manner," while at the same time he immediately informed the *Ballhausplatz* "that at least the State Department now shares our opinion that Austria is not the place to grant great masses of refugees a lasting stay." Gruber, who did not forget about bringing up the Suez crisis, provided an analysis which Undersecretary of State Kreisky spoke of as "excellent."[56] Aside from acts of humanitarian assistance, Austria once again pursued a policy of national interest. Too many Hungarians should not and were not allowed to stay. In the end, fewer than 20,000 remained out of approximately 180,000 refugees.[57]

In spite of voting for the U.N.-resolution of 4 November, which called upon the U.S.S.R. to withdraw the Soviet troops from Hungary,[58] the Austrian government had every reason to act extremely cautious when deciding their policy, always with a view toward its neutrality. The Soviet deputy foreign minister Valerian A. Sorin reminded

Austria's diplomatic representative in Moscow, Norbert Bischoff, that in these times, "it is of the highest importance that Austria maintains its neutrality with the greatest acuity." The smallest deviation, the slightest inattention would be "exploited not by us [the Soviets], but by others as an undermining of neutrality."[59] Vienna was warned. Even with the best intentions, the recommendation of neutrality status by Austria to rebellious Hungary was not thinkable.

The State Department, however, reacted differently than what would have been expected from Sorin's statement. Regarding the maintenance of Austrian neutrality, a U.S. declaration was issued to counter Soviet allegations that the United States had assisted the rebels from Austrian territory. It stated that this did not match the facts. In an addendum, it was pointed out that "The United States has respected the neutral character of Austria and will continue to respect it. It is of the opinion that the violation of the territorial integrity or the internal sovereignty of Austria would of course signify a serious threat to peace." Austrian newspapers construed this as a declaration by the U.S. president that a violation of Austria's integrity was a "casus belli," an interpretation which in no way corresponded to the text of the declaration, as had been accurately pointed out by the *Ballhausplatz*.[60] Ambassador Karl Gruber reported to Washington that the reason for the State Department's declaration was the desire "to blunt the various attacks against Austria before the United Nations." The United States did not expect any special publicity, but through this it hoped to make clear to the U.S.S.R. "that interference in Austria would not be tolerated."[61]

The Belgian foreign minister, Paul-Henri Spaak, who was on a visit to the U.S.S.R. during the suppression of the Hungarian uprising, was, after his return, "severely shaken" and "quite depressed" by the events, because he saw no possibility "to really help Hungary with the exception of purely humanitarian measures and actions." His sobering summary was: "One has to have the courage to admit that any military intervention by the United Nations or the Western Powers in Hungary would most probably trigger a World War. There is no responsible government in the Free World which would or could undertake such a risk." Spaak made it clear to Martin Fuchs, the Austrian ambassador to Brussels, that during his stay in Russia the political decisions had not yet been made and Moscow was still prepared to yield. According to him, the Soviet government, that is, the leadership of the Red Army, had decided to violently suppress the Hungarian uprising only as a last resort:

As late as 48 hours before the intervention by Soviet units in Budapest, the responsible Soviet functionaries in Stalingrad had with clear satisfaction brought to his attention the Moscow Communiqué about the intended new regulations concerning the relationship between the Soviet Union and the satellite states and had spoken of the probability of a rapid withdrawal of Russian troops from Hungary. At that time the leading circles in the Soviet Union apparently still counted on the possibility of heading off and quelling the Hungarian uprising and to be able to channel it toward a moderate national communism just as with the Polish model. Once this expectation was overrun and obsolete because of the rapid development of events, the unforeseeable consequences of a victorious democratic revolution for the entire satellite area were immediately realized in Moscow, and this recognition led to the most extreme consequences. In doing this, they must have hardly overlooked the probability of far-reaching and lasting reactions of the free world to such an action. Against the background of immediately placing Soviet rule in Eastern and Central Europe in jeopardy, however, these reactions and the threat caused by them to Moscow's policy of reduction of tension and coexistence, which had been successfully pursued up to that point, were accepted as the lesser of two evils. Precisely because of the fact that the Soviet Union found and still finds itself in such a dilemma, subjectively considered, it cannot be reasonably expected to yield to such strong diplomatic pressure from the United Nations, that is, from the United States."[62]

Fuchs had nothing to add to this authentic illustration of the impressions which Spaak had gotten in the Soviet Union. In a discussion with Fuchs, the Belgian general secretary for foreign affairs, Ambassador Scheyven, asked whether Vienna had been disturbed about the Hungarian events, whereby Fuchs replied that it had been repeatedly shown since 1945 that they did not lose their nerve, even in critical times. The development of the situation, though, was not apt to strengthen the feeling of security and confidence in neighboring countries. Scheyven spontaneously expressed his conviction "that any attempt to violate the integrity and neutrality of Austria from the outside would meet with immediate and decisive resistance by the rest of the world." "An attack on Austria would mean the outbreak of World War

III," he stated, using exactly those words. Fuchs refrained from making any comment, although with regard to the character of his discussion partner he remarked "that he is generally considered a very responsible and level-headed functionary, almost cool and reserved."[63] At precisely the same time, after a discussion with J. Senard, the Austria expert at the Quai d'Orsay, legation counselor Franz Karasek stated in an official note that "any violation of the integrity of Austrian national territory would mean World War III." Senard was of the opinion that the Soviet Union would also respect Austrian neutrality, unless the Soviets intended to unleash the Third World War at all costs. The U.S.S.R. appeared, however, to be occupied with the quelling of the Hungarian uprising and the suppression of rebellious satellites. Austria could "feel completely safe." A threat to Austria would inevitably lead to an armed encounter between East and West.[64]

In the autumn of 1956 the U.S.S.R. was far from expanding its area of power. What was important for them was to eliminate these hotbeds of unrest in Poland and Hungary and to demonstrate concessions to the satellite states. The "Declaration on the Development and Further Strengthening of the Friendship and Collaboration between the U.S.S.R. and the Other Socialist States" from Moscow on 30 October, issued to the leaders of the non-aligned nations, provided for the following: "withdrawal of Soviet experts" (spies and agents, as a rule), "reorganization of relationships with the peoples' democracies, equal rights and full sovereignty, especially in the field of economic relations to the advantage of both; revision of the Warsaw Pact,"—i.e. primarily reduction or withdrawal of Soviet armed forces from Hungary and Rumania, and a return to the principals of the Potsdam Agreement for Poland. Austria's envoy in Warsaw, Stephan Verosta, noticed immediately that some of the wording of the Soviet declaration matched almost verbatim with the "Five Principles of Coexistence" program of Zhou Enlai and Nehru, and that the Chinese influence on the Kremlin was clearly visible.[65]

Verosta also pointed out the connections between the events in Poland and Hungary up to the Soviet declaration of 30 October. In spite of all the differences with regard to diverse geographical positions and internal political conditions as well as the social structures of opposition groups, according to Verosta, the situation in Poland developed analogously. This date, though, marked the beginning of the difference. While the Poles took the U.S.S.R.'s declaration very seriously, the Hungarians did not. Although the latter admitted mistakes with the people's democracies and promised negotiations on a revision of the Warsaw Pact, in Hungary the very clear threats at the end of the declaration were ignored. In Warsaw, it had been assumed that the Kremlin, already worried because of unrests in Poland, had made its declaration on 30 October in order to give the Nagy-Kádár government a chance to divert the people's uprising into a moderate people's democracy of the Polish type. Added to these crises, however, was the British-French surprise attack on Egypt, which threatened to topple the position built there by Tito, Nehru, and Moscow, as well as fears of possible unrest in the GDR. With a Polish government that was considered unreliable, there was the threat of a chain of collapses with all the people's democracies and the loss of the entire European glacis of the Soviet Union. This assumption was reinforced on 1 November by Imre Nagy's proclamation of full democracy, the withdrawal from the Warsaw Pact, and the declaration of neutrality in Hungary analogous to the Austrian example. Nagy demanded of Yuri Andropov, the U.S.S.R. ambassador and later head of the KGB, the immediate withdrawal of Soviet troops, and he announced to the U.N. the Hungarian request for the support of the Four Powers in the defense of the neutrality of his country. On the part of Poland, these demands were regarded as "very dangerous" and "not realizable for the time being," as Verosta reported. According to him, the Soviets would have to be dealt with "very cautiously"; throwing troops out of a country would be unacceptable for any superpower that had any pride. The new Polish leadership was worried about the repercussions of the Nagy declaration on its own people. Developments in Hungary also ran counter to the interests of Yugoslavia. The consequences of an example of a people's democracy, that suddenly turns into a democratic neutral state possibly prospering with the help of U.S. loans, appeared risky and out of control. According to Verosta's assessment, the Imre Nagy - Pál Maléter - Anna Kéthly government had not considered even the most primitive precautionary measures: "The Poles, who had led popular uprisings against the Russians in 1795, 1831, 1863, and 1905, could not even believe the naiveté of the Hungarians. In spite of this, the brutality of the Soviet blitz was just as much of a shock here as in the West."[66]

His Polish sources emphasized with unbridled indignation that, with the events in Hungary, they were dealing with Russian superpower policy and not with "an unmasking of Socialism." Thus the whole matter had nothing to do with Soviet Communism. While arguing this way, history was used to demonstrate that this particular chapter had a way of repeating itself: in 1849 the Russians had, at the request of the Austrian ruler, suppressed the Hungarian revolution in a similarly bloody way. At that time, as well, it took no more than a declamation about the unfortunate Kossuth and the "heroic Hungarian people" until these people were able, under Déak, to fight for and win equal rights with Austria in the Austrian-Hungarian settlement of 1867.[67]

Conservative, though also socialist, sources repeatedly and bitterly pointed out (possibly with a view toward the negative experiences from the broken promises by the West toward Poland in the Guarantee Declaration of 1939) that the United States and Great Britain as superpowers had placed the people's democracies into the Soviet's hands and had also left their internal organization up to the Soviets. The Western Powers did not want to lead a crusade against the U.S.S.R., since that would mean a third World War. A liberation of Poland, which would result in world conflict, was not desired. Broadcasts by *Radio Free Europe* would have been heard by the Hungarians and would have led the people, who were in a state of agitation, to believe that the West would intervene, which yet again would not be the case. Millions, for whom the West had done nothing since 1945, had to pay for the unrealistic demands of the Hungarians, which had been stirred up by the West. Verosta made it clear to the *Ballhausplatz* that it would be easy "to join the general indignation about the brutal Soviet intervention in Hungary, but it is more difficult to defend the inconsistent policies of the West."[68]

7. "Probably the biggest and most shameful defeat" of the U.S.S.R.

The U.S.S.R., in fact, had hardly been given any other possibility by the unilateral Nagy declaration than to extricate itself while saving face. Based upon Verosta's report, Vienna had no reason to feed unrealistic hopes by publicly approving of Nagy's neutrality declaration. A telegram from Norbert Bischoff about investigations on the attitude of leading figures in the Kremlin could be interpreted as a confirmation of Verosta's report:

> Soviet government would have been ready in accordance with declaration of 30th previous month to give Nagy government broad-reaching additional freedom of action. Development toward neutrality would have been acceptable and accepted if it had taken place in orderly fashion and with suitable consider-

ation of security interests of remaining participants of Warsaw Pact. Intervention of Soviet troops had only become inevitable when clearly rabble-rousing revolutionary and terrorist forces took the lead in Hungary under absolutely chaotic conditions. With declaration of immediate withdrawal from Warsaw Pact, security of remaining participants in pact was placed in serious, direct jeopardy.[69]

In a later report, the very Soviet-friendly and russophile Bischoff noted self-critically that the bloody suppression would represent "probably the biggest and most shameful defeat that the Soviet Union has had to suffer in its forty years of existence." He debited *five negative points* from the Soviet account: *first*, a terminally compromised relationship to the Hungarian people; *second*, destruction of all successes which aimed at the recognition of moral-social coexistence; *third*, the shake-up of the just re-established friendship with Tito; *fourth*, the impairment of the relationship with India and the group of Asian nations sympathetic to him; and *fifth*, the worst crisis in Communist parties and "fellow travelers" in the West. Without the "Hungarian catastrophe," the U.S.S.R. would have won even greater advantages from the Israeli-Anglo-French attack against Egypt. Alluding to Nagy's neutrality declaration, Bischoff pointed out:

The Russians have offered for years to withdraw their troops from the countries in Eastern and East-Central Europe if America would remove its troops from Western and West-Central Europe. They stick by this offer even today, as can be concluded by the most recent manifestations, even though it has been made clear to a large degree that the people's democratic order would hardly survive very long after the withdrawal of Soviet troops.

According to this analysis, the basically positive attitude of the U.S.S.R. leadership to a neutralization of Europe did not appear to have changed, in spite of the Hungary debacle:

However, this means nothing more than that in the case of the demilitarization of Europe, which basically would be brought about by the withdrawal of Soviet and American forces from their respectively occupied halves of our continent, the Soviet leadership seems to be ready for the step-by-step transformation of the people's democracies into more or less socialist-oriented parliamentary democracies and to accept a generally much less aggressive form of state and society.[70]

Bischoff cited the Belgrade Protocol of 1955, the resolution of the 20th Party Congress of February, and the declaration of 30 October 1956, which seemed to speak for a consistent line of political leadership:

Now, however, since these resolutions received such a clear reinforcement and far-reaching interpretation in the declaration of 30 October at the highpoint of the Hungarian crisis, and with the Polish crisis not having been completely resolved, there can hardly be any doubt about the correctness of that conclusion, which is additionally supported by the fact that the leading local military attachés have for a long time been of the opinion that because of modern armament technology, the significance of the people's democracies for the security of the Soviet Union—the one factor which had doubtlessly played a decisive role in the old Stalinist concept—had lost its value to a large degree. The military significance of the people's democracies for the Soviet Union is today reduced to little more than the radar screen.

Therefore, it could be the case that now, in light of the Hungarian and Polish events, what to many had so far appeared to be only unrealistic wishful thinking would be realized: that a peaceful 'roll back' was in fact possible and that what could not be achieved through the cold war and the policy of 'strength position', could one day (which was unfortunately still far away) be made possible through the clearing out of Soviet and American occupation armies from Europe.[71]

Even though Bischoff spoke in the subjunctive mood, expressing possibilities rather than facts, his comments had their grounds. Austria's ambassador in Belgrade, Walter Wodak, found out that a conflicting attitude was predominant in Moscow regarding the suppression of the Hungarian uprising. The Finnish ambassador Vuori had the opportunity to speak to Khrushchev on the occasion of the anniversary of the Russian revolution. The latter emphasized the continuation along the path of de-Stalinization that had been adopted at the 20th Party Congress of the Communist Party of the Soviet Union, especially in connection with the relationship to the satellite states. Khrushchev added "that he did not consider it to be out of the question, after a calming of the situation in Hungary, to be able to create a status of neutrality similar to that which Austria enjoys today." Since, however (as Wodak added to Vuori's information), the resolution by Nagy's government declaring Hungary's neutrality was the immediate cause for the second Russian intervention in Budapest (on 4 November 1956), Khrushchev's statements could be interpreted, if desired, as a difference of opinion between him and the generals, who "have been the driving force behind the military suppression of the Hungary revolution."[72]

We now know from new Soviet sources (the so-called "Yeltsin-Dossier"[73]), that the second Russian intervention was ordered by the Kremlin leaders just before Nagy's declaration of Hungarian neutrality. It was on 31 October when the Politburo in Moscow made the decision. If Khrushchev had ever entertained the idea of Hungary's neutrality, in the end he gave the green light for the bloody intervention. In the very beginning of November 1956 he also came to an agreement with Tito to fight against this "Hungarian counterrevolution" and to make Prime Minister Nagy and his government disappear.[74] These are the facts.

8. Austria: officially neutral, but "not neutral at heart"
The spontaneous outbreak of unrest in Hungary and the ensuing security measures took Austria's political and military leaders by surprise. Austria was not sufficiently prepared for an attack against its territory. The national army (*Bundesheer*) had only been built up in the very beginning of 1956 and the first conscripts (*Präsenzdiener*) began service in October. There was a lack of both experience and knowledge in how to deal with the various different problems caused by an uprising in a neighbor state. During the first stage of the crisis there was even a lack of ammunition. The command-structure within the ministry of defense was not clear; units received contradicting orders. On the one hand the Austrian minister of defense, Ferdinand Graf (Austrian People's Party), acted on his own, on the other hand he asked his government what to do. No mutual agreement existed between the chancellery and the head of the military. Therefore, Graf made ad hoc decisions. In the course of the second Russian intervention he gave the order to fire if Soviet troops crossed the Austrian border and this order was carried out. But it seemed to be clear that Austria's military was too weak to adequately protect the borders. An effective control of air space did not exist. It was fortunate that no real danger existed, and the Red Army kept its distance from Austrian territory. Only a few border violations took place. The Austrian

army did their best to secure the territorial integrity of the country. In April 1957 this so-called *Sicherungseinsatz* ended.[75]

In the course of the uprising in Hungary, the Austrian federal government organized comprehensive shipments of aid and the transport of medical supplies. Peinsipp could only reestablish telephone contact with Vienna on 30 October, and he stated that the distribution of the aid by the embassy meant "real propaganda for Austria."[76] As early as 28 October, the national government made a courageous appeal to the U.S.S.R. to stop the fighting and bring an end to the bloodshed. Austria advocated "a normalization of conditions in Hungary with the goal that, through the reestablishment of freedom with respect to human rights, European peace would be strengthened and assured." For the Swiss observer, this call was "right on the border of all that was possible for a neutral state."[77] On 9 November the Austrian U.N. delegation presented a resolution to initiate large scale assistance for the Hungarian population in need. This was accepted by the general assembly with a vote of sixty-seven in favor and eight abstentions.[78] Austria's attitude toward the revolutionary events is *on the one hand* proof of courageous and self-confident behavior. Austria was the only Western nation which had called upon the U.S.S.R. to grant Hungary the right of self-determination, and envoy Walter Peinsipp was considered "the hero of Budapest." He went to all the hospitals and distributed penicillin. In a telephone call from envoy Haymerle, it was mentioned that "At times, it is only possible to do this in a hail of bullets."[79] *On the other hand*, however, Austria's attitude demonstrates to what a great extent the Austrian government was on the defensive in the course of the further developments beginning in November. This could only partly be made up for by spontaneous denials of corresponding accusations and evidence of submissiveness. In autumn 1956 Austrian foreign policy was formulated against the background of the crisis in its neighboring country.

In the course of the Hungarian crisis and the second military intervention of the Soviet Union, the federal government felt compelled to withdraw its application for membership in the European Coal and Steel Community (ECSC),[80] which had already been announced by Chancellor Raab and Foreign Minister Figl in October. *Pravda* later admonished Vienna with a warning about neutrality, while *Izvestia* stringently warned against participation in the Community.[81] With this action, which was without a doubt remarkable, the federal government had tried to sound out the existing maneuvering room regarding integration policy,[82] and, with the projected application for membership for 1957, had tried to push to the furthest limit. Aside from the feared Soviet reservations, Thomas Angerer also pointed out the excessive prices for steel in the ECSC, which allegedly caused Vienna to back off. They were 20 to 30 percent above the highly subsidized domestic prices, which favored the finished goods industry, and, had this membership occurred, wages and prices in other business sectors would also have increased. Apart from this, there were also considerations in the partnerships between labor and management. Thus, the protectionist misgivings were no newer than the Soviet objections.[83] In a presentation to Raab of the "MacMillan Plan" for a large free trade zone in Western Europe, Johann Augenthaler, the expert from the ministry of trade pointed out on 29 October, after the Austrian announcement of the ECSC application: "The plan for a free trade zone also has the advantage for both countries [Austria and Switzerland] that participation is possible in spite of their neutrality, whereas Austria joining the six country bloc which is in fact strongly tied to the NATO concept is still to be considered from a political point of view with regard to the reaction of the Soviet Union."[84] That was at a point in time when the government of Imre Nagy in Hungary seemed to have stabilized itself. The second Russian intervention was still to follow with strong attacks in the media against neutral Austria.

The fact remains that the maneuvering room for foreign policy was very limited against the background of the massive accusations coming from the East regarding an alleged violation of neutrality in the context of the events in Hungary. Furthermore, if Vienna had pushed its ECSC application request, this would have been grist to the mill for the critics of Austrian neutrality. This had to be avoided if at all possible. Therefore, the application to the ECSC was not pursued. The announcement in October 1956 that Austria would attain ECSC membership in 1957 can be interpreted as the Austrian intention to participate with respect to a "common market," and the European Economic Community (EEC) was in fact more important to Austria than the ECSC.[85] According to the author, Austria at that time had no realistic chance to become a member of the six state community, that is, either the ECSC or the EEC. The economic community was only in formation stages as a result of the ECSC Nations Conferences in Messina (1955) and Venice (1956). Participation in negotiations could not seriously be considered, though the course of events was carefully observed.

In spite of assurances to the Austrian government, the Hungarian government accused Austria of having smuggled arms, ammunition, and "Horthy fascists" (followers of the pro-fascist Hungarian politician Miklós Horthy) under the cover of the Red Cross.[86] Austria was accused of a violation of neutrality primarily because of the content of Austrian broadcasts and press reports and the behavior of its political parties. Austria's U.N. representative, Franz Matsch, corrected the actual situation in the Hungarian debate before the United Nations. There was no military organization of Hungarian immigrants in Austria, and the Austrian delegation to Budapest distributed only food and medicine, not weapons.[87] In the face of these strong and unfounded attacks, the recommendation of the 'Austrian model' on the part of the Austrian government was ruled out at once. Peinsipp, however, let the *Ballhausplatz* know "that the broadcasts of Viennese Radio have been anything but helpful during these times."[88]

Pravda joined the official Hungarian criticism of Austria. It asked the question, "What are the obligations of a policy of neutrality?" and referred to an article that appeared in the 10 November issue of the ÖVP organ *Kleines Volksblatt* entitled "Neutralität des Staates - aber nicht des Herzens" ("Neutrality of the State - but Not of the Heart"), which could not have better described the Austrian position.[89]

After the bloody suppression of the Hungarian uprising and Imre Nagy's capitulation, Peinsipp "urgently" pointed out that Austria "should not demonstrate any friendly attitude" towards the present regime under János Kádár, as this would "in no way be understood" by the population. The envoy requested "a renewed, energetic protest to be lodged most decisively against the accusations put forth against Austria."[90]

Austria further suggested that the aid action be overseen by a coordination committee of the United Nations. Such a resolution found no strong resonance at the U.N.; however, its execution should be insisted upon "with all energy." Austria also ought to be represented in the committee. If not, then the rumors about Austria smuggling arms to Hungary under the cover of the Red Cross would be granted an apparent confirmation. According to the *Ballhausplatz,* this ought to be the task of states who were not part of any military alliance, such as Sweden, Austria, if need be Burma and Yugoslavia, "to help Hungary out of the chaos that today represents a certain threat for all neighboring countries."[91]

In a meeting with Leopold Figl and secretary general of the Austrian foreign office Josef Schöner on 19 November 1956, Soviet foreign minister Dmitri T. Shepilov asked of what sort of people the masses of refugees consisted and whether any of them wanted to return. Figl responded that it was mostly women and children. Those who wanted to return were not impeded, but thus far no one had wanted to return. Figl emphasized that neutrality had been strictly adhered to and would continue to be so in the future. That is why the Austrian authorities had also called upon Ferenc Nagy to leave the country immediately after his arrival. Shepilov had already been informed of that. The U.S.S.R. did not have the intention "to threaten Austria in any way." Austria's neutrality would be respected.[92]

In mid-November the military resistance of the Hungarian rebels was broken. Sixteen Soviet divisions now controlled the country. The Anglo-American-dominated West reacted only with empty words. To it, Hungary was plain and simply "within the zone of Soviet interest."[93] Not only did the "roll back advocates" leave the rebels fighting for freedom and democracy in the lurch, but they also had no interest in Hungary's destiny.[94] According to Ambassador Gruber, the only reason for the spectacular visit to Austria of U.S. Vice President Richard Nixon in December 1956 was that in the beginning of January 1957 the U.S. Congress would have to be asked for financial support for Hungary and thus a direct report based upon immediate, on-the-spot impressions and discussions with the Austrian government would make the granting of such support less difficult.[95]

The process of reducing tensions between Austria and Hungary that had begun in 1953/54 had all of a sudden been interrupted by the uprising, the Soviet intervention, and the coming to power of the Communist regime of Kádár. Neutrality proved to be a dangerous instrument for the destabilization of Communist rule. For Austria, its neutrality was still too new to be able to be evaluated reliably, let alone to be recommended to others. It was not yet ready for export,[96] which led to the maintenance of the *status quo ante*. The absence of the export of Austrian neutrality was closely linked to the establishment of the division of Europe and, with it, political defeat for Central Europe in 1955 and 1956.

9. Vienna's position toward the Hungarian uprising:
Austrian consequences

The author agrees with Thomas Schlesinger and Manfried Rauchensteiner that the events in Hungary in 1956 were the real test of Austrian neutrality on the first anniversary of the end of the occupation.[97] From the very beginning of the uprising, the federal government took reasonable care not to overstep the bounds of neutrality in any way that could be interpreted as an intent to influence, instigate, or further stimulate the Hungarian revolution. Vienna was in a very difficult position and under enormous pressure. What kind of interests did the Austrian government have? Six points must be mentioned:

First, Vienna had to keep in mind Soviet comments that were skeptical, critical, and then aggressive concerning the reaction of the mass media and the attitudes of political parties. The government could not do anything that might have provoked further aggression and had to do everything to prevent the danger of a violation of its neutrality and a Russian intervention.

Second, just before the outbreak of the events in Hungary, Austria had announced its application for ECSC-membership.[98] Thus, Vienna did not want to have further additional troubles with the U.S.S.R. at this time.

Third, the government had to look after the interests of the other three signatories of the State Treaty. The Western Powers, especially the Anglo-Americans were watching Austria's behavior toward the Hungarian crisis very carefully.[99]

Fourth, on the one hand, since Austrians and her politicians after 1945 were Western-oriented, they reacted sympathetically toward the Hungarian freedom fighters in the autumn of 1956.[100] On the other hand, Austria as a new member of the United Nations took the role of a neutral state in Europe but did not play the role of an indifferent neighbor regarding the Hungarian crisis. The general assembly adopted an Austrian draft resolution to provide U.N. humanitarian aid to Hungary and to enjoin all parties involved to cooperate with U.N. efforts to promote peace and to ease suffering there.

Fifth, the government had to keep in mind the mood of its own population. The Austrians initially reacted very optimistically. After the second Russian intervention, they were alarmed and somewhat frightened. Fears began to surface that Austria's borders and independence could be threatened.

Sixth, with regard to the waves of refugees—the total figure up to
September 1957 was 180,000—Austria tried to combine the need
to give expression to all these expectations and feelings with a
response resembling one element of Swiss neutrality: to give
humanitarian, social, medical, and moral support. Massive shipments of medicine, food, and clothing were organized via the
Austrian embassy in Budapest under the direction of Walter
Peinsipp.

With regard to the political dimension of the Hungarian crisis, the
concept of neutralizing Europe, which was recommended by officials of
Soviet diplomacy in 1955, produced negative effects for Moscow's
foreign policy. With respect to the uprising in Hungary in 1956, this
concept came to be seen as a dangerous threat that could destabilize the
entire system of Soviet satellite states.

10. "An extremely delicate problem":
Raab's radio-speech of 20 January 1957 and the Mikoyan visit

Austria was aware of the widespread effects that its neutrality
policy had for Central and Eastern Europe and was therefore afraid of
exporting its political status. Just as in the case of the German question
in 1955, it did not lay in Vienna's interest to recommend the 'Austrian
solution' for Hungary in 1956. Hoping to guarantee its own neutrality,
the political elite was nowhere close to recommending the 'Austrian
model' to the Hungarians. The country had no experience with its new
political status. Austria's neutrality was too young and too little rooted
in the political culture to serve as a well-developed export good.

The question as to whether Austria should support the Hungarian
claim for neutralization was not part of official statements in 1956.
There are two phases to be examined. In November and December 1956
Raab left the question open. And on 20 January 1957 he made a cautious
public statement. In a radio speech he added a few sentences: "The
proposal which was recently made, to adopt a kind of neutrality-status
for Hungary, has to be considered. This could lead the country on its
way to a pleasant future development."

In addition, it can be confirmed by material from the state archives
in Vienna that the Hungarians were stimulated by the Austrian solution
of 1955. The thesis of the 'model case' should neither be exaggerated
nor underestimated: the absence of Soviet troops on Eastern Austrian

soil created an attractive and promising idea of a Red Army troop withdrawal from the satellite nations. Austria's freedom caused a kind of psychological stimulus. However, in 1956, Austria was neither able nor willing to export its neutrality status to Central or Eastern Europe. Chancellor Raab remarked during the radio speech on 20 January "that any kind of neutrality would be gladly accepted by the Hungarian population. Neutrality would pave the way for calming down the situation at the demarcation line and would contribute to a political stabilization of Central Europe."[101] And Raab added:

Hungary borders directly on Austria, and any form of neutrality would surely be gladly accepted by the Hungarian people. However, the creation of a neutral state on both sides of the ideological line of demarcation, which was referred to in Churchill's speech at the time as an 'iron curtain', would certainly contribute considerably to a general calming in Central Europe, even more so since through such a construction nobody would have to feel that his security was threatened.[102]

Raab's speech of 20 January in which he proposed that Hungary be given "a type of neutral status," caused the Austrian envoy in Warsaw to attentively observe how his Polish dialogue partners would react. According to their assessment, the entirety of Raab's speech could be understood in the final paragraph, which included the following words: "Even though the present situation might seem turbulent, chaotic, and threatening to some people, I believe that the moment has arrived precisely now to look for a lasting and peaceful solution." These, at least, were the words of the Austrian chancellor. For Verosta, consequently, only one solution was possible: "A lasting and peaceful solution can only be reached when a still-to-be-defined part of Central Europe—and the current people's democracies absolutely must be considered as part of Central Europe—is released from the East and West blocs." Consequently, Verosta could only have meant a neutralization of Central Europe as a peaceful solution. It is difficult to imagine that Verosta would not have spoken to his Polish dialogue partners as instructed. Until such a solution was reached, the Russians would have to maintain their sphere of influence, even at the cost of high material and moral sacrifice. "The Russians also have to hold on to Hungary at all costs until there is a solution for all of Central Europe," Verosta analyzed.[103]

He accurately recognized that Western passivity was the decisive factor for the Soviet Union not being able to realize its real maximum Euro-political ideas:

> With the complete inaction of the West, there was nothing left for the time being for the Russians to do than to continue to pursue the strong arm policy in Hungary. The Poles are convinced that the Russians would also accept a Nagy-Kéthly government in Hungary if it were moderate, once the West got involved in discussions about Yalta and the final postwar structure of Europe, including the reunification of Germany. That remains to be seen.

For Verosta, a revision of Russia's Central Europe policy was not out of the question, rather it was definitely conceivable.[104]

According to another information, it was the U.S.S.R. itself that prevented the release of Hungary from the Warsaw Pact, as Alois Vollgruber, the Austrian ambassador to Paris, reported to Figl from Paris: "France would gladly welcome a Hungary that was somehow neutral, as it appears it would in general for all the states of Central Europe with the exception of Germany. But as the most recent events showed, Russia was not in the least inclined toward such a solution nor even considering it."[105]

In the run-up to the visit by deputy prime minister of the Soviet Union, Anastas Mikoyan, it was clear that the question of Austria's membership in the ECSC could not be a topic of conversation. However, a phrasing had been prepared to justify the acceptance of Austria in the Council of Europe the previous year. With regard to the Soviet position, Raab's secretary, Ludwig Steiner, pointed out:

> There are great worries about the unification of Europe into a common market. It doesn't matter what form this would take. They take for granted that Austrian membership could not occur without political consequences for its neutrality. Statements by Austrian politicians about a speedy Austrian membership in the common market, in a Free Trade Zone, or even in the ECSC, were always registered with great disapproval.

Considerations of a 'model case' were implicitly proposed by the Austrians, but "statements by the Russian dialogue partners have again and again left the impression that a really constructive solution of the German question is presently unthinkable, since it appears that at this point in time the Russians lack the necessary internal equilibrium and prestige to reach such a solution." In connection with the quoted statements by Raab, the future of Austrian neutrality and "a possible expansion to countries in the Danube area was also discussed. It is also clear here, however, that there are no constructive possibilities before the Hungarian events are fully digested."[106]

Moscow could not and would not react to Raab's trial balloon—was it still fixated on the German question or oriented toward global issues? In January 1957 the Austrian legation counselor in Paris, Franz Karasek, held a discussion with the legation secretary Radzig from the Russian embassy in Paris. After the usual, well-known accusations against Austria for its behavior during the Hungarian crisis, they both turned to more serious topics. Karasek asked what the reaction was on the part of the Soviets to Raab's suggestion "to grant Hungary a similar neutral status." Radzig answered that a Hungarian neutrality could only be addressed when problem number one in Europe, that is, the German question, had been resolved. Karasek went on to ask whether the Soviet Union would also agree to a reunification of Germany if this would entail that, after free elections, there would not be a Communist government but a democratic one, upon which his dialog partner replied that it would suffice if such a Germany would not participate in the Atlantic pact. Radzig pressed on: "To go even further, if the Atlantic pact were to be renounced, then the Soviet Union would even be moved to renounce the Warsaw Pact." Karasek stated in an unimpressed manner that this kind of argumentation made him assume that the Russian intervention in Hungary could be explained as "simply strategic." Radzig blurted out an affirmative response which he then corrected. He then returned to the subject of Austrian neutrality. It had shown that solutions could be reached with the Soviet Union if goodwill and consideration for the security concerns of the U.S.S.R. were present. Russia was, however, surrounded by the United States with atomic weapons and by military bases from Japan, the Philippines, the Baghdad Pact, SEATO, and NATO. The relationship with the Soviet Union could be no different if the fact of an armed Germany was stuck to. The U.S.S.R. could imagine allowing a reunified Germany with armed forces of approximately 200,000 soldiers. Such a Germany would have to exclude itself, "like Austria", from any military alliances.[107] Thus the Soviet representative had returned to the starting point of Karasek's question: the 'model case' of Austria was clearly meant for Germany for the time being, and seemingly applicable to Hungary only later. Was

Soviet policy once again getting in its own way? Those in the Kremlin were still too shocked by the crisis scenario in Poland and the people's uprising in Hungary. When Mikoyan visited Austria in April 1957 (he had already intended to visit the country in the autumn of 1956, but his trip to Vienna had to be postponed[108]), he referred to Raab's radio speech of 20 January. Mikoyan stated that Austria's neutrality status represents a "special case" and "under current circumstances is not repeatable."[109] This 'message' was not a surprise for the *Ballhausplatz.*

Nothing sensational was to be expected from the very beginning of the visit of the Hungarian satrap and his entourage to the rulers in Moscow—Peinsipp spoke of a "command to Kádár." The result was "the end of any hope for an evolution in this country which could gradually lead it out of slavery." The Austrian observer diagnosed a harsh setback with respect to the situation before the revolution, "since even under Rákosi, Communist cadres could at least show revisionist tendencies, which now were finally choked off or at least banned from any public debate." Peinsipp's summation was depressing:

> In summary, the results from Moscow mean nothing more than that Hungary has now become a satrapy of Moscow to an extent that did not even exist during Rákosi's times: administrated through mediocrity, which lacks any revolutionary facet, Moscow's parrot, its only quality being technicians of terror, and, what is most evil, they are so frightened that they themselves are glad to only have to play the roles of satraps, and if they behave well towards their ruler, they will enjoy his protection. It is no coincidence that the reconstruction of the Iron Curtain and the command from Moscow occurred at the same time.[110]

Had Moscow learned its lesson from the Austrian neutrality being, as the French diplomat François Seydoux or the U.S.-secretary of state John Foster Dulles referred to it, a Trojan horse for Central and Eastern Europe? With the Hungarian uprising and the brutal suppression of it, a neutralization of the country was out of the question for the U.S.S.R. "For the Russians, Hungary is the front and is treated according to special rules and principles, and above all else it is looked on with mistrust," Peinsipp reported in August 1957.[111]

At the end of August 1956 the Hungarian government had removed the Iron Curtain from the Western border of Hungarian territory. Peinsipp referred to the process of normalization, which had set in

between 1953 and 1956 between Hungary and Austria, and which was
brutally brought to a halt with the bloody autumn of 1956. When the
envoy let Vienna know "the sad fact that for the foreseeable future we
will no longer be in a position to influence the course of events and to
support them in accordance with our wishes, as we did in the previous
year up until 23 October," he made it understood that some influence
from Austria could not be completely discounted.[112]

The neutralization of Central Europe remained a Hungarian pipe
dream. The former finance minister (1945-1946) and final envoy of the
civic Hungarian postwar government in Bern, Franz Gordon, who many
years ago emigrated to Argentina, held the position that an "Austro-
Hungarian confederation based upon armed neutrality" would not only
be in the interest of both countries but also appeared to be a desirable
solution for the superpowers. Furthermore, it would offer the Soviet
Union the possibility "to finally give up the senseless occupation of
Hungary without the loss of prestige." Austria's ambassador to Buenos
Aires, Meinrad Falser, considered Gordon's ideas to be unrealistic. In
addition, with regard to Austrian neutrality, Falser made clear that for
the Austrian government "it may be impossible for the time being to
take any initiatives along this path before domestic and foreign policy
in Hungary do not undergo fundamental changes." Gordon wanted to get
to know important Austrian personalities in order to subsequently exert
his influence on the central leadership of Hungarian immigrants in the
United States. Falser once again made it clear that this was "an
extremely delicate problem."[113]

In a directive to Falser, the *Ballhausplatz* instructed him to exercise
"extreme restraint" with regard to the thoughts expressed by Gordon. If
the latter should bring up the topic again, the answer could be that "his
proposal had been forwarded on" and that "the competent authorities
had taken note of it."[114] In Vienna, the memory of the recommendation
by Mikoyan must have been fresh. In the event that the 'model case'
could not find an application in Hungary, Raab would try to apply it to
the German question.

11. Too late: Raab's proposal to use the 'Austrian Model' as a negotiation solution for the German question in 1958

In December 1957 a dialogue partner of the Soviet embassy in
Vienna raised the question to Ludwig Steiner "whether it were not
possible that Austria could *support* [italics in original] a peaceful
solution to the German problem. Austria and particularly the chancellor

have proven that they could come through the most difficult problems with the possibility of solution." Steiner answered that for Austria's part "it would be difficult to pursue an initiative on its own, but some kind of incentive should come from one of the two sides for it to mediate. Of course Austria is very interested in a reasonable solution to the German problem. Perhaps a discussion about this question is possible on the occasion of the chancellors visit." Steiner referred to signs of mutual trust (in Austria's case this was the abolition of the demarcation line, the permission to build the *Autobahn*, the solution of the peripheral communities question, etc.) in order to create "the necessary climate" for discussions. In the future Austria would not be lacking in goodwill.[115] Gruber, who at that time was special advisor to the International Atomic Energy Agency (IAEA) in Vienna, held talks soon thereafter with the Soviet disarmament specialist Samyatin, who asked about Austria's interest in a solution to the German question. In accordance with Raab's considerations, Gruber answered: "General interest in peaceful relations, detoxification of the dangerous German question, conviction that once Germany were at the negotiating table there would be the chance to diminish the problem in the course of the year and to solve it." Samyatin pointed out that the question of reunification was not a matter for the Four Powers but for the two German states. The Soviet Union, though, was ready to put "the preparation of a German peace treaty" on the agenda of the Four Power Conference and also would have nothing against the establishment of a Four Power Commission for that purpose. This information seemed to Gruber to be "significant," but it required "that the persons interested in this question [to] adapt their language to this circumstance." According to Samyatin, the Soviet Union currently wanted "to avoid anything [...] that would give the appearance that it was ready to sell out the East German government." Gruber further reported to Raab: "For the purpose of consideration, it is of course irrelevant which name this commission receives. Its founding would in any case represent decisive progress in international relations and would furthermore confirm and support your views."[116]

In April 1958 Raab let Khrushchev know that the Austrian government would welcome any initiative that "would bring about general understanding between the major powers concerning a moratorium on atomic tests." The U.S.S.R. had decided to temporarily and unilaterally cease tests of atomic and hydrogen bombs starting 31 March. Raab emphasized that "Austria had concretely demonstrated its readiness to actively contribute to the promotion of the peaceful use of atomic energy through the hosting of the International Atomic Energy Agency." He made simultaneous assurances that Austria was making the effort "within the framework of its possibilities to contribute at any time and everywhere to the systematic tearing down of international mistrust that unfortunately was too frequently present today, to reduce tension among the peoples, and to pave the way for a peaceful and flourishing coexistence of all peoples and nations." Raab referred to similar declarations already issued earlier by the Austrian government.[117]

Suggestions regarding possible chances of an Austrian solution for Germany had been inopportune before the integration of the Federal Republic of Germany into the Western defense system. Austria subsequently saw the solution of the German question coming less from its 'model case', that is, a neutralized Germany, than from negotiations leading to a Four Power solution, which should not exclude the possibility of a reunification of Germany. In internal deliberations such considerations were made, and they come to light with the "Raab plan."[118]

Raab presented the Austrian way as a model solution for resolving the German partition in the form of a mediation attempt in February 1958 between Bonn and Moscow on the basis of an expert commission at par. This commission was not to discuss more than a small number of clearly defined topics. The contacts went via Raab, Figl, Gruber, the German ambassador to Vienna, Carl-Hermann Mueller-Graaf, and the German minister for foreign affairs, Heinrich von Brentano. Possibly related to that was Adenauer's proposal for neutralizing the GDR in March 1958 in exchange for renouncing reunification. In May 1958 Raab once again suggested a Four Power Conference for the solution of the German question. According to Mueller-Graaf's opinion, the "Raab plan" concealed the idea of "bridging the gap between the Soviet claim for negotiating the question of 'two German states' and the German or Western refusal of such negotiations." This was the idea of Vienna's balancing policy between the blocs. According to Gruber's view, the Four Power Conference should not negotiate with official representatives but with "experts" from the FRG as well as from the GDR. It should further reach an agreement on some fundamental steps which should lead to reunification. The concrete idea was an electoral law to form a basis on which a constituent assembly would have had to be convened. This assembly—regardless of the further functioning of the two states—would have had to work out a joint constitution later on.

The necessity of an amnesty law was emphasized. This law was to grant amnesty to the rulers and the apparatus of the Soviet zone. In this way, "golden bridges should be built for the Soviet zone," obstacles should be removed, and Soviet appearance should be kept up. The mediation attempt was met with resistance in Bonn; the U.S.S.R. as well as the GDR also spoke clearly against this plan in public.[119] Thus, in 1958, there was no more chance for the 'model case'.

III. The End of an Illusion: Summary

Four important questions should be answered at this point: Could the 'Austrian solution' be seen as a 'model' for a normalized situation in Middle Europe or even a unified Europe? Was the Hungarian revolution conceivable without Austria's gained freedom in 1955?[120] What kind of effects did the Hungarian crisis have on Austria? Did the new conjuncture of Austria's neutrality have an influence on the country's attitude towards the applicability of the 'model case'?

To begin with, it must be pointed out that the idea of creating a neutral belt of states remained theory. Neutralizing Central Europe as a first step to weakening capitalism and strengthening socialism turned out to be counterproductive from Moscow's point of view: from the very beginning, neutralization concepts were connected with the risk of destabilizing Soviet communism and of weakening the U.S.S.R.'s position within the satellite system. Soviet representatives—especially those who favored the 'Austrian solution' of 1955—had to accept that the so called 'model case' was much more suited to acting like a Trojan Horse for their own political system than to weakening the positions of Adenauer and the West. The shot backfired. So in the long run, the non-applicability of the Austrian 'model case' served Western, American-capitalist interests. The Western 'policy of strength' was confirmed, although without offering a real alternative to the population of Eastern Europe. The 'roll back' philosophy excluded a mutual troop withdrawal from Europe. Thus, the defeat of the Hungarian revolution was a great victory for 'cold warriors' and for political *status quo*-oriented politicians.

Regarding the second question—whether the Hungarian revolution was conceivable without Austria's freedom of 1955—a distinction has to be made between general and Austro-specific aspects: the Hungarian uprising was part of the general development that began with the death of Stalin in 1953 and continued with Titoism spreading in Soviet

satellite states, unrest and disturbances caused by the lost soccer final of
the World Championship in 1954, the 'new look' of Soviet policy
("peaceful coexistence") under Khrushchev's leadership, high expectations connected with the "spirit of Geneva" in 1955,[121] and the demonstration of Western unity through German NATO-membership and the
foundation of the Western European Union (WEU). All these steps were
decisive for the blood bath in Budapest. The 'Austrian example'
represented at minimum a very great temptation and a strong attraction
for the political opposition of Rákosi as well as for malcontented
intellectuals and huge segments of the population. Vienna showed 'how
the Russians can be gotten rid of'. This represented a strong stimulation
to the people of Hungary, who wanted a political change.

To answer the third question about the effects the Hungarian crisis
had on Austria, ten points of interest can be mentioned:[122]

first, the opposition to strengthening the Austrian army was weakened,
and the need for an active defense force was established;[123]

second, tensions in the coalition government were reduced;[124]

third, the Communists were heavily attacked, isolated, and they finally
lost; in 1959 they did not get one single seat in the parliament;[125]

fourth, the two positions of 'neutrality' versus 'Western allegiance'
were brought closer together with a significant increase in value of
the former. The Swiss envoy observed the rapid change in how
Austrians themselves perceived the new foreign policy status:
What at that time was the price paid for regaining this sovereignty, that is, the neutrality of the country, is now virtually
regarded as a gift from heaven, since this neutrality of Austria,
according to widely held opinion, facilitates its historical role
as a mediator between East and West. However, this neutrality
does not prevent it from raising its voice for freedom and
justice and against the regime of terror which currently is
subjugating Hungary.[126]

fifth, Austria could play a very active role at an early stage in its
membership in the United Nations;

sixth, self-confidence and national pride were enhanced—thus, Austria's
management of the Hungarian crisis served to strengthen political
self-consciousness. Apart from 1955 (gaining national freedom),
1956 (defending the new political status) was another milestone for
the Austrian nation-building process after 1945. On 12 November
1956 the young diplomat Franz Karasek wrote to Raab about his
impressions of the events in Hungary:

When an Austrian thinks today how just a few years ago we ourselves had been the recipient of alms (from the UNRRA [United Nations Relief Rehabilitation Administration] to the Marshall Plan), Austrians should now be even more conscious of how prosperous they are. This is convincing proof of the prosperity which our country has achieved under the leadership of you and your staff. We could also finally show ourselves as givers to our poor neighbors in a situation of distress and thus feel even happier than during that time when we ourselves were on the receiving end.

Karasek also mentioned that "Austrian neutrality is politically an enormous point of attraction for the peoples in the Eastern prison," as was shown by the attempt of Nagy's government "to cling to neutrality as a sheet anchor;"[127]

seventh, Austria's own status was convincingly defended even though the people had not known what shortcomings in crisis management there had been. The military had made itself partially independent from politics. The feeling of being left alone was thus also present;

eighth, a Western guarantee for neutrality did not exist, but many verbal assurances were given to Austrian diplomatic representatives that a violation of Austria's territorial integrity would mean World War III;

ninth, there was a stronger awareness of the necessity of an Austrian policy toward Central Europe and the East. All of a sudden, Austria was much more conscious of the existence of Central European neighbors. Up until then, no noteworthy contact with these countries had existed, and Austria had been isolated, almost cut;

tenth, the further development of neutrality as a 'model' for this area appeared as a thinkable if not a necessary consequence.

To answer the last question raised at the beginning of this summary, 'Austrian solutions', that is, the political aims and diplomatic methods of Raab, Figl, Kreisky, etc. in the spring of 1955, which had become possible through the consent between the ÖVP and the SPÖ, could definitely (theoretically) have served, easing a path for negotiations, as a model for the solution of the German or the Hungarian question. This is indirectly confirmed by fears and/or hopes that were repeatedly voiced by respected Western diplomats and politicians especially concerning possible results. When the 'Austrian solution' became known the German chancellor rejected the idea of creating a neutral belt categorically. Konrad Adenauer, one of the strongest allies of the Americans in Western Europe, feared that this would be the end not only of Germany but of the entire continent as well.[128] The Austrian miracle provoked his hysterical reaction. In contrast to Adenauer, Hungarian politicians, especially Imre Nagy, were eager to get the Austrian status of neutrality.

It was not so much the basic position, that is, the alleged or real incomparability of the questions, that made attempts such as establishing direct contacts with the Kremlin before fixing the status of the FRG or the political status of Hungary impossible. Rather, concrete political interests and a lack of preparation and readiness on the part of decision makers in Austria, in the East and the West, caused their failure. In this way, Raab overestimated in 1958 the possibility of presenting the Austrian way of dealing with the U.S.S.R. and of his country serving as a mediator and 'model' for the solution of the German question. The chances to bring itself in as an active builder of confidence were only minimal. No détente existed in the second half of the 1950s such as there was in the 1970s.

Oliver Rathkolb[129] has already brought up the question of whether Austria's policy toward the East in the 1950s and 1960s was that of an honest broker or that of a double agent. The overall situation did not appear to be so clear-cut to the *Ballhausplatz* diplomats, who thought that there was not necessarily and not always a clear contradiction between these two extreme points of view. I think, Vienna did both. Austria was economically and politically Western-oriented and concerning its *Ostpolitik* backed by the West and secured by NATO. With regard to Hungary, Austrian foreign policy was positioned to carry out a normalization of relations as far as cautious rapprochment. In this way, it indirectly contributed to a destabilization of the Rákosi regime. In general Austria's maneuvering room was limited, though. However much Vienna tried to pursue an active neutrality policy with strong humanitarian aspects within the context of the Hungarian crisis[130] and the mass upheaval in the neighboring country, recommendation for an application of its own status was denied. In 1955-56 Austria had not yet progressed to the point that it could recommend itself as a 'model'. In 1957-58 this changed: especially Raab tried to play a role as honest broker but with limited success. Raab and the *Ballhausplatz* had partly been prevented from doing so and partly hesitated on its own, recognizing the futility of the endeavor. A necessary reduction in tensions of the political situation in Central Europe in the second half of the 1950s by means of a neutrality solution, which would bring about an understanding between East and West, was not really possible, let alone desired.

Notes

1. See for this and the following remarks Peter Gosztony, "Der Volksaufstand in Ungarn 1956. Eine Nation wehrt sich gegen die sowjetische Diktatur," *Aus Politik und Zeitgeschichte* B 37-38 (6 September 1996): 3-14; idem, "Neue Dokumente zum Ungarnaufstand 1956," *Neue Zürcher Zeitung*, 24/25 October 1993, no. 247, 7; also the different bulletins and working papers published by the Cold War History Project (CWHP) of the Woodrow Wilson International Center for Scholars in Washington, especially Csaba Békés, "The 1956 Hungarian Revolution and World Politics" (working paper no. 16 of the CWHP), Washington 1996, 30 pages.

2. See Christoph Kleßmann and Bernd Stöver "Das Krisenjahr 1953 und der 17. Juni in der DDR in der historischen Forschung," as well as the contributions by Christian F. Ostermann, Michael Lemke, and Klaus Larres in Christoph Kleßmann and Bernd Stöver, eds., *1953 – Krisenjahr des Kalten Krieges in Europa,* Zentrum für Zeithistorische Forschung Potsdam, Zeithistorische Studien, vol. 16 (Cologne: Böhlau, 1999), 9-28, 115-139, 141-154, 155-179.

3. See Rainer Eger, *Krisen an Österreichs Grenzen. Das Verhalten Österreichs während des Ungarnaufstandes 1956 und der tschechoslowakischen Krise 1968. Ein Vergleich* (Vienna: Herold, 1981), 15-20; see the different contributions on Poland by Antoni Dudek, on the Polish October by A. Orlow, on Hungary and the U.S.S.R. by Walentin A. Pronko, and on the Hungarian Revolution and the Great Powers by Csaba Békés in Winfried Heinemann and Norbert Wiggershaus, eds., *Das internationale Krisenjahr 1956, Polen, Ungarn, Suez,* Militärgeschichtliches Forschungsamt, Beiträge zur Militärgeschichte, vol. 48 (Munich: Oldenbourg, 1999), 27-42, 43-57, 75-94, 353-374.

4. See Günter Bischof and Saki Dockrill, eds., cold war *Respite: The Geneva Summit of 1955* (Baton Rouge, LA), 2000 forthcoming.

5. "Depesche" Zl. 20770, 1 November 1956, Österreichisches Staatsarchiv (ÖStA), Kriegsarchiv (KA), Nachlaß Josef Schöner E/1773: 214-221, Mappe 216.

6. For the text of Nagy's declaration of neutrality see Paul Zinner, ed., *National Communism and Popular Revolt in Eastern Europe: A Selection of Documents on Events in Poland and Hungary, February-November 1956* (New York: Columbia University Press, 1956), 463-464.

7. Email from Günter Bischof to the author, 29 December 1999; see also Günter Bischof, "Österreichische Neutralität. Die deutsche Frage und europäische Sicherheit 1953-1955," in *Die doppelte Eindämmung. Europäische Sicherheit und deutsche Frage in den Fünfzigern,* ed. Rolf Steininger et al., Tutzinger Schriften zur Politik 2 (Munich: V. Hase & Koehler, 1993), 163-164.

8. In order to give answers to all these aspects, documents from the Austrian state archive, which have never before been systematically assembled, will be utilized. This article is part of a bigger working project by the author about "The Hungarian Crisis 1953-58."

9. Vojtech Mastny, "Kremlin Politics and the Austrian Settlement," *Problems of Communism* (July-August 1982), 37-51; the master work on the history of the State Treaty is Gerald Stourzh, *Um Einheit und Freiheit. Staatsvertrag, Neutralität und das Ende der Ost-West-Besetzung Österreichs 1945-1955,* 4th ed., Studien zu Politik und

Verwaltung, vol. 62 (Vienna: Böhlau, 1998), 487-578; for a more recent work, which is stronger from the international perspective than Stourzh see Günter Bischof, *Austria in the First Cold War, 1945-55. The Leverage of the Weak,* Cold War History Series (London: Macmillan Press, 1999), 142-149.

10. See Mihály Fülöp, *La paix inachevée. Le Conseil des Ministres des Affaires Étrangères et le traité de paix avec la Hongrie (1947),* Association des Sciences Historiques de Hongrie (Budapest: Presses de Neotipp SCN, 1998), 359-371.

11. Report Zl. 9-Pol/56, "Ungarn und die Sowjetunion," Braunias to Figl, 6 January 1956, Österreichisches Staatsarchiv (ÖStA), Archiv der Republik (AdR), Bundeskanzleramt/Auswärtige Angelegenheiten (BKA/AA), II-pol, Ungarn-2, Zl. 511.192-Pol/56.

12. Ibid.

13. Report Zl. 31-pol/55, Braunias to Figl, 31 March 1955, ÖStA, AdR, BKA/AA, II-pol, Ungarn 2, Zl. 319.156-pol/55 (GZl. 321.061-pol/55).

14. Report Zl. 69-pol/54, Rességuier to Figl, 29 December 1954, Ibid., Zl. 319.156-pol/54.

15. "Amtsvermerk," 18 August 1955, Ibid., Zl. 324.298-pol/55 (GZl. 324.298-pol/55).

16. Report Zl. 321-pol/55, "Die Rede des Herrn Bundeskanzlers im Nationalrat," Braunias to Figl, 3 November 1955, Ibid., Zl. 320.705-pol/55 (GZl. 325.932-pol/55).

17. Report Zl. 5-Pol/56, "Neujahrsempfang beim Staatsoberhaupt," Braunias to Figl, 12 January 1956, ÖStA, AdR, BKA/AA, II-pol, Ungarn-1, Zl. 511.195-Pol/56.

18. Report Zl. 21-pol/56, "Zur Normalisierung der österreichisch-ungarischen Beziehungen," Braunias to Figl, 21 January 1956, ÖStA, AdR, BKA/AA, II-pol, Ungarn 2, Zl. 511.368-pol/56 (GZl. 511.049-pol/56).

19. Ibid.; Eger, *Krisen an Österreichs Grenzen*, 29.

20. Peter Haslinger, *Hundert Jahre Nachbarschaft. Die Beziehungen zwischen Österreich und Ungarn 1895-1994* (Frankfurt am Main: Lang, 1996), 239-240; see also Felix Butschek, "EC-membership and the `Velvet´ Revolution: The Impact of Recent Political Changes on Austria's Economic Position in Europe," in *Contemporary Austrian Studies*, vol. 1, *Austria in the New Europe*, ed. Günter Bischof and Anton Pelinka (New Brunswick: Transaction Publishers, 1993), appendixes 1-3, 76-78.

21. Report Zl. 21-pol/56, "Zur Normalisierung der österreichisch-ungarischen Beziehungen," Braunias to Figl, 21 January 1956 plus "Beilage", ÖStA, AdR, BKA/AA, II-pol, Ungarn 2, Zl. 511.368-pol/56 (GZl. 511.049-pol/56). The official version states Hungary was the tenth country.

22. For the latest account about this topic see Michael Gehler, "Österreich und die deutsche Frage 1954/55: Zur`Modellfall´-Debatte in der internationalen Diplomatie und der bundesdeutschen Öffentlichkeit aus französischer Sicht," in *20. Österreichischer Historikertag*, Bregenz 1994, Tagungsbericht (Vienna: Verband Österreichischer Historiker und Geschichtsvereine/Österreichisches Staatsarchiv, 1998), 118-123.

23. Report Zl. 126-pol/55, Braunias to Figl, 23 June 1955, ÖStA, AdR, BKA/AA, II-pol, Ungarn 3, Zl. 323.397-pol/55 (GZl. 322.857-pol/55).

24. Report Zl. 385-Pol/55, "Ungarns Innenpolitik im Jahre 1955," Braunias to Figl, 31 December 1955, ÖStA, AdR, BKA/AA, II-pol, Ungarn 3, Zl. 511.197-pol/56 (GZl. 511.190-pol/56).

25. Ibid.

26. Report Zl. 10-Pol/56, "Zwischen Verzweiflung und Hoffnung," Braunias to Figl, 7 January 1956, ÖStA, AdR, BKA/AA, II-pol, Ungarn 3, (GZl. 511.190-pol/56); see also Manfried Rauchensteiner, *Die Zwei. Die Große Koalition in Österreich 1945-1966* (Vienna: Österreichischer Bundesverlag, 1987), 336; Paul Lendvai, *Die Ungarn. Ein Jahrtausend Sieger in Niederlagen*, (Munich: Bertelsmann, 1999), 112-124, 254-293.

27. Report Zl. 105-Pol/56, "Einladung einer österreichischen Parlamentsdelegation nach Ungarn," Peinsipp to Figl, 19 July 1956, ÖStA, AdR, BKA/AA, II-pol, Ungarn 1, Zl. 517.199-pol/56 (GZl. 511.957-pol/56).

28. Letter Figl to Hurdes, 13 October 1956, ÖStA, AdR, BKA, II-pol, Ungarn 2, Zl. 519.106-Pol/56 (GZl. 511.957-Pol/56); Eger, *Krisen an Österreichs Grenzen*, 29.

29. "Akte," "Einladung einer österreichischen Parlamentsdelegation nach Ungarn," ÖStA, AdR, BKA/AA, II-pol, Ungarn 2, Zl. 520.935-Pol/56 (Zl. 511.957-pol/56).

30. János M. Rainer, "Demokratievorstellungen in der Ungarischen Revolution 1956," *Österreichische Zeitschrift für Geschichtswissenschaften* 2, no. 4 (1991): 119-121.

31. "Rundschreiben" by the BKA/AA, "Die Opposition gegen Rákosi," 23 July 1956, ÖStA, AdR, BKA/AA, II-pol, Ungarn 2, Zl. 516.510-Pol/56.

32. Report Zl. 29-Pol/56, "Horváth, Imre, Ernennung zum ungarischen Außenminister," Falser to Figl, 1 August 1956, ÖStA, AdR, BKA/AA, II-pol, Ungarn 2, Zl. 517.377-pol/56 (GZl. 511.721-pol/56).

33. Copy of the report Zl. 123-pol/56, Peinsipp to Figl, 24 November 1956, Ibid., Zl. 791.077-pol/56.

34. Secret report Zl. 110-Pol/56, "Das Interview des Herrn Bundeskanzlers an Szabad Nép," Peinsipp to Figl, 21 September 1956, ÖStA, AdR, BKA/AA, II-pol, Ungarn 1, Zl. 518.691-pol/56 (GZl. 511.049-pol/56).

35. See György Litván and János M. Bak, eds., *Die Ungarische Revolution 1956. Reform, Aufstand, Vergeltung* (Vienna: Passagen Verlag, 1994), 50-57.

36. Report Zl. 116-Pol/56, "Nochmals der Fall Imre Nagy," Peinsipp to Figl, 17 October 1956, ÖStA, AdR, BKA/AA, II-pol, Ungarn 3, Zl. 519.385-pol/56 (GZl. 511.190-pol/56); Haslinger, *Die Beziehungen zwischen Österreich und Ungarn*, 241.

37. Report Zl. 40-pol/56, "Österreichisch-ungarische Beziehungen; Gespräch mit dem ungarischen Gesandten in Brüssel," Fuchs to Figl, 18 October 1956, ÖStA, AdR, BKA/AA, II-pol, Ungarn 1, Zl. 519.668-pol/56 (GZl. 511.049-pol/56).

38. See Gosztony, "Der Volksaufstand in Ungarn 1956," 6-12.

39. "Verschlußakt," "Ungarischer Aufstand, Situationsbericht LS Dr. Liksch vom 30. Oktober," Vienna, 19 November 1956, ÖStA, AdR, BKA/AA, II-pol, Ungarn 3 A, Akt Zl. 520.736-pol/56 (GZl. 511.190-pol/56); Rainer, "Demokratievorstellungen," 122; György Litván, "Die ungarische Revolution," in *Das internationale Krisenjahr 1956*, ed. Heinemann and Wiggershaus, 154-156.

40. Ibid. ("Verschlußakt," "Ungarischer Aufstand").

41. Ibid.

42. Ibid.

43. Ibid.

44. For a very good account see Eger, *Krisen an Österreichs Grenzen*, 31-72.

45. Ibid.

46. François Seydoux to the Quai d'Orsay, 4 July 1955, Ministère des Affaires Étrangères (MAE), Paris, Série Europe 1944-1960, vol. 30, fol. 205-206; see also Michael Gehler, "'L'unique objectif des Soviétiques est de viser l'Allemagne'. Staatsvertrag und Neutralität 1955 als `Modell' für Deutschland?," *Österreich in den Fünfzigern*, ed. Thomas Albrich et al., Innsbrucker Forschungen zur Zeitgeschichte 11 (Innsbruck: Studienverlag, 1995), 270-272.

47. This aspect was not reflected by Stourzh, *Um Einheit und Freiheit*, 494.

48. Julius Raab to Karl Gruber, 2 November 1956, Archiv des Julius Raab-Gedenkvereins (AJRGV), Vienna, Karton Außenpolitik. Raab wrote to Gruber: "Wir haben jetzt infolge der Ereignisse in Ungarn nicht sehr angenehme Zeiten, doch hoffe ich, daß schließlich und endlich alles gut ausgehen wird und Ungarn seine Freiheit bekommt."

49. "Telegramm in claris und Verbalnote," "Lage in Ungarn, Appell an die Sowjetregierung," 28 October 1956, ÖStA, AdR, BKA/AA, II-pol, Ungarn 3, Akt Zl. 519.625-pol/56 (GZl. 511.049-pol/56); "Abschrift," "Gegenwärtige Lage in Ungarn und die sich dadurch ergebende Situation an der Grenze für Österreich, Appell d. Bundesregierung," Ibid., Zl. 519.872 (GZl. 511.190-pol/56); and report Haymerle to Peinsipp, 31 October 1956, Ibid., Zl. 519.736-pol/56 (GZl. 511.190-pol/56); see also Rauchensteiner, *Die Zwei*, 341.

50. "Telegramm in Ziffern," 28 October 1956, Ibid.

51. "Depesche" by the BKA/AA, Zl. 50981 "Abschrift für Abt. Pol." concerning "Behauptete Verletzung der Neutralität durch Österreich; Information der Botschaft Moskau," ÖStA, AdR, BKA/AA, II-pol, Ungarn 3 C; see also Manfred Rauchensteiner, *Spätherbst 1956. Die Neutralität auf dem Prüfstand*, Eine Veröffentlichung des Heeresgeschichtlichen Museums (Vienna: Österreichischer Bundesverlag, 1981), 22-51.

52. "Vertraulicher Aktenvermerk," Platzer, 28 October 1956, ÖStA, AdR, BKA/AA, II-pol, Ungarn 3 C, Zl. 519.701-pol/56 (GZl. 511.190-pol/56).

53. "Telegramm in Ziffern," Zl. 88150, 29-30 October 1956, ibid.

54. See Békés, "The 1956 Hungarian Revolution and World Politics;" Heinemann and Wiggershaus, eds., *Das internationale Krisenjahr 1956*; and the useful conference report by Wolfram Kaiser, "Die internationale Politik während des Ungarnaufstandes 1956. Neue Forschungsergebnisse," in *Deutschland Archiv* 30, no. 1, (1997): 130-133.

55. "Information für den Herrn Bundesminister betreff 'Beabsichtigte Ungarndebatte im Parlament'," 30 October 1956, ÖStA, AdR, BKA/AA, II-pol, Ungarn 3, Zl. 519.696-pol/56 (GZl. 511.190-pol/56).

56. Report Zl. 11-pol/56, Karl Gruber to Leopold Figl, 3 November 1956, ÖStA, AdR, BKA/AA, II-pol, Pol. Berichte 1956; for a reference to the refugees as a security-problem see Oliver Rathkolb, *Washington ruft Wien. US-Großmachtpolitik und Österreich 1953-1963. Mit Exkursen zu CIA-Waffenlagern, NATO-Connection, Neutralitätsdebatte* (Vienna: Böhlau, 1997), 158.

57. See the figure of 18,000 by Eduard Stanek, *Verfolgt, Verjagd, Vertrieben. Flüchtlinge in Österreich von 1945-1984* (Vienna: Europaverlag, 1985), 72; Brigitta Zierer, "Willkommene Ungarnflüchtlinge 1956?," in *Asyland wider Willen. Flüchtlinge in Österreich im europäischen Kontext seit 1914,* ed. Gernot Heiss and Oliver Rathkolb (Vienna: Picus, 1995), 157-172.

58. Haslinger, *Hundert Jahre Nachbarschaft*, 243-244.

59. "Depesche" Bischoff, Zl. 20862, 18 November 1956, ÖStA, AdR, BKA/AA, II-pol, Ungarn 3 C, Zl. 520.644-pol/56 (GZl. 511.190-pol/56).

60. "Pressemeldung," Washington UP, 8 November 1956, referring to the Washington Post, 7 November 1956; "Amtsvermerk," 26 November 1956, ÖStA, AdR, BKA/AA, II-pol, Ungarn 3 C, Zl. 520.881-pol/56 (GZl. 511.190-pol/56); The declaration of the U.S. State Department said, according to an Austrian source: "Die Vereinigten Staaten haben den neutralen Charakter Österreichs geachtet und werden ihn auch weiter achten; sie sind der Ansicht, daß die Verletzung der territorialen Integrität oder der inneren Souveränität Österreichs natürlich eine ernste Bedrohung des Friedens bedeuten würde;" "Fernschreiben Austroamb Paris," Zl. 16.947-A/56 (Zl. 520.011-Pol/56), ibid.; see also Rauchensteiner, *Die Zwei*, 347.

61. "Einlageblatt zu Zl. 520.006-Pol/56," "Austroamb Paris zu FS Zahl 10247" and 10249 (without date), ibid.

62. Report Zl. 44-Pol/56 "Gespräch mit dem belgischen Außenminister und mit dem Generalsekretär für die Auswärtigen Angelegenheiten über die internationale Lage," Fuchs to Figl, 9 November 1956, ÖStA, AdR, BKA/AA, II-pol, Ungarn 3 C, Pol-Berichte; see also Gosztony, "Der Volksaufstand in Ungarn 1956," 10.

63. Report Zl. 44-Pol/56, ibid.

64. "Amtsvermerk" by Legation Counselor Franz Karasek, 9 November 1956, ÖStA, AdR, BKA/AA, Pol-Berichte.

65. Report Verosta to Figl, 30 October 1956, ibid. (folder Warsaw).

66. Report Zl. 38-Pol/56 "Die Tragödie in Ungarn und die Polen," Verosta to Figl, 8 November 1956, ÖStA, AdR, BKA/AA, II-pol, Ungarn 3, Zl. 520.284-pol/56; see also Mark Kramer, "The Soviet Union and the 1956 Crises in Hungary and Poland: Reassessments and New Findings," *Journal of Contemporary History,* vol. 33, no. 2 (April 1998): 163-214; concerning Nagy see Johanna Granville, "Imre Nagy. Hesitant Revolutionary," *CWIH-Bulletin,* issue 5 (Spring 1995): 23, 27-28.

67. Ibid.; Lendvai, *Die Ungarn*, 254-274, 317-335.

68. Ibid. (Report Zl. 38-Pol/56 "Die Tragödie in Ungarn und die Polen.")

69. "Depesche" Bischoff/Moscow, Zl. 20815, 8 November 1956, ÖStA, AdR, BKA/AA, II-pol, Ungarn 3 A, Zl. 791.227-pol/56 (GZl. 511.190-pol/56).

70. Report Zl. 58/p, "Zu den Ereignissen in Ungarn. - Eine vorläufige Bilanz," Bischoff to Figl, 12 November 1956, ÖStA, AdR, BKA/AA, II-pol, Ungarn 3 A, Zl. 791.437-pol/56 (GZl. 511.190-pol/56).

71. Ibid.

72. Report Zl. 85-Pol/56, Wodak to Figl, 11 December 1956, ÖStA, AdR, BKA/AA, II-pol, Ungarn 3 A, Zl. 792.056-pol/56 (GZl. 511.190-pol/56); for a different attitude see Gosztony, "Der Volksaufstand in Ungarn 1956," 10-11; for a differentiated view see Vladislav Zubok and Constantine Pleshakov, *Inside the Kremlin's Cold War. From Stalin to Khrushchev* (Cambridge: Harvard University Press, 1996), 182-188, here 186-187; John Lewis Gaddis, *We now know. Rethinking Cold War History* (Oxford: Clarendon Press, 1997), 207, 210-211.

73. Éva Gál, et al., eds. *A "Jelcin-dosszié." Szovjet dokumentumok 1956-ról. (The Yeltsin File. Soviet Documents on 1956)* (Budapest: Századvég K. – 1956-os Intézet, 1993).

74. See Gosztony, "Neue Dokumente zum Ungarnaufstand 1956," 7; Kramer, "The Soviet Union," 188-190; Wilfried Loth, *Helsinki, 1. August 1975. Entspannung und Abrüstung, 20 Tage im 20. Jahrhundert*, ed. by Norbert Frei, Klaus-Dietmar Henke, and

Hans Woller (Munich: Deutscher Taschenbuch Verlag, 1998), 59; see also Igor V. Lebedev, "The Archives of the Ministry of Foreign Affairs of Russia as a Source of Open Documentation on the ´Double Crisis of 1956´," in *Diplomatic Sources and International Crises. Proceedings of the 4th Conference of Editors of Diplomatic Documents,* comp. Leopold Nuti, Ministero degli Affari Esteri, Commissione per il Riordinamento e la Pubblicazione dei Documenti Diplomatici, (Roma: Istituto Poligrafico e zecca dello stato, 1998), 159-163.

75. Rauchensteiner, *Spätherbst,* 22-30, 31-34; Norbert Sinn, *Schutz der Grenzen. Der Sicherungseinsatz des Österreichischen Bundesheeres an der Staatsgrenze zu Ungarn im Oktober und November 1956* (Graz: austrian medien service, 1996), 37-40, 65-69; Klaus Eisterer, "Die Schweiz und die österreichische Neutralität 1955/56," in *Österreich in den Fünfzigern,* ed. Thomas Albrich et al., 317-319.

76. "Amtsvermerk," 30 October 1956, ÖStA, AdR, BKA/AA, II-pol, Ungarn 3, Zl. 519.722-pol/56 (GZl. 511.190-pol/56).

77. Escher to Eidgenössisches Politisches Department, 30 October 1956, Bundesarchiv Bern (BAR), E 2300 Wien, Bd. 58-60.

78. See Document Nr. 3 ("Text der österreichischen Resolution zur Hilfeleistung für Ungarn"), in Eger, *Krisen an Österreichs Grenzen,* 192.

79. Report of a telephone conversation Haymerle-Molden/Balvany, 11 November 1956, ÖStA, AdR, BKA/AA, II-pol, Ungarn 3, Zl. 520.207-Pol/56 (GZl. 511.190-pol/56).

80. See Thomas Angerer, "Integrität vor Integration. Österreich und 'Europa' aus französischer Sicht 1949-1960," in *Österreich und die europäische Integration 1945-1993. Aspekte einer wechselvollen Entwicklung,* ed. Michael Gehler and Rolf Steininger, Institut für Zeitgeschichte der Universität Innsbruck, Arbeitskreis Europäische Integration, Historische Forschungen, Veröffentlichungen 1 (Vienna: Böhlau, 1993), 193-194.

81. *Archiv der Gegenwart,* 12 February 1957, 6256-6257.

82. Fritz Weber, "Austria. A Special Case in European Economic Integration?," in *Explorations in OEEC History,* ed. Richard T. Griffiths, OECD Historical Series (Paris: OECD, 1997), 55.

83. Thomas Angerer, "Exklusivität und Selbstausschließung. Integrationsgeschichtliche Überlegungen zur Erweiterungsfrage am Beispiel Frankreichs und Österreichs," *L'Élargissement de l'Union Européenne. Actes du Colloque Franco-Autrichien Organisé les 13 et 14 juin 1997 par l'Institut Culturel Autrichien et l'Institut Pierre-Renouvin, Revue d'Europe Centrale* 6, no. 1 (1998): 41-46.

84. "Informationen für Herrn Bundeskanzler betreffend Mac-Millan-Plan der Schaffung einer europäischen Freihandelszone," Johann Augenthaler to Julius Raab, 29 October 1956, AJRGV, Sonderakten.

85. Angerer, "Exklusivität und Selbstausschließung," 42-43.

86. "Akte," "Telephongespräch mit der Gesandtschaft Budapest seit der zweiten russischen Intervention," 14 November 1956, ÖStA, AdR, BKA/AA, II-pol, Ungarn 3 A, Zl. 520.419-pol/56 (GZl. 511.190-pol/56).

87. "Behauptete Neutralitätsverletzung durch Österreich, Information des H. Bundesministers, Pressemeldung durch APA New York," 5 December 1956, ibid., Zl. 520.659-pol/56 (511.190-pol/56).

88. Akte "Telephongespräch."

89. "Abschrift der Information des BMfI, Abteilung 2, Fernschreiben, Nr. 72," 15 November 1956, ÖStA, AdR, BKA/AA, II-pol, Ungarn 1.

90. "Amtsvermerk," "Lage in Budapest," 15 November 1956, ÖStA, AdR, BKA/AA, II-pol, Ungarn 3 A, Zl. 520.439-pol/56 (GZl. 511.190-pol/56).

91. "Akt," "Derzeitige Lage Ungarns; Information an den Herrn Bundesminister," 17 November 1956; "Telegramm" Zl. 58045, ÖStA, AdR, BKA/AA, II-pol, Ungarn 3 A, Zl. 520.595 pol/56 (GZl. 511.190-pol/56).

92. "Telegramm Austroamb Moscow 58070," 5 December 1956, ibid., Zl. 791.503-pol/56 (GZl. 511.190-Pol/56).

93. Hannah Arendt, *Die ungarische Revolution und der totalitäre Imperialismus* (Munich: Piper, 1958); see also idem, "Konnte der Westen in Ungarn eingreifen?," *Die Welt*, 20 September 1958, no. 219.

94. Gosztony, "Der Volksaufstand in Ungarn 1956," 11-12; see also Sándor Kopácsi, *Die ungarische Tragödie. Wie der Aufstand von 1956 liquidiert wurde* (Stuttgart: Deutsche Verlagsanstalt, 1979); László Borhi, Rollback, Liberation, Containment, or Inaction? U.S. Policy and Eastern Europe in the 1950s, *Journal of Cold War Studies*, Vol. 1 (Fall 1999), No. 3, 67-110.

95. "Depesche" Gruber/Washington to Vienna Nr. 28076, 10 December 1956, ÖStA, AdR, BKA/AA, II-pol, Zl. 791.705-pol/56.

96. Rauchensteiner, *Die Zwei*, 337, 351-352.

97. Thomas O. Schlesinger, *Austrian Neutrality in Postwar Europe. The Domestic Roots of a Foreign Policy* (Vienna, Stuttgart: Wilhelm Braumüller, 1972), 34-52; Rauchensteiner, *Spätherbst 1956*, 101-108.

98. See Angerer, "Integrität vor Integration," 193-194; more recently Angerer, "Exklusivität und Selbstausschließung," 41-46.

99. See for example Rathkolb, *Washington ruft Wien*, 157.

100. See for example Fritz Molden and Eugen Géza Pogany, *Ungarns Freiheitskampf* (Molden: Vienna: Molden, 1956).

101. Rauchensteiner, *Die Zwei*, 352.

102. Rauchensteiner, *Spätherbst 1956*, 107.

103. Report Zl. 28-pol/57, "Gomulkas Botschaft zum ungarischen Nationalfeiertag," by Verosta to Figl, 19 March 1957, ÖStA, AdR, BKA/AA, II-pol, Zl. 218.853-pol/57 (GZl. 215.393-pol/57).

104. Report Zl. 8-pol/57 Verosta to Figl, 19 November 1957, ibid., Zl. 216.075-pol/57 (ibid.).

105. Report Zl. 83-pol/56, Alois Vollgruber to Leopold Figl, 18 December 1956, ÖStA, AdR, BKA/AA, II-pol, Pol-Berichte.

106. Report Ludwig Steiner ad. Zl. 219.187-pol/57, 13 April 1957, Archiv des Karl-von-Vogelsang-Instituts (AKVI), Vienna, Deposit Mikojan-Besuch.

107. "Aktenvermerk" Zl. 10-Pol/57, Vollgruber to Figl, 29 January 1957, ÖStA, AdR, BKA/AA, II-pol Zl. 216.654-pol/57 (GZl. 215.393-pol/57).

108. Rainer Eger is absolutely right when arguing, that the Austro-Soviet-relations finally did not suffer from the events in Hungary: see Eger, *Krisen an Österreichs Grenzen*, 57-58; Rauchensteiner, *Die Zwei*, 338-339.

109. Rauchensteiner, *Spätherbst 1956*, 108.

110. Report Zl. 27-pol/57, "Die Befehlsausgabe an Kadar in Moskau," Peinsipp to Figl, 17 April 1957, ÖStA, AdR, BKA/AA, II-pol 1957, Zl. 219.502-pol/57 (GZl. 215.393-pol/57); Gosztony, "Neue Dokumente zum Ungarnaufstand 1956," 7.

111. Peinsipp to Figl, 2 August 1957, Ibid., Zl. 223.161-pol/57 (GZl. 215.394-pol/57).

112. Report Zl. 27-pol/57,"Die Befehlsausgabe an Kadar in Moskau."

113. Report Zl. 50-pol/57, "Finanzminister und Gesandter a.D. Dr. Franz Gordon zur Frage einer künftigen österreichisch-ungarischen Zusammenarbeit," Falser to Figl, 27 July 1957, ÖStA, AdR, BKA/AA, II-pol 1957, Zl. 223.129-pol/57 (GZl. 217.022-pol/57).

114. "Weisung" Zl. 223.129-pol/57 to Ambassador Falser, 24 September 1957, ibid.

115. "Notiz Dr. St. [Steiner]," 19 December 1957, Archiv des Julius-Raab-Gedenkvereins (AJRGV), Vienna, Karton 170, "Staatsbesuch d. HBK Moskau 1958."

116. Gruber (Privat) to Raab, without date [spring 1958], ibid.

117. "Amtliche Bekanntgabe," 24 April 1958, ibid.

118. Michael Gehler, "'Kein Anschluß, aber auch keine chinesische Mauer`. Österreichs außenpolitische Emanzipation und die deutsche Frage 1945-1955," in *Österreich unter alliierter Besatzung 1945-1955* ed. Alfred Ableitinger, Siegfried Beer and Eduard G. Staudinger, Studien zu Politik und Verwaltung 63 (Vienna: Böhlau, 1998), 265-266.

119. See Rainer Bollmus, "Die Bundesrepublik und die Republik Österreich 1950-1958," *Christliche Demokratie* 1, Heft 3 (1983): 19-21; Karl Seidel, "Bundeskanzler Raab und die Deutschlandfrage," *Deutsche Außenpolitik* 3 (1958): 755-759; Carl-Hermann Mueller-Graaf to Bundesminister Heinrich von Brentano, 27 February 1958, Politisches Archiv des Auswärtigen Amtes (PAAA), Bonn; "Aufzeichnung von Carl-Hermann Mueller-Graaf," 25 February 1958 (sic! The document quotes it correctly: 26 February), PAAA; Botschaft der Bundesrepublik Deutschland/Wien, Carl-Hermann Mueller Graaf to the Auswärtige Amt, 21 May 1958, VS-Vertraulich, "betr. 'Raab-Plan' - Politik des österreichischen Bundeskanzlers in der Frage der deutschen Wiedervereinigung" (10 Seiten), PAAA, VS-Akten; see also Christoph Klessmann, "Adenauers Deutschland- und Ostpolitik 1955-1963," in *Adenauer und die Deutsche Frage,* ed. Josef Foschepoth (Göttingen: Vandenhoeck, 1988), 65, 67-68; Matthias Pape, Die Deutschlandinitiative des österreichischen Bundeskanzlers Raab 1958, Vierteljahreshefte für Zeitgeschichte, Vol. 48 (2000); No. 2, 281-318.

120. See the statement by Rauchensteiner, *Die Zwei*, 340.

121. See the new extended edition of Wilfried Loth, *Die Teilung der Welt. Geschichte des Kalten Krieges 1941-1955,* ed. Martin Broszat and Helmut Heiber, dtv-Weltgeschichte des 20. Jahrhunderts (Munich: Deutscher Taschenbuch Verlag, 2000), 340-342.

122. For this, see Schlesinger, *Austrian Neutrality in Postwar Europe*, 51-52.

123. See also Eger, *Krisen an Österreichs Grenzen*, 71.

124. Ibid.

125. Ibid., 70, 72.

126. Escher to Eidgenössisches Department, 12 December 1956, BAR, E 2300 Wien, Bd. 58-60.

127. Franz Karasek to Julius Raab, 12 November 1956, AJRGV, Karton Außenpolitik.

128. See "Briefwechsel Bundeskanzler Adenauers mit Bundespräsident Heuss und dem designierten Außenminister v. Brentano, Adenauer an Heuss," 22 May 1955, in *Westintegration, Sicherheit und deutsche Frage. Quellen zur Außenpolitik in der Ära Adenauer 1949-1963,* ed. Klaus A. Maier and Bruno Thoss, Ausgewählte Quellen zur Deutschen Geschichte der Neuzeit, Freiherr vom Stein-Gedächtnisausgabe, founded by Rudolf Buchner and continued by Winfried Baumgart, vol. XLII (Darmstadt: Wissenschaftliche Buchgesellschaft, 1994), 188-189.

129. Oliver Rathkolb, "Austria's ´Ostpolitik´ in the 1950s and 1960s: Honest Broker or Double Agent," *Austrian History Yearbook,* vol. XXVI (1995): 129-145; idem, *Washington ruft Wien,* 292.

130. Rathkolb, *Washington ruft Wien,* 292.

The Austrian Legation in Prague and the Czechoslovak Crisis of 1968

Klaus Eisterer

The aim of this paper is twofold: first, to outline the political analysis elaborated by the Austrian legation in Prague and to show how the Austrian legation assessed the process, chances, and perils of the Prague Spring; this information is based on the 'political reports' to the *Ballhausplatz* (Austrian ministry of foreign affairs), recently made accessible in the Austrian State Archives. Second, this paper will show what impact the intervention of the "socialist brother countries," led by the Soviet Union, had on Czechoslovak-Austrian relations—with special focus on the actions of the legation in Prague in the crucial months of August and September and their consequences.[1]

1. The Austrian Legation in Prague on the Process, the Chances and Perils of the Prague Spring

On 5 January 1968, Alexander Dubcek was elected first secretary of the Central Committee of the Czechoslovak Communist Party. It was expected that he would carry through the economic reforms, which the XIIIth Party Congress had decreed already in 1966, and which were never realized because Dubcek's predecessor, Antonin Novotny, did not support them. His other field of action would be to eliminate "existing imperfections in methods and working-style" of the Communist Party and to make "the principles of democratic centralism and intra-party democracy" come true - as stated in the communiqué on the January session of the Central Committee. And simple people had the hope that for Dubcek "you did not have to be a party member to be considered a human being."[2]

Differing segments of Czech and Slovak society set a great amount of trust in Dubcek right from the beginning: his Slovak compatriots, who regarded him as 'their best man'; non-party-members, who hoped for more flexibility; economists, who expected speedy reforms and the successes they had predicted; artists, who wanted a wider margin for individual freedom in the artistic field; the West, which thought about a careful 'emancipation' from Moscow; and the Soviet Union, which was sure that the "fraternal and sincerely friendly relations between both parties and countries would continue, would be strengthened and further developed." Rudolf Kirchschläger, Austrian minister in Prague,[3] concluded: "So much trust is almost crushing. It will be very difficult for Alexander Dubcek in the next months and years not to disappoint those who believe in him and put their faith in him."[4] What this implied was that it would be a high risk balancing act .

The 'rigid immobility' which had characterized Czechoslovak internal policy up to January 1968 suddenly seemed gone: People who cared for the *res publica* but had their reservations about the Communist regime "began to plan and started to act." Already at the beginning of February, a surprising awakening, an 'evolution from below', could be registered. Not only intellectuals or artists started to reorganize and voice their ideas, ministries and party organs were swamped with proposals and ideas—ideas formerly considered too dangerous. Even high ranking officials started talking quite openly about the "chilly winds of spring" which might blow on the government and carry away, for example, the minister of the interior.[5] Especially the activities of the writers union with Eduard Goldstücker as their new president led Kirchschläger to ask the rhetorical question about the limits of this evolution—nobody knew, "but to have to think about these questions means to worry about the future already."[6]

But the process of "democratizing party and society" seemed to be the new party line, expressed in the new action program adopted by the party presidency several days before the 20th anniversary of the Communist takeover of 1948.[7] And the change seemed to be pervasive: The mass media spread "real news, that is, information about what really happened;" The students started to create their own organizations and demanded participation in public affairs; *Unpersons* (like Tomás and Jan Masaryk), "nullified for 20 years," were remembered and venerated in public. In social affairs two basic principles took hold, principles emphasized by Dubcek wherever he appeared: democratization and socialist humanism. The party secretary stressed over and over again "that he confided in the democratic tradition in Czechoslovakia, with what the C.S.S.R. 'could contribute substantially to democratization on a global basis'." In March 1968 this confidence seemed justified. Regarding the interior development of the C.S.S.R., the evolution might be successful, although the enemies of this process "not only stayed alive but also frequently in office."[8]

But what about the foreign policy within the setting of the *'Czechoslovak Renaissance'*—as more and more Czechs and Slovaks called the new developments in their country? This was an area where the "joy of the new and the experiment" had scarcely penetrated—and understandably so. Kirchschläger stated:

> Those who stand within the 'socialist commonwealth' cannot claim a certain amount of freedom in their foreign policy as well as in their domestic policy. It requires courage and wisdom to demand just one. The new Czechoslovak leadership has chosen freedom in its internal affairs. If it wants to make the best of the freedom in this sector to its utmost possibilities, it has to try to dissipate fears of its Communist brother states, especially Moscow, in the sector of foreign policy and therefore has to conduct a moderate, traditional foreign policy.[9]

The Austrian minister therefore did not expect fundamental changes in this field, although there were signs that Prague would at least "put forward its own arguments" in the big struggle for peace and freedom in the world.[10]

Some voices advocating neutral Finland as a model were quickly disavowed in the press; that they had even been voiced was a clear sign to the Austrian observer that some people ignored the obvious limits. But in Czechoslovak society the idea of neutrality was stronger than assumed: not only Finland but also Austria as well as Yugoslavia—the non-alignment model—were discussed publicly. According to *Rude Pravo* the Communist Party—following its new line—did not want "to ignore these considerations but convince with better arguments;" the deputy foreign secretary insisted that these ideas showed "a lack of understanding of Czechoslovak interests *and possibilities.*" He quoted (the bourgeois) Jan Masaryk, who had stated that "Czechoslovakia was not situated between East and West but between Germany and Russia and that this fact had to determine its foreign policy." And after Dubcek himself had called these ideas politically wrong and unethical,[11] they had to disappear from public debate. The resolution of the Central Committee of 6 April stated very clearly: "Non-socialist or possibly even anti-communist voices cannot count on resonance or support in public."[12]

Almost every day politicians on all levels emphasized two central points of their policy: loyality to the Warsaw Pact and loyality to the socialist form of society. No Western observer had reason to doubt their sincerity. But Eastern European diplomats and politicians were full of mistrust and misgivings. For Kirchschläger Austrian history held an interesting parallel:

> With how much concern and unspoken or open mistrust by its western friends was Austria confronted when in 1955 it chose the path of permanent neutrality—reaffirming constantly and sincerely its continuing ties with the West—, that path which made Austria for years the only showcase of a democratic society and an economy accessible to the people behind the iron curtain and which influenced the movement within the states of the Eastern block, which in those days was still rigidly formed in an essential way.[13]

Here we have a clear allusion to a "model-C.S.S.R." as showcase for a communism 'with a human face'—an idea, a possibility, dear to many people in the West but unacceptable to many in the East: The new developments disquieted those in the East, who feared the consequences of the Czechoslovak example. The leaders in Prague understood these worries; their aim was to "gain the trust of all brother parties in the Czechoslovak way of Renaissance, as it is proudly called." Nobody in Prague believed in or even faintly hinted at a possibility of a break with Moscow.[14]

As for the Western observer, there were clear limits to the program of democratization the new Czechoslovak leadership proposed in its "action program of the Czechoslovak Communist Party" of April 1968: Better guarantees of civil liberties, more freedom to travel, freedom of speech, freedom of association—all these elements would contribute to a democratization of public life in the C.S.S.R. and would "make the life of millions of people more beautiful and more worth living." But there were at least two "taboos," two points, which could not be discussed: the alliance with the Soviet Union and "the socialist character of the state or - in other words - the leading role of the Communist Party."[15]

The Central Committee thought it necessary at the beginning of June to clearly state the dogma, which could be summed up in the following points:

- The leading role of the Communist Party guarantees the socialist character of the country.
- The Communist Party is the strongest political force in the country; it alone has a scientific program, and without the party there is no progress.
- The Party is the uniting force between the Czech and the Slovak people.
- No opposition parties or movements are allowed; the National Front holds the monopoly of political action; only organizations or parties, which accept socialism as the guiding force in state and society can be accepted into the National Front.
- The Communist Party is the best guarantee for friendship with the Soviet Union and the other socialist states.

The confirmation of these points was directed towards forces in the interior, where discussions apparently had gone way beyond the acceptance of Dubcek's light-handed phrase: "He knew no better party than the Communist Party and there was no need of an opposition against the best." It was also directed towards Moscow.[16]

At the beginning of July the Austrian minister in Prague summed up the situation and gave his estimate of the near future under the title: "It will be a hot summer full of tensions."[17] He predicted the near-impossibility of liquidating a dictatorial system, which had the support of and strong contractual ties with one of the superpowers through the convincing force of the argument and the secret ballot alone - especially when the ones trying to change the system from within worked with democratic means but denied the logical consequences of their work by insisting on the monopoly of power of one party. This contradiction was one of the factors which weakened the drive of the reformers. Others were the "rumble and sometimes very clear warnings from Moscow," as well as the lack of solidarity from some of the leading men, as e.g. the first secretary of the Slovak Communist Party, Vasil Bilak, who had come back from Moscow (where he had been in May together with Dubcek, Josef Smrkovsky and Oldrich Cernik), "changed from Paul to Saul."[18]

The new leadership could not claim immediate economic success—understandably so in such a short period of time—but the people's high expectations were disappointed. The progress in the social sector was undeniable: new passport laws, abolition of press censorship, reinforced rule of the law—changes which only four months before were just 'a wonderful dream' for many. But then, after the realization of these dreams, wishes went further. Party members, however, had always enjoyed certain privileges—and privileges for everybody were no privileges any more—so their disenchantment grew. This mood within party members was a suitable basis for the 'counterattack' of the 'conservative group', which had regained its composure, due to, among other reasons, the pressure Moscow began to exert. The means of this 'conservative group' were: a whispering campaign, anonymous leaflets, threatening or slandering letters, and ultimately the open discussion in all party or state organs, where it was still present.

Dubcek and his followers reacted with a double strategy: In order to relieve the external pressure from their 'socialist brother countries' they emphasized more than ever their loyalty to Moscow and the other members of the Warsaw Pact system. In order to cope with the internal challenge they stressed their concept of a competition of ideas. Svoboda, Sik, Goldstücker, and other, less prominent members of the 'new line' started an information campaign:

> In this almost daily argument between the past and the present the new line has shown remarkable political ability. That it is less successful in the task of standing its ground than in relieving the old, finds its explanation in the fact that—apart from a certain amount of external pressure—the overwhelming majority of the people supported them in relieving the Novotny regime whereas only those parts of the population which accept the leading role of the Communist Party support them in the task of self-assertion. The rest remains benevolently neutral.[19]

But in the end it was pressure from outside, which ended the experiment in democratizing the Communist system. For the Communist Party of the U.S.S.R., these developments in the C.S.S.R. were simply revisionism, even "counterrevolution,"[20] an experiment, which endangered the very existence of the other regimes of the Soviet bloc.[21]

There is no need to comment on the developments in July and at the beginning of August 1968, but I would like to point to the analysis of the declaration of Bratislava (3 August), where the Austrian Minister drew clear parallels to Austrian history.

The declaration of Bratislava—a result of negotiations between the leaders of the C.S.S.R. and of five socialist brother states (U.S.S.R., G.D.R., Poland, Hungary and Bulgaria)—seemed to mark an end to a phase in the relations between Czechoslovakia and the five other countries. In this phase all means short of actual armed intervention had been utilized in a war of nerves: formal protests and exchanges of notes at state and party level, an intense propaganda campaign, the political condemnation of Czechoslovak politicians as revisionists and even counterrevolutionaries, military exercises as impressive as possible along the borders, maintaining operational troops after the official end of staff exercises on Czechoslovak territory, the open support of the 'fifth column' through Moscow, and so on.

The Czechoslovak people— knowing they would stand alone in case of an armed intervention—as well as the Czechoslovak leadership had resisted this immense pressure up to and during the conference of Cierna nad Tisou. The Bratislava declaration could therefore be considered a partial success. It stated the "renewed recognition of the principles of the equality of states, of sovereignty, national independ- ence and territorial integrity—also within the socialist camp" and confirmed "the right that each party could solve its problems with regard to its national characteristics and conditions as long as it followed the goal of strengthening socialism." It further implied that no stationing of foreign troops in the C.S.S.R. was possible, no retraction of the action program of the Czechoslovak Communist Party, no reshuffling of party or state-posts (personal), and no excommunication from the socialist camp.

But the concessions the Czechoslovak representatives had signed were in more or less clear contradiction to the statement of principle and confirmation of policy. They had accepted the necessity:

• to educate the masses in the principles of socialist ideals and proletarian internationalism, for the relentless fight against bourgeois ideology, and to watch out for non-socialist forces;
• to coordinate their foreign policy;
• to reinforce the defensive potential of the Warsaw Pact system (instead of modifying the alliance) and therefore to collaborate not only militarily but also politically;
• to reinforce the potential of the Czechoslovak army;
• to orient their economic activities more towards the COMECON (Council for Mutual Economic Assistance).

There were grave differences in all substantial points, and Kirchschläger compared it to an armistice: "Doesn't the beginning of these conversations on the rail tracks of Cierna nad Tisou resemble very much the signing of the armistice of Compiègne, in this case, though, before the weapons have really spoken?"[22] He predicted conflict would soon start on the interpretation of this declaration and reported that the Czechoslovak side saw it simply as a reprieve, a sort of probation in order to "prove that the Czechoslovak way remains a way towards socialism."[23]

In his own interpretation of the Bratislava declaration, the Austrian observer saw clear parallels to the Austro-German accord of July 1936: Then—like now—he noted

the big state had recognized the independence and sovereignty of the small state in which his fifth column was at work, too, and had qualified the political developments in both states as internal affairs. Then, too, the small state had bound itself to basing its foreign policy in principle on its status as a German state, hence to harmonize it. Then, too, Austria obligated itself to forestall propaganda against National Socialism and to accept German nationalists into the government. Then, too, there was an inherent contradiction between sovereignty, independence, and non-intervention on the one hand and the obligations to shape the government and government policy in a certain way on the other hand. Finally, then, too, the international press and diplomatic circles registered this accord with relief and satisfaction, whereas radical elements on both sides rejected it.

Kirchschläger also noted similarities in motives: In 1936 both parties had needed 'breathing space'—the German Reich to shape up its international standing, Austria to consolidate its internal position. But then, Austria was not able to make use of this respite.

Kirchschläger concluded that the situation in the C.S.S.R. was another respite and that "in the interest of the developments in Central Europe and of the people living here one can only wish it will be put to better use now than it was possible for Austria from 1936 to 1938."[24]

One month later—and with hindsight—Kirchschläger had to revise his analysis: Full of wrath he inferred that the Bratislava declaration had been "not even an armistice and no parallel to 1936; it was only one of the stations on the way to armed intervention. ... Nothing has happened in Czechoslovakia between the 3rd and 21st of August which would have created a different situation ..."[25]

But, again, one last parallel lay at hand: In 1968 the Soviet Union needed a telegram, a letter of invitation, as Goering had needed one

thirty years earlier. But then again, this is 'standard operating procedure'.

2. The Impact of the Intervention of the Socialist Brother Coun-
tries on Czechoslovak-Austrian Relations

More than half a year after the occupation by the 'socialist brother
countries' the Austrian minister in Prague made a comprehensive
analysis of the state of Austro-Czechoslovak relations. Personal
meetings with the new Czechoslovak minister for foreign affairs as well
as the minister for external trade in February and March 1969 had
helped to clarify the Czechoslovak position; his assessment was partly
based on these conversations.[26]

The cultural, economic, political, and human relations had not
suffered through the tragic events in August—quite to the contrary:

In Austria—as well as in large parts of the world—the Czechs
and Slovaks as a people have gained respect which they did not
have before. As a consequence, public opinion made a constructive policy towards the C.S.S.R. easier. On the other hand,
just on the 50th anniversary of their separation from Vienna,
Czechs and Slovaks did not only realize the advantages of the
big Monarchy from times past more than before but also the
value of the permanently neutral Austrian Republic as a
neighbor.

A neutral neighbor—especially one which, "according to authorita-
tive Czechoslovak opinion," had a "useful relation of trust" with the
Soviet Union—was now very much in the interest of the Czechoslovak
Republic. On 27 August 1968, Deputy Foreign Minister Kohut had
confessed to Kirchschläger his personal views that "only the boundary
to Austria was a boundary with friends. All other surrounding states
would have to be considered enemies."[27]

The only real contentious point between Prague and Vienna was the
property question: as a compensation for lost property,[28] Austria
demanded a lump sum of four billion Schilling—a minimum claim
already adjusted to Czechoslovak near-insolvency—and had no illusions
about the willingness and the possibilities of its neighbor to comply with
these demands. Encouraging signals from Czechoslovak diplomats
during the Prague Spring had given rise to a certain degree of optimism,
but no real progress had been made. The Czechoslovak position had not

changed after August 1968, so that there was no real drawback in this field.

In other fields there were even positive developments: Austrian *trade* with its neighbor had risen in the winter of 1968/69, and various visits of Czech and Slovak politicians responsible for foreign trade had led to further intensification of commercial contacts. In spite of economic uncertainties within the C.S.S.R., a higher trade volume and better economic cooperation were to be expected. As the following graph (Table 1) shows, the Czechoslovak crisis in August 1968 did not have an appreciable impact on the volume of commercial exchange (not even in the third quarter of 1968: exports declined only in August, but imports rose—mainly due to higher gas imports). The volume of imports and exports in fact grew steadily in 1968/69 (see Table 1).

Table 1

Austrian trade with the CSSR 1968/69

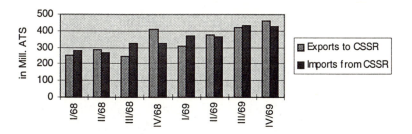

Source: *Monatsberichte des österreichischen Instituts für Wirtschaftsforschung* 41, no. 12 (1968): 508. The data on which the graph is based: *ibid.* 41, no. 6 (1968): 256; no. 9: 382; no 12: 506; *ibid.* 42, no. 3 (1969): 148; no. 6: 253; no. 9: 383; no. 12: 512; *ibid.* 43, no. 3 (1970): 124.

A qualitative jump in economic relations, though, did not seem possible as long as no real economic reforms were carried through in the C.S.S.R.

Austrian *cultural activities* in the C.S.S.R. had also been intense: An exhibition on the Hallstatt culture had opened in Brünn; the sculptor Fritz Wotruba's *oeuvre* could be admired in Prague; and the exchange of university professors continued to function without problems—even theologians could communicate their views; a visit of the *Wiener*

Staatsoper "attractive and overdue" was expected. So here there was at least business as usual. But what about the *political relations*?

During the crisis in August the Czechoslovak government had shown its satisfaction and gratitude about the attitude of the Austrian government and the Austrian people.[29] Vienna, nevertheless, had apprehensions that in the following months Prague would revise its stance and praise would change into reproach—just as the Budapest regime had done in 1956/57. But this did not happen. Even the reshuffled Czechoslovak government continued to confirm its respect for the political attitude Vienna had shown and their gratitude for humanitarian actions.

What political attitude? In one word: the strict 'non-intervention' in internal affairs; official declarations, which contained no condemnation of the forceful occupation, which gave no piece of advice in the critical days of August.[30] Declarations criticized in Austria as far too lame and too tame (especially when compared with the ones the Raab Government had issued during the Hungarian crisis of 1956), but which of course made relations with the slowly but surely 'normalized' Czechoslovak government easier and certainly did not constitute any obstacles.[31]

As for the humanitarian actions, the Austrian auto-stereotype contains the element that Austrians have always received refugees with open arms: at the end of the Second World War, during the Hungarian revolution, during the Czechoslovak crisis, during the Balkan wars following the break-up of Communist Yugoslavia. While this is true especially with respect to the Hungarian refugees of 1956, in all other cases some serious reservations have to be made.[32]

As for 1968, the open borders with Czechoslovakia and the availability of Austrian visa were not self-evident. We need to look more closely—and now, for the first time, with the help of documentary evidence—into the actions of the Austrian legation in Prague, all the more since there still is a public debate going on about what happened.[33]

The invasion on 21 August did not only surprise Czechoslovak citizens and politicians, it also found the Austrian legation without its head of mission. Although, Kirchschläger had predicted at the beginning of July that "It will be a hot summer full of tensions,"[34] he decided to leave for his vacation in Portoroz (Yugoslavia), possibly induced by the fact that the Czechoslovak foreign minister had announced his firm plans to go on vacation.[35] Kirchschläger would not be back at the Austrian legation in Prague until late afternoon of 22 August.[36]

Acting chief of the legation was Counselor of Legation Walter Magrutsch, who had come to the official building on the 21 August at about four o'clock in the morning, when Austrians as well as Czechs and Slovaks already asked to be allowed inside. Since more and more Czechoslovak citizens entered the Austrian legation and many declared they would not leave the building any more, the foreign ministry in Vienna had to be asked for guidance.[37] The central part of the instruction cabled back from the *Ballhausplatz* before noon on 21 August 1968 read: "You will have to lock legation building and only allow access to people with Austrian passport. Czechoslovak citizens already inside the building shall be brought to leave the building through friendly persuasion and by emphasizing the fact that the legation has to be reserved for the admission of own citizens."[38]

Although the necessary activities of the legation centered on the fate of the Austrians (various convoys bringing home Austrian citizens from Prague were organized), Austrian entry or transit visa were granted on the same lines as before—just that now the legation did not limit its office hours (!).[39] One of the achievements of the Prague Spring had been the improved freedom of travel: not only passports but also the additionally necessary specific permits to leave the country—*doluschka*—had been made available, and on this basis the Austrian mission had of course handed out visa, thus allowing many Czechoslovak citizens to enjoy freedom of travel to a Western country. This did not stop, but in the first days after the invasion of the Warsaw Pact Allies the number of visa applicants went down considerably—and pressure on those waiting in line seemed to grow. On 23 August, for example, a Czech subject who was taking photographs of the visa applicants waiting on the street was driven away. This seemed to be reason enough to allow the Czechoslovak citizens back into the office building.[40] Kirchschläger, back from Yugoslavia and in charge of the mission, apparently considered the instruction of two days earlier *caduque*.[41] Some days later a tank with mounted infantry demonstratively 'cruised' in front of the legation, apparently to intimidate waiting people, and once again these people were ushered inside the building.[42] But, in spite of the threats and efforts of intimidation—or because of the continuing tension in Prague—the number of visa applicants grew steadily. (According to Kirchschläger, everybody in the legation was stamping visa documents, including his wife and his son.)

On 25 August though, the Austrian ministry of the interior instructed the legation in Prague—via the channels of the foreign ministry—to stop granting visa to Czechoslovak citizens. The reason for this measure was that it had received information that "the occupation power had seized 10,000 blank Czechoslovak passports." The Austrian ministry of the interior feared these passports might be used "for purposes other than originally intended"—in other words, they might serve to infiltrate agents or even a fifth column into Austria.[43]

It seems strange that in the upper echelons of the Austrian ministry of the interior it was thought possible that the Soviets, wanting to prepare an action against Austria, relied on such blunt means to procure 'sanitized' documents. The Soviets were in fact known for a much subtler *modus operandi*. But apparently there was a certain nervousness in Vienna. There also existed other pieces of information on activities of foreign agents as well as 'covert' Soviet preparations—e. g. Danube barges from Warsaw Pact countries within Austria serving as caches.[44]

The Austrian minister in Prague, nevertheless, could not imagine such drastic consequences for the security situation in Austria. On the contrary, were he to obey these instructions, the consequences in Prague would have been drastic. So he cabled back:

> I ask to reconsider these instructions. To completely stop granting visa to Czechoslovak citizens would be such a terrible blow to the local population, which commands the unanimous admiration of all foreigners here because of their conduct, and it would also be in such contradiction to the humanitarian tradition Austria has followed since 1956, that this harsh provision would hardly be understood by anyone. I confess, I could hardly bring myself to obey these instructions without suffering the most severe conflict of conscience.[45]

He thus asked the legation be allowed to hand out visa as before and assured that an in-depth check of the passports would be conducted. In the meantime, though, the legation continued to give visa to Czechoslovak applicants.[46]

The instruction was later revoked by the *Ballhausplatz*, and the Austrian legation was again officially authorized to grant entry permits into or transit permits through Austria. A stop in the liberal practice of handing out visa might have had grave consequences since other Western missions—the Swiss embassy, the British embassy and the German trade delegation—had made it clear that they would cease handing out visa the moment the Austrians stopped.[47]

What seemed to have been the *political* motive for the Austrian minister—apart from the misery of the applicants he addressed in his cable—was his reflection, his conviction, that the Austrian style of neutrality had and should have a special humanitarian stamp. He felt that if the Austrian policy lost its humanitarian character it lost the legitimacy and the moral justification for its neutrality.[48]

The number of visa applications went up the next day: from the invasion day, 21 August, to Sunday, 25 August, some 600 visa were handed out in total. On 26 August alone some 900 visa were granted, rising to more than two thousand a day by the end of the week. The number of visa issued per day stayed between two and three thousand for quite some time:[49] From 22 August to 17 September more than 49,000 Czechoslovak citizens entered Austria (but also more than 78,000 returned to the C.S.S.R. from or through Austria).

In the third quarter of 1968 (July, August, and September) the Austrian legation in Prague alone—not counting the general consulate in Bratislava—granted 100,192 visa, 56,300 more than in the same period of the previous year (see Table 2).[50]

Table 2

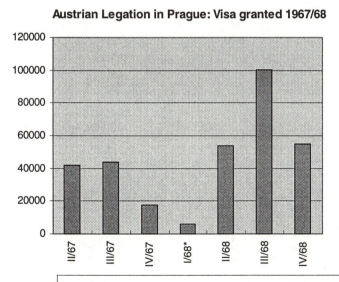

Austrian Legation in Prague: Visa granted 1967/68

(II/67 to IV/68:quarters; I/68*: only January and February)

Not many of those applying for visa wanted to go into exile; in fact, only 2,248 persons had sought asylum in Austria by 23 October.[51] Most of them simply could not bear the tension any more or feared imprisonment. They wanted to follow the developments from outside the country and went to visit friends or relatives.[52] And if they had left the country legally—i.e. with visa—they could re-enter legally.[53]

Thus, what happened in 1968 was not quite comparable to the flood of refugees Austria had to cope with in 1956, when some 160,000 people had fled from Hungary to the Western neighbor by the end of the year.[54] Still, from the day of the invasion until 10 October—when Czechoslovakia closed its borders again—some 96,000 Czechoslovak subjects had left their country for Austria. Another 66,000 Czechs and Slovaks had entered Austria mainly from Yugoslavia by 23 October—a total of about 162,000 people. 129,000 of them returned to their homeland and 12,300 emigrated to other countries, especially Switzerland (8,000), Canada (2,800), Australia (1,400), and the United States (100). On 23 October, there were still some 15,000 Czechoslovaks in Austria.[55]

So many thousands had come, and those who did not have friends or relatives in Austria had to be cared for by government or charity organizations. More than ten million Schilling were to be destined for the care of these refugees by the Austrian Republic.[56] Austria was in keeping with its humanitarian traditions it so proudly pronounces—in part due to the fact that its mission chief in Prague was not intimidated by an instruction he thought improper as well as politically and morally damaging.

The Czechoslovak people had gained immense sympathy in Austria (as probably in most countries of the West) due to their attitude in dealing with the occupants—an attitude full of courage, inventiveness, dignity and rage. Some examples should be mentioned which not only struck the foreign observer, but which—thanks to mass media still able to bring news from the occupied country—impressed the free world:

•   The Czechoslovak people invented the symbol of the Soviet star with the Nazi swastika in its core[57]—a daring but evident equation for Czech and Slovak citizens; and, accordingly, the political joke went as follows: "We have waited for seven, have suffered for twenty, and will curse you for a thousand years."[58]

•   They lined up in front of Soviet tanks in order to sign petitions calling for neutrality or supporting Dubcek, the symbol of their hopes.[59]

- They took down all street signs in order to make orientation difficult for the invading forces, flew state flags on official buildings at half mast in order to demonstrate the firm support for Svoboda, Dubcek, and the other members of the Czechoslovak 'delegation' under pressure in Moscow, discussed with the soldiers of the occupying forces in order to demoralize them, and invented a whole arsenal of peaceful means in a war of civil resistance.

The provocations to the occupying forces were such that the Austrian minister not only assumed they had stern orders not to react but also commented on their patience![60] In the words of Kirschläger:

The attitude of the Czechoslovak people in face of this armed intervention was so exemplary and heroic in its non-violent actions that it hardly has any parallel in the past. All the defiance, all disappointed friendship, all the scorn, the wit and the irony, all the courage and all the bitterness were expressed in the slogans on the streets and on the walls, in many thousand posters, in the signposts rendered useless and the street-signs taken down, in the radio and TV broadcasts of illegal stations, which were the legal ones, and also in the discussions with the soldiers somewhat helpless in their tanks. ... But most remarkably, the whole people was one, was so unified, that apparently it even surprised the five (occupying) powers. Because they did not dare to appoint one of those who had committed themselves to their cause to any office in this occupied state.[61]

All these actions of resistance, of course, could not achieve a 'roll back', but at least made it clear to the world that here a whole people had been raped. Two more things seemed clear: The traditional bonds of friendship between the Russian and the Czechoslovak people were broken. Even convinced Communists turned their backs on their socialist brother country to the East. Sympathies had turned into hatred.[62] What seemed clear, too, was that a people in this state of rage and courage could not be governed by a collaborationist government.[63] The so-called 'normalization' had to be slow ed down.

But slowly it came. Normalization turned into consolidation,[64] occupation turned into "fraternal help,"[65] and the C.S.S.R. turned into a "quasi-protectorate" of the U.S.S.R. Starting with the invasion and occupation in August 1968 and then fully since April 1969—when Gustav Husak took over as first secretary of the Czechoslovak Communist Party—Prague lost the little autonomy it had had in its interior decisions as well as in its foreign relations, and "the relations between Austria and Czechoslovakia had become part of the Austrian-Soviet relations."[66]

Notes

1. The policies of the Vienna government with regard to the Czechoslovak crisis are not a main subject of this paper. A first assessment of these policies of 1968—in comparison to the handling of the Hungrian crisis of 1956—was already presented in 1981: Reiner Eger, *Krisen an Österreichs Grenzen. Das Verhalten Österreichs während des Ungarnaufstandes 1956 und der tschechoslowakischen Krise 1968. Ein Vergleich* (Wien-München: 1981); a more recent book by two journalists, who had access to more substantial documents than Eger is Kurt Tozzer and Günther Kallinger, *"Marschmusik für Glockenspiel". 1968 Österreich am Rande des Krieges* (St. Pölten-Wien: 1998). It nevertheless seems very speculative in some parts, and the analysis as well as the interpretation of the documentation leaves much to be desired. For an interesting paper on the actions of the Austrian government see Walter Rauscher, "Austria and the Czechoslovak Crisis 1968," Fifth International Conference of Editors of Diplomatic Documents. The documentation on 'Prague 1968' is abundant. For a list of sources see the notes in Mark Kramer, "New Sources on the 1968 Soviet Invasion of Czechoslovakia (part one)," *Cold War International History Project Bulletin* 2 (Fall 1992): 1-12; one of the most interesting works in the German language—written after the opening of the archives in the East—is Jan Pauer, *Prag 1968. Der Einmarsch des Warschauer Paktes. Hintergründe – Planung –Durchführung* (Bremen: 1995); see also the edition of the documents *The Prague Spring 1968. A National Security Archive Documents Reader* (New York: 1994).

2. So the words of a Slovak poet, himself not a party member. Rudolf Kirchschläger, Austrian minister to Prague, to Lujo Toncic-Sorinj, Austrian foreign minister until 19 January 1968, 1-Pol/68, "Der Wechsel in der Führung der KPTsch," 12 January 1968, Österreichisches Staatsarchiv [Austrian State Archives, Vienna, ÖStA], Archiv der Republik [Archives of the Republic, AdR], BMfAA, II-pol 1968, C.S.S.R. 3, box 7.

3. Kirchschläger was envoy extraordinary and minister plenipotentiary in Prague from 1967 to 1970. In April 1970 he was appointed minister of foreign affairs in the Kreisky cabinet. In 1974 he was elected president of the Republic and got reelected in 1980.

4. Kirchschläger to Toncic-Sorinj, 2-Pol/68, "Vorgänge um die Wahl Dubceks zum Ersten Sekretär des Zentralkomites," 15 January 1968, ÖStA, AdR, BMfAA, II-pol 1968, C.S.S.R. 3, box 7.

5. Kirchschläger to Kurt Waldheim, Austrian foreign minister, 3-Pol/68, "Die ersten vier Wochen der neuen tschechoslowakischen Parteilinie," 2 February 1968, ibid.

6. Kirchschläger to Waldheim, 5-Pol/68, "Der csl. Schriftstellerverband und die neue Parteilinie," 10 February 1968, ÖStA, AdR, BMfAA, II-pol 1968, C.S.S.R., box 6.

7. Walter Magrutsch, counselor of legation, to Waldheim, 7-Pol/68, "Das Prager Februar-Jubiläum im Zeichen der neuen Parteilinie," 27 February 1968, ÖStA, BMfAA, II-pol 1968, C.S.S.R., box 6.

8. Austrian legation Prague to Waldheim, 9-Pol/68, "Zehn Wochen Dubcek," 12 March 1968, ÖStA, AdR, BMfAA, II-pol 1968, C.S.S.R. 3, box 7.

9. Kirchschläger to Waldheim, 10-Pol/68, "Die Außenpolitk im Rahmen der 'csl. Wiedergeburt'," 19 March 1968. ÖStA, AdR, BMfAA, II-pol 1968, C.S.S.R., box 6.

10. Quote from the resolution of the Communist Party workshop meeting in the foreign ministry, 14 March 1968.

11. His opening statement before the plenum of the Central Committee of the Communist Party, 1 April 1968.

12. Kirchschläger to Waldheim, 14-Pol/68, "Der Gedanke der Neutralität der C.S.S.R.", 8 April 1968, ÖStA, AdR, BMfAA, II-pol 1968, C.S.S.R., box 6.

13. Kirchschläger to Waldheim, 18-Pol/68, "Zwischen Bedenken und Vertrauen," 14 May 1968, ÖStA, AdR, BMfAA, II-pol 1968, C.S.S.R., box 6.

14. Ibid.

15. Kirchschläger to Waldheim, 15-Pol/68, "Nach der Verabschiedung des Aktions-programms," 16 April 1968, ÖStA, AdR, BMfAA, II-pol 1968, C.S.S.R. 3, box 7.

16. Kirchschläger to Waldheim, 20-Pol/68, "Die führende Rolle der Kommunistischen Partei," 6 June 1968, ÖStA, AdR, BMfAA, II-pol 1968, C.S.S.R. 3, box 7.

17. Kirchschläger to Waldheim, 23-Pol/68, "Ein spannungsreicher und heißer Sommer steht bevor," 1 July 1968, ÖStA, AdR, BMfAA, II-pol 1968, C.S.S.R. 3, box 7.

18. Ibid.

19. Ibid.

20. Kirchschläger to Waldheim, 29-Pol/68, "Die Preßburger Deklaration," 6 August 1968, ÖStA, AdR, BMfAA, II-pol 1968, C.S.S.R. 3, box 7.

21. Kirchschläger to Waldheim, 28-Pol/68, "Das Phänomen der Ära Dubcek," 30 July 1968, ÖStA, AdR, BMfAA, II-pol 1968, C.S.S.R. 3, box 7.

22. Kirchschläger to Waldheim, 29-Pol/68, "Die Preßburger Deklaration," 6 August 1968, ÖStA, AdR, BMfAA, II-pol 1968, C.S.S.R. 3, box 7.

23. The idea of a 'breathing-space' for the Czechoslovak side was probably brought up by Foreign Minister Jiri Hajek in a conversation with the Austrian minister after the conference of Cierna nad Tisou. See interview with Rudolf Kirchschläger in *Österreich II. 1968: Jahr des Aufbruchs, Jahr des Umbruchs. Eine Dokumentation von Hugo Portisch* (Vienna: ORF, 1995), 90 min., here minutes 65 to 67.

24. Kirchschläger to Waldheim, 29-Pol/68, "Die Preßburger Deklaration," 6 August 1968, ÖStA, AdR, BMfAA, II-pol 1968, C.S.S.R. 3, box 7.

25. Kirchschläger to Waldheim, 32-Pol/68, "Die Invasion," 2 September 1968, ÖStA, AdR, BMfAA, II-pol 1968, C.S.S.R. 3, box 5. Some years later, Kirchschläger came back to the comparison between the Austro-German accord of July 1936 and the final communiqué of the conference in Cierna nad Tisou on a more abstract level: "Collisions of interest between a small state and a bigger or big one cannot be solved through agreements, which, in order to create a text which both sides are able to sign, permit ambiguous readings. The interpretation of such agreements follows the version of the stronger party on principle." See Rudolf Kirchschläger, *Der Friede beginnt im eigenen Haus. Gedanken über Österreich* (Wien-München-Zürich-Innsbruck: Molden, 1980), 58-59.

26. The following is based on Kirchschläger to Waldheim, 7-Pol/69, "Die österr.-csl. Beziehungen; Stand März 1969," 7 March 1969, draft with handwritten parts. A copy of this document is held by the Institut für Zeitgeschichte, Innsbruck.

27. Kirchschläger to foreign ministry, Tel. 25 349, "Gespräch im Außenministerium und Lagebericht 27. 8. 1968," 27 August 1968, 16:00, ÖStA, AdR, BMfAA, II-pol 1968, C.S.S.R. 3, box 7.

28. See Oliver Rathkolb, "'Ein schwieriges Verhältnis'-Österreich und die CSR 1945 bis 1950," in *Kontakte und Konflikte. Böhmen, Mähren und Österreich: Aspekte eines Jahrtausends gemeinsamer Geschichte,* ed. Thomas Winkelbauer (Horn-Waidhofen/Thaya: 1993), 479-490, esp. 485, 489-490.

29. See Kirchschläger to foreign ministry, Tel. 25 349 [cable with #], "Gespräch im Außenministerium und Lagebericht 27. 8. 1968," 27 August 1968, 16:00, and Kirchschläger to foreign ministry, Tel. 25 367, "Gespräch im Außenministerium," 29 August 1968, ÖStA, AdR, BMfAA, II-pol 1968, C.S.S.R. 3, box 7.

30. Austrian documents and statements with respect to the Czechoslovak crisis are compiled in the dossier GZl. 129.266 - 6(Pol)/68, GrZl. 110.223 - 6/68, 12 November 1968, ÖStA, AdR, BMfAA, II-pol 1968, C.S.S.R., box 6. The most important ones have already been published in: Eger, *Krisen an Österreichs Grenzen,* esp. documents 6-9, 195-197.

31. These declarations were criticized, e.g., in Parliament: "If the Austrian government has been unable to arrive at this conclusion [that the occupation of the C.S.S.R. is a violation of international law and a infraction of the U.N.-Charter], then it is the duty of the people's representatives to state what the facts are." Bruno Pittermann in the Parliamentary debate on 18 September 1968, *Stenographische Protokolle über die Sitzungen des Nationalrates (XI. Gesetzgebungsperiode) der Republik Österreich,* 1968, vol. VII, Wien 1968; they were further criticized in the press: see Bruno Kreisky, "Um was es geht," *Arbeiter-Zeitung,* 27 August 1968: p. 2; and the declarations were finally criticized in inner-party circles of the governing ÖVP (Österreichische Volkspartei, Austrian People's Party): Chancellor Josef Klaus himself stated on 2 September 1968: "Chancellor and foreign minister have been too cautious, the press too little." Postsitzung am 2. September 1968, in Robert Kriechbaumer ed., *Die Ära Josef Klaus. Österreich in den "kurzen" sechziger Jahren,* vol. 1, *Dokumente* (Wien-Köln-Weimar: 1998), 201. Especially Foreign Minister Kurt Waldheim had advocated a moderate and mitigating low-key response; see "Verhandlungsschrift Nr. 91a über die Sitzung des a. o. Ministerrates am 21. August 1968," pp. 2 and 4, ÖStA, AdR, Bundeskanzleramt, Präsidium, Ministerratsprotokolle.

32. For a critical reflection of these questions with respect to 1945 and the following years see Thomas Albrich, "Fremde," *Historicum* (Summer 1996): 23-28 (also a very useful resumé of the literature). The open questions about the handling of the refugee problem caused by the Balkan wars in the nineties and the debate about Austrian practice concerning refugees and asylum-seekers have been constantly debated in the Austrian press; see especially the very critical reports and articles in *Der Standard.*

33. Kirchschläger's personal account can be found e.g. in "Besondere Achtung für bewundernswerten Widerstand," *Salzburger Nachrichten,* 20 August 1998, p. 7. Franz Soronics, minister of the interior from 1968-1970, recently criticized Kirchschläger's version stating that the head of the legation "was not in Czechoslovakia at all at that time" ("at that time" referring to the days when Kirchschläger reacted to the instruction of the interior ministry). Kirchschläger was there, as will be shown. See the report of the Austria Presse Agentur, 22 September 1998, Nr. 336; see also "'In Kürze': Franz Soronics," *Die Presse,* 23 September 1998, p. 10. In an interview with Franz Soronics by Helmut Wohnout and Michael Gehler, the contents of two cabled instructions of 21 August 1968 ("You will have to lock legation building …") and 25 August 1968 ("stop granting visas") are confounded and so Soronics' statement is unfounded as well as

incorrect. See Franz Soronics, "Prinzipiell wäre es uns genauso ergangen wie im Jahr 1938," in *Demokratie und Geschichte. Jahrbuch des Karl von Vogelsang-Institutes zur Erforschung der Geschichte der christlichen Demokratie in Österreich*, vol. 3, ed. Helmut Wohnout (Wien–Köln–Weimar: Böhlau, 1999), 96-126, 116-17.

34. Kirchschläger to Waldheim, 23-Pol/68, "Ein spannungsreicher und heißer Sommer steht bevor," 1 July 1968, ÖStA, AdR, BMfAA, II-pol 1968, C.S.S.R. 3, box 7.

35. After the meeting of Cierna nad Tisou (29 July to 1 August 1968) Foreign Minister Hájek had shown Kirchschläger his and his family's tickets to Yugoslavia as a sign of how relaxed he thought the situation was. Interview with Rudolf Kirchschläger, in *Österreich II*, minutes 66 to 67.

36. In a letter to the author (9 September 1999) Kirchschläger adamantly rejects the version cited in Tozzer and Kallinger, *"Marschmusik für Glockenspiel,"* 167, which is based on a note from the Austrian ministry of the interior. Tozzer and Kallinger claim that Kirchschläger returned to Prague as late as the evening of 23 August. This version is also proven false in the light of other documentary evidence: If Kirchschläger took over as head of mission as late as the evening of 23 August, how could he possibly have signed a cable dispached in the afternoon (16:35 hours) of the same day? See Kirchschläger, legation in Prague, to foreign ministry, Tel. 25 309, 23 August 1968, ÖStA, AdR, BMfAA, II-pol 1968, C.S.S.R. 3, box 6. In the same letter Kirchschläger states that he took over as head of mission on the afternoon of 22 August, a statement which is further corroborated by an entry of the diary of his son Walter, then 21 years of age, on Thursday, 22 August, 1968: "Um ca. 16.30 Uhr kamen wir nach Prag; [...] Wir fuhren zuerst zur Gesandtschaft [...]." A copy of this document is held by the Institut für Zeitgeschichte, Innsbruck.

37. Kirchschläger to foreign ministry, 369-Res/68, "Tätigkeit der Gesandtschaft Prag in der 1. Woche der Besetzung der C.S.S.R. (21.-26. August 1968)," 26 August 1968, GZl. 124.925, GrZl. 112.916, ÖStA, AdR, BMfAA, II-pol 1968, C.S.S.R. 3, box 6. The cable Magrutsch to foreign ministry, Tel. 25 283, not in the boxes C.S.S.R. 3.

38. *"Wollen Sie Gesandtschaftsgebäude abschließen lassen und nur Paßösterreichern Zutritt gewähren. Bereits im Gebäude befindliche tschechoslowakische Staatsbürger sollen unter Hinweis darauf, daß Gesandtschaft der Aufnahme eigener Staatsbürger vorbehalten bleiben muß, durch gütliches Zureden zum Verlassen des Gebäudes bewogen werden."* Foreign ministry to legation Prague, Tel. 55 143, GZl. 124.333-Pol/68, GrZl. 117.030 II/68, sent on 21 August 1968, 11:25, ÖStA, AdR, BMfAA, II-pol 1968, C.S.S.R. 3, box 8.

39. Kirchschläger to foreign ministry, 369-Res/68, "Tätigkeit der Gesandtschaft Prag in der 1. Woche der Besetzung der C.S.S.R. (21.-26. August 1968)," 26 August 1968, GZl. 124.925, GrZl. 112.916, ÖStA, AdR, BMfAA, II-pol 1968, C.S.S.R. 3, box 6.

40. Kirchschläger to foreign ministry, Tel. 25 309, "Lagebericht 23. August," 23 August 1968, 16:35, ÖStA, AdR, BMfAA, II-pol 1968, C.S.S.R. 3, box 6.

41. *"Diese Weisung ging in meiner Abwesenheit ein; ich habe sie nie zu Gesicht bekommen. Ich sah sie als überholt an und beschloß, sie zu ignorieren."* Quoted in "Besondere Achtung für bewundernswerten Widerstand." *Salzburger Nachrichten*, 20 August 1998, p. 7.

42. Kirchschläger to foreign ministry, Tel. 25 341, "Situationsbericht 26. 8., 13:30," 26 August 1968, ÖStA, AdR, BMfAA, II-pol 1968, C.S.S.R. 3, box 6.

43. *"bundesminister für inneres teilt mit, dass heute in prag von besatzungmacht 10.000 (zehntausend) cssr-blanko-reisepässe beschlagnahmt wurden. da gefahr besteht, dass diese reisepaesse zweckwidrig verwendet werden koenen [sic], hat innenministerium*

ersucht, bis auf weiteres keine visa auf C.S.S.R. paesse zu erteilen." Foreign ministry to head of legation, Prague, Tel. 55 171, 25 August 1968, 16:55. A copy of this document is held by the Institut für Zeitgeschichte, Innsbruck.

44. See the statement of Franz Soronics in Wohnout, ed., *Demokratie und Geschichte*, 113; see also Tozzer and Kallinger, *"Marschmusik für Glockenspiel,"* 78-81.

45. *"Ich bitte sehr, die Weisung einer neuerlichen Überprüfung zu unterziehen. Eine absolute Visasperre für csl. Staatsangehörige wäre ein so schwerer Schlag gegen die hiesige Bevölkerung, die ob ihres Verhaltens von allen Ausländern hier einhellige Bewunderung genießt und würde auch so im Gegensatz zu der seit 1956 erworbenen humanitären Tradition Österreichs stehen, daß diese harte Maßnahme von kaum jemand verstanden werden könnte. Ich gestehe, daß ich es kaum über mich bringen würde, dieser Weisung nachzukommen ohne in schwerste Gewissenskonflikte zu geraten. ..."* Kirchschläger to foreign ministry (General Secretary), Tel. 25 332, 25 August 1968.

46. Kirchschläger in an interview to the author on 16 June 1998 in his home in Vienna; Kirchschläger, *Der Friede beginnt im eigenen Haus*, 155; see also "Besondere Achtung," *Salzburger Nachrichten*, 20 August 1998, p. 7, and Interview with Rudolf Kirchschläger in *Österreich II*, minute 76.

47. *"Und dazu hatten die Schweizer Botschaft, die Britische Botschaft und die deutsche Handelsdelegation sehr engen Kontakt mit mir, und wenn ich aufgehört hätte, Visum [sic] zu geben, hätten die wahrscheinlich auch gestoppt. Zumindest wurde mir immer gesagt, solang Sie geben, geben wir auch."* Interview with Rudolf Kirchschläger in *Österreich II* 1968, minutes 75 to 76.

48. This is a point Kirchschläger emphasized again later, while in office as president of the Republic. In his book, published in 1980, he outlined the characteristics of the specific Austrian neutrality policy, giving prominence to the "unconditional willingness for humanitarian action" as one of the main Austrian contributions to peace and security in Europe. See Kirchschläger, *Der Friede beginnt im eigenen Haus*, 150 and 154-155.

49. Numbers of the visa granted can be found in the situation reports of the legation in Prague for the period of 23 August to 9 September 1968, (ÖStA, AdR, BMfAA, II-pol 1968, C.S.S.R., box 6, and C.S.S.R. 3, box 7); see also the data given in the "Erklärung der Bundesregierung vor dem Nationalrat," 18 September 1968, *Stenographische Protokolle über die Sitzungen des Nationalrates (XI. Gesetzgebungsperiode) der Republik Österreich*, 1968, vol. VII; see also "Entwurf eines mündlichen Berichts des Herrn Bundesministers für Inneres an die Bundesregierung über die Betreuung der csl. Flüchtlinge und Staatsangehörige [sic]. Vortrag an den Ministerrat. Beilage A zur Verhandlungsschrift Nr. 92 über die Sitzung des Ministerrates am 10. September 1968," ÖStA, AdR, Bundeskanzleramt, Präsidium, Ministerratsprotokolle.

50. Kirchschläger to Waldheim, 7-Pol/69, "Die österr.-csl. Beziehungen; Stand März 1969," 7 March 1969, draft with handwritten parts. A copy of this document is held by the Institut für Zeitgeschichte, Innsbruck.

51. Bericht des Bundesministeriums für Inneres, 23 October 1968, qtd. in Eduard Stanek, *Verfolgt, verjagt, vertrieben. Flüchtlinge in Österreich von 1945-1984* (Wien-München-Zürich: publisher, 1985), 93.

52. Kirchschläger to foreign ministry, Tel. 25 342, "Situationsbericht 26. August, 18:00," 26 August 1968, ÖStA, AdR, BMfAA, II-pol 1968, C.S.S.R. 3, box 7.

53. Kirchschläger to foreign ministry, Tel. 25 354, "Situationsbericht 28. 8., 8:30," 28 August 1968, ÖStA, AdR, BMfAA, II-pol 1968, C.S.S.R. 3, box 7.

54. In total—by September 1957—some 180,000 Hungarians had fled to Austria. By that time, though, 160,000 had already left this country for other states which accepted the refugees; see the chart in Manfried Rauchensteiner, *Spätherbst 1956. Die Neutralität auf dem Prüfstand* (Wien: 1981), 112.

55. A number of people had left Austria for other destinations without leaving any trace in Austrian statistics. See Bericht des Bundesministeriums für Inneres, 23 October 1968, in Stanek, *Verfolgt, verjagt, vertrieben*, 93.

56. Stanek, *Verfolgt, verjagt, vertrieben*, 90.

57. Kirchschläger to Waldheim, 32-Pol/68, "Die Invasion," 2 September 1968, ÖStA, AdR, BMfAA, II-pol 1968, C.S.S.R. 3, box 5.

58. Magrutsch to foreign ministry, 8531-A/68, "Parolen gegen die Besatzungsmächte der C.S.S.R.," 23 September 1968, GZl. 126 558, GrZl. 110 223-6/68, ÖStA, AdR, BMfAA, II-pol 1968, C.S.S.R. 3, box 5.

59. Kirchschläger to foreign ministry, Tel. 25 309, "Lagebericht 23. August," 23 August 1968, ÖStA, AdR, BMfAA, II-pol 1968, C.S.S.R., box 6.

60. Kirchschläger to foreign ministry, Tel. 25 323, "Lagebericht 24. 8., 15:30," 24 August 1968, ÖStA, AdR, BMfAA, II-pol 1968, C.S.S.R., box 6.

61. Kirchschläger to Waldheim, 32-Pol/68, "Die Invasion," 2 September 1968, ÖStA, AdR, BMfAA, II-pol 1968, C.S.S.R. 3, box 5.

62. This was evident immediately after the invasion; see Magrutsch to foreign ministry, Tel. 25 298, 22 August 1968, ÖStA, AdR, BMfAA, II-pol 1968, C.S.S.R., box 6.

63. Kirchschläger to foreign ministry, Tel. 25 326, 24 August 1968, ÖStA, AdR, BMfAA, II-pol 1968, C.S.S.R., box 6.

64. [Kirchschläger] to foreign ministry, 16-Pol/69, "Von der Normalisierung zur Konsolidierung," 10 June 1969 (draft). A copy of this document is held by the Institut für Zeitgeschichte, Innsbruck.

65. [Kirchschläger] to foreign ministry, 28-Pol/69, "Von der Okkupation zur brüderlichen Hilfe," 20 October 1969 (draft). Ibid.

66. [Kirchschläger] to foreign ministry, 4-Pol/70, "Die österreichisch csl. Beziehungen," 8 February 1970 (draft). Ibid.

HISTORIOGRAPHY ROUNDTABLE

Gerald Stourzh's Opus Magnum
Um Einheit und Freiheit: Staatsvertrag, Neutralität und das
Ende der Ost-West-Besetzung Österreichs 1945-1955,
4th revised and expanded ed. (Vienna: Böhlau, 1998)

Günter Bischof

Introduction

Gerald Stourzh, professor emeritus of modern history of the University of Vienna, has been one of Austria's leading historians for more than a generation. His scholarly *oeuvre* has the rare breadth and the depth of a renaissance man. He made signal contributions in at least three distinct scholarly fields:

1) He is the rare Austrian historian recognized in the U.S. for his important scholarly contributions to early American history. His books on Benjamin Franklin's foreign policy and on Alexander Hamilton's constitutional ideas are still regularly read and much admired in American seminars.

2) His thorough knowledge of American constitutional history has inspired him to do path-breaking work on Austrian/Austro-Hungarian constitutional history of the nineteenth century, particularly on individual, human, and minority rights.

3) He has also defined and redefined how we think about twentieth century Austrian foreign policy and national identity in general, and--with his work on the Austrian postwar occupation and the making of the Austrian treaty--how we conceptualize Austrian neutrality in the cold war after 1955 in particular.

Both Stourzh's sterling international reputation in all these fields and his many students' adulation and esteem can best be gathered from the two *Festschriften* his students and friends dedicated to him for his

60th and 70th birthdays. Cumulatively these two volumes also present complete bibliographies of his numerous publications.[1]

This *Historiography Forum* will specifically deal with Stourzh's contribution to the history of the Austrian Treaty and Austria's *locus* in early cold war history. The following four essays by three noted cold war historians and a well-known Austrian political scientist were first delivered in a panel dedicated to Stourzh's new State Treaty history at the annual meeting of the *German Studies Association* in Atlanta, Georgia in October 1999.[2] The particular foci of the following contributions are Stourzh's placement of the Austrian events in the larger trajectory of early cold war history and historiography, Austria's significance in the cold war, his utilization of the full range of archival materials from Austrian archives and the vast archival sources of the four occupation powers (particularly the new Soviet sources from Moscow's archives), as well as the Austrian domestic context in the making of the State Treaty.

American and British international historians are generally little aware of Stourzh's "masterpiece of diplomatic history"; this is less the case with German specialists.[3] The reason for this specific lacuna in Anglo-American cold war historiography is simple—Stourzh's state treaty histories were never translated. This has made them largely unavailable, particularly to the "tongue-tied" (Sen. Simon) American cold war historians. As Jonathan Haslam of Cambridge University has reminded his colleagues, "the days when a book on some aspect of international relations in the postwar period could be researched purely from American or, indeed, British archives are over."[4] Stourzh's polyglot approach to all these sources is exemplary, his is a *model* of multi-archival, multi-lingual international history.

Stourzh has been mining new sources on the Austrian treaty, which were consecutively opened in archives around the world according to national access rules, for thirty years. The first edition of his Austrian treaty history was published in 1975 and relied largely on Anglo-American archival sources.[5] The second and third updated editions appeared in 1980 and 1985 respectively, which were important anniversary years of the State Treaty. Easily affordable textbook versions (*Studienausgaben*) made these books widely available.[6] He updated these editions with newly available extensive sources from Western archives and new work done in British, French, and American archives by his best students. Stourzh also received privileged access to crucial sources in the Austrian State Archives and private Austrian collections. This gave his work an unmatched authority but also made it hard to challenge his interpretations from the Austrian sources.

Stourzh's work on the State Treaty has become signal both in defining Austrian *neutrality* and the role of neutrality in constituting a specific *postwar Austrian identity*. He was a key organizer, participant, and keynote speaker of the huge official 25th anniversary symposium commemorating the State Treaty with foreign ministers from all four former occupation powers.[7] With these contributions the historian Stourzh, in fact, has been making history himself. When his eagerly awaited fourth edition was launched in the late fall of 1998, it was done with a presentation at the Austrian Parliament.[8] A considerable number of Vienna's political, bureaucratic, and scholarly elite was present, giving it the quasi-imprimatur of an act of state. This is an indication of how much Stourzh's successive volumes of *Staatsvertragsgeschichte* have become a mainstay on the grand narrative of Austrian postwar history, shaping it and fortifying important parts of the "coalition history" penned by his generation of historians.[9] The following essays will assess the contribution Gerald Stourzh has made to both cold war and Austrian history with his weighty updated *Staatsvertragsgeschichte*. CAS thus continues its "Historiography Forums" about signal contributions defining the debates about and setting the parameters for Austrian twentieth century history.

Notes

1. Emil Brix, Thomas Fröschl, and Josef Leidenfrost, eds., *Geschichte zwischen Freiheit und Ordnung: Gerald Stourzh zum 60. Geburtstag* (Graz: Styria, 1991); Thomas Angerer, Bigitta Bader-Zaar, and Margarete Grandner, eds., *Geschichte und Recht: Festschrift für Gerald Stourzh zum 70. Geburtstag* (Vienna: Böhlau, 1999).

2. We are grateful to the Austrian Cultural Institute in New York, the Center for Austrian Culture and Commerce at the University of New Orleans, the University of Innsbruck, and the German Studies Association for sponsoring this session.

3. This is the judgement of Klaus Hildebrand, one of the masters of diplomatic history in Germany; see his review in the *Frankfurter Allgemeine Zeitung*, 19 October 1999, p. 10.

4. Jonathan Haslam, "Russian Archival Revelations and Our Understanding of the Cold War," *Diplomatic History* 21 (Spring 1997): 228.

5. Gerald Stourzh, *Kleine Geschichte des Österreichischen Staatvertrages: Mit Dokumententeil* (Graz: Styria, 1975). It contained 149 pages of text, 270 endnotes, and exactly 100 pages of appendices (a highly valuable parallel text analysis of the April 1947 treaty draft with the final draft signed in 1955).

6. Gerald Stourzh, *Geschichte des Staatsvertrages 1945-1955; Österreichs Weg zur Neutralität* (Graz: Styria, 1980/1985). The third (1985) edition is largely the same as the second (1980) edition but with an extensive historiographical essay in the new epilogue and updated bibliography, see the *Nachwort* of the third edition, pp. 319-33. It contained 212 pages of text with 443 endnotes, and 104 pages of appendices (including again the 1947 and 1955 treaty drafts).

7. Austrian Federal Government, ed., *25 Jahre Staatsvertrag: Protokolle des Staats- und Festaktes sowie der Jubiläumsveranstaltungen im In- und Ausland*, 4 vols. (Vienna: Österreichischer Bundesverlag, 1981).

8. His massive revisions and large portions of new text, particularly on events in 1955, amount to a new book, which resembles the older 1985 text only in the beginning. The book is now a brickbat of 606 pages of text, including 1,533 footnotes, and 172 pages of appendices, along with the best bibliography available anywhere on Austria's role in the early cold war. See also my review "Ringen 'um Einheit und Freiheit'. Das Opus magnum eines grossen österreichischen Historikers: Zu Gerald Stourzh neuer Staatsvertragsgeschichte," *Die Furche*, 14 January 1999, p. 22.

9. On the distinct historiographical school of "coalition history" see Ernst Hanisch, "Der forschende Blick. Österreich im 20. Jahrhundert: Interpretationen und Kontroversen," *Carinthia*, no. 189 (1999): 573-76.

The Soviet Godfathers of Austrian Neutrality

Vojtech Mastny

Austrian neutrality originated in Moscow. The 1955 State Treaty, which made neutrality possible, could only come about because the key Soviet leaders had changed their mind, and finally approved of a neutral status for Austria. A book that tells the story primarily from the Western, and in particular from the Austrian, perspective may therefore seem out of balance. It need not be so if, while taking into account the available Soviet sources, it uses them to ask, and preferably answer, the right questions. How does Gerald Stourzh's *magnum opus* measure up to these expectations?

For the revised and greatly expanded fourth edition of his work, first published in 1975, Stourzh took advantage of the limited access to former Soviet archives. He saw unpublished documents from the foreign ministry and party archives, besides those already published elsewhere. Like other scholars, he had to make do with what the custodians of those files deigned to share, without being able to penetrate the inner sanctum where the most important records of top decision-making are kept—the Kremlin Presidential Archives.

The value of such incomplete evidence is not to be overestimated, but neither is it to be treated lightly. The author of these lines analyzed Soviet policy on the Austrian State Treaty in 1982, and has found no reasons to alter the main conclusions since.[1] Still, the very existence of new sources requires them to be considered. They often raise important questions, which had not been apparent before. They also exude that unmistakable Soviet flair, reminding the scholar that they do not originate from a 'normal state'.

It is difficult for a historian steeped in the Western tradition to sort out what is important amid the mass of trivia, all obfuscated by the dreary Marxist-Leninist jargon. Stourzh tends to overrate diplomatic papers originating from Molotov's underlings, who were habitually kept in the dark about important matters. As attested by one of them, Vladimir S. Semenov, "responsible officials of the foreign ministry and even deputy ministers" were prevented by their boss from knowing what was discussed in the highest party councils.[2]

More revealing of Russian policy are the records of the Communist party, especially transcripts of the contentious July 1955 plenum of its central committee, where the Austrian settlement was retrospectively assayed behind closed doors. Though blatantly biased, these records convey not only the real issues but also the thuggish milieu in which Soviet 'high' policy was made. They are consistent with the other evidence we have. Of course, as Stourzh reminds us, since "the deliberations in the presidium ... cannot be reconstructed and documented from sources" (p. 453), interpreting the Soviet motives is difficult. But this makes it all the more important for historians to try to do so as best as they can and to share their expert opinion with their readers.

Long before the archives provided the evidence, the origins of the Soviet turnabout regarding Austria could be detected in the Kremlin power struggle, which led to the downfall of Malenkov and the mounting feud between Molotov and Khrushchev. But the true nature of the infighting among Stalin's former henchmen and its link to the concurrent turn in the German question—the November 1954 Paris agreements that opened up the prospect of West Germany's admission into NATO—could only recently be traced from internal Soviet sources. Most of these are in Stourzh's book, however not in the context of their Soviet setting.

The swift substitution of the Paris agreements for the defunct European Defense Community, whose debacle in the French National Assembly merely two months earlier had been greeted by Moscow with undisguised glee, cast doubt on the efficacy of Molotov's reliance upon driving wedges within the Western alliance. Living off his reputed foreign policy expertise, Molotov nevertheless insisted on that tactic as the only properly tough way of treating the capitalist enemy. Making the Austrian settlement contingent upon the prior solution of the German question, and thus postponing both solutions indefinitely, was integral to that Stalinist tactic, whose obsolescence became clear by late 1954.

Molotov's commissioning from his aides studies about the possible resumption of talks about the Austrian question indicated an awareness that his policy was not working. But nothing suggested that an alternative policy was found by the time he colluded with Khrushchev to get rid of Malenkov. While disagreements on domestic issues sufficed to engineer Malenkov's downfall at the secret plenum of the central committee at the end of January 1955, his disgrace provided the added opportunity to affix upon him, as was the Stalinist habit, failures of Soviet foreign policy as well. Doing so was made easier by Malenkov's susceptibility to unorthodox ideas about the settlement of the German and, by implication, the Austrian question as well. But Malenkov was too weak and soft (by the cutthroat Bolshevik standards) to give these ideas coherence, much less to act upon them—as Winston Churchill, in particular, deluded himself he might do. They were close to the similarly nebulous ideas about the unification of a neutral Germany as a way toward accommodation with the West entertained by the detestable Lavrentii P. Beria, Malenkov's former crony, dispatched to death by his peers in 1953.

Only after Malenkov's dangerously vague ideas had been disposed of along with their proponent could the remaining members of the Kremlin team address their foreign policy predicament without fear of setting into motion an avalanche they might be unable to control. Contemporaries rightly grasped that the victory of Molotov and Khrushchev marked the ascendancy of hardliners at that time. Retrospectively, however, Molotov's keynote foreign policy address of 8 February 1955, the day Malenkov's ouster was made public, has bred the optical illusion that it inaugurated Soviet commitment to the Austrian settlement.

Stourzh does not succumb to that illusion. He recognizes that Molotov's obiter dicta about the desirability of the settlement signified no departure from his axiom that this could only take place once the German problem had been solved to Soviet satisfaction (pp. 341-345). And Evgenii D. Kiselev, the knowledgeable former political adviser to the Soviet High Commissioner in Vienna, confirms that "until 1955, i.e., until the time [in April] when the central committee decided to resolve the Austrian question in conformity with the proposal by comrade Khrushchev, the basic line was to delay rather than achieve its resolution."[3]

Why did Moscow single out Austria as its priority? It could have responded in other ways to the timetable set by the Paris agreements for West Germany's admission into NATO, a timetable which gave the Kremlin leaders less than five months to try to avert their ratification or, more realistically, at least to mitigate their consequences by cutting their own losses. Lacking the record of their deliberations, Stourzh is reluctant to speculate about their motives. Yet there is enough evidence in his book to answer the question of what impelled the embattled Kremlin chiefs to move on the Austrian question.

As was often the case, well-placed observers with *Fingerspitzengefühl* for things Soviet, such as U.S. ambassador to Moscow Charles Bohlen, intuitively found the answer by reading between the lines of the official Soviet pronouncements against the alleged increased danger of another Anschluß. In Soviet parlance, this emotionally charged word was not to be understood literally as referring to a repetition of Hitler's triumphant march into Austria in 1938, but rather as a codeword for the possible integration of the Western-controlled bulk of Austria's territory into the West's expanding defense system, of which the ascendant West Germany was poised to become the key European pillar. Stourzh may be right in not setting as much store by the scope of the American effort to bring Austria into the "Western military club" (p. 384), as do other historians, such as Günter Bischof or Michael Gehler.[4] But the Soviets were evidently worried—less about the military than about the political implications of NATO's advance. "NATO is a political organization of our adversaries," Khrushchev pointedly reminded the East European party chiefs at a meeting in June 1956.[5]

The innovative streak in Soviet policy was the decision to respond to the military challenge inherent in NATO's forthcoming expansion by setting into motion political developments calculated to diminish the importance of the cold war's military dimensions and, as a result, enable the Soviet Union to turn the tables on its adversaries. This was unmistakably Khrushchev's thinking, expressed forcefully in the rhetorical question he asked the skeptical Molotov, challenging him whether he wanted war. If not, Khrushchev continued, "then what do you want to accomplish by having our troops stay in Vienna? If you are for war then it would be right to stay in Austria. It is a strategic area, and only a fool would give up a strategic area if he is getting ready to go to war."[6]

Professor Stourzh paraphrases Khrushchev's statement among other "remarkable details" (p. 459) without highlighting it for the insights it offers into the frame of mind that determined Moscow's extraordinary behavior in the *annus mirabilis* of 1955. Despite all its bluster about 'imperialist warmongers' and its exhortations for the need for military readiness, the party secretary was saying nothing less than that the Soviet Union was not going to war after all—implying, at the same time, that the West was not either. The stage was thus set for the 'first détente', and the Austrian settlement became the first item on its agenda.

When did this remarkable new thinking begin to prevail in the Kremlin? The decision to act on the Austrian question in response to the Paris agreements may have been reflected in the introduction of the Anschluß theme in the Soviet press on 19 January 1955.[7] However, the Kremlin could have reacted in different ways, and Professor Stourzh might have offered an opinion on why the Soviets chose the unusual way of approaching the Austrians first. Could it have been because Chancellor Julius Raab had just been to Washington, praising there the Paris agreements, which had a chilling effect on his country's relations with Moscow? If so, then it was Austria's rapprochement with the United States rather than its currying Soviet favor, which Austria's envoy to Moscow, Norbert Bischoff, had been busy trying to do, that prompted the Kremlin to act before it might be too late. "The Austrian question," Khrushchev remarked, alluding to Molotov's management of it, "is like a rotten egg," and might have to be thrown away (p. 459).

Ignoring the indispensable Soviet godfathers, Bischoff has been ludicrously described as the "father of Austrian neutrality" by the none too perceptive West German ambassador to Moscow, Hans Kroll (p. 424). According to documents in the Vienna archives, Bischoff's contribution appears to have been more dubious than previous authors, including the writer of this essay, used to believe. So acclimatized had the diplomat become to the Soviet capital that he composed on his own initiative a proposal to ensure Moscow's right to intervene militarily in Austria should "an immediate threat of the Anschluß" warrant it. (p. 372) Professor Stourzh has been intrigued by Bischoff's ability to communicate directly with both his chancellor in Vienna and the Soviet bosses in the Kremlin, sometimes bypassing the respective foreign ministries, and by Bischoff's shadowy meetings with Soviet contacts in Moscow bathhouses, especially the lack of documentation about these meetings (pp. 423-424). Such *liaisons dangereuses* held a certain fascination to Western officials convinced of their self-importance, both because of the thrill involved and because of the putative benefits that might accrue to their countries, besides the real benefits that accrued to their Soviet manipulators.

Bischoff's propensity for representing Soviet views to his government made him an ideal conduit for the Kremlin, once its leaders found a speedy conclusion of the State Treaty to be in their interest. Moscow tried to make a deal with the Austrians before presenting the Western powers with the outline of a settlement difficult to resist and envisaged a four-power conference on Austria to throw the timetable for West Germany's NATO entry into disarray—a last-ditch attempt to use the

245

rotting Austrian egg as a monkey-wrench. At a secret briefing of Soviet ambassadors to the Communist countries in mid-February, Molotov confidently maintained that "we are not afraid of the Paris agreements," for "whatever the form in which they might be implemented, we will stir up the capitalist bloc by taking advantage of its weaknesses."[8]

But by April it had become sufficiently evident that Molotov's policy was mostly wishful thinking and that it had to be replaced by a sounder one. Stourzh's study is the first to document from Soviet sources the crucial April 2 decision by the party presidium to substitute Molotov's concept for the Austrian settlement by Khrushchev's, which would also expedite its attainment. Khrushchev's concept entailed dropping Molotov's insistence on keeping some Soviet troops in Austria for a prolonged period to ensure its good behavior while reserving Moscow's right to intervene militarily should it judge Austrian neutrality to be in peril (pp. 405-408). Only now was the road to the State Treaty cleared.

The familiar story of the ensuing nine weeks of negotiations is enriched in Stourzh's book by interesting details. He justly dwells on the dexterity of the Austrian representatives who, once sensing how badly Moscow needed an agreement, managed to extract from it concessions that made the resulting treaty in several ways less favorable for the Soviet Union than the drafts it had previously rejected. The feat of the bipartisan team of Julius Raab and Adolf Schärf, Leopold Figl and Bruno Kreisky proved quite out of *Proporz* with their country's lowly status.

Moscow's uncharacteristic behavior merits pausing and pondering on what, beyond preventing the largely imaginary Anschluß, the Kremlin rulers wanted to accomplish. On the twenty-odd pages where the broader "context of the Soviet policy on Austria [is] discussed in four points" (pp. 463-485), Professor Stourzh gives no clear answer. Nor does he attempt to differentiate between the substantive and incidental tenets of the Soviet diplomatic offensive, of which the Austrian settlement was but one part.

Among those four points, the soothing effect of the withdrawal from Austria on Khrushchev's simultaneous effort to mend fences with Yugoslavia is duly noted but not related to the two countries' complementary role in the running dispute between Molotov and Khrushchev about the right Soviet policy. At the 1955 party plenum Khrushchev assaulted Molotov for his Stalinist rigidity and singled out his rival's mismanagement of both the Austrian and the Yugoslav questions—with an emphasis on the latter because of its deeper ideological implications. Moscow had been preoccupied with what Molotov described as the

danger of Yugoslavia joining "the North Atlantic bloc or any of its
international affiliates."[9] It was this twin specter of the Austrian
Anschluß that Khrushchev sought to exorcise by his risky rapprochement
with Tito, which he justified as having prevented the possible use of
Yugoslavia by NATO.

The intriguing question of whether Moscow conceived of Austria's
neutrality as an invitation to Germany to follow suit, understandably
tantalized contemporaries and has nourished the tiresome German debate
about the allegedly missed opportunities for the country's reunification.[10]
That heavily politicized debate has been more about the policies of
Chancellor Konrad Adenauer and his Social Democratic opponents than
about Soviet policy, and as such of interest mainly to Germans.
Historians detached from their quarrels—Professor Stourzh included (pp.
467-480)—find no mystery in Soviet officials dropping hints about their
government's alleged support for German unification, as long as such
hints could be expected to discourage West Germany's still pending
NATO membership. But when it came to specifics, Moscow's spokes-
men hedged. While they praised, in general terms, the Austrians'
forthcoming attitude as a model worthy of imitation by the obstreperous
Germans, they also pointed out the obvious—that the German situation
was complicated by the country's bigger size and its deeper division. In
any case, the instructions Molotov received from the presidium before
going to Vienna to sign the treaty stated unequivocally "that after the
ratification of the Paris agreements the situation in Europe has changed
and that the German question cannot be regarded in any way as being
ready to be successfully discussed at the present time" (p. 478).

In view of the Soviet concern about Austria becoming part of the
Western defense system, military-minded analysts—though not
contemporary NATO planners—have tended to attribute paramount
importance to the interruption of the alliance's North-South lines of
communication through Austria as a result of its neutrality.[11] Stourzh
gives short shrift to the military implications for either NATO or the
Soviet Union. Such a treatment would be justified if the West had not
been so much preoccupied by the imbalance of forces in Europe, and if
Khrushchev had not proposed to rectify the imbalance by submitting,
only a week before the State Treaty was signed, Moscow's most radical
disarmament proposal prior to Gorbachev. It was not by accident, as the
Soviets would have put it in their jargon, that their turnabout on Austria
occurred at a time when NATO had just initiated a major armament
program as a result of its December 1954 "MC-48" decision. This
program provided for a massive deployment of tactical nuclear weapons

in Western Europe, which Moscow had so far been reluctant to integrate into its own arsenal.

Concurrently with the Austrian *volte face*, Khrushchev embarked upon unilateral reductions of Soviet conventional forces. If, as he implied in his rhetorical question to Molotov, the likelihood of war had diminished, so did the utility of the vast army inherited from Stalin. Its size had become counterproductive by encouraging NATO's nuclear buildup. Rather than compete with the West militarily, Khrushchev wanted to rely upon what he believed was his country's ascendancy in political, economic, ideological, and other nonmilitary attributes of power—a belief which was later proved wrong. He sought détente to demilitarize the cold war just as the West accelerated its militarization.

Did Moscow consider the Austrian treaty a test of détente which it was prepared to follow by further concessions, as Günter Bischof and other historians suggest it was?[12] Citing contemporary Western estimates, Stourzh sees a *grand dessin soviétique* in Khrushchev's cultivating friendly ties with nonaligned states in Asia and encouraging the emergence of more such states in Europe as well (pp. 482-485). In Vienna, Molotov himself hailed the fact that "in addition to Switzerland, there will henceforth be a neutral Austria in the center of Europe," voicing hope "that this course will be followed by other states as well."[13] And Eisenhower seconded by suggesting that "there seems to be developing the thought that there might be built up a series of neutralized states from north to south through Europe."[14] Soon a whole cottage industry would develop in Western Europe, though not so much in the United States, turning out proposals for the creation of a zone of disengagement separating the two blocs.

Regardless of Molotov's statement, the widespread assumption that Moscow favored the idea is not supported by the evidence. A survey commissioned by the Soviet foreign ministry committee of information at the end of 1955 treated the different disengagement plans critically as Western artifacts.[15] The often mentioned Soviet troop withdrawals of that year, from the Lüshun (Port Arthur) naval base in China and then the Porkkala-Udd base near Helsinki, stemmed, like the evacuation of Austria, from primarily local considerations. The former withdrawal had been decided already in 1954 by Khrushchev's desire to placate Mao Zedong, the latter by his desire to secure the election of the Soviet favorite, Urho Kekkonen, to Finland's presidency.[16] None of these actions served as the starting point of a larger enterprise.

While always ready to advise NATO members that they would be better off as non-members, the Soviet Union never seriously encouraged a Western European state to follow Austria's example of declaring itself neutral and actively discouraged its own Eastern European dependencies from even thinking about it. This was a message implicit in the conclusion of the Warsaw Pact, signed just one day before the Austrian State Treaty. By tying the Soviet satellite states more closely to each other and to Moscow, the Warsaw Pact served unambiguous notice that the Austrian model was not for them. When three months later the Romanian party chief Gheorghe Gheorghiu-Dej tried to ignore the message by proposing to the Soviet Union to withdraw its troops from his country as well, Khrushchev fell into a rage, and the Romanian hastily denied in public that any such plan existed.[17]

Stourzh agrees that the coincidence of the Warsaw Pact with the State Treaty "must not be ignored" (p. 464), but does not elaborate why. Extensive documentation about the Warsaw prelude to the Vienna act exists in archives of the former member states of the Communist alliance, illuminating its larger purposes.[18] Beyond its role as a precautionary measure to keep the Eastern European 'sheep' within Moscow's fold, the Warsaw Pact—a product of the same shift in Soviet thinking that also produced Austrian neutrality—became the true test of détente as Khrushchev understood it. His objective was nothing less that the eventual establishment of a new security system in Europe, with the Soviet Union as its arbiter.

The new alliance, proclaimed at a time when East-West tensions were declining, was superfluous, for Moscow had in any case the military potential of its allies at its disposal because of the already existing network of bilateral mutual defense treaties it had previously imposed on them. Created as a diplomatic ploy without military substance, the Warsaw Pact organization was dispensable and therefore suitable to being negotiated away, together with NATO, if the conditions were right. The Soviet diplomatic campaign in the aftermath of the Austrian treaty, featuring proposals for the replacement of military blocs by a collective security system, was about creating such conditions. The Soviet assumption that such proposals could be taken seriously proved that Moscow had not quite outgrown those children's shorts and graduated into grownups' pants, as Khrushchev later suggested it had (p. 484).

Eventually, the Warsaw Pact became the cold war's preeminent military fixture whereas the establishment of Austrian neutrality remained a mere episode. Limited to that country, it was therefore hardly "one of the most important, successful, and lasting compromises in the history of Europe in the era of the East-West confrontation" (p. 450). It might be sufficient to say, as Professor Stourzh exhaustively shows, that it served his nation's interests remarkably well throughout the cold war. And it should be added that the neutrality status allowed Austria to become at that time, despite all its warts, a beacon of freedom and decency for the neighboring peoples of the Soviet empire, contributing a far from negligible share to its final breakup and the cold war's happy end. This was the historic accomplishment of the Austrian people and their astute leaders that the Soviet godfathers of Austrian neutrality had inadvertently made possible.

With the cold war over and no other war looming on the European horizon, however, the justification of Austrian neutrality became increasingly tenuous. It did not help the nation to overcome its inhibitions about whole-hearted participation in the European Union or, in contrast to the neighboring Switzerland, in NATO's Partnership for Peace. Nor did it help the Austrian people to come to terms with the unsavory legacy of their Nazi past. It has not prevented the country to find itself, as a result, in uncomfortable international isolation in the year 2000 and may have, in fact, substantially contributed to this outcome.

Notes

1. Vojtech Mastny, "Kremlin Politics and the Austrian Settlement,"*Problems of Communism* 31 (1982): 37-51.

2. Semenov to Shvernik, 17 October 1959, copy from the Russian State Archives of Contemporary History [RGANI] provided for the conference, "New Evidence on Cold War History," Moscow, 12-15 January 1993.

3. Kiselev to Shvernik, October 1959, ibid.

4. Günter Bischof, "Österreich—ein geheimer Verbündeter des Westens? Wirtschafts- und sicherheitspolitische Fragen der Integration aus der Sicht der USA," in *Österreich und die europäische Integration, 1945-1993: Aspekte einer wechselvollen Entwicklung*, ed. Michael Gehler and Rolf Steininger (Vienna: Böhlau, 1993), 425-450, and other items, listed in Stourzh's bibliography.

5. Record of Moscow meeting of Soviet bloc leaders, 22-23 June 1956, 64/230, Central State Archives, Sofia.

6. Record of the central committee plenum, 12 July 1955, 2/1/176/282-95, RGANI, copy at the National Security Archive, Washington, DC. Khrushchev rendered his statement almost verbatim in his conversation with Vice President Richard Nixon on 26 July 1959, *Foreign Relations of the United States*, 1958-1960, vol. 10, pt. 1 (Washington: U.S. Government Printing Office, 1993), 366.

7. Michael Gehler, "Österreich und die deutsche Frage 1954/55: Zur 'Modellfall'-Debatte in der internationalen Diplomatie und der bundesdeutschen Öffentlichkeit aus französischer Sicht," *Österreichischer Historikertag, Bregenz 1994: Tagungsbericht* (Vienna: Verband der österreichischen Historiker und Geschichtsvereine, 1998), 83-134, here 87.

8. "Vazhneishie vneshnepoliticheskie sobytiia" 'The Most Important Foreign Policy Events', preparatory material for the 20th party congress, pre-February 1956, copy from the Russian State Archives of Contemporary History provided for the conference "New Evidence on Cold War History," Moscow, 12-15 January 1993.

9. Record of the central committee, 9 July 1955, "Plenum Transcripts," *Cold War International History Project Bulletin* 10 (1998): 41.

10. For the Austrian dimension of the debate, see Michael Gehler, "State Treaty and Neutrality: The Austrian Solution in 1955 as a 'Model' for Germany?," *Contemporary Austrian Studies*, vol. 3, *Austria in the Nineteen-Fifties* (New Brunswick: Transaction, 1995), 39-78; Bruno Thoß, "Modellfall Österreich? Der österreichische Staatsvertrag und die deutsche Frage 1954/55," in *Zwischen Kaltem Krieg und Entspannung: Sicherheits- und Deutschlandpolitik der Bundesregierung im Mächtesystem der Jahre 1953-1955*, ed. Bruno Thoß and Hans-Erich Volkmann (Boppard am Rhein: Boldt, 1988), 93-136.

11. See P.H. Vigor, *The Soviet View of War, Peace and Neutrality* (London: Routledge & Kegan Paul, 1975), 182-83; report by Standing Group, MRM-100-55, 2 September 1955, International Military Staff, NATO Archives, Brussels.

12. Günter Bischof, "The Making of the Austrian Treaty and the Road to Geneva" (Paper delivered at the conference "The Dawn of Détente: The Geneva Summit of July 1955," New Orleans, 20 – 22 October 1995).

13. Quoted in William L. Stearman, *The Soviet Union and the Occupation of Austria: An Analysis of Soviet Policy in Austria, 1945-1955* (Bonn: Siegler, 1962), 164.

14. "The President's News Conference, 18 May 1955," in *Public Papers of the President of the United States, Dwight D. Eisenhower, 1955* (Washington, DC: Government Printing Office, 1959), 518.

15. "Plans of the Western Powers Concerning the Creation of a 'Zone of Reduced Tension' in Europe," pre-November 1955, 89/70/1, RGANI.

16. Constantine Pleshakov, "Nikita Khrushchev and Sino-Soviet Relations," in *Brothers in Arms: The Rise and Fall of the Sino-Soviet Alliance, 1945-1963,* ed. Odd Arne Westad (Washington: Woodrow Wilson Center Press, 1998), 226-245, here 228-229; Kimmo Rentola, "From Half-Adversary to Half-Ally: Finland in Soviet Policy, 1953 to 1958" (Paper delivered at the conference "The First Détente, 1953-1958," Helsinki, 29-30 October 1999) 11-13.

17. Dennis Deletant, *Communist Terror in Romania: Gheorghiu-Dej and the Police State, 1948-1965* (New York: St. Martin's Press, 1999), 273-274.

18. Vojtech Mastny, "The Soviet Union and the Origins of the Warsaw Pact in 1955," in *Mechanisms of Power and Soviet Foreign Policy*, ed. Erik Kulavig (London: Macmillan, 2000), forthcoming.

An American Perspective

Thomas Schwartz

To comment on a book this comprehensive and well-researched is a considerable challenge in and of itself. It is also difficult to comment on the work of an author whose *Benjamin Franklin and American Foreign Policy* was one of the first I ever read on American foreign policy, and whose interpretation I still rely upon in my undergraduate classes. In any event, my commentary on the Stourzh book will come less in the nature of criticisms and more in terms of the questions which this work poses. As definitive a history as this is—and I agree with Günter Bischof that this is a book that can be called definitive—it suggests a number of areas for further inquiry.

Simply put this book reflects the best of international history. Stourzh understands that the Austrian story can not be grasped without an extraordinary multiarchival research effort, and the use of American, British, French, and Russian sources brings this fact home. International history is a truly challenging endeavor, not only in terms of the languages necessary but also the research grants involved. This book is the type which diplomatic historians need to convince skeptical government agencies and private foundations that such work is truly necessary.The second point is the significance of this story. One of my graduate school professors was fond of saying "So what?" at the end of lengthy expositions by frightened graduate students about some set of underused documents or obscure past event. What, indeed, is the significance of the Austrian state treaty? Obviously it has enormous significance for the Austrians themselves, shaping the environment of their nation for close to forty years. However, what significance should the agreement have for students of American foreign relations? Stourzh has documented a true Cold War success story, and one small piece in the puzzle of explaining why the Cold War never did become World

War III. In their ability to reach an agreement on Austria, the two superpowers demonstrated a willingness to stand back from confrontation and remove at least one small source of tension in their relationship. The Austrian agreement did not lead to an end to the Cold War, but it did demonstrate that the conflict was not simply about strategic positions and holding on to every inch of territory. Rather, the Austrian settlement reflected an understanding on both sides of the essentially political struggle between the two ideological giants, a political struggle which offered opportunities for some compromises.

Finally, the Stourzh book does illuminate the important role played by the Austrians themselves in shaping their own history. There is not total agreement on how significant the "leverage of the weak" was in influencing the great powers to accept their version of neutrality.[1] The Stourzh book does make it clear that historians of international relations—no matter how consumed they may be with the Cold War power games going on—must consider the role of the smaller powers in both influencing and to manipulate great power patrons.These points aside, I would like to pose a number of questions to the author, questions which I hope might lead to new avenues of research. The first is actually quite simple: Do you have any reason to believe that there is any material in the Russian archives that you did not have access to which might substantially change or alter any interpretation in the book? Although the excitement generated by the new sources in Cold War history has tended to run its course, it is also clear that there is still a great deal that is unavailable about Soviet decision making.[2] On the other side, would access to a broader range of intelligence material from the United States, such as material from the archives of the Central Intelligence Agency, affect the book's interpretation of American policies? Could it help explain the relatively enlightened attitude of John Foster Dulles toward Austrian questions? After all, his brother was Director of the CIA!

The second question I would like to pose is which of the other four possible outcomes or variants (p.580) he identifies was most likely if the Moscow talks had failed. The book does an excellent job in underlining the series of fortuitous events that led to the "miraculous year" of 1955, but it also underlines the risks and real possibilities for failure. What would have been the most likely result of such a failure? Continued partition? Western Austria within NATO? What implications does this counterfactual question have for understanding Austria's subsequent history?

The third question concerns the relationship between the resolution of the Austrian question and the ongoing division of Germany. Which of these two formulations would Prof. Stourzh accept? Hypothesis 1: The Austrian treaty was evidence that a peaceful reunification of Germany was possible, but that would have required a commitment by German leaders similar to that evidenced by both Austrian political parties. To this extent, those German historians, notably Rolf Steininger and Wilfried Loth, who identify Adenauer as a central barrier to German reunification, are correct.[3] This viewpoint would also underline the degree to which the Eisenhower Administration forfeited a key opportunity to defuse the Cold War in Europe.

Hypothesis 2: The reunification and neutrality of Austria was only possible *because* West Germany was integrated into the Western alliance and the division of Germany was stabilized. Was the Austrian solution available because the Western powers had reached a decision on Germany, and the Soviets sought to undermine that decision with West German public opinion? Absent such West German integration into NATO, would the West have shown the same willingness to accept a neutral Austria? I would argue that even a West German leader committed to reunification above all else might have found his room to maneuver exceedingly limited.

The fourth comment and question I would like to pose has to do with the significance of the Austrian solution for Eastern Europe. It is obviously no surprise that this monumental study comes to an end in 1955, marking the end of ten years of "East-West" occupation of Austria. But for a number of reasons, 1955 really stands in the middle of a five year period, beginning with the death of Stalin and perhaps ending with the onset of the Berlin crisis, in which the Soviet Union begins to explore the possibilities of some type of détente with the West. The problem is, of course, that the Austrian solution, far from becoming a model for the West Germans, becomes a model for the Hungarians and even the Poles of a different future than continued Soviet domination. In many respects this period seems to demonstrate the very narrow limits that Nikita Khrushchev (a.k.a. the first Gorbachev) operated under in his attempt to reform Soviet rule in Eastern Europe. In this respect, does the book end too early, considering that the real shape and nature of Austrian neutrality only becomes clear after the Soviet suppression of unrest in Hungary and Poland? I am not asking Prof. Stourzh to write another book. But it does seem to me that one area that is opened up by this book is the impact of subsequent and related events—namely the unrest in Eastern Europe—on the character of Austrian neutrality. "Neutrality" was a large question in the Cold War, whether it applied to Austria in Europe or Laos and Vietnam in Southeast Asia. "Neutralization" was proposed for the latter, and in the case of Laos, it was officially agreed at the Geneva Conference of 1962. But we know that story did not end as happily as the Austrian case, and it is certainly worth pondering the conditions for a successful defense of neutrality.

The fifth question I would like to ask Prof. Stourzh to explore is connected with the Austria as "victim" myth, the decision by the great powers to allow Austria to enjoy the unique—and controversial—status as Hitler's first conquest. In this country this is sometimes referred to as the "Sound of Music" theory of Austrian culpability, taking its name for the enormously popular movie that depicts the courageous von Trapp family's resistance to the Anschluss. To what extent did this myth about Austria's real role in the Nazi Holocaust—a very substantial one and certainly not easily dismissed even by some examples of courageous resistance—influence the diplomacy surrounding the Austrian question? In the case of Germany it was always apparent, even if occasionally as an unspoken assumption behind the unwillingness of the Western powers to allow Germany real freedom of action, but rather to "bind" them into the West?[4] How did it influence issues on Austria, especially from the Russian perspective? Was the sense of Austrian culpability for Hitler's crimes an important element of Soviet rigidity on Austrian issues, especially economic ones?[5] Obviously this also played a role in Western concerns, perhaps above all for the French, but it does not seem that apparent in the documents. Are we dealing here with unspoken assumptions of Western diplomats about Austria's responsibility for Nazi crimes? Or are we dealing with willful ignorance?

Finally, the last question I would pose is whether the Austrian solution, and its durability during the Cold War, was a vindication of American Wilsonianism and its sentimental belief in the rights of small states to their independence? At the same time, the very success of Austria in maintaining its independence during the Cold War meant that 1989 was not only a vindication of its position, but also a revelation of the relative weakness of such independence. Indeed, the last ten years have shown the need for Austria to now pursue its goals within larger frameworks, in part the European Union, but also even the possibility of membership in NATO. Although that seems unlikely to happen in the near future, it is clear that the future holds an ongoing dilemma of the demands of integration with the weight of traditions of independence and identity. This change since 1989 however, underlines the degree to which the historical epoch that this work documents is a now a closed one, and that challenges Austria—and Europe and the United States—now face are fundamentally different. It will, nevertheless, help to have such a reliable guide to the past as this book to help in charting a new course.

Notes

1. For a different perspective, see Günter Bischof, *Austria in the First Cold War, 1945-55: The Leverage of the Weak* (New York: St. Martin's Press, 1999).

2. For the best discussion of these new sources, see John Lewis Gaddis, *We Now Know: Rethinking Cold War History* (New York: Oxford, 1997).

3. Wilfried Loth, *Stalin's unwanted child: the Soviet Union, the German question, and the founding of the GDR* trans. Robert F. Hogg (New York: St. Martin's Press, 1998) and Rolf Steininger, *The German Question: the Stalin Note of 1952 and the problem of reunification*, trans. Jane T. Hedges (New York: Columbia University Press, 1990).

4. This was the argument I presented in Thomas Alan Schwartz, *America's Germany: John J. McCloy and the Federal Republic of Germany* (Cambridge: Harvard University Press, 1991).

5. This argument is made concerning other Cold War issues in Melvyn Leffler, "The Cold War: What Do 'We Now Know'?", *American Historical Review* 104 (April 1999), 501-524.

The British Perspective of Austrian Neutrality*

Klaus Larres

The fourth and almost definitive edition of Gerald Stourzh's well-known work on the Austrian State Treaty is a massive and comprehensive volume dealing with the years 1945-1955 in great detail. At the same time it is a concisely argued scholarly opus of high quality covering the years of early occupation and the time of intricate but frustrating and unsuccessful four-power negotiations to end the occupation of Austria in the 1940s and early 1950s. The book also covers the years from Stalin's death in early March 1953 to the bilateral Austrian-Soviet negotiations in Moscow in April, 1955 which led to the rapid signing of the Austrian State Treaty in May 1955 by the Raab government.

Perhaps the most important period of time covered in the book—and incidentally the years I am most interested in—is the period of time after Stalin's death in March 1953. The weeks, months, and years following Stalin's death is the period, which is being discussed in scholarly literature as a time of 'missed opportunities' during which the cold war might have been overcome. It is not so much anymore the Stalin note of 1952,[1] but the developments after March 1953, which are considered the transition that offered a chance to relax the icy cold war atmosphere and to end the cold war for good. Thus, the time after Stalin's death is a crucial episode in cold war history as far as the solution of both the Austrian question and the German question are concerned. Moreover, it is also crucial with regard to the British (and in

* I would like to acknowledge the generous support of the British Academy by means of the 'Overseas Conference Grant' scheme for enabling me to contribute this article.

particular to British Prime Minster Winston Churchill's) attempts to terminate the East-West conflict.

After Stalin's death on 5 March 1953 a series of bold diplomatic initiatives from Moscow, coupled with more temperate public statements by senior Soviet officials and repeated pledges about Soviet commitment to peaceful coexistence with the West, suggested a potentially far-reaching shift in Soviet foreign policy. Within days of Stalin's passing, his successors moved to abandon the blustering approach of the Stalin years for a 'softer' line that emphasized compromise, diplomacy, negotiation, and accommodation. These changes raised hopes for a relaxation of tensions whereby the West might deal with the Soviets on a stable basis, reducing armaments expenditures, increasing East-West diplomatic contacts and trade, and perhaps even ending the cold war by reaching a 'status quo' peace settlement in Europe and elsewhere.[2]

Both, the Stalin succession in the Soviet Union and the election of Dwight D. Eisenhower as new American president signalled important changes in the nature of the East-West conflict. Within days of his accession to the premiership in Moscow, new Prime Minister Georgii Malenkov announced that there were no disputes between the United States and the Soviet Union that could not be settled by mutual agreement. And indeed within a matter of months after Stalin's death a settlement of the Korean War was achieved. The impressive 'peace campaign' the new Soviet leadership had embarked upon seemed to indicate that Moscow was prepared to cooperate with the West and slow down the escalation of the cold war. After all, the Soviets were, for example, ready to waive their long-standing claims over Turkish territory. After the collapse of the European Defence Community (EDC) the Soviet Union was even gradually (and grudgingly) prepared to accept West German rearmament. Moreover, no harsh reactions followed West Germany's rearmament within NATO (North Atlantic Treaty Organisation) although Moscow hat threatened for years that such a development would have dire consequences for East-West relations. The Kremlin was eventually also prepared to meet with the Western foreign ministers and then the heads of government at the conference tables in Berlin and then Geneva. And of course the Kremlin also signed the Austrian State Treaty in May 1955, which guaranteed the unity of the country and the withdrawal of all foreign troops from Austrian territory.

Yet, the Western Powers were more than suspicious about the sudden thaw and change of mind of the new leaders in Moscow. They believed that the Soviet Union simply wanted to be more accommodating in order to gain time for the consolidation of the new collective leadership at home. A general amnesty of political prisoners and the release of the doctors who had been imprisoned by Stalin because of their alleged plot to kill senior Soviet politicians showed that the new Soviet leaders were careful to be forthcoming and to avoid upsetting the Soviet people. It was apparent that Malenkov and his colleagues felt very insecure in their new positions, perhaps anticipating civil unrest and riots after Stalin's death. At this juncture it seemed to be critically important for the Kremlin to avoid trouble with their own satellite countries and, above all, with the West. A relaxation of international tension could be expected even though the Soviet Union would not waver in its determination to make world Communism succeed and to maintain a grip on the countries of Eastern Europe. These were the interpretations of the British Foreign Office and the American State Department. With regard to the Russian overtures, British Permanent Under-Secretary William Strang stated cautiously that "A few swallows do not make a summer," and Sir Alvary Gascoigne, the British Ambassador to Moscow, claimed: "a really genuine change of heart which might bring about a basic change of policy is out of the question."[3] British Foreign Secretary Anthony Eden basically agreed with these statements, although, in a cautious way, he was quite willing to exploit the more forthcoming attitude of the Soviet leadership by trying to conclude agreements about some long-standing minor issues in Anglo-Soviet relations and to promote movement on the Korean and the Austrian questions.[4] His reference to the latter was somewhat surprising given the fact that the Western Powers had used the propaganda device of an 'abbreviated treaty' (*Kurzvertrag*) in early 1952 to put the blame for the failure of solving the Austrian question squarely on the Soviet Union.

In general Stalin's death hardly made any real impact on the attitude of the British Foreign Office. For a long time contemporary historians were not overly impressed by this event either. The historical significance of the post-Stalin changes in Soviet foreign policy has only recently become more appreciated by scholars.[5] The orthodox view of Soviet history, which emphasized continuity between the policies of Lenin, Stalin, and their successors, combined with the closure of Soviet archives, perpetuated a simplistic view of Soviet foreign policy as one of implacable hostility towards the West. Thus, until the end of the cold war and the increasing availability of Russian and Eastern European primary sources, the opportunities Stalin's death provided for negotiating and solving the German and Austrian questions were only marginally considered in the scholarly literature. However, the end of the cold war and the availability of Soviet and Eastern European archival sources have set a new agenda for cold war scholarship, challenging the often sterile 'black-and-white'-interpretations provided by orthodox and revisionist historians.

To my mind there are two major findings from the use of what John Lewis Gaddis has called the "new cold war history:"[6]

1. The new archival sources and an increasing number of books based on these sources reveal many new insights about the intentions of Soviet foreign policy after Stalin's death. For example Vojtech Mastny, Zubok and Pleshakov, and many of the important working papers of the Cold War International History Project indicate that there was greater flexibility and pragmatism among some senior politicians within the Soviet leadership than previously assumed.[7] The new sources give us a glimpse of the internal discussions in the Kremlin. They suggest that at least one faction of the new collective Soviet leadership, led by the new Prime Minister Georgii Malenkov and KGB chief Lavrentii Beria, advocated greater cooperation with the West, including a settlement of the German and the Austrian questions and a reduction in armaments.[8] This side was opposed by another faction, led by Foreign Minister Vyacheslav Molotov, which argued for a continuation of the Stalinist policy of 'no concessions to the capitalists'. It was this faction which was eventually outmaneuvered by Khrushchev in 1955/56.[9]

The divisions within the Kremlin leadership raise the possibility that a less confrontational policy by the West, a more openly constructive policy of active engagement with Moscow after March 1953, might have found a receptive ear in Moscow and tipped the balance of power in the Politburo away from the orthodox hardliners. Above all, it appears that President Eisenhower's negative and less than constructive attitude towards the post-Stalin leadership is to blame for a lack of progress in East-West relations in 1953. I have argued elsewhere that his "Chance for Peace" speech on 16 April 1953 was in fact a psychological warfare offensive and had nothing whatsoever to do with attempting to extend a hand of friendship to Moscow, as was claimed by Eisenhower himself and is often maintained in the literature.[10] Eisenhower's refusal until late 1953 to agree to a foreign ministers' or heads of governments' conference with the Soviet Union meant that neither the German nor the Austrian question could be discussed throughout 1953. Thus, the option open to the new Raab government in Vienna appeared to be twofold: to take the initiative itself instead of relying on the Allied powers and to move towards 'neutrality' to placate the Soviets and thus be able to arrive at a compromise solution.

After all, in the summer and autumn of 1953 the Soviet Union made considerable concessions to Austria for which they were publicly praised by Chancellor Raab. Not only was the Soviet high commissioner replaced by an ambassador, but Moscow also abandoned the practice of making Vienna pay for the occupation costs (which meant Britain and France had to follow suit). The Kremlin also ended censorship, terminated trade restrictions, and returned many economic assets to the Austrian government. From now on, Raab would gradually move a little closer to Moscow and observe a somewhat greater distance than hitherto to Washington. He would also increasingly use the instrument of 'neutrality' to obtain Austrian sovereignty, thus precluding Austria's membership of NATO or the contemplated EDC. Austria's policy and the Soviet Union's peace campaign after Stalin's death, which both appeared to drive Austria away from the West, found little favor in Washington and London as there was broad agreement that Austrian 'neutrality' could only have negative implications for the rearmament debate in the Federal Republic of Germany.

However, the British Foreign Office was much more pragmatic than the Americans. Despite some misgivings, the Foreign Office began to advocate dealing separately with the Austrian and German questions. While, for largely geo-strategic and economic reasons, German neutrality was unacceptable and was not favored by the majority of West Germans, and certainly not by the Adenauer government,[11] the Austrian question seemed to be much less important and Austrian neutrality could thus be tolerated. Moreover, both the Austrian people and the new Austrian government appeared to approve of it. What was important was to ensure that no power vacuum would arise in Austria and that the country was able to defend itself. Furthermore, it appeared to be clear that despite official neutrality the Austrians would largely regard themselves as part of the Western world; in fact they could be relied upon to constitute a 'secret ally'. Eventually Dulles and the State Department—despite strong opposition from within the Pentagon—would adopt a similar position.

However, British Prime Minister Churchill further complicated matters for the West in the aftermath of Stalin's death. Churchill was not in favor of German rearmament within the EDC, which he regarded as a rather cumbersome and useless instrument. He was thus only half-heartedly behind Western efforts to propagate the EDC to the parliaments in France and elsewhere which had to ratify the treaty signed in May 1952. Churchill's skepticism regarding the EDC was largely shared by the British foreign policy elite. This skepticism was however strongly rejected and considered defeatist in Washington and Bonn.[12]

Another, more crucial, complication was Churchill's intention to overcome the cold war by organizing an informal and wide-ranging 'Big Three', Potsdam-style, summit meeting. As Churchill made clear in several secret memoranda, he intended to create a reunited and neutral Germany and was quite prepared to sacrifice the Federal Republic's rearmament and integration with the West as a suitable price for an end to the cold war. Churchill also believed that the Soviet Union and a reunited neutral Germany should conclude a security pact, rather like the Locarno pact of 1925, which would be guaranteed by Great Britain. Yet, these ideas were strongly opposed both, by his own Foreign Office and by the political elites in other Western countries.[13] Thus, not so much the British foreign policy elite but merely Churchill and a very few trusted advisers were behind Britain's summit diplomacy of 1953-1954. Still, Churchill's policy proved to be a major headache for American President Eisenhower.

2. In addition to the new knowledge about the intentions of Soviet foreign policy after Stalin's death, scholars owe another major insight to the new sources and the new interpretations based on these sources of cold war history since 1990. They have arrived at an enhanced understanding of the role of smaller 'third actors' (i.e. those other than the U.S. and the U.S.S.R.) in shaping the direction of postwar foreign policies and influencing the policies of the superpowers. Recent research, for example, has been able to reveal that East German, Chinese, and Cuban leaders exerted a far greater impact on the overall direction of Soviet foreign policy than was previously believed.[14]

The same applies to the friends and allies of the United States. Much work has already been done with respect to the great impact of European states on the United States, both in a theoretical and a more empirical way.[15] Gerald Stourzh in his important book, but also Günter Bischof in his just published analysis of the Austrian question during the early cold war years,[16] have convincingly shown that, despite all efforts and all displeasures expressed, in the last resort the United States was not able to impose its will on a small country under its protection. Instead Washington eventually had to witness Vienna's bilateral negotiation with the U.S.S.R., which would lead to Austria's armed neutrality. Although this solution could be tolerated, it was not Washington's preferred way to solve the Austrian question.

In my current work[17] I am attempting among other things to show the influence of third actors with regard to British Prime Minister Churchill's summit diplomacy. In Churchill's case, the Eisenhower White House could insist on its refusal to convene an East-West summit meeting only with great difficulty. It was above all German Chancellor Adenauer's collusion with American Secretary of State John Foster Dulles in the summer of 1953 which was decisive. Adenauer and Dulles quickly moved to exploit Churchill's stroke and temporary non-availability in the summer of 1953 to undermine his controversial proposals to meet with the new Soviet leaders at an informal summit conference.[18] However, even more important for the failure of Churchill's summitry was the Soviet Union's great mistrust of Churchill, which led the new men in the Kremlin to underestimate Churchill's seriousness. It resulted in the Soviet leaders' hesitation and eventual refusal to 'check out' his proposals by giving their quick agreement to a "parley at the summit."[19] Moscow was convinced that Churchill did not mean what he said in his speech of May 1953, when he called for an informal 'Big Three' summit conference to overcome the cold war by finding a solution to the division of Germany, and, by implication, also a solution to the partition of Austria.[20] Moscow therefore missed an important opportunity in the summer of 1953 to undermine the coherence of the Western world and the American leadership of the Western alliance. After all, Churchill was dead serious with his proposal.[21]

On the whole it appears to me that, as far as the years 1953-1955 are concerned, Gerald Stourzh neglects two important issues which might have proven illuminating.

1. It seems that the author is not convinced of the crucial importance of the demise of Stalin. He argues instead that, ever since autumn 1952, an increasing number of signals (from the middle level of Soviet politics) pointed towards the Russian acceptance of solving the Austrian question on the basis of neutrality. However, to my mind, it would have been more fruitful if Gerald Stourzh had not only paid great attention to

the continuities in Soviet foreign policy, but had also given greater consideration to the new developments after Stalin's death.

Considering the Soviet leaders' willingness to terminate the Korean War, to show greater flexibility in the German question (at least temporarily until the 17 June uprising in the German Democratic Republic [GDR]),[22] and to generally embark on a closer and more friendly relationship with the Western world, it could be expected that the Kremlin's Austrian policy was also influenced by the political shake-up after Stalin's death. If, between March and June 1953, Moscow even seemed prepared to sacrifice the GDR and to genuinely approve of the unification of Germany on a neutral basis, Soviet concessions to the Austrian question were likely too. After all, by the spring of 1953 it must have been obvious to Moscow—in view of the GDR's deep unpopularity in East and West Germany—that the establishment of a neutral reunited German state would have entailed German neutrality 'on the western side' and Germany as a 'secret ally' of NATO (as would be the case with Austria after 1955).

Thus, the conclusion of an Austrian State Treaty may well have been feasible in the spring of 1953. However, it is unlikely that such an event would have derailed West German rearmament, although Moscow may have hoped so. After all, German rearmament (and more importantly the country's irreversible integration with the West brought about by means of rearmament) was the West's top priority. The Western world would have attempted to realize this policy under almost any circumstances, even if the conclusion of an Austrian State Treaty prior to such an event could not have been delayed.

One can go even further: Considering that the Soviet Union was prepared to accept a neutral reunified Germany with a low level of armaments, Moscow may also have been prepared (if it had been pushed hard enough and offered real incentives) to accept a Westernized non-neutral Austria in the spring of 1953, if a more constructive policy had been pursued by Eisenhower and the Western alliance. Yet, due to the West's German policy and its intricate linkage with the Austrian problem, this was not desirable from a Western point of view. Therefore, no constructive Austrian policy came forth in 1953. So far this has not been substantially explored in the literature. Thus, the implications of Stalin's death on the Austrian question deserve greater attention than hitherto.

2. It appears that Prof. Stourzh neglects the influence of Britain, that is largely Churchill's activities, both between March and June 1953 (in

the immediate aftermath of Stalin's death and Churchill's stroke on 23 June 1953) and the second half of 1954. By summer 1954 Churchill had recovered from his illness and from his great disappointment over the failure of the Berlin Foreign Ministers' Conference in January/February 1954.[23] While acknowledging the deep split in the British government between the prime minister and almost all of Churchill's foreign policy experts in the Foreign Office, Prof. Stourzh does not pay much attention to Churchill's role in the Austrian question. While we have a fairly clear picture of Churchill's policy on Germany between 1953 and 1955, the same is not true of his Austrian policy. Indeed, here Churchill appears confused and contradictory. There is a definite need for clarification both with respect to his own policy and to the question whether or not his activities had an impact on Washington's changing attitude towards the Austrian question. After all, by late 1954 the American policy on this issue began to correspond with the views prevalent in London.[24]

In 1953 Churchill frequently addressed the German question; Austria hardly ever appeared to loom in his thoughts. Yet, on occasion, Churchill was ready to acknowledge that the activities of the Malenkov government had not been as accommodating as he wanted to believe. Churchill even admitted sometimes that Moscow's activities had only "taken the form of leaving off doing things, which we have not been doing to them."[25] Occasionally, despite his summit diplomacy, he realized himself that a comprehensive solution to all of the cold war's many problems would not necessarily be achieved at an international conference. Thus, he announced at times that it might be better to pursue solutions on an individual basis before convening a summit. Problems such as the continued division of Austria could perhaps be solved without linking it to other cold war issues. He argued that "Piecemeal solutions of individual problems should not be disdained or improvidently put aside." It would be a shame if the drive for an overall settlement of the cold war "were to impede any spontaneous and healthy evolution which may be taking place inside Russia."[26]

In late June 1954 Churchill visited Eisenhower in Washington to make a desperate final attempt to persuade the president to give his agreement to a three or four power summit conference. Churchill threatened that if the U.S. administration did not agree to participate in a summit conference, he would be prepared to go to Moscow by himself. The whole Western world viewed such a development with despair. It was generally expected that the aging and increasingly fragile Churchill would hardly be able to stand up to the shrewd Soviet leaders in the course of exhausting negotiations. In principle, Churchill still hoped to reverse the division of Germany, and by implication, the division of Austria by means of a negotiated settlement. However, by mid-1954, when he realized that his time as prime minister was running out and that it might prove impossible for him to overcome the many obstacles to convening a 'Big Three' summit meeting, he made use of both the nuclear armaments question and the Austrian question to persuade Eisenhower and Dulles to agree to a summit conference.[27]

Although Churchill was deeply worried about the lack of progress on both issues, it is unclear whether he used either or both of these issues merely as a means to an end, or whether he was really convinced of the political urgency to tackle them. When Dulles asked him in Washington what he intended to achieve if a summit was convened or if he traveled to Moscow as a lone peace envoy, the prime minister replied that he hoped to obtain a solution to the Austrian question. Yet, only a few months before he had told his Foreign Secretary Eden that he did not believe in dealing with the German and Austrian questions separately, as this would make a successful summit conference impossible from the start. Dulles was not impressed by Churchill's reply. He declared that the West had tried everything to solve the Austrian question during the Berlin Conference in early 1954. He was doubtful "about the possibility of getting it [an Austrian solution] by this method." Dulles "urged that the matter be very carefully weighed before any positive decision was made."[28] Churchill, however, still thought about meeting the new Soviet leaders alone. He now considered meeting Malenkov in Vienna to sign an Austrian peace treaty. "If that came off people would whoop with joy. I might pay a courtesy visit to Moscow after Vienna - perhaps staying forty-eight hours."[29]

Churchill's role in the Austrian question in 1954 is less than clear—at times it appears to be confusing and contradictory. It seems that the Austrian question merely served his ultimate goal of convening a 'Big Three' summit conference so that Churchill could go down in history both as a peacemaker and a war hero. Yet, a detailed analysis might result in interesting findings regarding British policy-making about the Austrian question. It appears to be clear that both the changes in Soviet policy after Stalin's death and Churchill's courageous attempt to criticize the Western world's cold war strategy and shake Western leaders out of their exaggerated caution and lack of imaginative thinking, may have contributed to the Raab government's policy of taking the initiative itself instead of relying on the great powers for deciding the destiny of Austria.

Moreover, it seems that the likelihood of a solution to the Austrian question increased considerably once a solution for the German problem had been found. Until late 1954 Western politicians always believed that any Soviet willingness to compromise over Austria would only come forth in order to obtain concessions with respect to the geo-strategically much more important Germany. Dulles in particular, but also Eisenhower and other important figures in Washington, were obsessed by the German problem. Moreover, they were clearly influenced by West German Chancellor Adenauer's shrewd use of personal relations for political ends. Adenauer was able to build up (and maintain until Dulles' death in 1959) a much more trusted relationship with the Eisenhower administration than Austrian Chancellor Raab managed to do.[30]

However, the post-Stalin leadership in the Kremlin was also greatly focused on the German question. For example, despite the notion of 'armed neutrality' put forward during the 1954 Berlin Conference, in Berlin Molotov still attempted to link the withdrawal of occupation forces to the signing of a German peace treaty (and he may also still have hoped to undermine German rearmament in the process). Yet, once West German rearmament and integration with the West was cleared by October 1954, it may well have been the case, as has been argued convincingly, that the U.S.S.R. viewed an Austrian State Treaty and Austrian neutrality as helpful for a relaxation of the East-West conflict.[31] Above all, in Moscow an Austrian treaty was viewed necessary to prevent a German-Austrian Anschluss—though it was already obvious at this stage that Austria would remain the West's 'secret ally'. Before late 1954, it was again Churchill who was the odd one out: He did not always adhere to the 'linkage' concept. Instead, on occasion—and this time in agreement with his Foreign Office—he proclaimed the necessity to treat the Austrian and German problems separately, a view initially not widely shared, neither in Washington nor in Moscow.

However, soon decisive events occurred: In October 1954 the Western countries agreed to admitting West Germany to WEU (Western European Union)/NATO membership; then, the demotion of Malenkov in early February 1955 occurred. Above all, Molotov's subsequent announcement that Moscow saw no reason to delay an Austrian State Treaty if the country would remain militarily neutral proved important. It was a decisive step towards the conclusion of an Austrian State Treaty and Austrian neutrality. However, by then Churchill had already decided to tender his resignation as prime minister. Failing health, pressure from his colleagues, but above all his deep frustration about his inability to shake up the settlements of Yalta and Potsdam by means of a summit conference were responsible for his retirement at this stage.

Thus, by way of conclusion, Prof. Stourzh's book is above all highly valuable in analyzing and clarifying convincingly the diplomatic maneuvers of the Austrian governments between 1945 and 1955. It also gives us an excellent insight into American policy making towards Austria. However, as far as the exploration of Soviet policy after Stalin's death is concerned, as well as the British and especially Churchill's Austrian policy, there seems to be room for an interesting 5th edition of this important book.

Notes

1. For the 1952 Stalin note see the still classic account by Rolf Steininger, *Eine Chance zur Wiedervereinigung? Die Stalin-Note vom 10. März 1952: Darstellung und Dokumentation auf der Grundlage unveröffentlichter britischer und amerikanischer Akten* (Bonn: Verlag Neue Gesellschaft, 1985); and for a contrary view see Gerhard Wettig, *Bereitschaft zu Einheit in Freiheit? Die sowjetische Deutschland-Politik 1945-1955* (Munich: Olzog, 1999).

2. See Klaus Larres, *Politik der Illusionen: Churchill, Eisenhower und die deutsche Frage 1945-1955* (Göttingen: Vandenhoeck & Ruprecht, 1995), Chapter III.

3. Public Record Office, Kew: FO 371/106 533/NS 1051/17 (27/3/1953).

4. For Eden's unsuccessful attempts to negotiate with the Soviet foreign minister in late 1951/early 1952 see Larres, *Politik der Illusionen*, 63-64.

5. For an overview of the literature see Klaus Larres, "Großbritannien und der 17. Juni 1953. Die deutsche Frage und das Scheitern von Churchills Entspannungspolitik nach Stalins Tod," in *1953 - Krisenjahr des Kalten Krieges in Europa,* ed. Christoph Kleßmann and Bernd Stöver (Cologne: Böhlau Verlag, 1999), 156-157.

6. John Lewis Gaddis, *We Now Know: Rethinking Cold War History* (Oxford: Clarendon Press, 1997).

7. Vojtech Mastny, *The Cold War and Soviet Insecurity: The Stalin Years* (New York: Oxford University Press, 1996); Vladislav Zubok and Constantine Pleshakov, *Inside the Kremlin's Cold War: From Stalin to Khrushchev* (Cambridge, Mass.: Harvard University Press, 1996).

8. See for example Amy W. Knight, *Beria: Stalin's First Lieutenant* (Princeton: Princeton University Press, 1993).

9. Albert Resis, ed., *Molotov Remembers: Inside Kremlin Politics; Conversations with Felix Chuev* (Chicago: Ivan R. Dee, 1993); James Richter, *Khrushchev's Double Bind: International Pressure and Domestic Coalition Politics* (Baltimore: John Hopkins University Press, 1994).

10. Klaus Larres, "Eisenhower and the First Forty Days after Stalin's Death: The Incompatibility of Détente and Political Warfare," *Diplomacy & Statecraft*, 6 (July 1995): 431-469.

11. On Adenauer's policy, see Henning Köhler, *Adenauer. Eine Politische Biographie* (Frankfurt/M.: Propyläen, 1994); also Klaus Larres, "Konrad Adenauer (1876-1967)," in *Portraits der deutschen Politik 1949-1969*, vol. 2, ed. Torsten Oppelland , (Darmstadt: Wissenschaftliche Buchgesellschaft, 1999), 13-24.

12. See Spencer Mawby, *Containing Germany: Britain and the Arming of the Federal Republic* (Basingstoke: Macmillan, 1999).

13. See Larres, *Politik der Illusionen.*

14. See for example Aleksandr Fursenko and Timothy Naftali, *"One Hell of a Gamble." Khrushchev, Castro, Kennedy and the Cuban Missile Crisis, 1958-1964* (London: John Murray, 1997); Hope M. Harrison, "The Bargaining Power of Weaker Allies in Bipolarity and Crisis: The Dynamics of Soviet-East German Relations, 1953-1961" (Ph.D. diss., Columbia University, New York, 1993); Odd Arne Westad, *Cold War and Revolution: Soviet-American Rivalry and the Origins of the Chinese Civil War, 1944-1946* (New York: Columbia University Press, 1993); Sergei Goncharov et al., *Uncertain Partners: Stalin, Mao, and the Korean War* (Stanford, Calif.: Stanford University Press, 1993).

15. See for example David P. Calleo, *Beyond American Hegemony: The Future of the Western Alliance* (Brighton: Wheatsheaf, 1987); Gunther Mai, "Dominanz oder Kooperation im Bündnis? Die Sicherheitspolitik der USA und der Verteidigungsbeitrag Europas 1945-1956," *Historische Zeitschrift* 246 (1988): 327-364; John G. Ikenberry, "Rethinking the Origins of American Hegemony," *Political Science Quarterly* 104 (1989): 375-400; Thomas Risse-Kappen, *Cooperation Among Democracies: The European Influence on U.S. Foreign Policy* (Princeton: Princeton University Press, 1995).

16. Günter Bischof, *Austria and the Cold War, 1945-1955: The Leverage of the Weak* (Basingstoke: Macmillan, 1999).

17. "Churchill's Summit Diplomacy: Britain, Germany, the Soviet Union and the United States from the First World War to the Cold War" [in progress].

18. See also "Eisenhower, Dulles und Adenauer: Bündnis des Vertrauens oder Allianz des Mißtrauens? (1953-1961)," in *Deutschland und die USA im 20. Jahrhundert: Geschichte der politischen Beziehungen*, ed. Klaus Larres and Torsten Oppelland (Darmstadt: Wissenschaftliche Buchgesellschaft, 1997), 119-150.

19. Churchill's phrase, used in his speech in Edinburgh on 14 February 1950, quoted. in Royal Institute of International Affairs, ed., *Documents of International Affairs, 1949-1950* (London: Oxford UP, 1951), 56.

20. See Larres, *Politik der Illusionen*, Chapter IV.

21. For a brief assessment of Stalin's view of Churchill based on his wartime acquaintance with the British leader and memories of British involvement in the Russian Civil War see Jonathan Haslam, "Soviet War Aims," in *The Rise and Fall of the Grand Alliance, 1941-1945*, ed. Ann Lane and Howard Temperley (Basingstoke: Macmillan, 1995), 24, 36-37.

22. See Larres, "Großbritannien und der 17. Juni 1953," 155-179.

23. Nikolaus Katzer, *"Eine Übung im Kalten Krieg." Die Berliner Außenminister-konferenz von 1954* (Cologne: Westdeutscher Verlag, 1995).

24. See for example Günter Bischof, 'Eisenhower, the Summit, and the Austrian Treaty, 1953-1955', in *Eisenhower: A Centenary Assessment*, ed. Günter Bischof and Stephen E. Ambrose (Baton Rouge: Louisiana State University Press, 1995), 136-161.

25. See Churchill's speech in the House of Commons, 11 May 1953, in Hansard: House of Commons Parliamentary Debates, 5th ser., vol.515, col.895.

26. Ibid.

27. See Larres, *Politik der Illusionen*, 267-273.

28. Memorandum of a conversation between Dulles and Churchill, 27 June 1954, in *Foreign Relations of the United States, 1952-54*, vol. 6, pp. 1111-12:.

29. Diary entry, 4 July 1954, Lord Moran, *Churchill. The Struggle for Survival, 1940-1965* (London: Constable, 1966), 574.

30. See note 18 above.

31. See John van Oudenaren, *Détente in Europe: The Soviet Union and the West since 1953* (Durham, N.C.: Duke University Press, 1991), 32; see also Bischof, *Austria in the First Cold War*, 140-142.

An Austrian Perspective

Anton Pelinka

Gerald Stourzh presents his view of post-1945 Austria from the perspective of international relations. Stourzh's focus is on Austria as an international actor dealing with the major powers, but also with other, smaller actors like Germany, Yugoslavia, India, Italy, and Switzerland. Stourzh's focus is not—at least not primarily—on Austria as a political system governed by the logic of domestic politics, by political parties competing for votes.

This distinction is necessary to understand what Stourzh presents so brilliantly, and what he presents insufficiently or not at all. Stourzh describes and analyzes Austrian foreign policy, including the domestic aspects, only to explain certain developments of Austria's foreign policy. And as Austria has been and still is a small country, foreign policy has to be seen rather independently from domestic politics: Major powers have the privilege of shaping their foreign policy as a secondary outcome of domestic politics; small powers have the tendency to frame foreign policy as an art in itself, created by rather independent artists (experts, brahmins) as far as possible from the plains of domestic politics. Stourzh is the historian of a foreign policy which was kept largely autonomous from domestic infighting and domestic trifles.

As Stourzh stresses and explains on many occasions (e.g. p. 35), the Austria of the period 1945 - 1955 must be considered a special case. Liberated from Nazi-German occupation, but occupied by its liberators for more than a decade, Austria was treated differently from other liberated countries, but also differently from defeated Germany. In the peculiar political situation between 1945 and 1955, Austria was under a dual authority. On the one hand, there was an Austrian government based on the constitution of 1920 and recognized by the international community, including the four occupying powers. On the other hand, there was the authority of the Allied Council, which claimed a quasi extra-constitutional power, based on international agreements—like Potsdam—in which Austria was not a partner.

This peculiar duality of authority was eased by the Second Control Agreement in 1946, and by the implications of the cold war, which prevented the Allied powers from taking a unified position vis-à-vis Austria. But the authority of the Austrian constitutional institutions was still officially limited by the presence of military and political agencies beyond Austrian control.

This situation was responsible for the high degree of autonomy from domestic politics which Austrian foreign policy was able to develop. Austrian foreign policy, unlike that of many other democracies, was seen as an instrument not to satisfy domestic demands but to deal with the Allied powers. Foreign policy was free to follow its own logic under the general assumption that there was an extremely broad domestic consensus regarding the government's responsibility to make the occupation forces leave.

The Two Contradicting Logics

The distinction between these two layers of Austrian politics—the domestic and the international—is useful to understanding Stourzh's book. The distinction also provides us with an understanding of the coexistence of two—seemingly contradictory—rules, two different logics:

*   The logic of a 'positive consensus': The Austrian political main-stream, represented by the two major parties and the major economic interest groups, was directed to focus on two goals—'Westernization' and 'sovereignty'. Austria should follow the example of liberal (Western) democracy, including participation in the process of (Western) integration. And Austria should try by all possible means to end the situation of dual authority, to end the occupation. To reach this goal, Austria constantly reminded the Allies of their promise given in the first part of the Moscow Declaration. To make this reminder credible, Austria did everything to portray itself as a victim, as a country which—had it not been paralyzed by German occupation—would have sided with the Allies in World War II (see Schöner's remark about Austria as one of the "victors," p. 41/n 65).

- The logic of a 'negative consensus': The Austrian political main-stream was extremely interested in integrating that rather significant portion of Austrian society which did not accept the official formula of 1945 'liberalization' and considered the outcome of World War II a defeat. These people were invited to adapt to the reality of Austrian independence. To make this possible, the political mainstream started to adapt itself to the needs and expectations of this social segment. In order to integrate them and dissolve their links with the Nazi past, the political mainstream tended not to discuss the most terrible aspects of that past. Austria went to great lengths to present itself as a country which welcomed (former) Nazis—by neglecting the specific nature of Nazism. (Probably the best example of this negative consensus is found in Knight's book, see bibliography.)

The coexistence of these two rules was not intellectually sound, but it was politically feasible. It was possible by keeping foreign policy separate from domestic policy, and vice versa. As everybody agreed that ending the occupation was basically not only a good idea but the most urgent priority, almost everybody was prepared to pay a certain price:

- The most credible opponents of Nazism—on the left as well as on the right—accepted the negative consensus. The consensus was seen as both a necessity to win acceptance by the Allies and an opportunity to implant a specific understanding of Austria and Austrian history in a society, which was hesitant to accept its role as a victim of a regime so many had welcomed and defended. One step in that direction was to delete the co-responsibility clause from the State Treaty's preamble (pp. 517 - 522). This seemed necessary because this clause corresponded not only with the second para-graph of the Moscow Declaration but also with the reality of an Austrian society deeply split along the lines of pro- or anti-Nazism.
- The former Nazis—a significant, strong minority—accepted the positive consensus as a precondition to the Allies' retreat from Austria. To make their former enemies leave, almost any means seemed justifiable. The former Nazis could live with an intellectual contradiction because the hidden agenda of this contradiction—an independent Austria free of Allied troops—was a lesser evil than an Austria occupied by these troops. And the former Nazis could also expect future benefits: an Austria declared free of any responsibility for Nazism could not credibly rethink and reevaluate this very

responsibility after the Allies had left. The former Nazis had every reason to perceive the elimination of the co-responsibility clause as a *carte blanche*, an acquittal of all personal responsibility.

The package of agreements which were signed and implemented in Austria's 'annus mirabilis' (pp. 335 - 578) was a kind of synthesis that brought the intellectually contradictory hypotheses together. In the euphoria over the State Treaty on 15 May 1955, the different factions were reconciled, and the friends and foes of the Nazi regime, which had been defeated a decade earlier, were united.

The public opinion in Austria was divided about the year 1945: for many Austrians, it meant liberation; for many others, it was a defeat. There was a consensus, however, about the year 1955: practically all Austrians could agree that the State Treaty was the best possible deal for all of them. In order to make this reconciliation work, the intellectually unsound aspects of the negative consensus had to be forgotten.

Stourzh describes, explains, and analyzes the path to Austria's 'annus mirabilis', the year in which Austria's (former) Nazis and anti-Nazis were reconciled. The events of 1955 were based on different contradictions:

- The liberators left after having occupied the country for more than ten years. The Austrian Foreign Minister Figl finally declared "Austria is free"—a decade after Austrian independence and his own personal liberation from Nazi terror by the Allies in 1945.
- The Austrian army was reestablished to defend Austria's independence despite the fact that most of its officers were veterans of an army which had fought *against* Austria's independence. Schärf's telling remark about the necessity of establishing a *"Wehrmacht"*(sic!) in 1946 underlines this continuity (p. 131; see also p. 217, for the Western—in this particular case British—interest in registering "Austrians with previous military experience" for a possible Austrian army in 1954).
- The Allies were never able or even willing to agree which part of the Moscow Declaration should primarily define their attitude toward Austria—the part declaring Austria a victim of Nazi aggression or the part declaring Austria responsible for Nazism. The Allies and their policies were part of the contradictions themselves.

The Price of Reconciliation

Gerald Stourzh writes about one side of this complex reality: Austria's political fight to end its specific status, to become a 'normal' country, an average European sovereign state. He is the historian of the positive consensus. He does not ignore the other side of the issue, the intellectual and moral costs of the negative consensus, but his emphasis is on the history of Austria's foreign policy. In that respect, he cannot be criticized for being consistent with his intention.

The traces of the negative consensus found in Stourzh's book should be mentioned here, not as a point of critique, but as a demonstration.

- Stourzh quotes several internal memoranda written as early as the summer 1945, in which Austrian diplomats vehemently argue against Austria's accepting any responsibility for Nazism—e.g. against a "feeble mea-culpa-mood" ("schwächliche(n) mea-culpa-Stimmung"). This argument was based not on any claim to 'truth' or reality but on tactical and strategic Austrian interests (p. 37).
- Stourzh quotes Adenauer's angry remarks about Austrian double standards: "... significant parts of Austria existed which were more effected by Nazism than all parts of Germany ..." (pp. 526f./n 117). Had it been possible, Adenauer would gladly have sent Hitler's remains back to his native Austria (p. 526).

Stourzh is fully aware of the Austrian attempt to make the world forget some of the aspects of recent Austrian history. But as he deals with foreign policy, important aspects are mentioned only with regard to foreign policy. Stourzh writes about the talks between Raab and Dulles concerning Jewish claims on Austria during Raab's visit to Washington in November 1954 and about the resumption of negotiations with representatives of the "Jewish Claims Committee on Austria" just one week before the signing of the State Treaty (p. 516). He indicates that some of the results were the product of Austria's interest in mollifying U.S. public opinion (p. 540). He also refers to research published by authors like Robert Knight, Thomas Albrich, Brigitte Bailer-Galanda, and Michael Wolffsohn about the specific Austrian tendency to postpone any significant restitution of Jewish property (p. 541f.).

Stourzh treats all these aspects, which are only indirectly linked to the positive consensus, as side tracks—because they are primarily aspects of the negative consensus (for the effects of the negative consensus, see Knight). Stourzh continues to concentrate on foreign relations, and for that reason he sets clear priorities. His name index, for example, does not include Taras Borodajkewycz or Walter Reder, two key figures for any understanding of the years between 1945 and 1955 (Pelinka, 188 - 190). He mentions the VDU (League of Independents) only with respect to this party's attitudes towards the State Treaty and neutrality (pp. 556f.). Fritz Stüber, the VDU's most outspoken pro-Nazi deputy, is not mentioned at all.

This does not mean that Stourzh tries to ignore the remnants of Austrian Nazism. But as a specialist for foreign policy, he is interested only in the impact these remnants had on his field, on foreign policy. In comparison to Austria's experience during the Waldheim crisis more than thirty years after the 'annus mirabilis', the immediate effects of Nazism on foreign policy were less visible between 1945 and 1955.

The Political Function of Taboos

Stourzh presents plenty of evidence for his 'annus mirabilis' argument. Austrian foreign policy was at its best making the most out of the window of opportunity that opened sometime after Stalin's death. The two goals—'Westernization' and 'sovereignty'—were combined in the best possible way. Stourzh's book is the history of a remarkable success in foreign policy. It is the tale not only of how a tiny country was able to defend its interests successfully on the bargaining table of international politics, but also of the high price it paid for that success: a loss of intellectual consistency and moral rectitude.

In Storzh's story, the main Austrian actors—Figl and Schärf, Raab and Kreisky—did not express anything that could compare to Vranitzky or Busek's, Klima's or Klestil's different declarations after 1988 on the Austrian responsibility for Nazism (Pelinka, 194). The 'fathers of the Second Republic', beginning with Renner, did not dare to speak about Austrian anti-Semitism. In the years after 1945 an admission of Austrian responsibility by the government—which ultimately came about after 1988—would have been counterproductive for Austria's foreign policy. Had Leopold Kunschak, speaker of the Second Republic's first National Council, been reminded of his rather vulgar anti-Semitic background (Pauley, 159 - 173) or Karl Renner of his manuscript praising the Munich agreement of 1938, it would have worked against the concept and the strategy of Austria's foreign policy.

Neglecting the Austrian roots of Nazism, the Austrian aspects of anti-Semitism, and the Austrian participation in World War II had a particular function: it lent a certain credibility to Austria's 'victim theory'. But it also helped integrate those who had reason to feel excluded from the broad consensus of 1945 into the mainstream of Austrian politics.

Stourzh's book vividly describes how well the undeclared politics of taboos served a foreign policy in which the players were experts—brahmin diplomats and top representatives of the two major parties. This policy was successful because the players kept it as isolated as possible from domestic politics. The logic of the first hypothesis should not be mixed with the logic of the second.

Stourzh emphasizes the importance of the diplomats—Schöner, Wodak, Bischoff, Verosta, Kirchschläger, and some others—and how they were able to play an increasingly vital role in designing Austria's foreign policy because foreign policy was kept isolated from the ups and downs of domestic politics. By their very nature, diplomats are professionals who are not directly dependent on electoral results and on public opinion. The more isolated foreign policy can be kept, the more influential diplomats become.

Austria's foreign and domestic policies were supported by the taboos established after 1945 in Austria. These taboos were a great help to the generation, which during its lifetime, had to deal with the fall of the First Republic, the civil war, authoritarian rule, occupation and annexation, the Holocaust, and aggressive warfare. For this generation, the taboos provided internal healing as well as external support.

The next generation has had reason to see things differently. It raised, and is still raising, the questions regarding the intellectual and moral costs of the great taboos. The 'Waldheim affair' was the catalyst which brought this generational difference out into the open (Wodak, pp. 59-120; Mitten). This is not only an Austrian phenomenon. As the international comparative study about the different responses to the Holocaust demonstrates, there have been generational gaps everywhere, including Israel. The next generation has tended to be more critical about the Holocaust, more outspoken, and less inclined to ignore and to forget (Wyman).

For the next generation, the social, political, and economic environment was rather different. In Austria, the most urgent needs of 1945—the stabilization of politics and of the economy—were more or less satisfied. The new generation was able to raise itself to a new quality of needs, moral needs as well as intellectual needs. For this generation, the great success of a policy based on taboos and contradictory logics has lost most of its glamor. The next generation has had the freedom to be intellectually and morally consistent.

Bibliography

Knight, Robert, ed. *"Ich bin dafür, die Sache in die Länge zu ziehen." Die Wortprotokolle der österreichischen Bundesregierung von 1945 bis 1952 über die Entschädigung der Juden.* Frankfurt am Main: Athenäum, 1988.

Mitten, Richard. *The Politics of Antisemitic Prejudice. The Waldheim Phenomenon in Austria.* Boulder: Westview, 1992.

Pauley, Bruce F. *From Prejudice to Persecution. A History of Austrian Anti-Semitism.* Chapel Hill: University of North Carolina Press, 1992.

Pelinka, Anton. *Austria. Out of the Shadow of the Past.* Boulder: Westview, 1998.

Steininger, Rolf, ed. *Der Umgang mit dem Holocaust. Europa - USA - Israel.* Vienna: Böhlau, 1994.

Stourzh, Gerald. *Um Einheit und Freiheit. Staatsvertrag, Neutralität und das Ende der Ost-West-Besetzung Österreichs 1945 – 1955.* Vienna: Böhlau, 1998.

Wodak, Ruth et al. *"Wir sind alle unschuldige Täter." Diskurshistorische Studien zum Nachkriegsantisemitismus.* Frankfurt am Main: Suhrkamp, 1990.

Wyman, David S., ed. *The World Reacts to the Holocaust.* Baltimore: Johns Hopkins University Press, 1996.

Reply to the Commentators

Gerald Stourzh

First I would like to express my gratitude to the convener of this panel, Professor Bischof, for his initiative in organizing the discussion at the Atlanta meeting of the German Studies Association in October 1999 and for the opportunity to publish the proceedings. I would like to express my great appreciation to the four commentators, Professors Mastny, Larres, Pelinka, and Schwartz, for their careful reading as well as for their thoughtful comments on the book under discussion.[1]

I shall reply first to the comments of Vojtech Mastny, Klaus Larres, and Anton Pelinka, who have put particular aspects or themes of my book into the center of their comments, and I shall conclude by trying to reply to the comment of Thomas Schwartz, who has raised the most comprehensive catalogue of questions concerning the book as a whole.

Now, first then to "The Soviet Godfathers of Austrian Neutrality":

If the Soviets were the godfathers, there was also a godmother, in the unlikely person of John Foster Dulles—"if Austria wants to be a Switzerland, US will not stand in the way, but this should not be imposed." Thus spoke Dulles to Molotov on 13 February 1954 in Berlin, in a person-to-person meeting, the Soviet interpreter Oleg Troyanovsky being the only other person present.[2] A little later on the same day, Dulles presented this position (previously approved by President Eisenhower[3]) a bit more elaborately to the Conference of the Four Foreign Ministers:

"A neutral status is an honorable status if it is voluntarily chosen by a nation. Switzerland has chosen to be neutral, and as a neutral she has achieved an honorable place in the family of nations. Under the Austrian State Treaty as heretofore drafted, Austria would be free to choose for itself to be a neutral like Switzerland. Certainly the United States would fully respect its choice in this respect, as it fully respects the choice of the Swiss Nation.

However, it is one thing for a nation to choose to be neutral and it is another thing to have neutrality forcibly imposed on it by other nations as a perpetual servitude . ..."[4]

A neutrality like that of Switzerland—this became the Soviets' most persuasive argument in their bilateral talks with the Austrians in Moscow in April 1955, and I am a bit surprised that Professor Mastny makes no reference to this at all. Among the preparatory papers for the Soviet-Austrian talks to be found in the archives of the Russian foreign ministry there is a particularly interesting one that refers in detail to Dulles' Berlin statement of February 1954.[5] The records of the Austro-Soviet talks demonstrate the central place of the 'Dulles formula'—neutrality on the Swiss pattern, no neutralization by treaty—in the Soviets' successful effort to overcome Austrian doubts (particularly on the part of the Socialist leader Adolf Schärf) about the acceptability of neutrality, chiefly in view of a possibly negative attitude on the part of the Western powers.[6] The 'Dulles formula' was employed by the Soviets as the 'consensus' formula apt to sway reluctant Austrians like Schärf and the Western powers into agreeing to Austria's newly emerging international status. That this consensus was the chief goal of the 'Swiss pattern' formula, rather than the insistence on Austria's close adaptation of the Swiss model, is demonstrated by the fact that the Soviets had no objections to the Austrians deviating from the Swiss pattern rights by joining the United Nations.[7]

Professor Mastny feels that I dwell "on the dexterity of the Austrian representatives," and he praises the feat of the "bipartisan team" of Raab, Schärf, Figl, and Kreisky extracting "concessions that made the resulting treaty in several ways less favorable for the Soviet Union than the drafts it had previously rejected." Without denying the dexterity of the Austrian negotiators, I think that a close reading of the pertinent chapter of my book will show that

a) the most important concessions on the part of the Soviet Union—the return of the oil production (oil fields, concessions on new findings, refineries and distribution) and the Danube Steamship Company holdings in the Soviet Zone against compensation—had been decided in Moscow before the Austrians' arrival;[8]

b) in addition, considerable differences of opinion among the Austrian top politicians (Raab and Schärf in particular) came into the open even during internal talks of the Austrians in Moscow (which no doubt will have been known to the Soviet side).[9] While Chancellor Raab no doubt came to Moscow with the firm determination to accept neutrality as the key to Soviet withdrawal from Austria,[10] his Socialist counterpart Adolf Schärf had considerable reservations with regard to the concept of neutrality.[11]

Neither Professor Mastny nor I have so far been able to penetrate to the minutes (presumably taken by Vladimir N. Malin) of those meetings of the Presidium (i.e. Politburo) of the Communist Party of the Soviet Union in the early months of 1955, where the line to be taken towards Austria was controversially discussed. But one should never abandon hope. There were three meetings of the Presidium where the Austrian question was discussed at greast length, if we believe what Mikoyan reported to the secret plenary meeting of the Central Committee in July 1955.[12] Professor Mastny quotes from a most interesting letter by Evgenii D. Kiselev to Nikolai Shvernik of October 1959, that "until 1955, i.e., until the time when the central committee decided to resolve the Austrian question in conformity with the proposal by comrade Khrushchev, the basic line was to delay rather than achieve its resolution."[13] However, it seems that the date inserted in brackets by Professor Mastny—"in April"—is not necessarily warranted by the text of Kiselev's letter. The process of pushing aside Molotov's reservations was a more protracted one—according to Mikoyan, as I have noted, it took three reunions of the Party Presidium. Professor Mastny seems to put too exclusive a significance on early April 1955 as the time of the decisive turn of Soviet policy toward Austria. Though, indeed, as a result of the talks at the Central Committee on 2 April 1955 (and quite obviously as a result of Presidium rulings), very important new concessions to be granted to Austria were envisaged, and much tougher earlier drafts of the foreign ministry had to be abandoned accordingly,[14] as important developments had set in earlier:

a) The drive to prepare bilaterally a settlement with Austria as a preliminary to the State Treaty became apparent in the series of talks between Molotov and Ambassador Bischoff in February and March and culminated in the invitation to Chancellor Raab to come to Moscow, which was issued on 24 March. I fully agree with Professor Mastny that the introduction of the "Anschluss" theme in the Soviet press on 19 January 1955—incidentally after a while of silence on things Austrian—is indicative of the beginning of a new response to the Paris agreements by initiating a new approach to the Austrian question. It is most interesting—and hardly a fortuitous coincidence—that the first of a new series of internal papers of the Soviet foreign ministry papers on the Austrian question is dated 19 January 1955.[15]

To the question raised by Professor Mastny as to why the Soviets chose the unusual way of approaching the Austrians first, my reply is this: It is an old rule of 'power politics' that the stronger will try to deal with the weaker 'bilaterally', if thereby he eliminates or at least weakens the interference of potential helpers—particularly strong helpers—of the weaker one. It was a regular feature of Soviet policy towards Austria since 1945 to attempt to deal with Austria 'bilaterally', as I have pointed out in the book under discussion on several occasions.[16] One early attempt at a bilateral deal, concerning the oil production in Eastern Austria in late August/early September 1945, was successfully thwarted by the Western powers.[17] The Soviet approach culminating in the bilateral understanding reached in the "Moscow Memorandum" of 15 April 1955 was the most successful attempt of Soviet 'bilateralism' toward Austria, its success depending however on the moderation of Soviet goals including the employment of the 'consensus formula' of neutrality after the Swiss pattern without neutralization by treaty, designed to win the West's acceptance.

b) The Austrian question was definitely split off from the German question when the Soviet note to Austria of 24 March recognized for the first time that the Austrian question should be regareded "separately."[18] This was a major, and from the Austrian point of view very hopeful, breakthrough in favor of the "autonomy" of the Austrian settlement, if one keeps in mind that the *"Junktim"* or "package," tying a solution of the Austrian question to a solution of the German question, had been part and parcel of the Soviet position since August 1953,[19] reaching its culminating point at the Berlin Conference of February 1954.[20] It should be noted that the final step of separating the Austrian from the German question took place four days after a remarkable confidential conversation between Edgar Faure, the Russian-speaking French prime minister, and the Soviet ambassador in Paris Sergei Vinogradov. Faure told Vinogradov three important things: First, that the ratification of the Paris Treaties in the French Upper House, the *Conseil de la République,* was assured; second, Faure promised Vinogradov to intervene with Eisenhower and Churchill on behalf of the Soviet desire to arrange a summit conference; third, he urged the Soviets to agree to the conclusion of an Austrian Treaty prior to the summit conference, and he expressed the Westen powers' willingness to accept an Austrian declaration of neutrality.[21]

Professor Mastny feels that concerning the broader context of Soviet policy on Austria I give no clear answer, nor do I, he thinks, differentiate between substantive and incidental tenets of the Soviet diplomatic offensive. I must leave it to the readers of the pertinent sections of the book under discussion to judge whether they agree or not with Professor Mastny's opinions.[22] To me it seems fairly clear that after the great Western success in bringing the Federal Republic of Germany into the Western fold with the Paris Treaties, Krushchev responded to this Western success with rather daring initiatives, which, in the spring of 1955, led to his *winning the diplomatic initiative from the West*. The West was startled and wholly taken by surprise by three initiatives: The approach to Austria culminating in the Austro-Soviet understanding of April 1955 in Moscow; the approach to Tito culminating in Krushchev's and Bulganin's trip to Belgrade in May 1955; and the invitation to Konrad Adenauer to come to Moscow, which he did in September 1955.[23] Compared with these three "surprise actions," the preparation and conclusion of the Warsaw Pact was a much more "orthodox" and unsurprising affair.

It was the new flexibility or '*souplesse*', to borrow the word used by a brilliant analyst, the French top diplomat Jean Chauvel, that included even vacating military positions previously held, which enabled the Krushchev leadership (against the recalcitrant Molotov) to "distinguish the essential from the accidental and if necessary to sacrifice the accidental to the essential," to borrow again from Jean Chauvel. What was most essential, I believe to have made clear. It was the world wide attempt to push back American influence with political rather than military means (here I agree wholly with Professor Mastny) by creating improved relationships to non-communist nations outside the orbit of the Western alliance system, trying to include non-communist countries into what was propagandistically called a "zone of peace," or even a "camp of peace," and improving simultaneously the direct contacts to the opposing camp, as witnessed both by the establishment of direct relations with Adenauer's West Germany and the drive for a conference at the summit.[24]

With regard to Professor Mastny's observations regarding the Yugoslav issue, it suffices to say that the reader will find references in the book under discussion to the primary place of the controversies concerning relations to Tito in the Krushchev/Molotov feud, including the fact that the reprint of Tito's strictures against Molotov in *Pravda* and *Istvestija* on 11 March 1955 was the very first public sign that Khrushchev had begun to move against Molotov.[25] The evidence I have presented on the vast significance of the Soviet withdrawal from Austria for Tito's Yugoslavia[26] needs to be supplemented, in the future, by research in the Soviet and particularly Yugoslav archival holdings—presumably no easy task.[27]

The close connection of Khrushchev's (virtually simultaneous) policies toward Austria and Yugoslavia in the spring of 1955 has been put into a larger context in some interesting contemporary reports by the Austrian ambassador in Moscow, Norbert Bischoff, who, notwithstanding his lopsided sympathies, was capable of shrewd insights, and who was obviously (at times) the recipient of important information. He reported toward the end of February 1955 that a role was intended for Austria, similar to that of Sweden, Finland, Switzerland and Yugoslavia (*"eine funktional ähnliche Rolle"*).[28] I quite agree, of course, with Professor Mastny that there never was a thought of letting any of the Soviet controlled countries of East Central and South Eastern Europe escape into neutrality—*vide* the Warsaw Pact.[29] After all, did not Machiavelli write in his *Principe*: "And it will always happen that the one who is not your friend will want you to remain neutral, and the one who is your friend will require you to declare yourself by taking arms"[30]

Professor Larres has concentrated on one period of particular interest, and one of his particular expertise, namely the time after the death of Stalin, early in March 1953, until the end of 1954, with particular emphasis on the policies of Winston Churchill as prime minister until the time of his stroke on 23 June 1953, and again in the second half of 1954.

Professor Larres raises two particular points of criticism.

First, he feels that I unduly minimize the crucial importance of the demise of Stalin, and thus underestimate the possibilities or chances for solving the Austrian question as a result of the tranfer of power from Stalin to his successors. Second, and related to it, he criticizes that I neglect the influence of Britain, or rather of Prime Minister Churchill's activities, both between March and 23 June 1953 and in the second half of 1954. To these points I would like to reply as follows.

a) I am fully aware of the changed atmosphere of the 'thaw' that set in after Stalin's death, and of the very considerable easing of the burden of Soviet occupation in the months following Stalin's demise, measures that are partly mentioned by Professor Larres. These measures included the appointment of a civilian high commissioner (with the rank of ambassador, thus following the example set by the Western powers in 1950) instead of a military high commissioner (the office of high commissioner expired only with the coming into force of the Austrian Treaty on 27 July 1955). Other measures like an amnesty for (some) prisoners of war and civilian prisoners held in the Soviet Union, the termination of the control of Austrians crossing the demarcation line between the Soviet zone and the British or American zones, the end of postal censurship (all this more than eight years after the end of the war!), and the Soviets' renouncing the payment of occupation costs by Austria, were of greater and more immediate relevance for the population.[31]

b) These manifestations of a 'thaw' were used by new Chancellor Raab (appointed early in April 1953) to explore new avenues of a direct (i.e. bilateral) approach to the Soviet government with a purpose of de-blocking the State Treaty issue. In May 1953 Raab began to develop personal contacts leading to relations of great personal confidence with the Austrian political representative in Moscow, Norbert Bischoff, a great critic of Western 'cold war'-policies and an advocate of the improvement of Austro-Soviet relations. On 16 June 1953 the Austrian Council of Ministers approved the text of a 'message' to be conveyed to Foreign Minister Molotov by Bischoff, who incidentally was the drafter of the government message he was about to carry to Moscow. This document was couched in very friendly terms indeed,[32] and it was presented to Molotov on 30 June 1953. Simultaneously, the Austrian Foreign Minister Gruber had attempted to enlist the good services of India and of Prime Minister Nehru, whom he met on 20 June 1953 in Switzerland on the latter's return trip from London to Delhi. As a result, the Indian ambassador in Moscow saw Molotov also on June 30 in Moscow, even conveying to Molotov the notion that Austria might be willing to be neutral between East and West. Molotov's reaction was not forthcoming at all. In the ensuing months, the Soviet government insisted with great energy, and finally successfully, that the West (and Austria) retract the draft of an 'abbreviated' treaty published in March 1952, omitting the Soviet Union's various economic claims on Austria.

c) Thus the Austrian government very definitely sought to take advantage of the the 'thaw'. Professor Larres, incidentally, has no comment to make on these two Austrian initiatives. They were not successful. Of course, the fateful 17 June had intervened in East Berlin and East Germany, and—unknown to the public and to the diplomats who approached Molotov with their Austrian errand on 30 June—the arrest of Berija had taken place on 26 June. Thus, literally speaking, by the end of June, the Soviet foreign minister—and the Soviet leadership—had other things on their mind.

d) One has to add that these two Austrian initiatives provoked the most angry reaction of the Western powers, particularly of the British and the Americans. British reactions in particular were quite furious, even more than those of the Americans. I have dealt with these British and American reactions quite extensively. Raab and Gruber were actually read the riot act because of Austrian insubordination.[33] After July/August 1953—and very visibly by the time of the Berlin Foreign Ministers' Conference in January/February 1954—the Austrians had dutifully returned from their 'foray' into bilateralism to the old practice of very close consultations with the Western powers, a practice they would once more abandon in March/April of 1955. Professor Larres does not comment on all this, and therefore his observation that Raab "would gradually move a little closer to Moscow and observe a somewhat greater distance than hitherto to Washington" suggests more of a one-directional movement than was the case. There was no gradual movement but rather, between the spring of 1953 and the spring of 1955, something of a zigzag line, which I have tried to retrace, and there were also, on the part of Raab, who held his cards very close to his chest, some less than candid statements vis-à-vis Western diplomats.[34] I may add here that I am somewhat less sanguine than Professor Günter Bischof regarding the "leverage of the weak."[35] The non-solution of the Austrian question in 1953 or 1954 , and its solution in 1955 depended less on the lesser or greater weight of Austrian "leverage," and more on different power constellations and policy determinations in the Kremlin—given the fact that the Soviet Union held part of Austria's territory (and of its oil production) as a "pawn" to be released only when it suited its interests, as seen by the power holders in Moscow.[36]

e) The question remains whether, prior to the events which proved troublesome for the Soviet leadership—namely, 17 June in Germany and the removal of Berija on 26 June—, chances existed for an early solution of the Austrian question. As the research of Vladislav Zubok and

Constantine Pleshakov has shown, Prime Minister Malenkov approached Molotov both in May and early June 1953 with regard to a renewal of the State Treaty negotiations, yet foundered on the latter's procrastinating position.[37] Similarly, Krushchev told the secret Plenary session of the Central Committee in July 1955 that after Stalin's death he and Malenkov had approached Molotov on the Austrian question, who considered it as "complex" and wanted its settlement to be delayed.[38] Again in rather similar terms, Krushchev retold the story of his unsuccessful approaches to Molotov after Stalin's death in his memoirs.[39] Thus it seems—and here I come to Professor Larres' second point—that Churchill's hopes for solutions on the summit in the months following Stalin's death—and I admit that I have paid more attention to British Austrian policy on the foreign office level than on the level of the prime minister's foreign policy designs—never had any practical impact on the day-to-day operations of the Austrian Treaty diplomacy. What did have an impact was the fact, perhaps not sufficiently taken into account by Professor Larres, that the 'thaw' following Stalin's death was accompanied by one 'icy' element: the return to power of Molotov, who had fallen into disgrace towards the end of the Stalin era. In 1953, at any rate, Molotov's 'countervailing power' at the foreign ministry proved strong enough to block whatever approaches in favor of an early Austrian solution might have been made. As far as the period after Churchill's recovery in 1954 is concerned, events rather beyond Churchill's summit interests dominated the European scene: the demise of the European Defense Community (EDC) in France in August 1954 and the amazingly quick replacement of the EDC by the Paris Treaties of October 1954. In this 'replacement diplomacy', Anthon Eden, rather than Churchill, was the prime mover, and things Austrian were quite secondary and remained subordinated to the German question.

Professor Pelinka, in his comment, diagnoses something like a bifurcation of Austrian history in the 1945-1955 decade: he speaks of the "logic" of domestic policy ("negative consensus"), and of a different "logic" of foreign policy ("positive consensus"). In particular, he says that small powers "have the quality of framing foreign policy as an art in itself, created by rather independent artists (experts, brahmins) as far as possible from the plains of domestic politics." Professor Pelinka says that I emphasize the importance of diplomats, and he mentions the Austrian diplomats Schöner, Wodak, Bischoff, Verosta, Kirchschläger, and some others. On the whole, I feel that some foreign diplomats play a larger role in my book than some Austrian diplomats—Llewellyn Thompson, for instance, or, in view of their particularly interesting reporting, Sven Allard, Jean Chauvel, or Roger Lalouette; among the Austrian diplomats mentioned, Bischoff, due to his special role between 1953 and 1955, and Verosta, due to his formula of *"Territorialgarantie"* worked out in March 1955, are given particular attention.[40]

However, Professor Pelinka points to an important fact: In addition to the diplomats, the foreign policy players also included "top representatives of the two major parties." And here I would like to stress the following: The top representatives of the two major parties, to whom Professor Pelinka is referring, were the chancellor, the vice-chancellor, the foreign minister, and (in view of his responsibility for security forces and for the secret rearmament measures in the Western zones) the minister of the interior, accompanied by the state secretary in the ministry of the interior. I would like to draw attention to two points: First, the role of these major political figures in the shaping of foreign policy was far more important than that of the "brahmin diplomats;" and second, through these very figures the close connection of those two realms which Professor Pelinka separates so carefully—foreign policy and domestic policy—was assured. It is, however, a fact worthy of notice that these politicians, inspite of domestic rivalry and deep antagonisms of political philosophy, were able and willing to cooperate in the fields of foreign and security policy—the latter particularly requiring considerable discipline in sharing confidential information 'on the top', yet not divulging it to other persons of their own political groups, except for a small number of trusted aides.

Professor Pelinka seems to regret that I have not written a book covering the whole of Austrian political history of those years. If I had done that, I would have had to renounce too much of the story told here, for the time, in such detail, with new sources, and, I would hope, with a vividness often absent from works trying to cover more comprehensive narratives. Thus, I have rather chosen the way of referring the reader to other works and other authors, and Professor Pelinka kindly cites some of these authors, like Brigitte Bailer-Galanda and others.

Finally, I will attempt to reply to five questions which Professor Schwartz has put to me.

First, Professor Schwartz asks whether I have any reason to believe that there is any material in Russian archives that I had not access to, which might change or alter the interpretation of my book. The answer is bound to be speculative, and one starts treading on treacherous ground. I feel that there is a deficit in my book on one particular point, due to insufficient evidence, namely on Soviet internal plans and possible policy shifts during the year 1949, in which the conclusion of the Austrian Treaty seemed to be quite near, though it was to finally come about only six years later. The possible impact of a) the creation of NATO, b) the breaking of the American nuclear monopoly, c) the Communist victory in China, d) the development of Soviet-Yugoslav hostility, and e) the creation of both the Federal Republic of Germany and the German Democratic Republic on the Austrian policies of the Soviet Union remains to be enlightend by future archival findings. Also, as observed already, I think that the further clarification of Yugoslav-Soviet contacts in the early months of 1955 might shed additional light on Soviet (and Yugoslav) attitudes toward Austria. This concentration on two points obviously does not exclude other discoveries or surprises in Soviet archives or elsewhere.

Second, Professor Schwartz asks—again speculatively—which alternative for Austria might have seemed most likely, if the Moscow negotiations of April 1955 had failed. No one can tell. There were speculations at the time about the considerable 'nuisance' potential of the Soviet control of the demarcation lines to the Western zones of Austria, without necessarily cutting the East off the West completely. Also the nuisance potential of unilaterally boycotting the Allied Commission, again without necessarily cutting Austria into two, would have been considerable. I have pointed to these possibilities in my book.[41]

Third, as to the relationship between the Austrian solution and the German question, Professor Schwartz posits two alternative hypotheses, which I need not repeat here in extenso. My book makes it clear, I think, that I favor the second of these hypotheses, to wit that the Austrian solution became possible because the Western powers had reached a decision on Germany. I agree with Professor Schwartz that "absent such German integration into NATO, it is difficult to imagine the West showing the same willingness to accept a neutral Austria."

Fourth, Professor Schwartz raises the important question as to the "follow-up" of the Austrian solution of 1955 for nations under Soviet control like Hungary or Poland. What happened in Poland and Hungary must be seen in the wider context of Kruschchev's de-Stalinization speech and policies of early 1956. Yet, for Hungary's attempt to quit the Warsaw Pact and to declare neutrality at the beginning of November

1956, it is quite clear that this could never have been attempted without what had (successfully) happened in Austria in the preceding year. The brutal squashing of the Hungarian uprising demonstrated indeed, as Professor Schwartz says, the narrow limits of Krushchev's reform policies.[42]

As to the fifth question, it turns, of course, on the meanings and interpretations given to the Allied Moscow Declaration on Austria of 1 November 1943, which both—in words taken straight from Churchill—declared Austria to have been the first vicim of Nazi aggression, and also engaged Austria's responsibility of having taken part in the war "on the side of Hitlerite Germany." I have shown that the Soviet government hardened the working of the declaration and also put "juridic" teeth into the responsibility clause of the declaration.[43] It was also, together with the British, responsible for rather harsh terms put into the preamble of the Austrian Treaty.[44] This "responsibility clause" was eliminated, as is well known, on Austrian request in the very last moment, one day before the signature of the Treaty. This elimination may have been a "Pyrrhic victory" for Austria, as has been suggested, and as I have noted in my book.[45] The Soviets stressed at times the first aspect of the Declaration, as immediately after the liberation of Austria at times the second, the "guilt," aspect for instance around 1947.[46] As to a connection between Soviet rigidity on Austrian issues and the sense of Austrian culpability of Hitler's crimes, it seems rather clear that policies in the first months after the end of the war, like dismantling and taking over of rolling stock, were dictated both by the dire needs of the Soviet Union and the consciousness of terrible suffering inflicted. In later periods, more pragmatic notions may have prevailed, still dictated by the needs of the Soviet economy—and also, if we may believe a remark made by Anastas Mikoyan during the Austro-Soviet talks in April 1955, by the costs of constructing nuclear weapons.[47]

As far as the Austrian 'use' of the Moscow Declaration is concerned, I have noted, in my book, my views which somewhat differ from those presented by Professor Bischof on several occasions. If the Austrian leaders in and after 1945 had not stressed the violence done by Hitler to Austrian independence, if the Austrians had considered themselves merely the vanquished inhabitants of the German Ostmark, of one of the insolvent remains of the Third Reich, the sense of Austrian identity, which was to develop more fully in the decades to follow, could hardly have emerged. I have critically commented, however, on the lack of that moral insight which makes it possible to feel and express shame for misdeeds and crimes of one's countrymen even if one is not personally responsible.[48] As Chancellor Franz Vranitzky stated at the Hebrew University in Jerusalem in 1993, there is a responsibility for the suffering inflicted not by the state of Austria, which did not exist anymore, but by Austrians on their fellow men and on humanity, and though there is no collective guilt, there is a collective responsibility for every Austrian to remember, and to seek for justice.[49]

Sixth, Professor Schwartz asks whether or not I might agree to the suggestion that the Austrian solution and its durability during the cold war was a vindication of American Wilsonianism and its sentimental beliefs in the rights of small states to their independence. I think rather not. I have noted a certain liberality, perhaps one should say, a remarkable liberality, in the views of John Foster Dulles on the Austrian case.[50] Yet, the name of the game was power politics all the same. In conclusion, I agree with Professor Schwartz that the change since 1989 underlines the degree to which the historical epoch, which my work documents, is now a closed one, and that the challenges Austria now faces are fundamentally different.

Notes

1. Further references to the book *Um Einheit und Freiheit. Staatsvertrag, Neutralität und das Ende der Ost-West-Besetzung Österreichs 1945-1955* (Vienna: Böhlau 1998), 831 pp., will be abbreviated as follows: *UEuF*, page reference.

2. *UEuF*, 309-10.

3. Ibid., 298.

4. Ibid., 310.

5. Ibid., 407-8.

6. Ibid., 434-35, as well as 640-41.

7. I would like to refer to the interesting book by the Swiss author Christian Jenny, *Konsensformel oder Vorbild? Die Entstehung der österreichischen Neutralität und das Schweizer Muster* (Bern: Haupt, 1995).

8. *UEuF,* 406.

9. Ibid., 423-32.

10. Ibid., 423. Prime Minister Bulganin told Raab that neutrality was "*the* condition," as Raab reported in a confidential meeting of the Main Committee of the Austrian Parliament, ibid., 495, 601. It seems that during a conversation in the Austrian Embassy in the evening of 12 April, the eve of the decisive negotiations of 13 April, Bulganin obtained from Raab assurances that prompted him to tell the other Soviet officials present on that occasion that "everything is all right." Conversation with Ambassador (ret.) Rostislav Sergejev in Moscow on 10 April 2000. As a young diplomat Ambassador Sergejew was interpreter to the Soviet leaders during their conversations and

negotiations with the Austrians in April 1955, and was present in the Austrian Embassy on 12 April 1955.

11. *UEuF*, 426-29.

12. Ibid., 456.

13. The materials collected by Shvernik as head of the Party Control Commission in connection with investigations concerning Molotov ("delo Molotova"), which include the letters by Semenov and Kiselev quoted by Professor Mastny and made available to a research conference in early 1993, were no longer accessible in 1997.

14. Ibid., 405-8.

15. On this and the following papers see ibid., 337ff.

16. Ibid., 88, 227-28, 347, 383, 599.

17. Ibid., 88-94.

18. Ibid., 366-70, with a careful analysis of the various drafts preceding the final version of the Soviet note of 24 March.

19. This position was first formulated in the Soviet note of 4 August 1953 addressed to the Western powers. See Klaus Larres, *Politik der Illusionen. Churchill, Eisenhower und die deutsche Frage 1945-1955* (Göttingen: Vandenhoeck & Ruprecht 1995), 214.

20. See *UEuF*, 312, 318-19; for the final demise of the Austrian/German "Junktim" see Premier Bulganin's speech at the Austrian Embassy in Moscow on 12 April 1955, ibid., 416.

21. Ibid., 365-66.

22. Ibid., 463-485; also 591-592.

23. The invitation to Adenauer and the inauguration of a firm 'two states'-policy for Germany incidentally belied Western (and particularly German) speculations that the Austrian solution was meant to be a (short term) example for Germany. Professor Mastny has quite rightly pointed to one document of particular relevance for Krushchev's German policy: the instructions to Molotov for the Vienna foreign ministers' meeting on 14 May 1955—that the German question could not "be regarded in any way as being ready to be successfully discussed at the present time," ibid., 478.

24. Ibid., 482-483. As to Jean Chauvel, see ibid., 481. I refer to an analysis by Chauvel, who was French High Commissioner in Austria from October 1954 to January 1955 and ambassador in London from February 1955 onwards, published in *Documents diplomatiques français 1955*, I, no. 243 (2 May 1955).

25. Ibid., 335, notes 2 and 3, 455.

26. Ibid., 465-66.

27. The contribution by Andrei Edemskij, "The Turn in Soviet-Yugoslav Relations 1953-1955," in *Cold War International History Project Bulletin,* no. 10 (March 1998): 138, is quite disappointing, consisting merely of two brief documents from the AVG RF, none of which are from the crucial period of January to May 1955.

28. *UEuF*, 481-82. Professor Mastny calls the establishment of Austrian neutrality "a mere episode" as opposed to the "permanent military fixture" of the Warsaw Pact in the cold war. I do not think so. The constellation emerging in 1955 of the five countries just mentioned with a *"funktional ähnlichen Rolle"* presents the source of the 'N+N' (neutral and non-aligned) group of European countries consolidated after 1975 in the CPSE process until the end of the cold war.

29. With respect to Scandinavia, I cannot quite agree with Professor Mastny's statement that the Soviet Union never seriously encouraged a Western European state to follow Austria's example. The question is of course what weight one gives to the word 'serious'. In late 1955/early 1956 Moscow was very active—though of course unsuccessful as far as Denmark and Norway were concerned—in Scandinavia, witnessed by quite a number of statements extolling the virtues of neutrality, and the invitation to the prime ministers of Norway, Denmark, and Sweden to visit Moscow, which they did in November 1955, March and April 1956, respectively. Even after the Hungarian crisis and the shock it produced in Scandinavia, as elsewhere, the idea of the Baltic Sea as a 'sea of peace' was aired by Moscow in 1957. See Heinz Fiedler, *Der sowjetische Neutralitätsbegriff in Theorie und Praxis* (Cologne, 1959), 228-231.

30. Niccolo Machiavelli, *The Prince*, ch. XXI, quoted in Gerald Stourzh, "Some Reflections on Permanent Neutrality," *Small States in International Relations,* ed. August Schou and Arne Olav Brundtland, (Stockholm, 1971), 96. In this context I have spoken of the "affinity paradox," i.e. neutrality will satisfy a potentially more hostile power or power block more than a potentially friendlier power or power block (ibid.). Machiavelli's reflection on neutrality was on various occasions referred to by Bruno Kreisky.

31. *UEuF*, 223-25.

32. Ibid., 226-28.

33. Ibid., 235-37.

34. Ibid., 396-97.

35. Günter Bischof, *Austria in the First Cold War, 1945-55: The Leverage of the Weak* (New York: St. Martin's 1999), 153. Stourzh, *UEuF,* 598-99.

36. UEuF, 591, 594-96.

37. Vladislav Zubok and Constantine Pleshakov, *Inside the Kremlin's Cold War. From Stalin to Krushchev* (Cambridge, MA: Harvard UP 1996), 156-63, particularly 157-58, referred to in *UEuF*, 235.

38. Ibid., 458-59.

39. See the publication of the chapter on Austria ("Mirnyj dogovor s Avstriej"—"The Peace Treaty with Austria") of Krushchev's memoirs in Russian (the English language editions are quite incomplete on Austria) in *Voprosij istorii*, no. 7 (1993): 73-87.

40. On the latter, see particularly the text of Verosta's position paper, *UEuF*, 609-14.

41. Ibid., 398-400, 402-3.

42. On this, see, though briefly, *UEuF*, 485.

43. Ibid., 21-23.

44. For the text of this clause see ibid., 683-84.

45. Ibid., 520.

46. Ibid., 70-73.

47. Ibid., 416.

48. Ibid., 25-27.

49. The text of Vranitzky's statement is quoted in ibid., 521.

50. Ibid., 297-98.

REVIEW ESSAY

Austria after 1945—Success Story? Heroic Age?
Review of Recent Literature

Günter Bischof

Robert Kriechbaumer, ed., *Österreichische Nationalgeschichte nach 1945 - Die Spiegel der Erinnerung: Die Sicht von innen* **(Vienna: Böhlau, 1998)**

Reinhard Sieder, Heinz Steinert, and Emmerich Tálos, eds., *Österreich 1945-1995: Gesellschaft – Politik – Kultur,* **2nd ed. (Vienna: Verlag für Gesellschaftskritik, 1996)**

Rolf Steininger and Michael Gehler, eds., *Österreich im 20. Jahrhundert: Ein Studienbuch in zwei Bänden,* **vol. II,** *Vom Zweiten Weltkrieg bis zur Gegenwart* **(Vienna: Böhlau, 1997)**

Kurt Richard Luther and Peter Pulzer, eds., *Austria 1945 - 95: Fifty Years of the Second Republic,* **Association for the Study of German Politics (Aldershot: Ashgate, 1998)**

Anthony Bushell, ed., *Austria 1945 - 1955: Studies in Political and Cultural Re-emergence* **(Cardiff: University of Wales Press, 1996)**

David F. Good and Ruth Wodak, eds., *From World War to Waldheim: Culture and Politics and the United States;* Austrian History, Culture, and Society, edited by Richard L. Rudolph, vol. 2 (New York: Berghahn, 1999)

David. F. Good, Margarete Grandner, and Mary Jo Maynes, eds., *Austrian Women in the Nineteenth and Twentieth Centuries: Cross-Disciplinary Perspectives;* Austrian Studies, edited by David F. Good, vol. 1, (Providence, RI: Berghahn, 1996)

I.

How to review some 4000 pages of recent historiography on the Second Austrian Republic without descending into the same vast diffusion and microscopic fragmentation or sweeping generalizations that characterize many of the chapters in these essay collections? Historians can be divided into 'lumpers' and 'splitters'. The 'lumpers' impose order on the past by making sense out of entire epochs and systematizing complexity. They make sweeping generalizations and fit the chaos and untidiness of history into neat patterns. The 'splitters' write the micro-history of vast phenomena. They dwell on the incongruities and paradoxes of given events. They quibble and qualify and refuse to address broad sweeps of the past. They acknowledge complexity and delve into the details of it without tackling the issue of what their results imply for the larger trajectory of history.[1] Most of the essays in these volumes are exercises in 'splitting'.

Next to Anton Pelinka's penetrating review of Austrian politics *Austria: Out of the Shadow of the Past,*[2] Ernst Hanisch's magisterial Austrian history of the twentieth century has been the only serious recent attempt at 'lumping'.[3] The highly respected Salzburg historian has recently also provided us with a useful tool to deal with the complexity of the historiography in and on twentieth century Austria.[4] Hanisch isolates four major historiographical schools and relates them to the generational experience of their chief practitioners. The first school included the 'German national' historians who wrote between 1918 and 1945. For them Austria was a member of the German *Volk,* and so they were desperately looking for the German past in the history of the small Austrian republic left over from the vast Habsburg Empire after World War I. In the old German Rankean tradition the likes of

Heinrich von Srbik wrote mainly *political* history and made sure that Austrian history would be reintegrated into the larger trajectory of German history.

The second school comprised the *Koalitionsgeschichtsschreibung* (coalition history) practiced from the end of the war until the early 1970s. Born in the 1920s, these historians had experienced National Socialism and World War II personally, often in the trenches. With the experience of World War II they became fervent postwar Austrian patriots, accepted the official 'victim's myth', and externalized Austrians' responsibility in the war. In contrast to the conflicts of the First Republic, they perceived Austria's postwar history as one of unmitigated success (*Erfolgsgeschichte*). Both the Christian conservatives (ÖVP) and the Socialists (SPÖ), the two major political camps, zoomed in on this version of the past, which regarded Austrian resistance to National Socialism as central and ignored Austrians' contribution to Hitlerite war crimes. While the Communists were included in this antifascist and patriotic history, the third, nationalist, camp (FPÖ) was ignored as if it no longer existed in postwar Austria. This school still largely wrote in the tradition of positivist Germanic *political* history. Erika Weinzierl and Kurt Skalnik's two-volume *Geschichte der Zweiten Republik* (1972) probably is the *summa* of this school. Important innovations in Western historiography, such as the turn towards a new social history (*Gesellschaftsgeschichte*), were ignored at the very moment when the next generation born during or after the war started to test with gusto these methodological innovations for the Austrian history between the wars.

This third school, the Austrian 1968 generation (from 1970 to 1988), resembles the American revisionist-with-a-vengeance New Left historiography practiced in the 1960s and 1970s. Both rebelled against the racist imperialism of their fathers' generations—the Americans' U.S. imperialism in Vietnam, the Austrians' annihilationist Nazi imperialism. The hidebound paradigm of political historiography was abandoned for the methodologically sophisticated and empirically rich new *social* and *structural* historiography practiced in France and Germany (Bielefeld). A younger generation of scholars, led by Gerhard Botz and including Hanisch, made the interwar period, Austrofascism and the coming of the Anschluss, and Austrian labor history their favorite subjects. This was soon complimented with the first serious investigations of the twentieth century 'heart of darkness'–Austrians' roles in and contributions to National Socialism and the Holocaust. They often took the accusatory (critics say a 'moralistic') posture of the prosecutor. The 'victim's myth', which had survived for two generations collapsed with Kurt Waldheim's election to the Austrian presidency; this new New Left historiography lost its prevalence with the end of the cold war (1989).

Hanisch loosely characterizes the fourth school of Austrian historiography as the inevitable advent of 'postmodernism' in Austria. The *fragmentation and atomization* of all historical writing has become pervasive in Austrian historiography as well. The reigning paradigm of master narratives collapsed in Austria. They were replaced by the usual postmodern "anything-goes"-attitude of the eclectic microhistory of daily life, society, and mentality. A plethora of new methodologies such as oral history, linguistic deconstruction, and anthropological approaches have become dominant. After the end of the cold war, Austrian history writing has become 'de-ideologized' and very eagerly follows all the trends in fashionable Western historiography–gender history, the new cultural history, sophisticated regional history, environmental history, minority history (the history of Austrian Jews, Gypsies, Slovenes etc.). The savvy new historical journals of the 1990s *Zeitschrift für Geschichtswissenschaft*, *Historicum*, and the feminist *L'Homme*, have been 'translating' all the latest fashionable trends in Western historiography quickly and conveniently for Austrian academic consumption. This still prevailing paradigm demonstrates that Austrian historiography is not longer separated by time lags from the ruling Western trends. Writing political history has been abandoned almost entirely and has become a preserve of the political scientists, who usually do not bother to consult archives. Many of these 'postmodern' historians are assembled in the Sieder/Steinert/Tálos volume under review here and predictably spoke up as the sharpest critics of Hanisch's brilliant grand narrative of an Austrian *Gesellschaftsgeschichte*.[5]

The dichotomy 'lumping' and 'splitting', along with Hanisch's useful historiographical distinctions, will help us develope patterns in the volumes under review here.

II.

The volume edited by Robert Kriechbaumer appears as a strange case of a 'postmodern' project. It presumes to be an Austrian "national history," yet many of its authors are still stuck in hidebound coalition history. In his preface Kriechbaumer sets an ambitious 'postmodern' agenda for the volume. His subjective "historical hermeneutics" is based on the individual's "selective perception and construction" of reality.

Instead of one historical reality, he posits the different layers of reality of active and passive contemporaries and scholars. His three principal historical layers ("mirrors") are those of collective, individual, and historical memory. Historical reality is "mirrored" in the tales of both the political practitioners and their contemporary commentators in the media and the "reconstructions" by scholars. The overall theme of the volume is the "modernizing" of society after World War II, without defining it precisely. At the end of the short preface to this ambitious "national history", which presupposes political history, comes an odd disclaimer—these essays represent only the first "brushstrokes" of a sketch on the vast canvas of postwar history (pp. 11–13).

Kriechbaumer concludes by noting that "three" postwar generations are directing their attention "inward" to write the history of the Second Republic. Yet the birth dates of the forty-three authors of this massive brickbat of a volume (932 pp.) reveal that the majority of the authors were born before the war (the oldest one in 1921). Of the twelve 'baby boomers' (and potential '68ers) the youngest one was born in 1957. In other words, the age structure and socialization of the contributors is such that the volume is predestined to be at best mostly 'coalition history'. The generation born after 1960, the most likely practitioners of 'postmodern' history, are missing entirely. Only two women grace this male-dominated volume (Freda Meissner-Blau's weak essay on Austrian identity and the journalist Katharina Krawagna-Pfeifer's minute three-page essay on federalism), so gender history is not represented either. Is there any hidden agenda here? Robert Kriechbaumer is the scientific director (or scholar in residence) of the "Dr. Wilfried Haslauer Library" in Salzburg. Named after the late governor of Salzburg, the 'library' functions more like a research institute for the conservative People's Party, which traditionally had its strength in provincial rural Austria and not in Vienna. The Haslauer Library's "Research Institute for Political and Historical Studies" has been very active publishing Austria's history of the regions, particularly with its outstanding series on the nine Austrian states' history. It appears that the Haslauer Library is the provinces' answer to the Kreisky Archives and Forum in Vienna with its Socialist and internationalist agenda. In tandem, these two institutions enshrine the continuation of partisan *Koalitionsgeschichtsschreibung* even as the political arena is changing dramatically. In February 2000 for the first time a united bourgeois bloc (ÖVP-FPÖ) has formed a coalition government and ended 30 years of Socialist predominance. Thus the odd institutionalization of *Proporz* and partisan equivalency is upheld in the arena of writing the history of Austria at a time when we witness its waning days. Even though the book has no imprint of coming from the Haslauer Library (as all the others do), the choice of the scholarly contributors betrays that it is beholden to the conservative *Lager*.

The volume addresses seven major themes: (I) the larger postwar historical trajectory, (II) parties and political culture, (III) identity, (IV) the economy and economic policies, (V) social and mental change, (VI) continuities and discontinuities in culture, and (VII) the challenge of federalism (the strong state in Vienna vs. the provinces). Each of the six sections has a scholarly lead essay, followed by half a dozen or so essays by political practitioners and concluded with a rumination by a leading journalist. No matter what their political *couleur* may be, the lead essays are good summaries of the state of scholarship, meticulously researched and with an extensive scholarly apparatus. Kriechbaumer, the only author without a scholarly apparatus, introduces the postwar historical trajectory with an analysis of the principal turning points and the chronological subdivision of the postwar era and their specific mentalities. It is now commonly accepted that the Second Republic did not start with a blank slate ('zero hour') in 1945. Rather the continuities with the First Republic prevailed. The difficult period of political and economic reconstruction in the late 1940s followed with its construction of the victim's mythology and the externalization of the crimes of National Socialism. Since "the war had an existential dimension and became the instrument of socialization for an entire generation" (p. 23), the fellow-traveling Nazis and the returning soldiers needed to be quickly integrated into the Austrian body politic to achieve its stabilization. The 'long 1950s' (ending with the end of the great coalition in the mid-1960s) brought about Austrian independence from the four-power occupation and the Austrian economic miracle.

During the 'short 1960s' Austria became a consumer society and joined the West. For the only time in the postwar period the ÖVP-government of the former governor of Salzburg Josef Klaus initiated dramatic reforms, which modernized Austrian society and positioned the ÖVP in the "*Mainstream* [sic] *des Zeitgeistes*" (p. 34). The rehabilitation of the Klaus government as the "*Wegbereiter der Moderne*" (trendsetters for Modernism) (p. 35) is an important underlying and recurrent theme of this volume. With his savvy media techniques, Kreisky and the Socialists pinched this mantle of modernity from the ÖVP and has left them in the dust ever since. The 'long 1970s' of the Kreisky years were a period of economic prosperity and consensus (in the huge public economic sector based on increasingly misdirected 'Austro-Keynesianism'). A serious recession in the Western economies, growing state debts, and a number of seedy corruption scandals brought about a short-lived SPÖ-FPÖ coalition government (1983-86) to be ended by the sea changes of 1986.

The Waldheim affair and its repercussions on Austria's international image and the country's volatile 'politics of history' is hardly mentioned while Foreign Minister Alois Mock's (ÖVP) 'paradigm change' in Austrian foreign policy towards EU-membership in the return of the grand coalition under Franz Vranitzky (SPÖ) is stressed. The ÖVP as the driving force of Austria's EC/EU integration is another recurring theme on the hidden agenda of this volume. Haider, "the most gifted politician of the 1980s and 1990s" (!) (p. 41), entered the political arena as FPÖ party leader (since he never exercised national office, should it not be 'gifted *populist*'?). The remaining years of the 'short 1980s' saw a 'Westernization' of Austrian politics. By 1993 a new five-party system replaced the old 2 ½-party system with the rise of fickle "postmodern" and "postmaterial" (pp. 43ff) values, which are characterized by the rejection of politics-as-usual (in Austria that means the *Proporzsystem*), uncertainty about the future (especially the blessings of the welfare state), and the advent of environmental worries. Austria joined the European Union and is now being buffeted by globalization concerns, so the 1990s promise to be long as well. This basic chronology provides a backdrop for the rest of the volume (and the other volumes under review as well). Even though there are no specific references given in this essay, Kriechbaumer barely acknowledges how deeply his analysis is indebted to the Hanisch and Pelinka monographs mentioned above, which is to say, it is an exercise in 'lumping' as well.

So are the seven essays of the political practitioners (most of the politicians in section II "Politics" could also be placed in section I). The general consensus among politicians of all camps seems to be that the Second Republic was a dramatic 'success story'. While the economically non-viable First Republic was the "state that no one wanted," the economic miracle of the Second Republic produced the enviable state that everyone approved of. Even Jörg Haider chimes into this genuine lovefest of tooting the horn of the success of the postwar Austrian nation (at times bordering on the nationalistic). Only Peter Pilz from the Green Party talks about the price Austria had to pay for its clientelist '*Proporz*-state' and extra-constitutional governance—the atrophy of democracy and the undermining of the constitution. This is happily ignored by the representatives of the grand coalition who, after all, want to celebrate the 'success story' of the Second Republic, which is their success story as well. The Socialist Fred Sinowatz, who led the small coalition (1983-86) as chancellor, is a case in point. He celebrates himself as a good party trooper—the quintessential 'functionary' in the SPÖ.

The majority of the essays by the practitioners return to hidebound 'coalition history'. Naturally, the trend is to present a defense of one's ideological positions or specific policies, and in this sense, politicians asked to write history present memoirs of *apologia pro vita sua*. Generally speaking, the chapters written by ÖVP politicians tend to be more partisan than those of the Socialists. Both the former ÖVP party leaders Josef Riegler and Alois Mock attack Kreisky's supposed long-term 'Machiavellian' strategy of trying to atomize the People Party into a number of smaller bourgeois splinter groups ("Swedish model") (pp. 71, 235) to get rid of any serious opposition. They ought to be reminded that there is nothing new or particularly sinister in this old Socialist strategy. It had worked before, when in 1948/49 the Socialists successfully pushed the creation of the 'fourth party' (the VDU, Verband der Unabhängigen). Riegler blames a power-hungry Kreisky for all the corruption scandals during his reign since he hindered Parliament to control these abuses of power (p. 70). This after all is the Second Republic, so he does not go as far as to intimate an *Ausschaltung* (elimination) of parliament but instead avers an accumulation of power not longer bothered by parliamentary control (*Macht ohne Kontrolle*). In Riegler's portrait Kreisky emerges as the last of the Austrian emperors, however, not a benevolent type such as Joseph II.

While the Communist Franz Murhi criticizes the "euphemisms" (p. 163) of the Austrian Declaration of Independence of 27 April 1945, Andreas Khol posits that it contains the "fundamental values" of the Second Republic and thus represents the state's consensus (pp. 121f). Historians agree today that this declaration was a hastily conceived document full of half-truths and an early exercise in amnesia when it comes to Austrians' role in World War II. To read a catalog of Austrian fundamentals into it may well be the most brazen exercise in old coalition-type *Geschichtsbeschönigung* (historical euphemism) in this volume. Khol goes on to attack Haider's fundamental opposition to the state as "prefascist"(!), his ideas on the "Third Republic" as being outside of the constitutional consensus ("constitutional arc") of the Second Republic. The self-proclaimed conscience of the ÖVP, Khol posits Haider's FPÖ as not governable (*"nicht regierungsfähig"*) (pp. 126ff). Today, in the first postwar government of what could be called the 'bourgeois bloc' (the very bloc that Adolf Schärf and Kreisky failed to atomize), the ÖVP governs with the FPÖ, and Khol is also lying in bed with the FPÖ as the ÖVP's party whip (*"Clubobmann"*) in Parliament. Clio's revenge: such are the pitfalls of surely practicing politicians writing contemporary history.

The painstaking attempt to give leaders from all political parties a voice (why not Heide Schmidt of the Liberal Forum?), leads to the inclusion of the apologetic propaganda tract by the unrepentant old Stalinist Franz Muhri. In this version the Communist Party supported a "free and independent Austria" (p. 170), fought against "militarism and war" and for "disarmament and détente" (p. 179). There is brief mention of *"Übergriffe"* (misbehavior), but the hoary details of the raping and looting Soviet Red Army in April/May 1945 are conveniently glossed over (p. 167). According to Murhi, the KPÖ (Communist Party of Austria) left the government coalition over currency reform in late 1947 (p. 167). In actual fact, the last Communist minister resigned because of first supporting Austria's participation in the Marshall Plan and then being embarrassed by Stalin's wild propaganda campaign against the European Recovery Program. Presumably, from the editor's perspective such factual inaccuracies do not matter in the age of postmodern arbitrariness as the genuine communist doctrinaire mirrors the distant past as well. Ironically this seems to mirror doctrinaire historical lies. Friedrich Peter, long-term leader of the FPÖ, is more felicitous in approximating the historical truth when portraying the postwar travails of his party so long isolated from power. He does not shy away from going into his fundamental disagreements with the opportunistic Haider. Not surprisingly, he still chafes under the "burden" (*"Bürde"*) of denazification (pp. 137ff). Haider meanwhile pontificates: "Hatred and isolation of people who have been persecuted, expelled and murdered for political, racial and other reasons, should never happen again" (p. 318). If only he practiced what he preaches. Peter Pelinka closes off the historical section with his summary of the changes in the Austrian political arena, in which he liberally lifts concepts from his brother Anton's scholarship without referencing it (the "Western Europeanization" of Austrian politics, p. 191).

Two simple tests for postmodern arbitrariness with firmly established facts accepted by scholarship might be these: first, is the importance of the 'victim's myth' acknowledged for Austria's unique postwar political trajectory?; secondly, is the unique contribution of the Marshall Plan for Austria's postwar economic reconstruction accepted? The authors from the ÖVP camps generally fail these tests, while the Socialists pass it. In section IV on the economy, Ferdinand Lacina, the long-term finance minister in the Vranitzky government, gives a warm tribute to the crucial importance of the Marshall Plan in firmly placing Austria on the road to a social market economy (p. 508). One would rather have expected such praise from Josef Taus, a former ÖVP leader in the 1970s. But Taus' rambling 50-page partisan tract concentrates on painstakingly looking for the Marxist roots of a planned economy in the postwar SPÖ. Meanwhile Lacina's essay is one of the few with a clear thesis—small postwar Austria's room to maneuver for an independent economic and fiscal policy was minute and the country's sovereignty was impaired long before it joined the EU (pp. 510, 516). The conservative politicians tend to gloss over the 'victim's doctrine', which was largely their creation, while Franz Vranitzky, who has done more to shatter it with his signal speeches in the early 1990s, dwells on it extensively (pp. 96ff). Haider warmly praises the World War II generation (presumably including the SS veterans) and their efforts in rebuilding the economy and democracy (no mention of the European Recovery Program!). On the same page he polemically castigates Austria's failure to master her past after 1945, as if it were not the same generation (pp. 315 ff.). Taus christens it the *"heroic age"* (*"Heldenzeitalter"*) of Austrian reconstruction (pp. 520 ff.), conflating the World War II generation like Haider with the postwar 'heroes of reconstruction'. This, presumably, is as close as one dares to tread in contemporary Austria calling the World War II generation, who ruled until the 1980s, "the greatest generation," as the American anchorman Tom Brokaw does in his fawning heroization of American World War II veterans.[6] Austrian war memorials built in the 1950s are not beating around the bush like the politicians today when they commemorate the "fallen" veterans for "dying the hero's death for their fatherland" (W. Manoschek, in the Sieder et al. volume, p. 95).

This book contains many nuggets, such as Fritz Fellner's and Emil Brix's brilliant chapters on Austrian identity. The diplomat Brix seems to be the only author in this volume concerned about the geopolitical changes of 1989 and what they proffer for Austria's international position and identity. Section III on identity is probably the best section of this book because it contains solid scholarly analyses in place of treatises by political practitioners, as well as an outstanding concluding essay by Heinz Kienzl. Kienzl takes his job seriously and presents a plethora of survey data to show how Austrian national identity has consistently strengthened since the end of the war to build a 'strong republic'. The German-born Freda Meissner-Blau, the co-founder and *grande dame* of the Austrian Greens, seems a strange choice to reflect on Austrian identity. One would expect from her an essay on how closely the Austrian character is related to its landscape and attuned to its unique environment (Kienzl partly delves into this Austrian trait). Instead one get a prolix rumination on the well-worn theme of how Austrian identity was forged in the cauldron of World War II and on the '*Piefke*'-repression of the Austrian character. She concludes with an intemperate polemic on how the 'success story' of the Second Republic has recently been threatened by the 'new Anschluss' to the European Union, dominated by the German powerhouse (the '*Piefkes ante portas*' once more?). Austria's remilitarization in NATO is around the corner, "fueled by the illusions of American global hegemony by the military industrial establishment" (p. 447). Primitive anti-Americanism seems to be alive and well in the diffuse Austrian Left.

Dieter Binder's lead essay in Section VI on culture is a lucid disposition on the long survival of anti-modern provincial culture in postwar Austria (there is much on this theme in the Bushell volume reviewed below). He uses a representative regional case study on Styria to show how hidebound emotional symbols of Austrian *Heimat,* such as the Archduke Johann cult, were revived in postwar Austria. Modernism arrived in the late 1960s in the provinces—in Graz with the iconoclastic *Forum Stadtpark.* The architect Gustav Peichl illustrates his 'lumping' essay on characteristics of Austrian culture, and the special role the 'creative' city Vienna plays in it, with a selection of "Ironimus" cartoons. Peichl's brilliant and often clairvoyant cartoons, regularly published in *Die Presse*, have provided one of the most insightful running commentaries on postwar Austria. Peichl's ironical historical reality is at once subtle and brutally honest on the ambiguous Austrian mentality. Peichl has become a postwar institution himself, and so has the "leading progressive" (Peichl, p. 756) of the arts scene, the modernist *enfant terrible* Hermann Nitsch. His essay is easily the quirkiest in this motley collection. Nitsch illustrates the process of deconstruction of all reality in language ("*Sprache als Gefängnis,*" i.e. language represents a reality that resembles a prison) by writing all his words in e.e. cummings-style lower case letters. Partly reflection on historical hermeneutics (here it fits Kriechbaumer's "project of mirrors" per-

fectly), partly *Pulikumsbeschimpfung* attack of all things Austrian à la
Peter Handke (and Thomas Bernhardt)—the typical pose of the Austrian
artist as conscience of the nation—Nitsch concludes his anarchistic
manifesto with the expression of his desire to become "emperor of the
Waldviertel" (p. 752). Here is a representative reality of the Austrian
artist as *poseur*. But since we learn so very little in this essay about the
postwar trajectory of Austrian culture, should it be included in this
volume? One gets the impression that the very peculiar practice of the
'postmodern' in this volume has left the editor without a job.

III.

The Sieder/Steinert/Tálos book *Österreich 1945-1995* is the
quintessential 'postmodern' history of postwar Austria (according to
Hanisch's categorization) without being heavy-handedly explicit about
it. It is a *summa* of some of Austria's top talents in the social sciences.
Of the forty-six essays in the tightly-edited 738-page volume, sixteen
have been (co)authored by women. Whereas the majority of the
Kriechbaumer authors come from the Austrian provinces, the majority
of the authors in this volume live in Vienna. The vast majority of these
authors were born in the postwar period, many of them 'boomers' and
'post-baby boomers'. It is all solid scholarship—no "mirrors." There is
virtually no coalition history left in this volume, which makes the
scholarly texts refreshingly de-ideologized. Clearly, the agenda is
postmodern and post-new Left, concentrating on the new social and
cultural history—social change, consumerism, right-wing populism,
women, mentalities, youths, leisure and private life, the environment,
minorities, new cultural history (television and film and the importance
of *Herr Karl*), and media. The structure applied to the Austrian postwar
era is lifted from Eric Hobsbawm's *The Age of Extremes*. Part I is
dedicated to the "golden years" (1945-1980); part II to the ruptures in
the "age of crisis" (1980-1995); these essays are 'splitting'
microhistories. The essays in part III, almost half of the book, present
dense analyses of the new social science themes over the entire
trajectory of the postwar period (as *Längsschnitte* daring but largely
successful exercises in 'lumping').

The tightly-argued introduction is as lucid a summary of social and
economic change in Austria as can be found anywhere in the books
under review here (only matched by Peter Pulzer's conclusion on the
postwar "political evolution" in the Luther/Pulzer volume discussed
below). The main framework of the book is Austria's postwar

'Westernization' and turn to 'Fordism'—rationalization and innovation in the workplace, mass production and rising productivity, and the resulting growing prosperity of workers and their turn to consumerism and leisure activities (p. 10). In the 1980s the communications and technological revolution hit Austria as well, leading to a further modernization of the means of production ("postfordism," p. 14). Culturally this led to the "Americanization" of Austria, particularly in youth cultures. While the parents were "re-Austrified" and caught up in the dutiful "National Socialist cult of sacrifice and performance," their children turned to the American cult of consumption (p. 18). The generational conflict is associated with the weak 1968 rebellion, which cannot be nailed down to a specific year but was gliding into the 1970s. In spite of Kreisky's successful reforms the old political orientations began to erode. The Zwentendorf anti-atomic power plebiscite (1978) and the Hainburg anti-hydroelectricity protest movement (1984)—electrical power was seen as the engine and symbol of capitalist productivity—led to more informal patterns of political participation in the 1980s and the break-up of the old party system. Environmental consciousness became the new paradigm and female politicians the new models of political activists—politics became "ecologized," and "feminized," and "diffuse" (pp. 30f).

This volume represents a quarry of useful information for the professional who writes lectures on postwar Austria or for advanced students. Yet its handsome illustrations should also make it attractive to the larger Austrian *Bildungsbürgertum* (the educated bourgeoisie), albeit it might be too 'left' or 'green' or 'feminist' or 'postmodern' for the staid burghers. It is not a volume to read cover to cover and one impossible to do justice to from the reviewer's perspective. One has to be very selective. The initial essays set the tone of economic, political, social and mental reconstruction of postwar Austria. There is no talk of 'success stories' and 'heroes' but a cool social science analysis of the ambiguities of daily life in a representative Lower Austrian village and in urban Vienna. Ernst Langthaler demonstrates how the war almost surreptitiously began to open up isolated Austrian villages. The needs of the Nazi war machine sent locals into the world (*"die Eigenen in die Fremde"*) and brought alien forced laborers and refugees home (*"Fremde ins Dorf gebracht"*) (p. 44). At the end of the war looting Red Army soldiers came to town. After the war followed the conundrums of denazification and the difficult reestablishment of traditional authority in the village, including the reassertion of male power. The returning soldiers had to mentally work through a "dual defeat"(p. 51)—their defeat in the war and the defeat of their women vis-à-vis the marauding Red Army. The postwar "*Heldenehrungen*" (honoring of the heroes) became complex rituals, attempts to give meaning to the death of their "comrades" and to their long imprisonment after the war. The veterans accepted the new Austrian patriotism instilled by the government, but their identity remained "German Austrian" (pp. 51f). Postwar male fantasies of Austrian veterans savored the "German success story"—a jarring notion, ill at ease with the celebrations of anti-German Austrian nationhood in the Kriechbaumer volume!

Ela Hornung and Margit Sturm's essay is a similar thoughtful gender perspective in assessing everyday life in Vienna's *Trümmerzeit*. In 1945 above all *women* were forced to secure the survival of their families in a "dysfunctional" city with a ruined infrastructure. Finding food and a place to live became the wherewithal of survival. Women organized *Hamsterfahrten* to the countryside where the farmers for a change dictated the price of food. The black market proliferated. When the half million Austrian POWs returned home they often encountered estranged children and uppity wives who refused to accept the reassertion of male control from their afflicted fathers and husbands. Strange 'heroes' they were, physically crippled and mentally broken. Many families, hastily started during the war, collapsed when these estranged fathers returned home (pp. 62ff).[7] This story, pregnant with the gender perspective of strong women and weak men, describes a reality totally missing from the celebration of the postwar *Heldenzeitalter* (heroic age) in Kriechbaumer's volume.

This volume succeeds in the above-mentioned tests of analyzing the importance of the 'victim's myth' and the 'Marshall Plan' for postwar reconstruction considerably better than Kriechbaumer's. Walter Manoscheck shows how the 'victim's mythology' was built on the legal 'occupation doctrine' to deny numerous Austrians' rich involvement in Nazi war crimes. He specifically demonstrates how the 'Declaration of Independence' (27 April 1945) denies the reality of more than one million Austrian soldiers,[8] who participated in Hitler's war of conquest and racial extermination. From the very beginning of the Second Republic it was the People's Party who boycotted thorough denazification and pushed for the integration of the Austrian Nazis.[9] Soon everyone was some sort of 'victim' in postwar Austria. Austria procrastinated in paying restitutions to Jewish victims of Aryanization or of the Holocaust, or to forced laborers. An ÖVP minister summarized

Austria's position succinctly in 1946: "since Austria has committed no crimes it is not responsible for restitution" (p. 100). Today we know that these defense mechanisms, based on a selective memory[10] only began to break down in the 1980s, with the result that Austria will be paying restitution into the 21st century for its post-1945 "domestic extraterritorialization and psychic externalization [and internalization!] of National Socialism" (p. 17). Manoschek tackles what has been called the postwar Austrian "living lie" ("*Lebenslüge*") head-on,[11] but his judgement is too harsh. Austria's pragmatic postwar founding fathers had little room to maneuver in rebuilding a destroyed and desperately poor country. Putting the 'Nazi problem' on ice was morally callous but politically expedient since it permitted them to tackle the monumental challenges of political and economic reconstruction.[12] Also, Austria paid much more than six million dollars in restitution to Jewish victims (p. 101), but it procrastinated, paid only in fits and starts over the entire postwar period, and established a victims fund only in 1995. Above all, the Austrian government failed to adequately inform the world about these disjointed efforts.

Fritz Weber prominently addresses the implementation of the Marshall Plan as the "crucial stadium of economic reconstruction" (pp. 76f), particularly in the Austrian West. In a book positing the American-ization/Westernization of Austrian society and culture after World War II as its principal theme, the Marshall Plan would have deserved a separate chapter, particularly when we consider that it's still operative in Austria via the annual investment billions distributed through the *ERP-Fonds*.[13]

The essays by Rolf Schwendter and Karl Stocker address the question whether the year 1968 was a crucial turning point in Austrian history. They agree that it was not, since there were no decisive revolutionary events like the demonstrations in Paris or Chicago.[14] There were, however, important 'micro'-cultural changes from the mid-1960s throughout the 1970s that amounted to distinct breaks with the past. Anti-nuclear-superpower pacifism, jazz and rock 'n' roll, and personal life style transformations were parts of it. Together they prepared the reformist climate of Kreisky's 1970s. The 1960s revolution in life styles came to flower in the 1970s, as Stocker points out in his case study of the '68 movement' in Styria. The sexual revolution did not take place at all. Austria lagged behind the rest of the West. Kurt Luger presents further detail about youth culture as the avant-garde of resistance to and emancipation from the dull traditional *Heimat* and high culture of their parents. While hippie culture hardly made inroads in Austria, rock music became the preferred form of resistance (p. 506). By the 1960s the 'Americanization' of Austrian popular youth culture was in full swing.[15] Not surprisingly, developments in popular culture are totally absent from the culture section of the Kriechbaumer volume, which operates with the traditional outdated definition of Austrian culture as high culture (another sign of the survival of 'nationalistic' coalition history). While Austrian youth culture has been thoroughly 'Americanized' throughout the Second Republic, Thomas Klestil, a former diplomat who is now the president of Austria, asserts the old myth of Austria as an "intellectual and cultural superpower" (p. 53).

Among the most fascinating essays in the Sieder et al. volume are Wolfgang Kos' analysis of Austrians' relationship with their environment, as well as Kurt Luger and Franz Rest's essay on tourism. "Landscapes manifest people's ideas, evaluations and desires vis-à-vis nature," is Kos' programmatic statement (p. 601). Since Austria emerged as the "alpine republic" ("*Alpenrepublik*") after World War I, the landscape became the stage for a specific Austrian metaphysics. The dear image of an Austrian "harmony of landscape, historical buildings and culture" made Austria's *Landschaft* an "article of consumption and export" (p. 601). While Austrian tourism lived off this "aesthetization" of the Austrian landscape, it began to destroy it with over-consumption. Kos shows how the same photographers contributed their pictures of *"erhabene Bergstimmungen und pathetischen Schollenkult"* (majestic impressions of mountains and pathetical cult of the earth) (p. 605) to volumes published during the Nazi era as well as in the postwar years. The contributors to such Austria-books were often politicians who perpetuated the old stereotypes of Austria's manifest destiny in the world as a peaceful "bridge between East and West" and as a perfect representation of god's creation (p. 607). After the war the hydroelectric power plants and the many gondolas built in the high mountains became a symbol of a new "euphoric belief in technology" (p. 615). The takeover of the Austrian Alps by tourism led to the "urbanization" (ibid.) of the Austrian landscape. The Greens set out to save Austria's endangered, but still 'intact' ecology from permanent economic exploitation and destruction. A new paradigm of "nature-under-siege to be nurtured" replaced the old view of "nature to-be-conquered and consumed" (p. 620). Luger and Rest show how modern tourist critics attack tourism for "devouring nature" ("*Landschaftsfresser*"). They discuss how the complex postwar trajectory of tourism turns much of

Austria's backward alpine areas based on subsistence agriculture into highly developed service economies (pp. 664f). By the 1980s tourism has become Austria's most important industry, transforming Austria into the "world champion of tourism" with the global lead in per capita income earned from *Fremdenverkehr* (tourism). In 1993 Austria booked an astounding 127 million overnight stays by guests. The authors show how Marshall Plan investment dollars have started and fueled much of this postwar tourism boom (p. 657).[16]

It is fair to say that Austria's broad postwar prosperity, particularly in the most backward alpine regions, would not have been possible without this tourism boom. Income from tourism also equalized Austria's chronically negative balance of trade. It is astounding that a book as voluminous as Kriechbaumer's manages to totally ignore one of the most important elements of Austria's postwar 'success story', particularly when considering that the University of Salzburg is the Austrian leader in tourism research, and Luger and Rest are among the leading scholars there.

IV.

Both these volumes almost exclusively concentrate on domestic history and, in that sense, are isolationist and *nabelbeschaulich* (introverted). Austria's foreign and security policy is almost totally ignored. It is surprising that a volume written in the spirit of old-fashioned coalition history, with its hegemony of political history, fails to address foreign policy in a separate section. Foreign policy only appears in the *apologias* of party politicians, who claim success such as EU-integration. Only Emil Brix briefly discusses Austria's changed security situation after 1989. The Sieder et al. volume does not fare much better in this area. It only dedicates three slim essays to foreign policy: Manfred Rotter discusses the State Treaty of 1955 and its position after the changes of 1989-92; Gerda Falkner looks at Austria in the EC/EU integration process; Christoph Reinprecht analyzes the *Umbruch* (transformation) in Eastern Europe. Rotter is an international law professor, and his prose is about as lively as that of the dry Austrian civil code. His essay on the Austrian State Treaty betrays that he is obviously not familiar with the vast historical literature and the fascinating debates around the making of the treaty, particularly in its final stage. The Moscow talks of April 1955 are moments of highest political drama with a large significance for general cold war history.[17] Falkner and Reinprecht give similarly lifeless factual accounts of the

EU-*Beitritt* (joining) and the Eastern European revolution, ignoring the security issues altogether.

Given that the international arena has changed so dramatically around Austria after 1989, it is perplexing that books as thick as these succeed in ignoring it altogether. In both books Austria's military defenses and intelligence services in the postwar period are totally ignored.[18] This is a signal lacuna indicating how deeply *the neutralist mindset* has settled over Austria, where the younger generation of academic historians has almost totally abandoned the study of international power and national security. The authors in the Sieder volume are perfect examples of young social scientists, who reared in the new social history devoid of an understanding of power and national security.[19] Cynical Austrian politicians and blue-eyed pacifists have comfortably settled in the ostrich's pose of proudly accepting their dubitable status as free riders (*Trittbrettfahrer*) of Western security efforts. They have lived with the illusion that NATO (North Atlantic Treaty Organization) will take care of them if push comes to shove, and that nuclear war would not affect them (predictably the Chernobyl disaster in 1986 was a reality check, and the anti-nuclear Austrians were more paranoid than the rest of Europe). The huge holes in these volumes are eloquent testimony to these specifically Austrian blind spots.[20]

V.

One needs to go to the *Studienbuch* edited by Michael Gehler and Rolf Steininger to fill some of these gaping holes. Of the massive, more than 1200-page, two-volume *Studienbuch* only the second volume is reviewed here. Designed as an American-type textbook for students, each chapter features appendices of key documents, specific study questions and bibliographies as well as an extensive and useful postwar chronology at the end of the book. As a textbook the chapters are by nature exercises in 'lumping' vast amounts of data into easily readably lengths. The design is not as colorful and aesthetically attractive as American textbooks. But a more appealing layout might not help sales. The grapevine has it that in the typical mode of the Austrian *Neidgenossenschaft* (culture of envy), those professors who are not included as authors refuse to assign it as a contemporary history textbook. Another reason might be that for the above-mentioned practitioners of the new social and cultural history, who nowadays often dominate history departments in Austrian universities, the *Studienbuch* probably represents a peculiar throwback to a more traditional political history paradigm. What I consider its strength—a solid survey of postwar Austrian domestic and foreign policy—the postmodern historian most likely considers its fatal weakness. It contains no specific chapters on social change, history of everyday life, cultural, environmental, or gender history. Franz Mathis presents a useful survey of postwar economic history, Manfried Rauchensteiner of domestic history until the mid-1960s (the 'grand coalition' of 1945-66), Oliver Rathkolb of the Kreisky era, and Thomas Albrich in the most brilliant chapter of this book, a dense sixty-five page survey of Austria's failure to "master" the Holocaust ("Holocaust und Schuldabwehr. Vom Judenmord zum kollektiven Opferstatus").

The rest is foreign policy! The Canadian historian Robert Keyserlingk drives, once again, his valuable point on the Moscow Declaration of 1943 home - it was an Allied propaganda instrument, in its wartime genesis not designed as the *Magna Carta* for postwar Austrian independence. Günter Bischof and Klaus Eisterer's chapters on the crucial occupation period complement each other—Bischof concentrating on the larger cold war international arena as the specific background in which Allied occupation policies were formulated, Eisterer on the domestic context, namely the specific zonal implementations of these policies. Rolf Steininger gives the epic moment of the conclusion of the Austrian Treaty in 1955 the attention it deserves. Steininger also contributes as tight a summary of the South Tyrol issue in postwar Austrian foreign policy as one is likely to get, short of perusing his much larger studies on this subject matter. Steininger and Gehler's analytical studies, based on a vast research in international archives, have single-handedly exorcised the bathetic emotional elements from the South Tyrol question so typical of postwar Austrian historiography.[21]

This volume represents what one might call the *new Innsbruck School of Contemporary History,* with its singular concentration on international history, a much needed but rare exception in the Austrian academic history landscape. If one could combine some of the shrewd analyses on gender, social change, culture, and the environment from the Sieder/Steinert/Tálos book with the foreign policy perspectives of the Gehler/Steininger texts, one would arrive at a rather complete survey on postwar Austria, representative of the current state of scholarship.

VI.

Such a smorgasbord volume could also benefit from many of the essays of recent volumes on postwar Austria published by Anglo-American scholarship. The forty essays of the four books in English impress with their combination of top Austrian scholars (some not represented in the above volumes) with recent Anglo-American scholarship on postwar Austria. Many of the essays are 'splitting' microhistories. These volumes add depth in the areas of international relations, cultural and gender history, missing in some of the hitherto reviewed volumes in German. Above all, they fill a lacuna curiously absent in the German volumes: the postwar impact of the forced intellectual prewar migration on the United States and Great Britain, as well as Austria.

The 'lumping' texts in the Luther/Pulzer volume come closest to a balanced survey of postwar Austrian politics and society among the entire lot reviewed here. Erika Weinzierl, the *grande dame* of contemporary Austrian history, retells the story she has often told before, of the end of World War II in the *Ostmark* and the origins of the postwar Austrian political life. Robert Knight reviews the difficult international environment which the provisional Renner government had to operate in after the war ended. In spite of a few new documents from Soviet archives, the problem with Weinzierl's account is that it is still deeply stuck in the paradigm of coalition history, failing to incorporate the entire last generation of scholarship. The Luther/Pulzer volume has a solid section on recent external relations. Two interesting case studies are Walter Lukan's review of Austro-Slovene relations and Lázsló J. Kiss' account of Austria's 'special' relationship with Hungary. Kiss stresses the new situation in Austrian/EU-Eastern European relations after 1989/95. Hungary's anarchic pre-modern relations with the Communist sphere have been replaced by "*post-modern*" relations, "denoting greater security and prosperity gained through greater openness, the adoption of multiculturalism, an end to the significance of frontiers, and a process of integration and transnational development based on intensive mutual interference in each other's internal affairs" (p. 186). This is as precise a definition of the 'postmodern' condition in the international arena as we find anywhere in these volumes, and one that the current Austrian Schüssel government should take to heed to understand its isolation in Brussels.

Hanspeter Neuhold, the prolific professor of international law at the University of Vienna and Austria's most solid analyst of international relations, gives as good an analysis of Austria's post-1989 search for "its place in a changing world" as can be found anywhere in the literature. Neuhold has no illusions about the romantic infatuation of Austrian public opinion with neutrality in the changed security architecture of the post-cold war world, when Austria is not threatened by superpower nuclear wars but by the "spillover of military hostilities from its neighboring countries" (pp. 209f). Neuhold operates with an up-to-date ('postmodern'?) definition of international security, where small nation states can solve trans-boundary ecological hazards, mass migration, Mafia-type cross-border international crime and terrorism only through international cooperation and collective security responses. Similarly, old 1968ers of the 'free riding' Socialist Party, with their anti-American opposition to NATO integration, should heed Neuhold's considered conclusion that "the logic of integration also calls for common defence": "Austrian solidarity *à la carte* will not be appreciated by the other states that are ready to incur the high costs of repelling armed aggression" (p. 217). Austria as a 'secret ally' of the West under Raab, and its active neutrality à la Kreisky were shrewd cold war strategies, as Oliver Rathkolb reminds us in his essay in this volume. Yet the international arena has changed so dramatically after 1989 with the end of the cold war and Austria's EU integration that the country needs a new security doctrine.

These chapters should be complemented by Richard Mitten's thoughtful analysis of the Waldheim crisis in the Good/Wodak volume. The American Mitten, who teaches at Central European University in Budapest, is not stuck in flaccid Austrian partisan debates over who is responsible for publicizing Waldheim's World War II past. Mitten rather places the U.S. 'watch list'-decision on Waldheim in the international context of President Reagan's treatment of the Bitburg affair in 1985. While Reagan cravenly gave in to a strong ally, and went with Kohl to a cemetery where SS soldiers were buried, subsequently facing a firestorm of criticism, he played to the galleries of American public opinion and placed Waldheim on the 'watch list', facilely upsetting a weak neutral state, which was not an ally and without a lobby in Washington.

The essays on culture may well be the highlight of the solid quality of these volumes. The volume edited by Bushell is particularly strong on the literary scene. It shows how a reactionary educational establishment 'restored' Austrian culture and identity by lionizing '*Heimat*' writers' like Heimito von Doderer, who had sat out the war at home and had served the Nazis ably. Once a younger generation emerged in the 1960s (Peter Handke, Thomas Bernhard, Franz Inerhofer, Hans Lebert), they rang in a massive paradigm shift with their picture of "a cold, uncaring, early post-war Austria," where "the soil revolt[ed] against the war crimes committed upon it" (p. 8).

This reviewer's favorite essay among some 130 chapters reviewed here is Edward Timms' fascinating analysis in the Luther/Pulzer volume of "schizophrenic" Austrian identity through the eyes of the writer Hilde Spiel, an Austrian Jewish exile in Great Britain.[22] He notes how the Austrian writers who stayed put during the war in the *Ostmark* "declared themselves to be German"—some of them becoming "fanatically pro-Nazi"—while the Austrian writers in exile were the "principal Austrian patriots" (pp. 55f). Timms maintains that "the concept of a 'Free Austria' was largely sustained by writers, artists and intellectuals in exile." During the war they organized exhibits and lecture series on Austria in Great Britain, which leads Timms to the conclusion that "*the cultural capital of Austria was London*" [my emphasis] (p. 58). After the war most of the exiles, such as Hilde Spiel, did not return. One of the reasons was that in collusion with the conservative and cultural consensus, the writers Friedrich Torberg and Hans Weigel played anti-communist gatekeepers à la McCarthy against any elements on the Left who considered returning. When in the spring of 1946 Spiel returned to her native Vienna as a British war correspondent in uniform, she penned this devastating commentary on the political climate: "Here everything is delightful apart from the attitude of the Viennese, who are either Nazis (whose sting has admittedly been completely drawn), or charming, politically absurd members of the Volkspartei, or prosaic bourgeois Social Democrats, or doctrinaire Communists, or charming but absurd Communists. That is roughly the extent of it. They are either corrupt or exhausted or politically obtuse or fanatical, but one thing does speak in their favour: their great love of art" (p. 59). Compare Timms' subtle portrait of Austria's difficult postwar reconstruction of "schizophrenic" identity with Bruckmüller's smooth portrait of the same process in the same volume (which, over larger portions, is a translation of his essay in the Kriechbaumer volume), and you think you are reading about two different countries.

Timms' essay should be read in conjunction with the thoughtful essays by Egon Schwarz, Bernhard Handlbauer, and Jonathan Munby in the Good/Wodak volume. The two latter analyze the huge influence of Austrian Jewish émigrés on psychoanalysis and Hollywood in the

United States. Schwarz' story of personal and intellectual uprootedness as a young man who experienced the Jewish exodus from Austria in 1938, is a haunting tale of the enormous toll such flight took on the individual, not to speak of the loss of such great talent for Austria. Reinhold Wagnleitner concludes correctly in his introduction, written in a prose given to hyperbole, that Austrians "indulged in what amounts to the most massive and violent export of culture, scientific knowledge, practical expertise, artistic quality, and human beings in history! After all, what other country would kick out all Nobel Prize winners active in its universities?" (p. 10). Klestil's notion of the "*geistige und kulturelle Grossmacht Österreich*" (the spiritual and cultural superpower Austria, in Kriechbaumer, p. 53) may be true for *fin-de-siècle* Vienna, when Jewish intellectuals and artists made their marks, but is pure myth when it comes to postwar Austria sans Jews. The deeper one delves into these issues of failed return of the exiles after the war, the more one has to question the notion of the 'heroic age' of Austria's postwar reconstruction years. The more one reads the Spiels and Schwarzs, the more one realizes how jarringly dissonant are the complacent views from inside Austria in the Kriechbaumer volume, and these alert observations from the outside in the Luther/Pulzer and Good/Wodak volumes.

The sophistication of the new gendered history of postwar Austria is coming to light in Maria Messner's comparative analysis of the feminist struggle for legal abortion in the United States and Austria. She first presents the historical context of the long abortion struggles in both countries and shows how different institutional and political cultures are. The culmination came with the 1973 *Roe vs. Wade* decision in the U.S. and the Austrian law legalizing abortion of 1974, positing not only a chronological confluence but also the American "model" for Austria (pp. 199f). Messner's thoughtful analysis ("war and containment," pp. 201ff) shows how *Roe vs. Wade* rallied the grass-roots 'pro-life' forces in the United States, which began their still-ongoing long and violent struggle against 'pro-choicers', but also how in the statist Austrian political culture the 'pro-life' movement quickly petered out once reigning political establishment had made its decision. Messner is one member of a new and young generation of female Austrian social scientists fully conversant with the scholarly debates on both sides of the Atlantic, which is also true for the authors in the Good/Grandner/Maybes volume *Austrian Women*. Brigitta Bader-Zaar and Gerda Neyer are prime examples of this, with their essays on the long march of Austrian women into the political arena. Today the representation of

Austrian women in Parliament and governing cabinets is much higher than in the United States. This would indicate that women attaining positions of political power by way of slow ascendancy through the political parties seems to be a more successful approach than the U.S. way of feminist grass roots and lobbying efforts, which allows the entrenched male powers to dismiss them as radicals. In the new Austrian Schüssel government we have women as vice chancellor and foreign minister. It is save to predict that Austria will have a woman as president or chancellor before the United States.

What might be the conclusion from reading such a torrent of writings on postwar Austria? The 'postmodern' historiographical paradigm is in excellent hands if practiced by a younger generation of social scientists conversant with both the current methodologies and international discourses in their fields. If, however, presented as un-reflected apologetic memoir, the unedited 'hall of mirrors' becomes delusion. It deteriorates into patriotic and nationalistic coalition history with all its blind spots about the seamy sides of Austria's recent past. It ends up being a throwback to past historiographical patterns long overcome by discerning professional historians. Beware of the politicians writing current history!

Notes

1. See the preface to John Lewis Gaddis' *Strategies of Containment: A Critical Appraisal of Postwar American National Security Policy* (New York: Oxford University Press, 1982), vii; this categorization was first suggested by J.H. Hexter, *On Historians* (Cambridge, MA: Harvard University Press, 1979), 241-43. Gaddis' book is an impressive example of 'lumping'.

2. It was published in Wesview's useful *Nations of Modern Europe* series in 1988. See Kurt Tweraser's review in *Contemporary Austrian Studies [CAS]* 8 (2000): 569-74, and Günter Bischof's review in the Minnesota Center for Austrian Studies *Newsletter* (April 2000).

3. Ernst Hanisch, *Der Lange Schatten des Staates: Österreichische Gesellschafts-geschichte im 20. Jahrhundert* (Vienna: Ueberreuter, 1994).

4. Ernst Hanisch, "Der forschende Blick. Österreich im 20. Jahrhundert: Interpretationen und Kontroversen," *Carinthia: Zeitschrift für geschichtliche Landeskunde von Kärnten* 189 (1999): 567-83; for a useful critique of "coalition historiography" see also Anton Pelinka, "Von der Funktionalität von Tabus: Zu den 'Lebenslügen' der Zweiten Repbulik," in *Inventur 45/55: Österreich im ersten Jahrzehnt der Zweiten Republik,* ed. Wolfgang Kos and Georg Rigele (Vienna: Sonderzahl, 1996), 23-32, transl. and repr.as "Taboos and Self-Deception: The Second Republic's Reconstruction of History" in *CAS* 5 (1997): 95-102. Hanisch's analysis can be fine-tuned with Robert Knight's essay "Narratives in Post-War Austrian Historiography," in Bushell, *Austria 1945-1955,* 11-

36. Knight subdivides postwar historiography into benign schools (collective education in the cauldron of World War II; odyssey of occupation; benefits of neutrality), followed by the critical narrative of the 1980s.

5. Ernst Hanisch, "Der lange Schatten der Historiographie oder: Barocke Aufklärung," *Österreichische Zeitschrift für Geschichtswissenschaft* 6 (1995): 85-118, and Hanisch's reply "Anklagesache: Österreichische Gesellschaftsgeschichte," ibid., 457-66.

6. For the American World War II generation, who "saved freedom and democracy," see Tom Brokaw's *The Greatest Generation* (New York: Random House, 1998).

7. One should complement this essay with Frank Biess' analysis on German returnee POWs, "Vom Opfer zum Überlebenden des Totalitarismus: Westdeutsche Reaktionen auf die Rückkehr des Kriesgefangenen aus der Sowjetunion, 1945-1955," in *Krieggefangenschaft im Zeiten Weltkrieg: Eine Vergleichende Perspektive,* ed. Günter Bischof and Rüdiger Overmans (Ternitz: Verlag Gerhard Höller, 1979), 365-89.

8. Manoschek at one point speaks of more than one million Austrian soldiers in the Wehrmacht (p. 95), at another point of more than 1,2 million. Such vague guess work with huge margins is no longer acceptable. A thorough recent statistical analysis has determined that 1,286,000 Austrian soldiers served in the German armed services (1,075,000 million in the Wehrmacht), see Rüdiger Overmans, "German and Austrian Losses in World War II," *CAS* 5 (1997): 293-301.

9. See also Walter Manoschek, "How the Austrian People's Party Dealt with the Holocaust, Anti-Semitism and National Socialism after 1945," *CAS* 4 (1996): 304-16.

10. See also the review essay by Günter Bischof, "Founding Myths and Compartmentalized Past: New Literature on the Construction, Hibernation, and Deconstruction of World War II Memory in Postwar Austria," *ibid.*: 302-41.

11. In Kriechbaumer's volume the economic historian Felix Butschek cynically dismisses the entire effort by contemporary historians to deconstruct the making of the victim's doctrine (*"ergrimmte Zeithistoriker,"* p. 495). Butschek is an archetypical dinosaur of coalition history, harboring the traditional 'enemy image' of contemporary historians being on the Left and too critical; his perspective ignores twenty years of historiographical development.

12. See also Pelinka, "Taboos and Self-Deception," *CAS* 5, 95-102.

13. See Günter Bischof, Anton Pelinka and Dieter Stiefel, eds., *The Marshall Plan in Austria*, *CAS* 8 (2000).

14. For a fascinating comparative portrait of 1968 see Carole Fink, Philipp Gassert, and Detelf Junker, eds., *1968: The World Transformed,* Publications of the German Historical Institute (Cambridge: Cambridge University Press, 1998); see also the magisterial Arthur Marwick, *The Sixties* (New York: Oxford University Press, 1998).

15. Reinhold Wagnleitner, of course, is the intellectual mentor of "Americanization" studies in Austria and an international leader in the study of global "Americanization"; his most recent contribution is Reinhold Wagnleitner and Elaine Tyler May, eds., *"Here, There and Everywhere": The Foreign Policy of American Popular Culture* (Hanover: University of New England Press, 2000).

16. On the intense struggle of the Austrian tourist industry to secure ERP investment funds vis-à-vis the more powerful state-owned sector, see the essay by Günter Bischof, "'Conquering the Foreigner': The Marshall Plan and the Reconstruction of Postwar Tourism," *CAS* 8 (2000): 357-401.

17. Gerald Stourzh' master narrative of the Austrian state treaty dedicates almost half of the volume to the complex 1955 treaty diplomacy; see *Um Einheit und Freiheit: Neutralität und das Ende der Ost-West-Besetzung Östereichs 1945-1955* (Vienna: Böhlau, 1998); see also the "Historiography Roundtable" in this volume.

18. For a good survey of defense and intelligence issues in the first twenty years of the cold war in Austria see Erwin Schmidl, ed., *Österreich im frühen Kalten Krieg 1945-1958: Spione, Partisanen, Kriegspläne* (Vienna: Böhlau, 2000). Siegfried Beer has been a lonely practitioner of World War II and cold war intelligence history in Austria and has kept the field alive single-handedly; e.g. see his "Early CIA Reports on Austria, 1947-1949," *CAS* 5 (1997): 247-88; and idem, "The CIA in Austria in the Marshall Plan Era," *CAS* 8 (2000): 185-211.

19. The editors were also too lazy to prepare at least a name index.

20. I have lamented about this phenomenon on other occasions; see Günter Bischof, "Spielball der Mächtigen? Österreichs aussenpolitischer Spielraum im beginnenden Kalten Krieg," in *Inventur 45/55*, ed. Kos, Rigele, 126-56, and guest commentary "*Österreichs Scheu vor Machtpolitik*," *Die Presse*, 7 February 1996, p. 2.

21. Rolf Steininger has recently published a long and a short version of a history of the South Tyrol conflict in the twentieth century and complemented it with a massive 3-volume documentation; see also Michael Gehler, ed., *Verspielte Selbstbestimmung? Die Südtirolfrage 1945/46 in US-Geheimdienstberichten und österreichischen Akten* (Innsbruck: Wagner, 1996).

22. Interestingly, Hilde Spiel seems to emerge as one of the major Austrian writers in exile in the Austrian literary canon. Andrea Hammel has an essay on her *Rückkehr nach Wien* in the Bushell volume (pp. 84-98).

BOOK REVIEWS

Austria's Escape from the Cold War

Alfred Ableitinger, Siegfried Beer, Eduard G. Staudinger, eds., *Österreich unter Alliierter Besatzung 1945-1955*, Studien zur Politik und Verwaltung, vol. 63 (Vienna: Böhlau Verlag, 1998)

Günter Bischof, *Austria in the First Cold War, 1945-55. The Leverage of the Weak*, Cold War History Series edited by Saki Dockrill (London-New York: Macmillan Press-St. Martin's Press, 1999)

Hans-Jürgen Schröder

Austria's postwar role in the international arena had been neglected for decades. Historians of the cold war had first concentrated their research on U.S.-Soviet relations and the major battle fields of the cold war. In this context, the German problem was of particular importance. Research on Germany's neighbors, including Austria, seemed to be less urgent. Ironically, the Austrian State Treaty of 1955 might have contributed to this development, since it seemed to create the impression that the Austrian question had been 'solved'. But why could it be solved? And what factors shaped Austrian history during the decade from unconditional surrender to the conclusion of the Austrian State Treaty? During the 1980s, access to Western archives improved due to the thirty years rule and offered new opportunities for empirical historical research. And the collapse of the Soviet Union seemed to have further improved access to unpublished sources. As a matter of fact, the archival situation since the 1980s has stimulated historical research on postwar Austrian history. This is particularly true for the years 1945 to 1955.

Developments in Austria during this crucial period were extensively dealt with at a symposium in Graz in late 1994. The publication of the conference papers under the title *Österreich unter Alliierter Besatzung 1945-1955* documents quite well the progress that has been made in the field. Austrian postwar history has become a concern of international scholarship. According to the general conference subject the essay collection is primarily focused on the policies of the four occupying powers.

The seventeen studies offer excellent insight into the four powers' specific goals and methods of dealing with postwar Austria. All four powers could finally claim to have been successful. The Russians exploited their zone economically and finally presented themselves as the most ardent proponents of Austrian unity and neutrality. The United States would have favored a long range American military presence, but were ready to accept Austrian self-determination. By informal means they were able to achieve their main goals—namely, to gradually draw Austria into the Western orbit economically as well as ideologically and to retain or rebuild a certain extent of secret military presence in Austria. The British government, well aware of Great Britain's decline as a great power, was nevertheless able to influence the course of events. This was demonstrated by Britain's role in the drafting of the second Control Agreement of February 1946. As in Germany, British cultural policy had a significant impact in parts of Austria. Two regional studies are devoted to this subject. As to the French aims in Austria, the government in Paris could claim to have realized its main objectives: sovereignty for Austria and her economic viability. However, French diplomacy was dependent on the preferences of the United States, a situation well-known from its position in Germany.

The close interaction of developments in Germany and Austria's gradual emancipation in domestic affairs and in the field of foreign policy is extensively dealt with by Michael Gehler, one of the contributors to the volume under discussion. His comparative approach helps to clarify the importance of Austrian politicians in determining the course of events in Austria. Adenauer's political strategy—i.e. absolute priority for West Germany's integration into the West—left no room for any credible West German drive to regain national unity. Austrian decision-makers, on the other hand, regarded national unity as their top priority.

In the field of bilateral Austrian-West German relations Vienna steered a middle course. There was neither a desire for any kind of Anschluß nor plan to build a "Chinese Wall" (pp. 205-268).

Obviously, the essay collection is a heavy weight for specialists in the field, and every library on contemporary history should have it on its shelves. However, this volume and similar essay collections are unlikely to attract a larger audience beyond the specialists in the field. What had been lacking for quite a time was a compact survey on Austrian history during the crucial years 1945-1955. Recently, this gap was bridged by Günter Bischof with his book *Austria in the First Cold War, 1945-55.*

Austrian postwar history has repeatedly been haunted by the past. Up to the conclusion of the Austrian State Treaty of 1955 one of the central questions was "what price Austria would have to pay for its role in Hitler's destructive conquests" (p.105). If Austrian responsibilities for the past could be reduced or rejected altogether, less would have to be paid in the future. From an Austrian perspective the solution was a genial one: Austria declared herself a victim. How could one expect a victim of Nazi aggression to be held responsible for the Third Reich's destructive policy? This important issue, which, up to the present, had been largely neglected by most authors, is dealt with by Professor Bischof in a provocative and brilliant manner. Members of the Austrian Foreign Office "invented" what Bischof refers to as the "occupation theory." It became the "official state doctrine" repudiating the so-called "annexation doctrine" (pp. 61-62). As one foreign policy expert remarked: "We were rather liberated after seven years of forced occupation and are legally speaking the same state, which was invaded and overcome by Hitler. There are numerous legal arguments for this thesis as well; above all else, the entire conduct of the Allies and the proclamations of their statesmen since 1940 seem to be ample proof that they hold this point of view as well." (ibid.) Any kind of "annexation theory" Bischof argues, "would have given Austria joint responsibility for Nazi war crimes and could make it liable to pay reparations . ... The 'occupation theory' held that Austrian statehood had lain dormant during the war. Since Austria had not declared war on anyone it could not be held legally responsible for German war crimes. Thus was born the *Austria's Rip Van Wrinkle legend* - a country blissfully sleeping through seven years of war while the Germans committed horrific war crimes" (p. 62).

The downplaying of Austria's share in the Third Reich's destruction of Europe had the advantage of combining foreign policy goals and the restoration of collective self-confidence within the Austrian society. This might explain the overall success of the victimization thesis. One must not be a prophet to predict that Bischof's revisionist approach will be criticized by some of his Austrian readers, since the notion that Austria was the victim of Nazi aggression has become an important element of Austrian postwar identity, which was also justified in historical terms. The Second Republic was seen in continuity with the 1920s rather than the Anschluss period. While the victimization thesis was a useful instrument in Austria's relations with the West, it could not be exploited vis-à-vis the Soviet Union which needed a legal basis for her reparation policy. This reparation policy is one of the key issues in Günter Bischof's book.

As in Germany, the Soviets systematically exploited their zone of occupation. This rigid reparation policy must be seen against the background of the extensive war damages caused by Nazi aggression. Reparations from Austria and Germany (in combination with reparations from Korea) were the Soviet Union's only significant source of foreign supplies to compensate for extensive war damages inflicted by the Nazi occupation. While the Soviet's brutal reparation policy was in accordance with the Potsdam reparations compromise on Germany and Austria, it was a direct threat against economic stabilization and reconstruction that would soon be pursued by both the Americans and the British. In Austria the problem was aggravated by Soviet seizure of "German assets." There is no doubt that the "Soviet legal claim under Potsdam was a maximalist interpretation of what constituted German assets in their zone" (p. 85).

The Soviet seizure of German assets had two major political effects. It pushed the Figl government, which had been elected in November 1945, more closely into the political orbit of the United States and it also alarmed American observers. In February 1946, General Clark sent a detailed political analysis to Washington. This report, referred to by Bischof as a "long telegram" (p. 85), alerted Washington that Soviet seizure of German assets would result in the "eventual political strangulation" (p. 86) of Austria. From the American perspective this had to be avoided.

There is ample evidence that Soviet economic exploitation provoked American reactions. But this is only one side of the coin. American policy should also be seen in a broader context of U.S. postwar policy towards Russia. Washington was not prepared to advance any direct aid for postwar Russian reconstruction unless the Soviet leadership shaped their behavior in international affairs according to American wishes. The abortive American loan of early 1945 might be cited as an example.

While the Soviet Union was denied access to American capital, Washington generously supported most West European countries, including Austria, with Marshall Plan aid. By supporting Austria financially, the Truman administration wanted to stimulate the economy and thereby contribute to a political stabilization as well. Austria became a vital element of the European Recovery Program (ERP). During the past few years Austria's role in the context of the Marshall Plan has become a field of detailed historical analysis. The broad spectrum of research was well represented at the 1998 University of New Orleans conference on "The Marshall Plan in Austria. An Economic and Social History." The conference results were published in two important essay collections in both German and English.[1] These publications inform about the immediate impact on and the long range perspectives of the European Recovery Program for Austria. The collapse of the Austrian economy was avoided, confidence restored, and political stability regained. In addition, ERP funds initiated the modernization of industry and agriculture. In the political field, the Marshall Plan decisively influenced Austria's orientation towards the West.

United States policy in Austria did not exclusively rely on economic means to influence the course of events. To contain potential Soviet expansion, Washington supplemented the Marshall Plan strategy by militarizing Austria's Western zones. Austria was seen as an important domino for Western defense. Günter Bischof quotes General Keyes who repeatedly drew attention to Austria's geostrategic importance:

The strategic importance of Austria cannot be overemphasized. The abandonment of the country to a possible Communistic infiltration or penetration would expose the south flank of Germany as well as the east flank of Switzerland to similar veiled aggression. ... From the military viewpoint, if occupied Germany is considered a bridgehead in Europe pending the peaceful settlement of our current political conflict with the USSR, it appears unwise to withdraw occupation forces from Austria until the treaty is concluded which will give reasonable assurance that the south flank of our occupation forces in Germany is not being exposed by creation of another potential Soviet satellite. In addition, by withdrawing from Austria and

particularly from Vienna we would lose prematurely valuable
facilities for gaining intelligence relative to the USSR and
Balkan States. (p. 113)

By 1948, the Truman administration had become convinced that the
falling of the Austrian domino had to be avoided. This is reflected in
numerous National Security Council statements as well as in the Truman
and Eisenhower administrations' key security decisions. As a consequence, Austria was included in military preparations for Western
defense. While Western Germany was to be formally integrated into the
Western defense system, Austria's militarization was shaped by
informal or secret measures. This indirect approach is also reflected in
the transformation of Marshall Plan aid. In 1950 the term 'European
Recovery' was substituted by 'Mutual Security'. The outbreak of open
hostilities in Korea brought about the militarization of the Marshall
Plan. This had immediate consequences for Austria since the republic—in terms of per capita aid—was one of the most important
recipients of Marshall aid.

Austria's geostrategical importance for Western defense and the
Soviet threat, which was intensified in the late 1940s and early 1950s,
turned out to be a safeguard against any significant reduction of
economic aid from the United States. This is convincingly presented by
Bischof: "The Austrians' most effective strategy for securing the bounty
of American aid was their contention of being a special case. The Figl
Government felt that as long as it prevented Soviet encroachments and
ensured the country's Western orientation, 'it has delivered its side of
the bargain'. ... in the ice age of the cold war during the conflict in
Korea the Austrian treaty was not concluded, for both the defence of the
country against internal foes and larger North Atlantic security needed
to be guaranteed first. Meanwhile, the largesse of American military and
economic aid made the Austrians feel secure, led them into growing
prosperity and made the endless occupation tolerable" (p. 129).

From an Austrian perspective, the year 1953 seemed to offer new
opportunities to negotiate for Austrian independence. Post-Stalinist
diplomacy created the impression that it pursued what has been
characterized as 'peaceful coexistence'. In Washington, a new president
had moved into the White House. And in Austria herself, the elections
of March 1953 brought about a change in government: When Julius
Raab of the People's Party became chancellor, this had to be seen as an
indication for a modification of Austrian foreign policy strategies. While

Raab was prepared to test the Soviet 'peaceful coexistence' propaganda drive, the new American president was reluctant to seriously explore Soviet cooperation. Therefore, 1953 might have been, as Bischof puts it, one of the great 'missed opportunities' not only for Austria. Why did Soviet diplomacy fail to pursue the model of Austrian neutrality as early as 1953? Could this have been an opportunity to derail West German rearmament? Why did Molotow's approach lack flexibility? It is still difficult to answer these questions. This is a clear indication that the opening of former Soviet archives did not yet produce enough evidence to explore the underlying assumptions of Soviet foreign policy.

It was not until Khrushchev's ascendancy in 1955, when Kremlin diplomacy became more flexible. The 'peaceful coexistence' slogan gained more credibility, since it had become obvious that Khrushchev took a more realistic approach. And it was Khrushchev who sent signals to the Vienna government. Chancellor Raab took the initiative. A successful bilateral Austro-Soviet summit meeting in Moscow paved the way for the 1955 State Treaty. While the Western occupying powers wondered whether Khrushev's fresh approach on Austria had to be regarded as a tactical maneuver rather than a significant shift in Soviet diplomacy, Raab grasped the opportunity. The concessions Austria had to make, namely neutrality and anti-Anschluss guarantees, were tolerable, since Austria's unity could be preserved. This was of primary importance, as Günter Bischof reminds us:

> Lest we forget, from the beneficial position of historical hindsight, the alternative outcome of a partition of Austria still frightened many observers in Vienna on the eve of the Moscow trip. Both superpowers were still deeply suspicious that the other side's ultimate motive was the division of Austria. The Soviets feared an integration of Western Austria into the NATO defence pact while the West was wary of an absorption of Eastern Austria into the Soviet empire. In both scenarios the partition of Austria would have been the end result. (p. 146)

In his conclusion, Günter Bischof explicitly points out that the personal factor was of primary importance for the course of postwar Austrian history. The author reminds us "that an extraordinary group of individuals made vital contributions to the 'Austrian solution' - the making of postwar Austrian recovery and independence. ... Among the Austrian 'founding fathers' Renner and Fischer, Figl and Gruber, Schärf and Helmer, and in the later stages Raab and Kreisky, along with diplomats of Kleinwaechter's and Bischoff's extraordinary talents, showed enormous skill and wiliness to steer the Austrian ship through the rough waters of the first Cold War." However, without the "persistent support of Western diplomacy a unified Austria might not have been attained" (p. 155).

Finally, Günter Bischof describes Khrushchev's key role, which was to overcome opposing forces within the Soviet camp. While "structural factors such as geopolitics and empire building, the international system and ideology, domestic politics and public opinion also played a role," the "Austrian solution" of 1955 was brought about by "self-effacing skillful and patient cold war diplomats" (p. 156). These architects of Austrian independence had to work in the framework of East-West confrontation, of course, but their permanent struggle for independence created a high degree of preparedness. They could therefore immediately grasp the opportunity when it arose. These men and women, "who have made such an extraordinary contribution to postwar Austrian independence 'certainly deserve' a monument" (p. 156), as the author concludes in his final remarks.

Why could Austria achieve what was denied to the Germans: independence and national unity? Was the Austrian State Treaty a model for a solution of the German problem? Certainly not. In the context of the cold war Austria was a special case. And this special case can best be elaborated by a comparison between postwar Austria and postwar Germany. Neither the Soviet Union nor the Western Allies were prepared to accept German neutrality: "In all likelihood the Kremlin did not design Austrian neutrality as a model for Germany - the two cases were too dissimilar. An armed neutral Austria (with all its military restrictions) was barely tolerable to its neighbours, but only ten years after the war a reunified and rearmed neutral Germany was not at all tolerable. The deep-seated apprehensions over a re-militarized Germany that was already economically resurgent were simply too great" (p. 151). Basically, this was also the Western Allies' position. In February 1958, for example, Secretary of State John Foster Dulles stated his opinion "that with respect to Germany the policies of the United States and the Soviet Union have something in common - namely, that it was not safe to have a unified Germany in the heart of Europe unless there were some measure of external control which would prevent the Germans from doing a third time what they had done in 1914 and 1939."[2]

Describing the Western position, Bischof leaves no doubt that "the Germans were needed to contain the Soviet Union; NATO was needed to contain the Germans; and Adenauer felt he needed Western integration to contain the Germans, whom he did not trust" (p. 151). However, such kind of *"triple containment"* (ibid.), the author argues, was not necessary for Austria. From their differing perspectives neither the Soviet Union nor the three Western Allies had any interest in the reunification of the two German states.

Another difference is to be seen in the respective domestic constellations. For Chancellor Adenauer integration into the West had priority. Despite the political rhetoric, which pointed to the contrary, the division of Germany was accepted for the time being. While Austrian diplomacy was prepared to accept Austrian neutrality, this was not the case for Western Germany. Konrad Adenauer was one of the most prominent cold warriors. For him, neutrality or neutralization was anathema. For the Austrian elites, on the other hand, the defense of national unity was far more important. Admittedly, it also was an easier task for Austria, since the country was never divided into separate states. Ironically, Austria's relative weakness was a key to success, since it opened an avenue for compromise. None of the great powers had to give up too much. All occupying powers could afford to withdraw from Austria without the risk of a serious shift in the cold war struggle. "The Leverage of the Weak" was effectively used by Austrian politicians.

Bischof's book is a masterpiece of cold war scholarship. The author's empirical basis is impressive. He consulted relevant documents from Austrian, British, German, U.S., and former Soviet archives. This multiarchival research approach is supplemented by the author's sovereign handling of the broad spectrum of cold war historiography. The compact presentation of historical evidence is combined with a subtle interpretation of Austria's role during the crucial years 1945 to 1955 in the context of international relations. At no stage does Bischof hesitate to formulate his positions. Finally, it must be pointed out that the book does not only address the professional historian but any reader interested in international relations after World War II. The publication gives both a compact summary of Austria's role in the first cold war and a convincing interpretation of political decisions that finally culminated in the conclusion of the Austrian State Treaty. In addition, the book contains many suggestions for further research. It is an important contribution to the Cold War History Series edited by Professor Saki Dockrill.

Notes

1. Günter Bischof and Dieter Stiefel, (eds.), *"80 Dollar." 50 Jahre ERP-Fonds und Marshall-Plan in Österreich 1948-1998* (Vienna: Ueberreuter, 1999); Günter Bischof, Anton Pelinka and Dieter Stiefel, eds., *The Marshall Plan in Austria*, Contemporary Austrian Studies, vol. VIII (New Brunswick, NJ: Transaction, 2000).

2. Memorandum of Discussion at the 354th Meeting of the National Security Council, 6 February 1958, in *Foreign Relations of the United States, 1958-1960*, vol. IX, *Berlin Crisis 1959-1960; Germany; Austria*, (Washington, DC: United States Government Printing Office, 1993).

Claudia Kuretsidis-Haider and Winfried Garscha, eds.
*Keine Abrechnung: NS-Verbrechen, Justiz und Gesellschaft
in Europa nach 1945*. Leipzig-Wien: Akademische
Verlagsanstalt, 1998. Paper. Pp. 488.

Norman J. W. Goda

In 1950, the Right Honorable Lord Hankey wrote a confidential
letter to the British Foreign Office. Hankey, a former Cabinet member
from both World Wars, had heard that His Majesty's Government would
create a clemency board to review the sentences of the German war
criminals sentenced by British military courts and incarcerated at Werl
prison, located in the British zone of Western Germany. An enthusiastic
advocate of closer Anglo-German relations, Hankey was not worried
that Germans convicted of war crimes would be released; on the
contrary, his concern was that they might have to stay in prison. Thus he
urged the Foreign Office to see to it that such a review board would not
be comprised primarily of jurists, who, as practitioners of the law, may
feel themselves bound by it. Politicians, he said, who understood the
dominant trends of German public opinion and the importance of closer
ties with the Federal Republic, must be included in any such hearings.[1]
Wittingly or not, Hankey put his finger on the fundamental problems
faced by those who wish to understand trials for war crimes, crimes
against humanity, and other offenses, such as treason, that follow armed
conflicts—trials which are far from being legal issues alone. Straddling
an especially shaky fence between justice and politics, their study is by
nature an interdisciplinary field where jurists, historians, political
scientists, and members of other disciplines should and in fact must
meet. Such interdisciplinary dialogue is ever more important at the dawn
of the twenty-first century. The next few decades will tell whether truth
commissions in Latin America and South Africa will bring the social
stability that the concerned countries sought when they opted away from
trials in a conscious trade of justice for truth. These next decades will

also tell whether the U.N.'s latest experiments in war crimes trials at The Hague and in Arusha will bring satisfactory results to the countries (Yugoslavia and Rwanda), in which (some of) the latest rounds of twentieth-century barbarism have been committed. The hopes for such institutions are high indeed. Depending on the local circumstances, truth commissions and criminal tribunals are expected to reinforce respect for the basic laws of humanity. They are expected to bring a greater degree of domestic tranquillity and to bring peace to war-torn regions. As the lawyer Michael P. Sharf has commented in his study of the recent trial of Dusko Tadič, there can be no peace without justice.[2]

Given what seems to be at stake, it is curious how little research has been done on overall political and societal effects of the thousands of war crimes trials that have already occurred this century. Aside from studies concerning Germany—most of which aim to link postwar trials with the development of democratic society in the Federal Republic—research concerning postwar trials in the remainder of Europe (to say nothing of Asia) is only now beginning to appear. There are many reasons for the scarcity, such as the narrowness of focus and the poor availability of documentation under the rules of access in Western state archives. Studies on postwar justice in the 1970s and early 1980s focused on the earliest and most visible trials, namely those of the major war criminals at Nuremberg and Tokyo.[3] A close look at subsequent atrocity trials and the issue of clemency for convicted war criminals in the 1950s had to wait until the later 1980s and 1990s. The increasingly crucial issue of West German *Vergangenheitsbewältigung* (coming to terms with the past), though, meant that most such studies would focus almost exclusively on the Federal Republic, whose past was believed to actually need mastering.[4] The opening of Russian and East European records over the past decade have, meanwhile, rekindled interest in the rethinking of Nazi crimes themselves rather than the issue of retribution—to say nothing of the tremendous interest in what such records reveal about the diplomacy of the cold war.[5] Atop the scarcity of wide research is a relative dearth of interdisciplinary dialogue about postwar trials between legal scholars and members of other academic disciplines, most notably historians. This is once again a question of emphasis and current interest. Jurists with an interest in war crimes trials have taken the lead in the past decade, aiming their efforts at moving the U.N. tribunals from theory to reality. Thus their interest in the application of the Hague and Geneva Conventions, the Nuremberg Charter, and the Genocide Convention to atrocities in the Balkans and

Central Africa via the human rights clauses of the U.N. Charter. Historians, meanwhile, generally turn their gaze toward the long-term political, societal, and intellectual effects of retribution—facets that many jurists assume must be intrinsically positive and beneficial. Thus law schools in recent years, particularly at the University of New England and the De Paul University, have been the primary sponsors of symposiums and programs on war crimes trials, with few scholars outside of the legal discipline involved in such programs.[6]

It is in this context that the volume under review should be understood. It is a collection of more than thirty-five papers from the conference "Entnazifizierung und Nachkriegsprozesse" (Denazification and Postwar Trials) held in Vienna in June 1996 and sponsored primarily by the *Dokumentationsarchiv des österreichischen Widerstandes* (*DÖW*, Archive for the Austrian Resistance) and the Austrian *Bundesministerium für Justiz* (ministry of justice). The former institution, originally founded in 1963, has been unique in its recent efforts to promote interdisciplinary dialogue on the issue of postwar justice, along with the undertaking of many other tasks in this area of study. The conference thus included jurists, but also historians, archivists, and political scientists. It also had a number of aims. One was to examine the Austrian postwar judicial experience and to place it within the context of Austria's postwar history. In fact the *DÖW* has sponsored preliminary work in this area already.[7] Another aim was to indicate the availability of postwar trial documents in light of lost records, East European archival openings, and national privacy laws. Finally, an effort has been made toward interdisciplinary and comparative histories of various states and the societal effects of postwar trials, primarily on the collective memory of affected societies. The result is a book at times very uneven in approach and in quality. But the volume is very useful as a catalogue for what we know regarding postwar trials in Europe and as a collection of comparative national and disciplinary approaches to the issue of postwar trials. It is thus a valuable jump-off point for anyone interested in pursuing historical research into the complicated world of postwar justice.

The study of postwar justice begins with sources, and here archivists and criminal justice scholars lead the discussion. Sources are most easily available and best organized in the Federal Republic of Germany, thanks primarily to two institutions. One is the *Zentrale Stelle der Landesjustizverwaltung* in Ludwigsburg, created in 1958 in the wake of the Ulm *Einsatzgruppen* trial of that year in order to coordinate local investigations into Nazi crimes. In a helpful essay on the *Zentrale Stelle*'s history, lead prosecutor Alfred Streim explains the expansion of its staff and scope, its formidable obstacles in garnering evidence and witness testimony, and its usefulness as a research base into Nazi criminal activity (pp. 130-143). As is pointed out elsewhere in the volume (especially by Austrian scholars), the *Zentrale Stelle* is an institution unique in Europe not only in function, but also for the statistics and information that it has compiled. The other key institution here is the Institute for Criminal Justice at the University of Amsterdam, which, thanks to the exhaustive work of the criminal attorney C.F. Rüter, has compiled the massive set (twenty-two volumes as of 1996) of West German trial judgments.[8] Rüter's group is currently at work on judgments issued by courts in the German Democratic Republic, and has already issued a very helpful guide to all West German trials from 1945 to 1997[9], as well as a CD-ROM version of all available judgments, searchable by key words. Rüter himself is a major contributor to this volume, not least concerning the ways historians might use the *Justiz* (justice) volumes to discern the facts of certain episodes, the motives of Nazi criminals, and the priorities and legal reasoning of the West German judicial system over the postwar period (pp. 265-279). In a comment on one of Rüter's presentations, the eminent historian Henry Friedlander differentiates between law and justice, arguing that lenient sentences and acquittals tell us something about the politics of the postwar age too. Friedlander also points out that unlike the volumes of the Nuremberg Trials, the *Justiz* volumes do not contain the protocols of entire trials or documents entered into evidence, even though many of the trials judgments are quite comprehensive (pp. 280-284).

Regardless, scholars of other countries, none of which have an organization as developed as the *Zentrale Stelle*, would be pleased to have such published sources at their disposal. Polish archivist Stanisław Kaniewski of the Polish High Commission for Research on Nazi Crimes describes the Commission's source collection on Nazi and Soviet crimes in Poland. He also mentions the support that the Commission has provided since its foundation in 1945—even to West Germany during the cold war—in criminal investigations (pp. 204-206). Yet the Commission is still working on a lexicon of all persons sentenced in Poland after the war for Nazi crimes, and presumably will continue to do so for years. Austrian archivists (Franz Scharf, Rudolf Jerábek, pp. 303-313) and researchers (Martin F. Polaschek, pp. 285-302, Hellmut Butterweck, pp. 314-318), meanwhile, describe a maze of disintegrating, lost, destroyed, or simply unorganized documents in Austrian repositories, along with unevenly applied 50-year release and personal privacy laws. According to Scharf, the trial records of Austria's *Volksgerichte* (people's courts) kept by the *Oberösterreichischen Staatsarchiv* (Upper Austrian State Archive) are still in a sorting process whereby records from 1947 were not catalogued until the end of 1997. It is a small wonder that Hellmut Butterweck and Eva Holpfer (pp. 421-429) tout the benefits of using newspaper accounts of earlier trials, which are rather comprehensive, even reporting on the courtroom atmosphere. There are no contributions from archivists from other key states (Russia, Yugoslavia, France, etc.) in this volume. One is left to hope then that the daunting task described by this volume's editors—to create within ten years a great *Handbuch der europäischen Nachkriegsprozesse* (Handbook of European Postwar Trials)—will one day come to fruition (pp. 326-332). In late 1998 the possibilities of such a work improved with the foundation of the *Zentrale österreichische Forschungsstelle Nachkriegsjustiz* (Central Austrian Research Center on Postwar Justice). The task of this center includes the systematization and microfilming of Austrian trial records and the creation—in collaboration with its institutional counterparts in Germany, Poland, and the Netherlands—of a European database for postwar trials in those states.

A second aspect of this volume moves historians more to center stage, namely the degree to which postwar trials have served as an effective means to make nations face their past. Seen in isolation, it is easy to become cynical about the Federal Republic's efforts in this matter if one looks only at the numbers. Of only 1,874 defendants tried on murder charges in West German-conducted trials from 1945 to 1999, 14 received the death penalty, 150 received life imprisonment, 817 received shorter prison terms and 893 escaped their sentence through acquittal, suspension, or age considerations.[10] Such numbers, according to state prosecutor Helge Grabitz, result from a variety of legal problems including the assemblage of evidence and the German penal code's heavy burden for proving murder (pp. 144-179). Explaining another deficiency in West German justice—the fact that trials there deliberately focused on the *Täter* (culprit) rather than higher policy makers—Rüter compares Germany with the Netherlands (pp. 180-184), and postulates that the answer may lie in the nature of justice itself, rather than national circumstances. The tendency of the Germans and Dutch both was to prosecute *Täter* even though policy makers were available for prosecution in both nations (including judges who had sent Dutch resisters to their deaths). Criminal codes, it would seem, lend themselves more easily to prosecutions of those furthest down the ladder of command and closest to the physical criminal act. But as Peter Steinbach's essay argues, the issue of collective reckoning cannot be measured in numbers or legal debate anyway—what matters is the broader public discussion generated by the trials regardless of their quantitative results (pp. 397-420). The major German trials (e.g. the first Auschwitz trial) began in the early 1960s as a younger generation came of age. Regardless of individual punishments, they forced a shift in research emphasis at German universities to Nazi crimes and the eventual abolition of the statute of limitations for murder. The trials helped German society to look harder and longer at its past, and this gaze, together with the bitter arguments that it has engendered, was upheld by generations. Despite its imperfections then, the Federal Republic's judicial record in confronting Nazi crimes compares rather agreeably to other successor governments attempting the same—to say nothing of the successor states of the Communist era. The East German record in trying Nazi crimes is especially troubling and will make rich ground for researchers to plough. In terms of numbers, the 786 trials of 1,222 defendants held in Eastern Germany from 1945 to 1999 compare nicely with the Federal Republic's number of trials—912.[11] But as Grabitz demonstrates, East German trials came in politically motivated bunches (either designed to please the Soviets or to embarrass the Federal Republic of Germany) with the majority held between 1948 and 1950. The chief source material for East German trials, after all, is the archives of the Ministry for State Security (*Stasi*). This ministry ran loaded investigations in which guilt was assumed, witnesses prepared, audiences handpicked, and crimes against humanity were essentially crimes against Communism.

Most interesting are the essays by the various historians in this collection who study states in which justice against collaborators was both a means of political purge and a foundation on which to build a new national consciousness. Gabriella Etmektsoglou, in an especially rich essay (pp. 231-256), reflects on the political nature of Greek justice during the civil war from 1944 to 1949. Here, Left and Right used trial and punishment against political and ethnic enemies, the charges ranging from collaboration to espionage depending on the defendants and the circumstances. Truly, justice in Greece was hardly an ethical exercise, especially given the mild sentences for right-wing collaborators from anti-Communist courts in 1945—the same courts which, in the same year, prosecuted over eighty thousand on the political Left, executing many without appeal. Szabolcs Szita, in an essay on Hungarian people's courts, examines the problems of justice versus political purge in liberated Hungary (pp. 207-216). The formula for a treason conviction here was broad enough to include everyone from Arrow Cross members to general staff officers, from journalists to doctors. Thus anti-Fascist people's courts carried out a political purge of Fascists and feudal elements in nearly 20,000 cases until October 1945. Peter Romijn's paper on the Netherlands raises the West European trade-off between justice and democracy (pp. 257-264). The Dutch experience displays a wide gap between the number of collaborators on whom dossiers were assembled and the number actually tried and punished. Though sentences were not mild, former resisters were disappointed in the low number of collaborators tried, especially given the high percentage of deported Dutch Jews and the high number of voluntary Dutch SS members. As in France, the myth of limited collaboration seems to have been the price of democratic consensus. In one of the best essays in this volume, Baard Herman Borge examines Norway, where of a population of three million, forty-nine thousand were judged in a six-year period, mainly on treason charges (pp. 217-230). Borge's assessment of the social consequence of this high percentage of trials is that it was a key step in the creation of a young state's national identity, not unlike the effect of the Eichmann trial in Israel.[12] In the larger sense Borge also challenges the accepted orthodoxy among historians that broad justice and democracy are mutually exclusive.

The largest group of papers concern postwar justice in Austria, and it is of special interest for three reasons. First, in contrast to the number of studies on justice in Germany, the number of such studies for Austria is small indeed. There is thus new information here, supplemented by helpful statistics. Second, as Claudia Kuretsidis-Haider, Manfred Schausberger, and Eleonore Lappin note in their fine papers (pp. 16-53), the Austrian experience is an odd mix between war crimes trials on the one hand and political purge on the other. Austrian *Volksgerichte* in each of the four occupied zones tried a total of 136,829 cases from 1945 to discontinuation these courts in 1955, with most cases being heard in the first three postwar years. These overburdened courts, whose judges, prosecutors, and juries were to come (ideally) from lists provided by the Socialist Party, Communist Party, and the People's Party, dealt mostly with cases of treason in the form of pre-1938 Nazi party membership and denunciation. Only one in five *Volksgericht* cases dealt with war crimes or crimes against humanity, which generally concerned the murder of Hungarian Jews within Austrian borders. The 1957 *Amnestiegesetz* (amnesty law) virtually ended the concept of war crimes as tried in 1945 and made convictions for atrocities all the more difficult, so that from 1955 to 1975 only forty-six cases of physical crimes were brought forward, which resulted in but eighteen guilty verdicts. Thus, while Austria seems to follow patterns similar to those in other European countries, it pales in comparison to West Germany in terms of the number of war crimes trials conducted after 1955 as well as the number of post-1960 trials, in which the accused committed crimes against Jews.[13] Third, the Austrian experience adds to the picture of Allied justice administered in central Europe, the statistics of which are generally considered separately from the *Volksgerichte*, but the overall effects of which cannot be separated so easily. Siegfried Beer, Kurt Tweraser, and Stefan Karner provide essays supplemented with statistics on British, American, and Soviet justice in the respective zones (pp. 54-129). Though Karner's account of Soviet justice is fascinating for the reasons one would expect from the rough Soviet style of arrest and trial, the surprises come in the other two articles. For while the U.S. military authorities displayed no interest whatever in the trial of suspects who committed crimes against non-American personnel, the British military authorities, highly suspicious of the *Volksgerichte*, were determined to try those involved in the forced labor and death marches of Hungarian Jews. Part of the reason for British stringency lay in the geography of their zone—the crimes had taken place there. Still it is curious that the British, who had backed the idea of war crimes trials only reluctantly,[14] were so eager to punish such crimes in Austria. The amnesty and repatriation process undertaken by the three powers in the 1950s, meanwhile, closely resembled the process in Germany, which challenges the notion that it was primarily Bonn's participation in the Western defense community that inexorably forced the amnesty issue.[15] In the end, the overall effect that these nearly forgotten cases in Austria had on the general Austrian consciousness awaits study, as does the effect that they had on the Allied and Soviet picture of Austria and vice versa.

Tying this vast array of papers together is no easy task, but István Deák's essay (pp. 389-396) aims to place the various national experiences with postwar justice into some sort of unified historical perspective. It is ironic, he says, that while postwar justice in the years after 1945 affected between five and ten percent of the adult male population in what had been Nazi-occupied Europe, the proportion of those tried was lowest in Germany itself. Yet the phenomenon of postwar justice, says Deák, must be understood within the context of European political and ethnic struggles, which had begun under Nazi occupation. The resurgence of the Left with the defeat of Nazism made trials possible, and the concomitant need by the Left for popular legitimization made trials necessary. The exceptions to the general rule are in Italy and Greece where the Right held onto power and in Germany where the Allies, not the Germans, conducted the trials. Thus postwar justice, at least in its initial, pre-cold war phases, was an integral part of the European political and ethnic struggle of the early twentieth century and national catharsis was greatest in those states that conducted their own trials. Fair enough—the essays in this volume bear out the argument that justice, either sharpened or dulled by its application, was used after the war at least partly as a political tool within the context of a larger political process.

Yet given the fact that trials for crimes committed during World War II have pressed into the 1980s and 1990s, outlasting the cold war itself, it is hard to leave the issue there. Trials for war crimes, crimes against humanity, and even treason are unlike other criminal proceedings in that they involve the national identity to a larger extent than a common murder trial. They are also divorced from the political process in the popular mind to the extent that, as legal processes, they are understood—at least in the ideal sense—to stand above politics. It is plausible then, given our perspective of the five and a half decades since Nuremberg, that a better justice, a better popular acceptance of justice, and thus a better national catharsis from justice ultimately demand time—perhaps decades—to become truly effective. The cooling of political flames (however slight), historical perspective, and shifts in national, international, and generational perceptions would seem to be essential elements for having such trials move closer to their ideal ends—if more recent trials in France, Germany, Austria, Croatia, and elsewhere are indicative. In the meantime, the nature of such trials—which combine debate on national and international law, domestic and international politics, national identity and international perception of certain nations, and the self-image of changing generations—is such that they will always fall shorter of the ideal standard than regular trials. Despite the trials inherent and serious flaws, however, all of the authors here would surely agree that we should hold them anyway.

This volume is not perfect. It lacks an index, the glossary of contributors and their professional affiliations is incomplete, and the binding is so poor that some pages fall out on the first reading. The essays on contemporary tribunals, i.e. the U.N.'s International Criminal Tribunal for Yugoslavia, are rather pedestrian and already dated by subsequent events; they thus add nothing to what an informed newspaper-reader would already know. There are no contributions on the major issues of French or Yugoslav justice after World War II, nor are there any contributions on the International Military Tribunal at Nuremberg and the subsequent occupation tribunals in Germany, on which new research is still appearing. Yet the strengths of this volume outweigh its inconveniences and omissions. The footnotes and statistics in the articles mentioned above are alone worth the price of the volume. But most importantly, the *DÖW* has shown here that on the crucial issue of international justice, meetings between the legal and social science communities are essential and fruitful enterprises that must continue.

Notes

1. Hankey to Lord Henderson, 13 December 1950, Public Record Office, Kew, FO 371/85898.

2. Michael P. Sharf, *Balkan Justice: The Story behind the First International War Crimes Trial since Nuremberg* (Durham, N.C.: Carolina Academic Press, 1997).

3. On Nuremberg see Bradley F. Smith, *Reaching Judgment at Nuremberg* (New York: New American Library, 1977); idem., *The Road to Nuremberg* (New York: Basic Books, 1981); Ann Tusa and John Tusa, *The Nuremberg Trial* (New York: Athenaum, 1983). More recently see Telford Taylor, *The Anatomy of the Nuremberg Trials: A Personal Memoir* (Boston: Little Brown, 1992); Arieh J. Kochavi, *Prelude to Nuremberg: Allied War Crimes Policy and the Question of Judgment* (Chapel Hill, N.C.: University of North Carolina Press, 1999). On Tokyo see Philip R. Piccigallo, *The Japanese on Trial: Allied War Crimes Operations in the East 1945-1951* (Austin: University of Texas Press, 1979); Arnold C. Brackman, *The Other Nuremberg: The Untold Story of the Tokyo Trial* (New York: Morrow, 1987).

4. Frank M. Buscher, *The U.S. War Crimes Program in Germany, 1946-1955* (New York: Greenwood, 1989); Tom Bower, *Blind Eye to Murder: Britain, America and the Purging of Nazi Germany – A Pledge Betrayed* (London: Granada, 1981); Jörg Friedrich, *Die kalte Amnestie: NS-Täter in der Bundesrepublik* (Munich: Piper, 1994); idem., *Das Gesetz des Krieges: Das deutsche Heer in Rußland – Der Prozeß gegen das Oberkommando der Wehrmacht* (Munich: Piper, 1995); Ulrich Brochhagen: *Nach Nürnberg: Vergangenheitsbewältigung und Westintegration in der Ära Adenauer* (Hamburg: Junius, 1994); Dick de Mildt, *In The Name of the People: Perpetrators of Genocide in the Reflection of their Postwar Prosecution in West Germany – the "Euthanasia" and "Aktion Reinhard" Trials* (Amsterdam: Martinus Nijhoff, 1996); Norbert Frei, *Vergangenheitspolitik: Die Anfänge der Bundesrepublik und die NS-Vergangenheit* (Munich: Beck, 1996).

5. On Nazi crimes see especially the work of Dieter Pohl, *Nationalsozialistische Judenverfolgung in Ostgalizien 1941-1944: Organisation und Durchführung eines staatlichen Menschenverbrechens* (Munich: Oldenbourg, 1997); Götz Aly, *"Final Solution": Nazi Population Policy and the Murder of the European Jews*, trans. Belinda Cooper and Allison Brown (London: Arnold, 1999).

6. See for example the International War Crimes Project at the University of New England's School of Law's Center for International Law see http://www.nesl.edu/ center/ ctrbro.htm for the De Paul University College of

Law's International Criminal Justice and Weapons Control Center see http://www.law.depaul.edu/centers/icjwcc/cherifweb.html. On the various legal forums and programs see for example "War Crimes Tribunals: The Records and Prospects, A Regional Meeting of the American Society of International Law," March-April 1998, American University, http://www.wcl.american.edu/pub/ humright/wcrimes/war_conf.html; The Balkan Institute, *Bringing War Criminals to Justice: Obligations, Options, Recommendations — A Workshop Held at the University of Dayton March 19-21, 1997* (Dayton, OH: Center for International Programs, 1997), http://www.nesl.edu/center/ warcrim1.htm# participants; Yoram Dinstein and Mala Tabory, eds., *War Crimes in International Law: Based on a Colloquium Held at Tel-Aviv University in December 1993* (The Hague: Martinus Nijhoff Publishers, 1996). For human rights approaches see especially Arieh Neier, *War Crimes: Brutality, Genocide, Terror, and the Struggle for Justice* (New York: Times Books, 1998). Recent political science-based surveys include Yves Beigbeder, *Judging War Criminals: The Politics of International Justice* (New York: St. Martin's Press, 1999); Howard Ball, *Prosecuting War Criminals and Genocide: The Twentieth-Century Experience* (Lawrence, Ks.: The University Press of Kansas, 1999); Kevin Bass, "Judging War: The Politics of International War Crimes Tribunals" (Ph.D.diss., Harvard University, 1998). One of the very few true interdisciplinary approaches to the issue is Mark Osiel, *Mass Atrocity, Collective Memory, and the Law* (New Brunswick, N.J.: Transaction Books, 1996).

7. Gerhard Jagschitz and Wolfgang Neugebauer, eds., *Stein, 6. April 1945: Das Urteil des Volksgerichts Wien (August 1946) gegen die Verantwortlichen des Massakers im Zuchthaus Stein* (Vienna: Dokumentationsarchiv des österreichischen Widerstandes,1995); Winfried R. Garscha and Claudia Kuretsidis-Haider, *Die Verfahren von dem Volksgericht Wien (1945-55) als Geschichtsquelle* (Vienna: Dokumentationsarchiv des österreichischen Widerstandes, 1993); Winfried R. Garscha and Claudia Kuretsidis-Haider, *Die Nachkriegsjustiz als nichtbürokratische Form der Entnazifizierung: Österreichische Justizakten im Vergleich* (Vienna: Dokumentationsarchiv des österreichischen Widerstandes, 1995).

8. *Justiz und NS-Verbrechen: Sammlung deutscher Strafurteile wegen nationalsozialistischer Tötungsverbrechen* (Amsterdam: Universität, Institut für Strafrecht, 1968-).

9. C.F. Rüter and D.W. de Mildt, *Die westdeutschen Strafverfahren wegen nationalsozialistischer Tötungsverbrechen 1945-1997. Eine systematische Verfahrensbeschreibung mit Karten und Registern* (Amsterdam: APA Holland University Press, 1998).

10. "Some Statistics on Postwar German Trials concerning Nazi Capital Crimes, 1945-1999," compiled by C.F. Rüter and D.W. de Mildt, special print for the Twenty-Third Annual Conference of the German Studies Association, 7-10 October 1999 (Amsterdam: Foundation for Scientific Research of National-Socialist Crimes, 1999).

11. Ibid.

12. On Eichmann and national identity in Israel see Tom Segev, *The Seventh Million*: *The Israelis and the Holocaust* (New York: Hill and Wang, 1993), especially 323-386.

13. See Rüter and de Mildt, *Die westdeutschen Strafverfahren*, ix-xiv.

14. Kochavi, *Prelude to Nuremberg*, passim.

15. The argument that amnesty decisions must be understood independently of defense negotiations has been made by Thomas A. Schwartz, "John J. McCloy and the Landsberg Cases," in *American Policy and the Reconstruction of West Germany, 1945-1955*, ed. Jeffry M. Diefendorf, Axel Frohn, Hermann-Josef Rupieper (New York: Cambridge University Press, 1997), 443-454.

Egon and Heinrich Berger von Waldenegg, *Biographie im* *Spiegel: Die Memoiren zweier Generationen* (Vienna: Böhlau, 1998)

Alexander N. Lassner

Perhaps the most regularly cited sources among historians are memoirs. They are compact, often available in translation, and easily obtainable at libraries or for purchase. Moreover, they purport to give the reader an inside look into the workings of the world with which the author was most intimately connected. It is all too common, however, for the authors of memoirs to obscure the very events that they profess to describe. The chief problem is the idea of a memoir itself: *ex post facto* writing is done with the knowledge of the results of the actions, policies, and/or decisions under discussion.[1] The negative impact of such knowledge upon the accuracy of memoirs can hardly be overestimated. With reputations at stake, authors are prone towards self-aggrandizement, the concealing of guilt, and the shifting of blame. Tactics include distortions, outright lies, and the omission of unpleasant evidence. Recently, one historian has commented precisely upon such tendencies in connection with the memoirs of leading members of the Austro-Hungarian political and military leadership in World War One.[2] Too often the memoir has become both apologia and propaganda for its author.

Unsurprisingly, such problems affect the memoirs of British, French, and Austrian statesmen connected with the history of the Austrian First Republic. For example, British Foreign Secretary Anthony Eden distorted the historical record while French Ambassador to Austria Gabriel Puaux omitted embarrassing details. Austrian memoirs are equally burdened with dishonesty and inaccuracies. In former Austrian Chancellor Kurt Schuschnigg's two apologias one finds truth and falsehood so closely intertwined that it is difficult to extricate the two. Although historians were suspicious enough of Schuschnigg's motivations that they continued to interview and question him throughout his life, the former chancellor never deviated from the essential framework of his story. One fares little better with the memoirs of other leading Austrians such as Ambassador to Britain Georg Frankenstein, or General Secretary of the Fatherland Front Guido Zernatto. The former omitted key events from the period of 12 February to 12 March 1938, while the latter was so vague and brief in his memoir as to make it almost useless. Indeed, among the memoirs of the leading members of the Schuschnigg regime, it is the one chapter memoir by Chief of the Austrian General Staff Alfred Jansa that stands up best to documentary scrutiny, though it too suffers from significant distortions and omissions.[3]

The recent publication of the memoirs of Egon and Heinrich Berger Waldenegg presents the critical reader with the hope for further insight into the history of the late First Republic, even as that hope must be tempered by knowledge of the aforementioned weaknesses. Egon was a minister in the cabinets of Dollfuß and Schuschnigg and was later demoted to Austrian ambassador to Italy, while Heinrich—his son—experienced life as an Austrian exile during the war. As the title indicates the book is also part biography and includes substantial descriptive elements regarding the lives of both men.

For the historian of the First Republic, Heinrich's account is necessarily of lesser import: Heinrich was a mere youth in the 1930s, unconnected to the high level decision-making processes with which his father was so intimately involved. Heinrich's memoir, therefore, is primarily of interest if one seeks a description of life for the young son of a well placed aristocrat, forced into exile in Italy during World War II.

Heinrich begins his account describing his family history and childhood. Thereafter he moves on to his experiences as a military cadet at a school in Liebenau. The account of his life there and during the period 1936-1938, constitutes the most interesting portion of his story, even if it is short. The author observes the increasingly strict measures taken by the Schuschnigg regime to control the cadets and prevent Nazi penetration into their ranks. Unfortunately he fails to provide the reader with a judgement as to how effective he felt these measures were. This is something he surely could have done and which would have been of considerable interest to historians. Heinrich also notes the steps taken by the Austrian Nazis to show their strength whenever possible. The effect of this aggressive propaganda on the Austrian population has been generally recognized by historians, but the effect that this had on Mussolini and his willingness to aid Austria is less examined. At the *Palazzo Chigi*, the Mussolini regime was already attempting to gage the real strength of Austrian Nazis in 1933, and these efforts continued until the Anschluß. Indeed, by the end of February 1938, it was the conviction in Rome that Austria was already lost which was partly responsible for Italy's inaction in the face of the German *Einmarsch* (invasion).[4]

Heinrich also provides interesting details on the behavior of the people close to him during the Nazi seizure of power on 11-12 March. After the virtual disappearance of the senior leadership at the *Ballhausplatz* (office of the chancellor), and cowed by the German *Wehrmacht* and the aggressive steps of the Austrian Nazis throughout the small Danubian country, many Austrians sided with the victors. Thus the author recounts that "the commander of the school, an old *Kaiserjäger* [imperial guard], who, up to now [had been] a spotless patriot, held a short address [and] welcomed the annexation to the Third Reich . . ." (pp. 65 – 66). Although fascist owned Italian newspapers confined themselves to a decidedly banal reporting of the Anschluß, the few still independently owned (legal) Italian newspapers, like *Il Piccolo,* highlighted this 'sitting on the fence' in their reporting:

Austria [was] overwhelmed by an indescribable wave of Nazi enthusiasm. Less than 24 hours were enough to change in a surprising way, the face of this country, that yesterday afternoon was ready for an anti-Nazi plebiscite. . . . Like in *un prodigio di scenotecnica*, after a moment of darkness, the picture appears radically changed and almost unrecognizable. . . [many people], following their leaders, at the decisive moment have stepped back. The Nazi idea created in a vast strata of the population that this was their destiny – there is no other explanation. In the general disorientation created by the resignation of Schuschnigg, and by the disappearance of his closest collaborators, and by the announcement that German troops [would] [cross] the border, the masses have decided in favor of the winners and even the most convinced anti-Nazis have had to abstain from any action.[5]

After the Anschluß, Heinrich departed for Italy, becoming a citizen and serving in the Italian army variously as an artillery officer, a liaison between Italian and German units engaged in anti-partisan operations, and finally as an intelligence officer. After the collapse of Italian forces in 1943, he was covertly recruited by the British to help build an *österreichische Widerstandsorganisation* (Austrian resistance organization). By May 1945 he was back in Austria, helping to set up a provisional regional government in Kärnten. The last several pages of the author's account shortly cover his troubled attempts to establish himself financially after the war.

Egon is present throughout Heinrich's memoir, but the author never recounts exact conversations with his father, referring to him in the third person. The result is that Heinrich's father takes on a rather distant, if still essential, role. As regards Egon's politics, Heinrich categorically supports the political actions and beliefs expressed by his father later in the book with little critical analysis. It is here that the reader will see the real 'reflection' noted in the book's title.

According to Heinrich, Egon never mentioned the existence of his memoirs while alive. Only after his father's death did they come into Heinrich's hands, and he decided to have them published. During the 1930s Egon served Austria as *Landeshauptmannstellvertreter* (vice governor) of the province of Styria, minister of justice in the Dollfuß regime, foreign minister in the Schuschnigg regime, and finally ambassador to Italy. As Georg Christoph Berger Waldenegg notes in the introductory remarks to the book, some amount of controversy surrounds the politics of Egon. Some historians have argued that he was anti-German while others maintained that he was pro-axis (p. 9–11). As we shall see, however, Egon's memoir is more honest than many, though not without serious faults.

Egon, like his son, starts his memoir with a detailed family history and pedigree. Although such aristocratic exercises may have seemed essential to Egon, it is unfortunate that he wasted so much verbiage describing oriental rugs and family castles instead of concentrating on the really meaningful portions of his recollections.[6] The reader is also informed of Egon's intellectual interests and his first steps into politics. Perhaps Egon's most interesting observations from his youthful days, at least for the casual reader, concern his first experiences at the *Ballhausplatz* as a young official. Reflecting the relaxed spirit of 'old-Vienna', for example, he describes the typical work day at the *Ballhausplatz* as one which did not start until 10:30 a.m. for most employees, or even 12:30 p.m. for some key ministers. In the period before World War I, the author worked at the Austrian embassies in Dresden and Durazzo, and upon the war's outbreak he made his way back to Austria. The largest single chapter in his memoirs concern his activities as a soldier in the Austro-Hungarian Imperial Army on the eastern front during World War I, including a brush with death during the army's retreat from Lemberg in 1914. In August 1917, he rejoined the Foreign Office in Vienna, and served as part of the Austro-Hungarian contingent to the peace treaty signed at Brest-Litovsk.

Predictably, Egon shows little sympathy for the post-war Socialist leaders such as Otto Bauer. Egon argues that his dismissal from the Foreign Office, initiated by Bauer, was the result of his anti-Anschluß stance; this may well be true. But historians will not readily agree when the author declares that the only goal of the *Heimwehr* (right-oriented paramilitary forces), as early as 1918-1922, was a positive and patriotic one: the maintenance of the independence of Austria (p. 361-362). The *Heimwehr*'s aim of eradicating Marxism and opposing the Socialist paramilitary *Schutzbund* (left-oriented paramilitary forces) is conveniently forgotten here. Further, by framing the debate as one in which the *Heimwehr* pursued the 'idealistic' goal of Austrian independence, Egon imparts a negativity to pro-Anschluß views, held among others by the Austrian *Sozialdemokratische Partei*'s (Social Democratic Party, or SDP), at a time well before such a desire for union had the sinister aspect it came to have after Hitler's 1933 seizure of power.

The author finally came to prominence after being named *Landesführer des Österreichischen Heimatschutzes* (provincial leader of the Austrian Home Defense Forces) in Styria by Ernst Rüdiger Starhemberg early in 1934. Clearly, Starhemberg was important to the rise of Egon, and it is perhaps for that reason that he scrupulously avoids any criticism of Starhemberg. No mention is made, for example, of Starhemberg's disruptive and intense rivalry with Dollfuß.[7] In June 1934 Dollfuß and Starhemberg brought Egon into the newly formed cabinet as minister of justice. Egon's judgements regarding Dollfuß border on the obsequious, going so far as to claim that Dollfuß was an *"überzeugter Demokrat"* (convinced democrat) forced to use authoritarian methods in order to rule (pp. 385). Although the SDP must share blame for Austria's then malfunctioning democracy, the available evidence indicates that Dollfuß did indeed believe in the precepts of the corporate state, which he espoused as a more effective way of ruling Austria.[8]

For the historian, however, it is Egon's recollections from the period when he served as Austrian foreign secretary and, subsequently, ambassador to Italy, that hold the most potential interest. There is some accurate material here, although disappointingly superficial: the 'Little Entente' and Germany's obsessive fears about a Habsburg restoration; the ongoing British disinterest in Austria; and French ambassador Gabrielle Puaux's diplomatic efforts in Paris on Austria's behalf (pp. 409-410, 423-424, 446, 449). Most significant is Egon's truthfulness about his conviction that Austria's independence could only be secured against Nazi Germany through a close relationship with Italy (pp. 408, 462, 465, 467, 475, 479, 482, 486). A thorough examination of the historical evidence supports him here, perhaps more than he would like.

Early in 1936, while still foreign secretary, Egon received assurances from Benito Mussolini and Undersecretary for Foreign Affairs Fulvio Suvich that no deal would be made with Nazi Germany at Austria's expense—declarations which Egon requested and received once more after he became ambassador to Rome in June 1936. But, as the *Duce* revealed, these assurances were only for a "Dollfuß Austria," one that was authoritarian and closely aligned with Italy. The ambassador was confident that "under no circumstances would Mussolini sacrifice Austria."[9] In this, Egon's essential outlook never changed. His friendship to Italian Foreign Minister Galeazzo Ciano, and his belief that Italy alone could provide immediate and effectual military aid to Austria against German aggression prevented him from reassessing his view.[10] As pressure by the Nazis on the Schuschnigg regime rose in early 1938, Egon believed that Italy's friendship for Austria was warmer than it had been throughout the previous year. Also, in his opinion the *Duce's* trip to Berlin in September 1937 and the display of German military power might well have made Mussolini even more interested in an Austrian buffer state, although this was difficult to judge.[11] Three days before the Anschluß Egon wrote that Italy was still the dominant power between Rome and Berlin. Mussolini did not want an expansion of the Reich in central Europe or the loss of a friendly Austria. Therefore, Egon concluded, Austria had to remain closely bound to Italy and carry out an "Anschluß to axis politics" as the price for Italian protection.[12] The author's frankness stems from the fact that he never doubted, *ex post facto*, that the key to Mussolini's passivity in the face of the Anschluß lay in the poor relationship that developed between Vienna and Rome after Dollfuß' death. In Egon's opinion, the person most at fault for this state was his replacement as foreign secretary, Guido Schmidt. Unfortunately, in trying to prove the wisdom of pro-Italian politics and Schmidt's culpability in disrupting them, the author resorts to frequent misrepresentations and omissions.

Although the available evidence indicates that Schmidt helped to undermine the *Ballhausplatz* by actively working with Berlin, Egon singles out Schmidt for more than his fair share of responsibility[13]: in the author's view Schmidt was the main architect of a regrettable 11 July 1936 *Abkommen* (settlement); Schmidt influenced Schuschnigg negatively *vis-à-vis* Italy; and, therefore, Schmidt was largely responsible for Italy's waning interest in Austrian independence. The author depicts Schuschnigg as naïve and easily influenced (pp. 413, 415, 418-419, 460, 462, 465, 467, 475, 479, 482, n. 59, n. 60).

Such a view leaves much out of account. First, it assumes that the 11 July 1936 *Abkommen* was the death knell of Austrian independence. This was not the case. The *Abkommen* was only one part of a comprehensive and subtle strategy by the Schuschnigg regime to prevent Nazi aggression, especially military action. Although the *Abkommen* may not have delayed the Anschluß significantly in the end, neither did it accelerate the end of Austrian independence. The Schuschnigg regime remained in control, and it was partially due to the checks imposed on Germany by the *Abkommen* that Hitler and his cronies resorted to violence and blackmail during the 12 February 1938 meeting at Berchtesgaden.[14] Egon's pro-settlement attitude is made clear by his statements at the 18 September 1935 cabinet meeting, and, thereafter, by his participation in refining portions of what became the 11 July 1936 *Abkommen*.[15] Indeed, the author would have found himself virtually alone if he had actually objected to a settlement with Germany: even the most ardent anti-Nazi members of the Schuschnigg regime—including chief of the general staff Alfred Jansa—understood the need for a respite, however brief, from the *de facto* war with Germany.[16]

Although Egon may have objected Schuschnigg's inclusion of the phrase that Austria "*bekennt sich als deutscher Staat*" (recognizes itself as a Germanic state) in the body of the *Abkommen*, this was little different from the proclamations of previous chancellors, including Dollfuß. The Austrian ambassador failed to realize that Schuschnigg's doubts about Italy came less from his own biases or from the baleful influence of Schmidt, than from a shrewd appraisal of the *Duce's* ideology, his commitment to the axis, and the fact that by mid-1937 the Italian military forces had become so weakened in Abyssinia and Spain that its real military value was in question.[17] Nevertheless, the author correctly detected Mussolini and Ciano's desire for a nominally independent Austria even as late as March 1938. Thus, to a lesser extent, Egon is also correct in criticizing Schuschnigg's failure to exploit that desire. A gangster of Mussolini's ilk could never trust the promises of an equally corrupted Hitler or Göring about the inviolability of an Italo-German border. Nor could Italy escape the very real threat of a furiously rearming Germany on its northern border, and the danger that necessarily posed to Italian influence in central-southeastern Europe.[18]

Another serious omission by the author concerns his account of the events surrounding Göring's January 1937 visit to Rome and the April 1937 meeting in Venice between Schuschnigg and Mussolini (pp. 474-475). Egon purposefully gives the impression that the *Reichsfeldmarschall*'s visit was unremarkable. In fact, news of the aggressive and inflammatory remarks made by Göring to Mussolini set off a panic at the Austrian embassy in Rome and at the *Ballhausplatz*. The direct results were repeated requests by Schuschnigg for a meeting with the *Duce*. Originally scheduled for February, the meeting was pushed back until April by Mussolini due to his displeasure with Schuschnigg's measures against Nazi and pan-German sentiments in Austria.[19]

Overall, *Biographie im Spiegel: Die Memoiren zweier Generationen* is of mild interest to the historian. Its most notable aspect, Egon Berger-Waldenegg's truthful admission that in his opinion Austria could only secure herself against Nazi Germany through closely Italian-oriented politics, which he tried to advance, could also be gleaned through archival research. But significant portions of Egon's story are inaccurate or omit important details. This makes at least Egon's portion of the memoir a minefield of misinformation for the layperson or student. Although the author hints at some interesting details, almost none of them are brought out in sufficient detail to be of great interest. In the final analysis, memoirs—including those of Egon and Heinrich Berger-Waldenegg—cannot replace lengthy and difficult archival research. Although in certain limited instances they may help to illuminate what can already be substantiated by the documentary record, they are problematical at best.

Notes

1. Baruch Fischoff, "Hindsight is not Equal to Foresight: The Effect of Outcome Knowledge on Judgement under Uncertainty," *Journal of Experimental Psychology: Human Perception and Performance* 1 (1975): 288-299; S.A. Hawkins and R. Hastie, "Hindsight: Biased Judgements of Past Events after the Outcomes are Known," *Psychological Bulletin* 107 (1990): 817-829; Philip E. Tetlock and Aaron Belkin, eds., "Counterfactual Thought Experiments in World Politics: Logical, Methodological, and Psychological Perspectives," in *Counterfactual Thought Experiments in World Politics:*

Logical, Methodological, and Psychological Perspectives (Princeton: Princeton University Press, 1996).

2. Holger H. Herwig, "Of Men and Myths: The Use and Abuse of History and the Great War," in *The Great War and the Twentieth Century*, ed. J. Winter, Geoffrey Parker, Mary Habeck, (New Haven: Yale University Press, 2000), upcoming. For a discussion of the distortions by Austrian historians such as Oskar Regele see Manfried Rauchensteiner, "Die Militärgeschichtsschreibung in Österreich nach 1945," in *Militärgeschichte in Deutschland und Österreich vom 18. Jahrhundert bis in die Gegenwart: Vorträge zur Militärgeschichte* (Herford: E.S. Mittler, 1985), and Rudolf Jerábek, "Die österreichische Weltkriegsforschung," in *Der Erste Weltkrieg, Wirkung, Wahrnehmung, Analyse*, ed. Wolfgang Michalka (Munich: Piper,1994).

3. Schuschnigg's own distortions and omissions have been the principle obstacles to a thorough understanding of what he tried to do between July 1934 and March 1938. For details on the manifold inaccuracies and omissions contained in the memoirs of Schuschnigg, Zernatto, Frankenstein, and Jansa (among others) see Alexander N. Lassner, "Austria, Europe and the Anschluß," (PhD. diss., Ohio State University, 2000), introduction, chapter 1.

4. Ibid., chapter 4, chapter 6.

5. *Il Piccolo*, 11 marzo 1938, p.3, MFP 33, *Biblioteca Nazionale Centrale, Roma* [hereafter referred to as BNC/R]; *Il Piccolo*, 12 marzo 1938, p.1-2, MFP 33, BNC/R; *Il Piccolo*, 13 marzo 1938, p.1, MFP 33, BNC/R.

6. Egon spends more than two hundred pages on the period up to his nomination as *Landeshauptmannstellvertreter* of the province of Styria in 1934, but only one hundred and twelve pages on the period thereafter.

7. Conversation Mussolini and Starhemberg, 6 September 1933, *I Documenti Diplomatici Italiani*, 7 serie, volume XIV, (Rome: Istituto Poligrafico e Zecca Dello Stato, 1989), document 154 [hereafter referred to as DDI, series, volume, document]; Preziosi a Mussolini, 22 November 1933, DDI, 7, XIV, 400; Preziosi a Mussolini, 18 December 1933, DDI, 7, XIV, 489; conversation Mussolini and Starhemberg, 17 April 1934, DDI, 7, XV, 110.

8. On the Austrian corporate state, in which parties were to be replaced with professional bodies the mission of which was to resolve any class conflict, see Wolfgang Putschek, *Ständische Verfassung und autoritäre Verfassungspraxis in Österreich 1933 – 1938 mit Dokumentenanhang: Verfassung und Verfassungswirklichkeit* (Frankfurt: P. Lang, 1993). That Dollfuß was less than a "convinced democrat" see Alfred Diamant, *Austrian Catholics and the First Republic, 1918-1934* (Princeton: Princeton University Press, 1960), 194. See also the introspective and excellent article on Dollfuß by John Rath, "The Dollfuß Ministry: The Intensification of Animosities and the Drift Toward Authoritarianism," in *Austrian History Yearbook*, 30 (1999), 65-101. Dollfuß told Mussolini in July 1933 that even "the most resolute Austrian patriots are convinced that parliamentarianism in its old form no longer corresponds to the exigencies of the times," meeting Dollfuß and Mussolini, 20 July 1933, DDI, 7, XVI, 9.

9. Berger to Berger-Waldenegg, 3 April 1936, Österreichisches Staatsarchiv/Archiv der Republik, Bundesministerium für Äußeres/Neues Politisches Archiv, box 85, document No. 61/Pol., Österreichisches Staatsarchiv, Wien [Hereafter referred to as ÖSA/AdR, BMfA/NPA, box, document]; Berger-Waldenegg to Schuschnigg, 24 June 1936, ÖSA/AdR, BMfA/NPA, #85, No. 118/Pol.; Berger-Waldenegg to Schuschnigg, 26 June 1936, ÖSA/AdR, BMfA/NPA, #85, No. 122/Pol.

10. Berger-Waldenegg to Schmidt, 26 April 1937, ÖSA/AdR, BMfA/Hinaus- und Hereintelegramme, #26, 389; Berger-Waldenegg to Schmidt, 18 May 1937, ÖSA/AdR, BMfA/NPA, #285, No. 108/Pol; H. James Burgwyn, "Italy, the Roman Protocols Bloc, and the Anschluß Question 1936-1938," in *Austrian History Yearbook*, 22 (1988), n. 65.

11. Berger-Waldenegg to Schmidt, 2 January 1938, ÖSA/AdR, BMfA/NPA, #86, No. 1/Pol.; Berger-Waldenegg to Schmidt, 3 October 1938, ÖSA/AdR, BMfA/NPA, #86, Zl. 184/Pol.

12. Ibid.; Berger-Waldenegg to Schmidt, 9 March 1938, ÖSA/AdR, BMfA/NPA, #86, No. 32/Pol.

13. Immediately after the 12 February 1938 meeting between Austrian Chancellor Kurt Schuschnigg and Adolf Hitler, Schuschnigg believed that Schmidt was a likely traitor. Paris and London had been suspicious of Schmidt since 1937, and by 20 February 1938 Whitehall condemned Schmidt as a turncoat. Soon after the Anschluß, Schmidt met with Hermann Göring for his 'reward'. Vansittart to Selby, 14 October 1937, *Documents on British Foreign Policy*, second series, volume XIX, (London: Her Majesties Stationary Service, 1982), document 250; Puaux a Delbos, 12 September 1937, *Documents Diplomatiques Français*, 2e série (1936-1939), Tome III, (Paris: Imprimerie Nationale, 1966), document 435 [hereafter referred to as DDF, series, volume, document]; Puaux a Delbos, 2 December 1937, DDF, 2, VII, 298; Lassner, "Austria, Europe, and the Anschluß," chapter 4, chapter 7, chapter 8. After the war, Schmidt was tried but acquitted: see *Der Hochverratsprozess gegen Dr. Guido Schmidt vor dem Wiener Volksgericht* (Vienna: Druck und Verlag der Österreichischen Staatsdruckerei, 1947).

14. Historians have argued, with mind-numbing regularity, that the conclusion of this agreement represented nothing less than a *de facto* abandonment of Austria by Italy. Jürgen Gehl's often cited landmark, *Austria, Germany, and the Anschluß,* and multitudinous other accounts portray Germany in general, and Papen in particular, as the initiators of the *Abkommen*, Mussolini as a willing or (at best) apathetic accomplice, and Schuschnigg as an arch appeaser. Jürgen Gehl, *Austria, Germany, and the Anschluss 1931-1938* (London: Oxford University Press, 1963), 110-111, 130-131. No less a scholar than Gerhard Weinberg has taken much the same view as Gehl: Gerhard Weinberg, *The Foreign Policy of Hitler's Germany: Diplomatic Revolution in Euope 1933 – 1936* (Chicago: Chicago University Press, 1970), 267-268. Luigi Salvatorelli, perhaps the first author to put forth this view, decried the 11 July 1936 *Abkommen* as the death knell of Austrian independence. See Luigi Salvatorelli, *Il Fascismo nella politica internazionale* (Modena: Guanda, 1946). That this Italian interpretation appeared in the chaotic and highly emotional year of 1946 explains its paltry evidence and categorical tone. Less clear is why scholars have continued to make only weak attempts at critical reevaluation of the 11 July 1936 *Abkommen*. For an in depth treatment of the strategy of the Schuschnigg regime and a more balanced interpretation of what the 11 July 1936 *Abkommen* represented see Lassner, "Austria, Europe, and the Anschluß," chapter 2, chapter 4, chapter 6.

15. Cabinet meeting, 8 September 1935, *Protokoll des Ministerrates der Ersten Republik*, vol. 3, *31. Mai 1935 bis 30 November 1935* (Vienna: Verlag Österreich, 1995), document 1008; Papen to Hitler, 27 May 1935, *Documents on German Foreign Policy 1918-1945,* series C, vol. IV (Washington: U.S. Government Printing Office, 1962), document 111 [hereafter referred to as DGFP, series, volume, document]; minute Papen, 11 July 1935, DGFP, C, IV, 203; Berger-Waldenegg to Papen, 1 October 1935, DGFP, C, IV, 319.

16. Jansa told French military attaché C.R. Salland that "I [Jansa] have personally insisted with Schuschnigg about a normalization of our relationship with Germany." Salland to Daladier, 25 August 1936, *Documents Diplomatiques Français*, 2e série (1936-1939), Tome III, (Paris: Imprimerie Nationale, 1966), document 202.

17. Lassner, "Austria, Europe, and the Anschluß," chapter 1, chapter 3.

18. Ibid., chapter 6.

19. Ibid., chapter 4, chapter 6.

Borders, Self-Determination, and the Emerging Concept of "Self-Governance"

Wolfgang Danspeckgruber

Ekkehard W. Bornträger, *Borders, Ethnicity and National Self-Determination* (Vienna: Braumüller, 1999)

The drive for self-determination has been one of the major causes of the world's humanitarian crises in the post-cold war era. Struggles for autonomy and secession have been the source of tremendous human suffering and destruction in Africa, Europe, and Asia. The dilution of the international system's bi-polar rigidity, global interdependence, intensified economic-technological cooperation, and real-time communication have added a fundamental challenge to the traditional problems between ethnic communities and central authorities. Today many communities are torn between their desire to participate in the global market place, maximizing their international contacts, and their strive to obtain maximum freedom for their cultural and religious traditions, and to assert themselves vis-à-vis their respective central authorities.

However, the bloody and destructive events accompanying the disintegration of Yugoslavia (i.e. Bosnia-Herzegowina and Kosovo), the upheavals in the Caucasus (i.e. the Russian Republic of Chechnya) and in South Asia (i.e. Kashmir)—to name just a few—have proven that separation by force and the intention to redraw international boundaries can lead to large-scale suffering and destruction. Moreover, ruthless leadership and commercial interests, combined with an increasingly global interaction among organized crime networks and easier access to weapons of mass destruction, have made self-determination crises much more dangerous, costly, and difficult to manage. Finally, the establishment of new borders unavoidably creates winners and losers and in many cases mobilizes the attention of outside powers.[1]

In his new book *Borders, Ethnicity and National Self-Determination,* Ekkehard Bornträger argues that particularly in Europe the concept of borders remains as valid today as it has been historically—and this in spite of "wishful thinking about the end of borders" (p. 17). In sometimes convoluted and 'philosophic' prose, supported by a wealth of materials, the author attempts to demonstrate the "dynamics" of the development of borders (p. 3). In so doing he offers interesting analyses and discussions, like the one regarding the possible uncertainty of international borders' final status ("finality"), which is especially fascinating in light of some of the old *limae* dividing the European and—to a lesser degree—the African continent. Bornträger also cites the example of one particularly meaningful boundary in (European and world) history: the border between France and Germany.

The ensuing historical debate could have brought to light that not only administrative, national, and ideological developments have influenced the shape and meaning of inter-state borders, i.e. hard external boundaries, but particularly technological progress, industrialization, and trade. In the strategic realm, power projection capability, economic interests, and military technological and strategic advancement all have influenced the degree to which national governments and/or ruling houses could push the external limits of their power—hence the extent of their boundaries. In the contemporary evolution of the international system, advanced technologies are prone to provide for other challenges: from real-time transfer of data and information on a global scale, to precise determination of geographical location (GPS – Global Positioning System) anywhere on the globe, maximum global mobility, and nearly unlimited access to all kinds of information virtually everywhere.[2]

Sovereignty is at bay, borders are challenged, but the state does 'fight back'.[3] Whenever the central government and its institutions feel challenged in their authority, they will try to find new ways to reassert themselves—through laws and technological or administrative means from censorship to acquisition of yet more advanced, defensive technologies. All this holds true also for the central authorities' intent to uphold their existing sovereign rights and boundaries—governments are by definition interested in maintaining the geopolitical *status quo.* However, any of this 'tit-for-tat', *actio-reactio* pattern depends on the overall 'cost benefit calculation' of the central authorities.[4] This is particularly relevant when it concerns international boundaries, since under certain conditions states will opt for accepting a weakening or erosion of their external boundaries in exchange for palpable benefits. These may include teaming up with others in a military alliance, the adhesion to a regional trading group, or—in the most advanced way—the joining of a supranational organization like the European Union (EU). Rather surprisingly Ekkehard Bornträger devotes little to no attention at all to the four liberties in the European Economic Area (EEA) and to the successful implementation of the *Schengen* Agreement as part of the EU with the aim to permit citizens, goods, services, and products free travel and transfer throughout the entire EU territory. This means that the sovereign territory of EU members has become extended to encompass the territory of the supranational unit 'EU' in matters of travel and transfer.[5]

Another, 'third' way would be, as Bornträger argues, to simply ignore or "obscure the continuing importance of inter-state (inter-nation) boundaries" (p.17). But then again, coming to grips with the emerging fundamental challenges to borders at this junction of international relations is perhaps quite a daunting and unsettling task for those dominating the contemporary system.

Boundaries

Borders can be anything with geographical meaning: just a line on the ground or in the sand, a mountain top, a mountain pass, a valley, a river, etc. In his latest book *States and Power in Africa*, Jeffrey Herbst demonstrates the relevance of 'boundary politics' in Africa. Of general international value is however his assertion that boundary really demonstrates "the extension of authority."[6] Bornträger's book addresses the fundamental question whether the role and impact of boundaries in their contemporary/traditional form continues, or whether some kind of new, perhaps limited or divided meaning of external borders will evolve. In our time a significant distinction exists in international relations between borders in the regular setting of the international system, i.e. state to state relations, and those in the newly emerging supranational setting, as seen within a tight regional organization such as the European Union.[7] Tension rises from such conflicting developments as these: industrial economic development and cooperation, trade, etc. will operate in an increasingly borderless environment, while socio-cultural dimensions, important and dear to the well being of a society, will continue to strive to exclude 'the others'. It seems that highly integrated, wealthy, and developed societies have a tendency to be less prone to such exclusionary policies, though experiences in Austria, Germany, Scandinavia, etc. would not support this assumption. External borders can on the one hand be nearly meaningless, especially in view of transnational projects and exchange. On the other hand, however, once a society perceives an influence as a 'threat' to its security and wellbeing, the withdrawal to the "'sacrosanct' character" of its border becomes premiere national interest.

Bornträger believes that in a global context the continued "traditional" meaning of boundaries will persist as "nation-building . . . whether in its assimilationist integrative or separatist variant is still far from its conclusion." He consequently assumes that "cross border horizontal social differentiation will give way to vertical national differentiation," which will increase with "the quest to make political boundaries coincide with cultural fault-lines ..."(p. 59). Interestingly Bornträger does perceive the issue of cultures and 'civilizations' as one of the more critical ones for the future, though he remains critical—and rightly so—of Samuel Huntington's assumption of a "clash of civilizations" (p. 61). Although Bornträger correctly states that the examples of Kuwait, Bosnia, and Kosovo have actually demonstrated the "strikingly little evidence of Pan-Muslim solidarity" (p. 62), one could still ask whether this can be explained by the lack of an efficient power projection and, concomitantly, of appropriate weapon systems, including weapons of mass destruction. Unfortunate references such as these to a suddenly available "Islamic bomb" could be heard when Pakistan successfully detonated its first nuclear devices in May 1998.[8]

Inversely, one may argue that the Kosovo crisis was 'solved' militarily—for better or worse—only due to a determined superpower action (United States). The ramifications of this rather unilateral military operation on the relationship with Russia and China are obviously not solely positive and impact not only NATO itself but also the future of military defense policy within the EU, i.e. the new European Security and Defense Initiative (ESDI).[9]

Conceptually argued, the strategic weight and determination of *the one* power in a seemingly 'uni-polar' international system, with all its military might, helped overcome fissures even within the NATO military alliance (for a short period of time), though it could not avoid ensuing problems with other major powers. The lesson however is that in case there was a comparable Islamic power, or the like, this may indeed serve to assert cohesion within its own religious or ethnic camp. It is difficult to predict that particular relationship and whether a new availability of major weapon systems and determination to use them could indeed change the situation between civilizations. Still, Bornträger's argument that this would be "unlikely ... [to] invalidate inter-nation borders" holds (p. 62). He finds hence that national boundaries will not only continue but also that 'cultured nations' (*Kulturnationen*) will continue to obtain their own territory and external boundaries.

Bornträger introduces another criterion of whether a community can justifiably claim right to its own territory and state: namely "critical size" (p. 63). Over the decades—particularly since the League of Nations (LN)—this has become an all too convenient tool of the powerful to tailor argumentation as it regards the acceptance of a small or micro state among those in power (i.e. LN membership, etc.).[10] However, President Woodrow Wilson has clearly addressed the issue of 'size' when he argued that the "equality of nations ... must be an equality of rights ..., must neither recognise nor imply a difference between big nations and small, between those that are powerful and those that are weak."[11] In our times the potential impact of a state versus its size even plays a role in organizations and their institutions such as the EU and the U.N.. In many cases, though, not only size and popula-tion count, but also the availability of weapons of mass destruction in a state's defense arsenal. Jeffrey Herbst has proven that in view of sophisticated technology and highly trained human capital such arguments, which evaluate a potential state's capability on the basis of territorial size and 'man power', may be misguided.[12] As will be discussed later, the issue of size has lost much of its importance in today's international system. Particularly in combination with regional integration and the will of the population to engage in activities as a "trading state"[13] in the global market place, many of the dimensions which originally influenced economic well-being and prosperity of a state have lost their relevance. However, the 'traditional dictum' still holds that the strategic setting, i.e. the safe environment, decides about a state's future: consider the blessed settings of Hong Kong, Andorra, Liechtenstein, etc. A strategically hostile environment can bring the role of size, manpower, and capabilities back to the fore.[14] Finally, in a rather convincing argument, Paul Krugman brings about that the location where industry, i.e. production, is located does matter.[15] Modern communications technology, i.e. real-time transmission of data and information on a global scale, has, however, made a dent into the importance of space, location, and distance. A working phone line, computer equipment, and a modem can transform any place into an office capable of communicating at once with nearly any place elsewhere on the globe. This kind of communication-capability has brought possibilities as well as challenges to communities and states. The degree of transborder-cooperation adds a new meaning to sovereign 'boundary' and 'exclusivity'. States and organizations do have an impetus to maintain their *status quo*, so they intend to confront any such challenge with the effort to reassert influence and limit under-washing. It may be interesting to discuss when and under what circumstances borders can be changed. The fundamental inviolability of borders is assumed as a guiding principle of the current international system. The emergence of a new state means change of international boundaries and—most importantly—requires international recognition. Existing governments and those who wish to create a new independent entity are supposed to settle any boundary dispute without the use of force. In case of necessity a new government can join "relevant arbitration conventions and submit to the compulsory jurisdiction of the International Court of Justice in The Hague."[16]

This raises another critical issue in the international system: when and under which conditions should the international community take the decision to intervene within a sovereign state where communities search for greater self-determination. Unfortunately, post-cold war history has demonstrated that such concerted international operations depend first and foremost, in the words of Richard Falk, on "geopolitics of ambivalence," namely on the national and strategic interest of the leading powers in a given struggle for autonomy and the respective geo-strategic ramifications.[17] Unfortunately—highlighting the cruelty and injustice of this parameter—geography, natural resources, energy, etc. are the deciding factors in such strategic considerations, and they have little to do with justice or with the suffering of the communities involved.

One may assume a fundamental obligation of the international community to stop flagrant violations of human rights. Two kinds of 'intervention' can be seen: The first, more benign 'intervention from within', really comprises outside support and assistance for democratization movements, the creation of civil society, and encouragement to the formation of working state structures. This should encourage peaceful process and discourage violence and destruction. Once a conflict has already emerged, and casualties, suffering, and destruction take place, the international response should be different. Then it should consider the degree and scope of violations of human rights and the resulting humanitarian costs (casualties, displaced persons, and refugees) as well as material and economic damages. When the scale of human suffering transcends acceptable standards—and exerts a great toll both in casualties and refugees—then the outside community has a right and indeed an obligation to intervene and stop the fighting and casualties. The timing is critical: early intervention can limit further suffering and devastation, and thus reduces collateral damages and reconstruction and peace implementation costs for the international community. It may also help avoid a dangerous contagion across borders, especially in highly multi-ethnic areas (e.g. the Caucasus and Southeastern Europe). In addition, dealing with self-determination interests early, and thus restraining outside influence, can help reduce military-strategic escalation and potential employment of weapons of mass-destruction. In a highly charged, highly armed regional environment, particularly along the post Soviet border (the Black Sea area, the Caucasus, and Central Asia), such anticipatory attention may be critical for limiting the scale and suffering caused by secessionist movements.

Self-Determination

Theoretical issues surrounding self-determination range from the obvious questions regarding sovereignty, exclusive state authority, and the inviolability of international boundaries, to the 'supra-national' validity of human rights, intervention, political-strategic interests, economic viability, as well as legal, economic, ethnic-cultural, and sociological dimensions. At the core are theories of state, membership in and structure of the international system, and the rights of groups and communities. The essence of the theoretical debate is how principles of sovereignty can be redefined to permit progress in autonomy and self-determination without provoking violence in defense of narrowly conceived state authority.

During the cold war the rigidity of the bipolar international system and the influence of the respective leading powers curtailed the opportunity for communities to seek greater autonomy or secession. Then self-determination was accepted by the international community—in accordance with the Charter of the United Nations—only if it concerned gaining freedom from colonial regimes. The Wilsonian dual meaning of self-determination, namely the freedom to choose one's government and the freedom to choose one's allies internationally, was further restricted to cases that fit the superpowers' interests. Those communities which did not receive independence through decolonization faced disaster when they attempted to fight for what they saw as their legitimate group rights (e.g. Biafra, Kashmir, Tibet, East Timor). In Europe the quest for self-determination was paralyzed by the rigidity of the cold war strategic confrontation, which divided the continent into an Eastern and Western part and rendered any attempt for separation or state formation futile. This stability lulled the international community into erroneously thinking that self-determination issues—besides decolonization—had essentially been solved and become matters of the past.[18]

Once the Soviet Union and its empire disintegrated, however, the rigidity of the global system softened, and those interested in self-determination and secession intensified their objectives. As a consequence, at the end of the twentieth century struggles over self-determination have emerged in many different places on the globe—from Central to Southeastern Europe via the Black Sea Region, Africa, the Caucasus, to Central and South Asia. But secessionist movements have arisen also in highly industrialized states such as Belgium, Canada, France, Italy, the United Kingdom, and Russia. Each case harbors its own, very specific background, causes, and level of development, and certainly differs in intensity and orientation. Causes range from economic challenges and interests of the leadership to quests for sovereignty by communities and lingering, unresolved inter-ethnic problems. Responses vary from suppression and domination to deliberate manipulation and incitement, as well as outside power involvement.

However, the international community, continuing the attitudes and strategies toward self-determination that were developed before and during the cold war, has responded neither effectively, nor consistently. For instance, in the case of Bosnia-Herzegovina and Kosovo, the local population had to suffer massive human rights violations and significant destruction had to take place before a concerted international reaction could garner momentum—which, in the case of Kosovo, led to NATO's largest air operation in Europe since World War II. In Chechnya, however, within the sovereign territory of the Russian Federation, even rampant human rights violations could not induce any meaningful international reaction.[19]

Self-Governance – an Emerging Concept

It has proven difficult to persuade leaders of communities interested in secession and traditional statehood of the advantages of regional cooperation and integration, to make them leave behind their ideas for classical sovereignty in exchange for participating in regional integration. In order to surmount that insistence for independence, the community should be offered—and convinced to accept—maximum autonomy and the largest possible freedom to participate in the global market place. In practice, this would comprise autonomy in all internal agenda, encompassing religious cultural, linguistic, educational, even fiscal, and local security and judicial administrative autonomy, as well as the right to participate in the central authority's decision-making process. However, that degree of self-governance would exclude national defense, currency, and complete international treaty-making power, i.e. an independent foreign service. Successful examples of international treaty-making powers, such as the German State of Bavaria, the Spanish region of Catalonia, and the Italian region Bolzano-Südtirol, demonstrate the extent of power such far-reaching autonomy may encompass.[20]

Parallel to this extensive self-governance, an incentive for transborder inter-regional cooperation and integration has to be launched.[21] Over time such integration on a regional as well as international scale, and among self-governing communities in sovereign entities with their traditional boundaries intact, would most certainly enhance local, cross-border cooperation and eventually erode the hardness of the separating international boundaries—both in practice and in perception.[22] Resulting prosperity, mobility, and openness to other cultural influences may further influence the regional setting and possibly ameliorate inter-communal tensions there. Hence, regional integration in combination with maximum autonomy—self-governance—may be an effective, albeit longer term recipe to satisfy the aspirations of freedom of ethnic communities, bring about greater prosperity, peace, and stability, while slowly alleviating the relevance of the respective international boundaries—and, perhaps, finally abrogating the traditional state shattering meaning of self-determination.

Notes

1. See Wolfgang Danspeckgruber, ed., "Introduction" in *Self-Determination of Peoples—Communities, Nations, States in Global Interdependence* (Boulder: Lynne Rienner Publishers, forthcoming).

2. For a fine discussion of this matter see Walter B. Wriston, "Bites, Bytes, and Diplomacy," Foreign Affairs, 76 (September/October 1997): 172-183.

3. See the path-breaking contribution by Raymond Vernon, *Sovereignty at Bay* (New York: Basic Books, 1971).

4. See the debate in Robert G. Gilpin, Jr., *War and State in World Politics* (Cambridge: Cambridge University Press, 1985), where the author clearly demonstrates that states may decide whatever they like, as long as it fits their respective interests.

5. For an extensive discussion of the Schengen Agreement see Andrew Moravcsik, *The Choice for Europe* (Ithaca, N.Y.: Cornell University Press, 1998).

6. Jeffrey Herbst, *States and Power in Africa,* (Princeton, NJ: Princeton University Press, 2000), p. 24.

7. A possible model for the future can be found in the combination between 'Schengen' and Erasmus, i.e. regional integration, technological progress, and generational change.

8. Wolfgang Danspeckgruber, "A third way?," *Defence Review* (London, Winter 1998): 26.

9. 'Unilateral' is to be seen here more as a term referring to the actual involvement of military hardware in the strategic bombing campaign of NATO, forcing Belgrade back to negotiations and stopping the forceful expulsions of Kosovars from Yugoslav territory. The political will to act was in joint agreement between the EU and the United States.

10. For instance, the League of Nations assessed that countries of some 500,000 citizens or less would be too small to become members.

11. Address to the United States Senate on Essential Terms of Peace in Europe, 22 January 1917, Baker and Dodd, *The New Democracy* II, 410-11, qtd in Alfred Coban, *The Nation State and National Self-Determination* (New York: Thomas Y. Crowell Company, 1969), 76, n. 50.

12. See Jeffrey Herbst, "Global Change and the Future of Existing Nation-States," in *Self-Determination of Peoples*, ed. Wolfgang Danspeckgruber.

13. Richard Rosekrance, *The Rise of the Trading State – Commerce and Conquest in the Modern World* (New York: Basic Books, 1986).

14. Sir John Thompson argued convincingly that the Hong Kongs, Liechtensteins, and Singapores of this world can only exists due to the absence of serious threat against them; see Sir John Thompson, "A Comment," in *Self-Determination and Self-Administration: A Sourcebook* ed. Wolfgang Danspeckgruber with Arthur Watts (Boulder, Co.: Lynne Rienner Publishers, 1997), p. 96.

15. Paul Krugman, *Geography and Trade* (Cambridge, MA: MIT Press, 1993).

16. Morton Halperin and David J. Scheffer, with Patricia L. Small, *Self-Determination in the New World Order* (Washington, D.C.: A Carnegie Endowment Book, 1992), 87. In addition the authors expect a new state to adhere to the Nuclear Non-Proliferation Treaty (NPT) and sign a comprehensive inspection agreement with the International Atomic Energy Agency (IAEA), as well as to voluntarily limit the size of its armed forces.

17. Richard Falk, presentation, Woodrow Wilson School, Princeton University, September 16, 1998.

18. Antonio Cassese, *Self-Determination of Peoples: A Legal Reappraisal* (Cambridge: Cambridge University Press, 1995).

19. Report, "The Crisis in Chechnya," Princeton University, LRPSD, 2000.

20. As concrete examples see the basic proposals of the "Hill-Plan," 1998, the points regarding self-government as proposed by the EU/U.S. negotiators at the negotiations at Rambouillet, and as enumerated by UNMIK (United Nations Mission in Kosovo). See the Chairman's Summary of the Liechtenstein Colloquium on "*Peace and the Future in South-Eastern Europe,*" Document of the UN Security Council (A/54/641-30/5/1999/1210). Regarding Chechnya, see the Khasavyurt Agreement, August 31, 1996, which laid the grounds for extensive independent legal and administrative authority of the Chechen government.

21. See the EU Stability Pact for the Balkans, which enumerates a whole series of concrete projects and steps to encourage intra-regional cooperation and development, as well as steps towards integration into the EU.

22. Wolfgang Danspeckgruber, "Self-Governance: A Futuristic Concept for Traditional (European) Problems," in *The Implementation of the Right to Self-Determination as a Contribution to Conflict Prevention*, ed. Michael C. van Walt van Praag with Onno Seroo (Barcelona: Centre UNESCO de Catalunya, 1999), 174-181.

Lothar Höbelt, *Von der vierten Partei zur dritten Kraft. Die Geschichte des VdU* (Graz: Leopold Stocker, 1999)

Kurt Richard Luther

Lothar Höbelt's history of the *Verein der Unabhängigen* (VdU)—*"eine ungewöhnliche, extrem zeitgebundene Partei, die eigentlich keine Partei sein wollte"* ("an unusual, extremely transitory party, which did not really want to be a party," p.7)—is timely in at least two respects. First, its appearance marked the 50th anniversary of the founding in 1949 of the short-lived VdU, a political party, which has to date been the focus of remarkably little academic investigation. Second, this account of the immediate predecessor of the Freedom Party of Austria was published just before the latter (and its then leader Jörg Haider) made once more headline news around the world—this time as a result of the party's entry into Austria's federal government on 4 February 2000.

The first two chapters of the volume analyze the background and the genesis of the VdU. They are followed by four chapters that document the party's rapid transition from dramatic early success to a seemingly unending catalogue of crises. Chapters seven to nine deal with the collapse of the VdU and its replacement by the Freedom Party. Finally, the main points of the book are succinctly summarized in twelve theses. The volume also contains about forty photographs of key persons and places, as well as two appendices. The first comprises a short retrospective by Herbert Kraus, one of the two founders of the VdU. The second has useful information on the VdU's internal organization, as well as on the political geography, membership, and election results of the VdU and the Freedom Party between 1949 and 1959.

Its second appendix notwithstanding, the book is written not from the perspective of a political scientist, but from that of an historian. Moreover, it draws upon a very impressive range of historical sources. These include interviews with dozens of *Zeitzeugen*, internal party documents, and the personal archives (many hitherto unexplored) of contemporary political activists. This material is painstakingly woven together into a fascinating chronicle of political intrigue and backroom machinations that involve a colorful collection of conservatives, monarchists, German-nationalists; former Nazis, secret service agents, liberals, the disgruntled and the dispossessed. The almost palpable atmosphere Höbelt's narrative creates is in many ways reminiscent of another product of the year 1949: Orson Welles' *The Third Man,* which also deals with conspiratorial activities on the outer fringe of postwar, occupied Austria.

Yet the chief merit of this volume lies not in its atmospherics, however fascinating. Instead, it is to be found in the volume's insights into two matters. The first is the nature of the VdU. Here, the following aspects deserve special praise. The first is the skillful manner in which Höbelt teases out the most salient ideological, organizational, and strategic differences within this complex and regionally extremely diverse party of notables. Second, not least by virtue of the numerous interviews he conducted, and the access he obtained to personal archives, Höbelt provides a unique insight into motivations and actions of key political activists of the period, be they from the VdU, the ÖVP, or (albeit less frequently) the SPÖ. Third, by linking the motivations of these actors to the socio-economic context in which they were operating, he manages to demonstrate the very contingent nature of the VdU's political demands. For example, he shows how the VdU's early support for economic liberalization was linked to the fact that the market price for agrarians' goods was then considerably above the price fixed by the government and how, once the situation was reversed, the farmers were much more susceptible to being recruited into the ranks of the more protectionist ÖVP. Fourth, the book provides a fascinating account of the tensions between the party leadership on the one hand and the grass-roots on the other hand. It strongly suggests that whilst such conflict was often rationalized in ideological terms, the reality is that both within the VdU and the later Freedom Party, it often had more to do with the personal animosities and political ambitions of individual politicians.

The second aspect of postwar Austrian politics into which this book offers welcome insights concerns the relationship between the VdU and what with hindsight we can recognize as the emerging system of neo-corporatism and two-party dominance, which was to characterize Austria for decades to come. First, whilst the existing literature emphasizes how the licensing of the VdU was supported by the SPÖ (which thought it would help split the bourgeois vote), and opposed by the ÖVP, Höbelt's research suggests that many VdU activists regarded their party as an instrument to ensure a bourgeois majority and thus prevent a possible *Volksdemokratie* (people's democracy). Second, the book is noteworthy for the way in which it details the ÖVP's considerable (and ultimately largely successful) efforts to recruit the VdU's supporters, often regardless of their political views or their track record under the National Socialist regime. Third, Höbelt points out the very real internal tensions which this 'inhalation' strategy created within the ÖVP. Thus, early attempts by ÖVP leaders, such as Gorbach and Graf, to pursue this strategy led to fear within the Catholic-social and employees' wings of the ÖVP that an influx of anti-clerical and market-oriented sentiment would tip the delicate balance of intra-party power decidedly in favor of the ÖVP's business wing. Fourth, Höbelt shows how the prospects of the VdU were fatally undermined by the growth of neo-corporatism and proportionality, which gave the two major parties patronage opportunities against which the VdU was unable to compete. There are a few aspects of Höbelt's book that can—and no doubt will—be criticized. First, some may question how appropriate it is for this account of the VdU to have appeared in the conservative publishing house named after someone, who himself played a significant role in the early years of the VdU. Second, especially in the light of current allegations that Austrians are all too prone to neglect the unsavory aspects of their country's 20th century history, some readers may consider the book to underplay the role and significance of Nazi and revisionist sentiment within the ranks of the VdU. Third, it might have been interesting to have had greater coverage of the relations (good or bad) between the VdU and the Socialists.

Such criticisms notwithstanding, this remains a valuable book. It provides a much overdue account of the internal life and external relations of the VdU, a party that was important in its own right and by virtue of the fact that it sought to challenge what were to become key features of the Second Republic. Having failed in its opposition to two-partism, neo-corporatism, and *Proporz*, it was replaced by the Freedom Party, the electoral prospects of which were considerably more constrained than those of the VdU had been in 1949. This was in large measure a result of the radicalized discourse with which the Freedom Party sought to rally the remnants of the 'Third *Lager*'. However, the fact that the Freedom Party was restricted to this German-national rump and the political impotence to which it was consigned must also be seen as a product of the political skills exercised during the lifetime of the VdU by the leaders of Socialist and Catholic-Conservative subcultures. They had after all, on the one hand, integrated a large proportion of that *Lager* into their own subcultures and, on the other hand, established a system of party-political control that was to last for decades to come.

ANNUAL REVIEW

Survey of Austrian Politics Austria 1999

The Avalanche
Elections to the State Diet in Carinthia, Salzburg and Tyrol
Marcus Omofuma
EU-Elections
Elections to the State Diet in Vorarlberg
National Council Elections

The Avalanche

Due to outstanding snowfall, in February 1999 a huge avalanche destroyed parts of the small village Galltür in the Paznaun Valley (Tyrol). 38 people—both inhabitants of Galltür and tourists from Germany, the Netherlands, and Denmark—were killed. This was one of the most destructive avalanches Austria had experienced in history. During the winter 1998/1999, Switzerland and France were also affected by disastrous avalanches.

State Diet Elections in Carinthia, Salzburg, and Tyrol

On 7 March, the state diets of Carinthia, Salzburg, and Tyrol were reelected. In Carinthia, the FPÖ gained—for the first time in history—the first place. Though it was not very surprising that the FPÖ was the winner, the difference to the former leader in Carinthia, the SPÖ, was remarkable. The FPÖ won 42.1 percent (+ 8.8 percent) and the SPÖ got 32.9 percent (- 4,5 percent). The ÖVP—with governor Christoph Zernatto—could not win either: 20.7 percent was a minus of 3.1 percent in comparison to the 1994 elections.

The FPÖ was led by the right-wing populist Jörg Haider, who was elected governor of Carinthia. Haider had been governor from 1989 to 1991. In 1991 he was dismissed because of his remark about *"ordentliche Beschäftigungspolitik im Dritten Reich"*: he had pointed out that in the Third Reich there was a better employment policy than in Austria at the end of the 20th century.

Table 1: Carinthia State Diet Elections

	Votes/ Percentage	+/- (in percent)	Seats	+/-
FPÖ	138,816/42.1	+ 8.8	16	+3
SPÖ	108,469/32.9	- 4.5	12	- 2
ÖVP	68,308/20.7	- 3.1	8	- 1
Demokratie 99*	12.895/3.9		0	+/- 0

*A coalition of Greens, Liberals and the Slovene minority in Carinthia.
Source: Compiled from official data.

In Salzburg, the ÖVP could keep its majority (38.8 percent, - 0.2 percent), the SPÖ received 32.4 percent (+ 5.3 percent), and the FPÖ 19.6 percent (+ 0.1 percent). The Greens lost a little bit but are still represented in the state diet (5.4 percent; - 1.9 percent). The Liberals couldn't get enough votes to be represented in the state diet (3.7 percent; - 2.1 percent). Though the SPÖ won most of all parties, the new (and old) governor is Franz Schausberger (ÖVP).

Table 2: Salzburg State Diet Elections

	Votes/Percentage	+/- (in percent)	Seats	+/-
ÖVP	97,649/38.8	+ 0.2	15	+ 1
SPÖ	81,562/32.4	+ 5.3	12	+ 1
FPÖ	49,345/19.6	+ 0.1	7	- 1
GRÜNE	13,536/ 5.4	- 1.9	2	- 1
LiF	9,207/ 3.7	- 2.1	0	+/- 0

Source: Compiled from official data.

On the evening of 7 March, the state diet of Tyrol still seemed to have an absolute ÖVP majority. The ÖVP got 19 seats, the SPÖ 8, the FPÖ

7, and the Greens 2. Due to the fact that many votes were declared invalid, a re-count of the votes in Innsbruck brought a different result: The ÖVP lost the 19th seat (in favor of the Greens) and thus lost the absolute majority, too. Finally, the ÖVP got 47.2 percent (- 0.1 percent), the SPÖ 21.8 percent (+ 2 percent), the FPÖ 19.6 percent (+ 3.5 percent), the Greens 8.0 percent (- 2.7 percent) and the Liberals 3.2 percent (- 0.1 percent).

Table 3: Tyrol State Diet Elections

	Votes/Percentage	+/- (in percent)	Seats	+/-
ÖVP	163,970/47.2	- 1	18	- 1
SPÖ	75,585/21.8	+ 2	8	+ 1
FPÖ	68,108/19.6	+ 3.5	7	+ 1
GRÜNE	27,862/ 8.0	-2.7	3	- 1
LiF	11,119/ 3.2	-0.1	0	+/- 0

Source: Compiled from official data.

The ÖVP lost its absolute majority in Tyrol for the first time since 1945. In general, the time of absolute majorities is fading away in the 1990s. Certain parties used to have, absolute majorities in certain regions: in Vienna the SPÖ from 1945-1996; in Lower Austria the ÖVP from 1945-1993; in Upper Austria the ÖVP from 1945-1949, 1955-1967 and 1979-1991; in Styria the ÖVP from 1945-1949, 1965-1970, and 1974-1991; in Salzburg the ÖVP from 1945-1949 and 1984-1989; in Carinthia the SPÖ from 1970-1989; in Burgenland the ÖVP from 1945-1953 and then the SPÖ from 1968-1972 and from 1977-1987. Only Vorarlberg was left with an absolute majority (ÖVP; since 1945)—until September 1999.

Marcus Omofuma

The Nigerian-born Marcus Omofuma was remanded pending deportation. On 1 May Omofuma was sent to Sofia, Bulgaria, in an airplane—accompanied by three Austrian policemen. On arrival in Sofia, though, Omofuma was dead. He died from suffocation, allegedly caused by the fact that he was gagged by the policemen.

In Austria this incident triggered a discussion about deportations and about Austria's foreigners and asylum policies. Not much, though,

changed. One of the most noteworthy remarks came from the FPÖ MP
Helene Partik-Pable. On 10 May she said in Parliament: "Ask civil
servants about the behavior of black Africans. They do not only look
different ... they are different, actually they are especially aggressive.
The reason for this is obviously their nature." This was the clearest racist
remark given in the Austrian Parliament in 1999. And not much
happened.

EU-Elections

On 13 June Austria—as all fifteen member states of the European
Union—elected its representatives for the EU-Parliament. In 1996 the
ÖVP, SPÖ, and FPÖ were very close: the ÖVP gained 29.6 percent, the
SPÖ 29.1 percent, and the FPÖ 27.5 percent.

In 1999, the SPÖ, the ÖVP and the Grünen were the winners, while
the FPÖ and the Liberals (LiF) lost:

Table 4: EU-Elections 1999

	Votes/Percentage	1996-1999 +/-	Seats	1996-1999 +/-
ÖVP	851,343/30.64	+ 1	7	+/- 0
SPÖ	882,005/31.74	+ 2.5	7	+ 1
FPÖ	652,458/23.48	-4	5	-1
GRÜNE	257,043/ 9.2	+ 2.5	2	+ 1
LiF	73,276/ 2.64	-1.7	0	-1

Source: Compiled from official data.

Two other parties ran for election: the CSA—*Christlich Soziale
Aktion*—with party leader Karl Habsburg—and the Communist KPÖ.
Both were without chances: the CSA got 1.53 percent and the KPÖ 0.73
percent. Karl Habsburg had been on the ÖVP list in 1996 but was not re-
nominated in 1999 because of various (alleged) scandals and internal
conflicts with party leader Stenzel.

The result of the CSA was not surprising, but the result of LiF was:
The Austrian Liberals had had one seat between 1996 and 1999 but
could not succesfully run for re-election in the 1999 ballot.

The FPÖ was among the losers, too. The SPÖ (pro-neutrality) and
the ÖVP (pro-NATO-membership) represented the major topics, and

neither the FPÖ nor its top EU-parliamentarian Daniela Raschhofer could successfully place other topics. Besides, Raschhofer and (more importantly) Sichrovsky allegedly even misused EU-money.

Probably the most outstanding result of the EU-parliamentary elections in Austria was the turnout: only 49 percent of those entitled to vote went to the ballots (compared to 67.7 percent in 1996). Throughout all of Europe, though, the turnout was very low (with Great Britain at an amazing low of 23 percent).

State Diet Elections in Vorarlberg

Table 5: Vorarlberg State Diet Elections

	Votes/Percentage	+/- (in percent)	Seats	+/-
ÖVP	87,542/45.8	-4.1	18	-2
SPÖ	24,844/13.0	-3.3	5	-1
FPÖ	52,444/27.4	+ 9.0	11	+ 4
GRÜNE	11,862/ 6.0	-1.7	2	-1
LiF	6,424/ 3.4	-0.1	0	+/- 0

Source: Compiled from official data.

The state diet elections in Vorarlberg were held a few weeks before the National Council elections, thus the result of the former was seen as kind of a test-vote for the latter elections on 3 October. The ÖVP and the SPÖ lost 4.1 and 3.3 percent respectively; the SPÖ went down to a historic low of 13 percent. Greens and Liberals lost, too, and the FPÖ could increase its percentage from 18.4 to 27.4 percent. The ÖVP, thus, lost the absolute majority and continued its coalition with the FPÖ. Herbert Sausgruber remained governor.

In 1988 eight out of nine state diets had an absolute majority of either SPÖ or ÖVP. At the end of 1999 all absolute majorities were gone.

National Council Elections

Table 6: National Council Elections

	Votes/Percentage	+/- (in percent)	Seats	+/-
SPÖ	1,532,448/33.15	-4.95	65	-6
ÖVP	1,243,672/26.91	-1.39	52	+/- 0
FPÖ	1,244,087/ 26.91	+ 5.01	52	+ 11
GRÜNE	342,260/ 7.4	+ 2.6	14	+ 5
LiF	168,612/ 3.65	-1.85	0	-10

Source: Compiled from official data.

The 1999 National Council elections, the last elections in the 20th century, were remarkable for several resons: The turnout went down to a historic low of 80.42 percent. Though the EU-elections had a turnout of only 49 percent, up to the late 1980s National Council elections usually had a turnout of some 90 percent. Since then, the turnout went down to 86 percent in 1990, 82 percent in 1994—up to 86 percent in 1995—and now down again to 80 percent. For the first time in post-war history, the ÖVP was replaced by the FPÖ in the second place. The ÖVP went down to a historic low of 26.91 percent, and the SPÖ did not much better with 33.15 percent. The FPÖ gained a remarkable share of the vote. Thus the SPÖ and the ÖVP, who together used to gain 80-90 percent (or even more) during the Second Republic, fell to 60 percent. The elections were followed by party negotiations (*Sondierungs-gespräche*). The SPÖ claimed that they would never form a coalition with the FPÖ; the ÖVP said they would go into opposition if being third (and they were third); and the FPÖ stated that they would build a coalition with both the SPÖ or the ÖVP. The *Sondierungsgespräche* were led until mid-December, and, finally, President Klestil asked Chancellor Klima to negotiate a new government.

If there will be a renewed SPÖ-ÖVP coalition in the year 2000, it will be for the first time that it is not a 'grand coalition' (first and second) but a 'small coalition' (first and third). The only small coalition so far was between SPÖ and FPÖ (1983-1986/7).

Racism and xenophobia was one element in the FPÖ-election campaign 1999. In Vienna, one could see posters entitled "*Stop der Überfremdung*" and "*Stop dem Asylmißbrauch*" ("stop to foreign infil-tration" and "stop to asylum misuse"). The FPÖ went even further when it pointed out that black asylum seekers were drug dealers with cell phones and trendy suits (FPÖ election announcement in Vienna 1999; http://www.fpoewatch.at).

Economic Data

In 1999 on average 3,106,000 people were employed, 221,000 unemployed; the rate of unemployment was 4.4 percent (International Labour Organization) and 6.7 percent respectively.

GNP was at 2,611 billion ATS (157 billion EURO) in 1998; inflation at 0.6 percent—with an increase in the first quarter of the year 2000.

Exports amounted some 881 billion ATS (64 billion EURO; + 5.5 percent), imports 819 billion ATS (59 EURO; + 5.8 percent).

According to Maastricht criteria public deficit was at 54 billion ATS (4 billion EURO; 2 percent of GNP) and public debt at 1,742 billion ATS (127 billion EURO; 64.9 percent of GNP).

Sources

Austrian newspapers and magazines; internet-archives

List of Authors

Gertraud Benke is a researcher at the research center *Discourse, Politics and Identity*, Vienna

Günter Bischof is professor of history and executive director of *CenterAustria* at the University of New Orleans

Wolfgang Danspeckgruber is a lecturer in international relations, Woodrow Wilson School, Princeton University, and director of the Liechtenstein Program in Conflict Mediation

Klaus Eisterer is assistant professor of contemporary history at the University of Innsbruck

Heinz Gärtner is a senior research fellow at the Institute of International Relations in Laxenburg

Reinhold Gärtner is associate professor of political science at the University of Innsbruck and secretary of the *Gesellschaft für politische Aufklärung* in Innsbruck

Michael Gehler is a professor of contemporary history at the University of Innsbruck

Norman Goda is an associate professor of history at the Institute of Contemporary History, Ohio University

David Irwin is professor of linguistics at the University of Belfast

Klaus Larres is a senior lecturer at the Institute of Politics, Queens University, Belfast

Alexander Lassner has completed his PhD in history at Ohio State University

Karin Liebhart is a lecturer of political science at the University of Vienna and the secretary of the Gesellschaft für politische Aufklärung, Vienna

Paul Luif is a senior research fellow at the Institute of International Relations in Laxenburg

Kurt Richard Luther is research fellow and lecturer in political science at the University of Keele

Vojtech Mastny is an independent historian in Arlington, VA, and a senior fellow at the Cold War International History Project at the Woodrow Wilson Center, Washington, D.C.

Anton Pelinka is professor of political science at the University of Innsbruck and director of the Institute of Conflict Research in Vienna

Oliver Rathkolb is professor of contemporary history at the University of Vienna and the research director of the Kreisky Foundation, Vienna

Hans-Jürgen Schröder is a professor of contemporary history at Giessen University

Gerald Stourzh is a professor emeritus of history at the University of Vienna

Thomas Alan Schwartz is an associate professor of history at Vanderbilt University

John Wilson is professor of linguistics at the University of Belfast

Ruth Wodak is professor of linguistics at the University of Vienna and research director of the research center *Discourse, Politics and Identity*, Vienna